WHITE GUYS

THE HAYMARKET SERIES

Editors: Mike Davis and Michael Sprinker

The Haymarket Series offers original studies in politics, history and culture, with a focus on North America. Representing views across the American left on a wide range of subjects, the series will be of interest to socialists both in the USA and throughout the world. A century after the first May Day, the American left remains in the shadow of those martyrs whom the Haymarket Series honors and commemorates. These studies testify to the living legacy of political activism and commitment for which they gave their lives.

WHITE GUYS

*Studies in Postmodern Domination
and Difference*

—◆—

FRED PFEIL

VERSO
London · New York

First published by Verso 1995
© Fred Pfeil 1995
All rights reserved

Verso
UK: 6 Meard Street, London w1v 3hr
USA: 180 Varick Street, New York, ny 10014

Verso is the imprint of New Left Books

British Library Cataloguing in Publication Data
A catalogue record for this book is available from the British Library

Library of Congress Cataloging-in-Publication Data
A catalogue record for this book is available from the Library of Congress

isbn 1 85984 937 7
isbn 1 85984 032 9 (pbk)

Typeset in Monotype Garamond by Lucy Morton, London se12
Printed and bound in Great Britain by Biddles Ltd,
Guildford and King's Lynn

CONTENTS

INTRODUCTION

I conceived the project of writing a book on changing representations of white straight masculinity in contemporary popular culture in the fall of 1990, submitted a proposal on the subject to Verso at the end of that year, and shortly thereafter received and signed a contract calling for delivery of the manuscript in the fall of 1992. Today, as I write these words as part of the work of completing the project, it is October 1994. In effect, it has taken me twice as long to write this book as I had thought; and that has come to seem such a telling fact that the best way to introduce what follows to its readers might well be to talk awhile about why writing it has taken so much longer than I anticipated.

There are three reasons, really – the two most socially significant of them having to do with fear, the third and most personal with grief. The first, and in many ways the largest of my fears centered on whether there was any point in – or audience for – my writing on this subject at all. Could there possibly be any interest, let alone approval, for a book on (a) "white guys" written by an avowedly (b) pro-feminist (c) white guy? I had reason to think that at least within the left-feminist community, academic and not, in which I work and for which I write, the answer might be No on each count, and all the more so to their concatenation. On the one hand, thanks to a variety of factors, from justly angry interventions into white middle-class feminism by women of color, to the influence and imported example of the Birmingham Center for Contemporary Cultural Studies, American feminists themselves were increasingly being guided, at least in theory, by the "theoretical assumption that gender is not a unified category, but a many-faceted one, open to change and variation."[1] But it was, and remains, much less clear that that assumption could or can be stretched to include white straight men. Of the nineteen essays on gender in contemporary American culture in the anthology from whose introduction I have just been quoting, for example, not one is written by a man, white or otherwise; nor, with the partial exception of Carol Stack's "Different Voices, Different Visions: Gender, Culture, and Moral Reasoning," which confronts Carol Gilligan's hypothesis on the supposed difference between the moral reasoning of men and the ethical grounding of women with empirical evidence of intersubjective moral norms shared by African-American men and women alike, is any group of men or category of masculinity ever taken up as a subject. Of course, there is nothing amiss in an anthology whose contributions are all women-authored, and whose subject matter concerns women's lives; and I do not doubt that there have been any number of books published on gender in American culture that were written by men from beginning to end. Still, in a book whose subtitle is "Negotiating Gender in American Culture" and whose founding assumption is that just quoted above, one might have expected some writing about the meanings and power relations of masculinity in general, and perhaps even of white straight masculinity in particular. Or, conversely, one might take the absence of any such attention as an indi-cation that some gender categories – once again, masculinity in general, and white straight masculinity in particular – are pretty unified, indeed monolithic, and imperiously closed to change after all.

Likewise, to the extent that one – man or woman – does choose to write about constructions of white straight masculinity, folks in my circles tend to assume that you're either gonna whomp 'em or join 'em. These alternatives showed up and sorted themselves out with particular vividness whenever I mentioned to colleagues and/or fellow activists that I was writing a piece on the mythopoetic "men's movement" of a few years back. Invariably, among both the men and women I know best, such an announcement was greeted with either a snarl of enthusiasm ("Oh *good* – I hope you're gonna *cream* those idiots!") or a sudden narrowing of the eyes and backward shuffle ("Oh *really* – huh...") towards the exit, often enough no matter how quick my desperately stammering rejoinder that I was hardly going to *affirm* it, fur crissake... The corollary to the notion that white straight masculinity is a single monolithic category here is, obviously enough, that it is simply, unambiguously, essentially evil as well: shot through with violence, megalomania, instrumental rationality, and the obsessive desire for recognition and definition through conquest.

As Rowena Chapman and Jonathan Rutherford define it, for instance, the contemporary crisis of white straight masculinity is precisely a function of the degree to which those incarnating it have been forced to see it for what it is: "a subjectivity that is organized within structures of control and authority." "For men who were promised recognition and a secure place in the world," they write, "there lies ahead a frightening prospect: that masculinity will be shorn of its hierarchical power and will become simply one identity among others."[2] Correlatively, Chapman and Rutherford call on men "to redefine masculinity ... to produce a masculinity whose desire is no longer dependent on oppression, no longer policed by homophobia, and one that no longer resorts to violence and misogyny to maintain its sense of coherence."[3] All of which is good left-feminist orthodoxy in my neck of the woods, and contains a great deal of important, even essential, sound political sense. But notice, first of all, that here, too, white straight masculinity comes in only one flavor; or, to approach much the same point from a different direction, that it is implicitly assumed that all be-penised humans whose skins lack melanin and whose sexual preferences run towards humans with vaginas are thereby "promised recognition and a secure place in the world," regardless of – for example – their class background, socioeconomic status, or ethnic heritage. Nor is there even a hint in this definition or the project that flows from it that masculinity, in this presumably singular white straight form or any other, might itself be a dialectical co-construction whose ongoing existence is at least partially dependent on the very forms and modalities of femininity it seeks to dominate and control: no hint, that is, that men and women in general, and heterosexual men and women in particular, make gender together, even if they do not do so – especially not women – just as they choose.[4]

So there is but one white straight masculinity, and it is bad; and white straight men must stop putting and living it out, and put out something else instead. But even if we grant the doubtful possibility that any group of men has the freedom and power to author a new gender script for itself – quite apart from, for instance, the pressures of the economic and/ or the gender norms and discursive regimes of so many versions and variants of femininity or womanhood – it is by no means clear to me that there is much room within progressive culture for any version of white straight masculinity to take its place in the ensemble of other racial, sexual, and gender identities as "simply one identity among others." Rather, it has at least occasionally seemed to me in my readings, experiences and encounters within left-feminist culture over the past decade or so that these "others" are dependent for their sense of affiliation and equivalence with one another, and all the more so for their self-approving understandings of their own lability, fluidity, and positionality, on the founding assumption of their opposition to another tribe whose mode of being is essentially immobile, oppressive, and unchanging; and that, accordingly, such others have little interest in interrogating the folkways or representations of that other tribe for any evidence that it, or any members within it, might be changing or moving around.

So, as I have scribbled and clacked away on the book that follows, I have been accompanied by the fearful expectation that wherever I have suggested that the modalities of white straight masculinity are multiple, and/or riven by contradictions and fissures, and/or subject to flux and change, I will be assailed by those women and men with whom I have worked and played and done most of my thinking for the past twenty years. When such fears have taken over, it is as though all the air had been sucked out of the room – all the space, that is, in which one might be able to say that even though *Die Hard* is indeed a disturbing, offensive film, it is nonetheless *also* a very busy and in some ways symptomatically incoherent one that is therefore well worth reading. And if at such points in my most paranoid fantasies I imagine myself accused, condemned, and dismissed as merely another crypto-macho Bruce Willis fan under a feminist sheepskin, what about those moments to come in which I presume to relate certain contemporary models of white straight masculinity to a part essentialist, part bourgeois-liberal feminist common sense that, in my view, those new models seek both to placate and to oppose? Can the question of such relationships be raised by anyone within my political-intellectual community – let alone by a white straight man?

What the latter question comes down to, of course, is whether it is possible for any white straight man to critique any aspect of contemporary feminist discourse from a position within (but here the words themselves grow treacherous: should it be "identified with" rather than "within," will that be okay; or do I need to shade it back to "sympathetic to"?) feminism itself. For it is not that long since, even in the academic circles I have frequented, it was a fairly tricky if not dangerous thing for straight white men to agree with feminism and announce their allegiance to it. For example, listen to the anticipatory flinches chopping the waves of Stephen Heath's prose in the essay that opens the influential anthology *Men in Feminism* by Alice Jardine and Paul Smith, and provides the pretext for most of the responses to follow in that book. "Men's relation to feminism," wrote Heath,

> is an impossible one. This is not said sadly nor angrily (though sadness and anger are both known and common reactions) but politically. Men have a necessary relation to feminism – the point after all is that it should change them too, that it involves learning new ways of being women *and men* against and as an end to the reality of women's oppression – and that relation is also necessarily one of a certain exclusion – the point after all is that this is a matter *for women*, that it is their voices and actions that must determine the change and redefinition. Their voices and actions, not ours: no matter how "sincere," "sympathetic" or whatever, we are always also in a male position which brings with it all the implications of domination and appropriation, everything precisely that is being challenged, that has to be altered. Women are the subjects of feminism, its initiators, its makers, its force; the move and the join from being a woman to being a feminist is the grasp of that subjecthood. Men are the objects, part of the analysis, agents of the structure to be transformed, representatives in, carriers of the patriarchal mode; and my desire to be a subject there too in feminism – to be a feminist – is then only also the last feint in the long history of *their* colonization. Which does not mean, of course not, that I can do nothing in my life, that no actions are open to me, that I cannot respond to and change for feminism (that would be a variant on the usual justification for the status quo, men are men and that's that); it just means that I have to realize nevertheless – and this is an effort not a platitude – that I am not where they are and that I cannot pretend to be (though men do, colonizing, as they always have done), which is the impossibility of my, men's, relation.[5]

I have few if any arguments with the sense of this passage; what I wish to draw your attention to is rather its motion and sound. Read it aloud, with all its desperate qualifications, interruptions, rephrasings, and you will hear what I mean: this is the sound of a person speaking, in effect, through the hands he has held up over his head, in expectation of the blows he believes will land on him for presuming to speak, to enter the dialogue, at all. (And land they do, as any reader of this conversation-stopping/starting volume will attest.)

In this book, though, for better or worse, I have sought not to speak from such a fearful, guarded position – but to push my fears back and take the hands down from my face. I have been emboldened to do so for a variety of reasons; and I hope it will not seem too perverse of me to confess that one of them has been precisely the example of the bravery of those feminists, people of color, and gays and lesbians themselves who throughout my life have continued to risk far greater penalties – for example, loss of employment and income, physical violence, even death – than the mere contempt and ostracism I fear might be my lot for speaking up. Yet another has been the encouragement I have been given in this project by others whose commitment to feminism is unimpeachable – among them, Judith Newton, Wahneema Lubiano, Betsy Traube, and my life partner Ann Augustine (though such encouragement, it must be added, does not imply their agreement with the positions I take up in the pages that follow).

And finally, I have assumed the right to speak about white straight masculinity from a general position which I take to be within feminism out of a sense that it is now not only possible but in some ways even necessary to speak up in the name of a version of the feminist project that, like many feminist women, I see in danger of being overwhelmed, occluded, and lost. In the early 1970s, when I was, as we used to say, radicalized, it was by and for the sake of a feminism that subsumed and transcended the socialist project whose sexism it rightfully critiqued. In the years since then, and, not coincidentally, at the same time as the historic linkage between the marketization of all social relations and their democratization was in the process of being curtailed or wholly decoupled throughout the ever-widening sphere of capitalism's worldwide reach, that feminism has been ever more eclipsed by the ascendance of other versions and voices less concerned to argue and organize for the material and ideological deconstruction of the mechanisms of the gruesomely asymmetrical, grievously binding binarism we call gender, than to protect, valorize, and enlarge the provinces of human activity and moral value assigned to the feminine. Needless to say, such a gender politics is not without its portion of good sense or its share of good effects. But a feminism that is not also anti-capitalist is subject to deformations and appropriations that inevitably cause it to lose sight of its most ambitious and, in the last analysis, most necessary goals: to end the oppression of women by unbinding the integuments of gender that wrap us all. To the extent to which the most hegemonic forms of contemporary American feminism posit masculinity – including and especially white straight masculinity – as a single, monolithic, absolute evil against which an interminable struggle for turf and power must be waged, such tribalized and market-friendly forms seem not only to have abandoned the most revolutionary aspirations of feminism for the human species, but increasingly to be in thrall to market-based logics of commodification and reification to which the more revolutionary feminism that preceded them was – and remains – intransigently opposed.

It is in the name and for the sake of that other, revolutionary feminism that the pages to follow have been written; if they have any value, it will be in the contribution they make to and the space they clear for that feminism to do its work – including, I would hope, that of critiquing this book! For it must be said that there is much more here for readers to take issue with than simply one white guy's presuming to speak for or within feminism. In fact, the second type of apprehension I have felt throughout this work – one that compounds and exacerbates in no small measure the fears attendant on the first presumption – concerns the critical method I have followed in most of the chapters to come, in which my arguments arise from and are grounded in close readings of a variety of cultural texts, from films to books to rock-and-roll bodies. The practice of close reading as a mode of cultural interpretation and argument has come in for its share of hard knocks over the past several years, and with good reason. At its worst, it ignores the active intertextuality of the objects it freezes in place, and seeks to elevate and authorize the prideful critic's sensitive, intelligent reading over the far more various and at least equally productive readings constructed by a host of other audiences and reading groups. My reliance on it here is therefore vulnerable to a charge that can neatly dovetail with the suspicion that there is something wrong with my claiming the right to critique feminism from a position sympathetic to if not within it: that the arrogance of producing readings claiming some measure of authority and comprehensiveness is at one with the arrogance of critiquing the assumptions and practices of some versions of contemporary feminism in the first place.

What, then, is my well-intended rationale for walking down this particular road to hell? It is, first and foremost, that I have found these objects and practices of sufficient complexity more or less in themselves to warrant the close attention and careful readings I have tried to give them – though I hope readers will also find that I have indeed made some effort in every case to embed those objects of study in at least the imme-diate context of their antecedents, regimes of production, and attendant texts. Another more prosaic but equally accurate way of putting this point might be to say that such readings have seemed to me to take up quite enough space all by themselves. Yet another, more polemical, way of stressing it is to note the prices that must be paid by other, if you will, more "horizontal" types of analysis, that move across a field of cultural objects and practices, shuttling across and back from texts to specific audiences, as in the work of Janice Radway, or, just as commonly, from one type of cultural practice to another, as in the work of Andrew Ross or Susan Jeffords.[6] For all the grip and sweep of the readings and arguments such methods and movements yield, and for all the refreshing iconoclasm of their refusal to reify and fetishize the text-in-itself, there is still something lost and some risk taken in doing cultural studies in only these ways. What gets lost is the complication and nuance of the single text, whose intricate motions and qualifications may be reduced to a single image or summary phrase to be thrown in and linked up with others glossed in the same way; and what is hazarded is a conflation of quite different levels of social practice that fails sufficiently to register the complexity and rivenness of their relatively autonomous internal workings, or to elucidate the specific cultural and political conjunctures in which they converge or overlap.

Besides, in all of this work – even, that is, in Radway's exemplary investigations of specific reading formations – it is not as though the moment of interpretation had been abolished and the critic's authority dissolved; what gets read is, in effect, a different sort of text, one composed of responses to books rather than to books themselves. Such responses, moreover, are notoriously difficult to gather in the case of such mass cultural phenomena as a rock superstar or blockbuster film, unless the critic focuses on one particular enclave – a group of bikers, say, watching *Lethal Weapon 2* on TV in a neighborhood bar. Finally, too, for all the criticisms levied against it, the activity of close reading has hardly been banned from feminist cultural studies – nor, of course, would I wish it to be. To cite only two recent feminist works whose concerns overlap with my own, both Tania Modleski's *Feminism Without Women* and most of the essays in the anthology edited by Constance Penley and Sharon Willis under the title *Male Trouble* generally employ the same critical method I am copping to here.[7] I have not read these works as though their authors were claiming absolute interpretative authority over the texts they explore, but rather as so many attempts, undertaken from their own determinate social and political positions, to listen as closely and attentively as possible to the full play of those texts, to the manifold meaning-effects they throw off and the complex circuitries of pleasure they invite us to enter. Our response to such attempts, especially when we too have formed part of the audience for the text, typically consists of comparing them to our own experience. Yes, we might say, from our own positions and perspectives:

Yes, it is like that, doing that, and connected up with these other things going on over here, and I knew it; or, Yes, it's doing that, and so on, and I never realized it; or, I'm not sure it really works or is connected up that way; or, I'm sure s/he's missing something here, or has gotten it wrong. At each such moment, in each response, the reader herself becomes critic, and enters into dialogue with the critic she has read, granting the critic no more authority than she does herself. That is, at any rate, how I hope the present work will be read, as a series of interpretations and linked arguments issuing from my own contradictory position as a left-feminist white straight male academic and activist; and all the more insofar as, to choose just one example, I myself have felt free to offer a different reading of both the *Lethal Weapon* and the *Die Hard* films from those proposed by Tania Modleski and Susan Jeffords.[8]

Before the conversation between us begins in earnest, however, and at the risk of belaboring the obvious, let me say one more thing about what this book is not trying to be or do. I never intended it to offer a comprehensive map of contemporary representations and renegotiations of white straight masculinity. What follows instead is a series of exploratory forays that at best have left a set of postholes tapped into the field in the region of US popular culture during the last years of the preceding decade and first few years of this one. Popular culture is, of course, hardly the only region of cultural practice where masculinities are modeled, renegotiated and/or reinforced; and a book that, like its author, pays no attention whatsoever to professional sports and from which, largely thanks to considerations of space and time, the mere mention of TV is almost wholly absent, can hardly claim to have done a half-decent job of "covering" white straight masculinity even in this realm. Still, I would like to think that the readings, speculations, and arguments I offer here might have some useful implications for further work in the fields of both gender studies and popular culture, particularly insofar as the chapters to come argue that contemporary mainstream masculinity too is in flux, in a period when at least practically every segment of white society is still inflected by the diverse discourses and effects of feminism, and every imaginable social group is ever more stressed, remolded, reformed and disarticulated by enormous, and largely grievous, economic restructuring – and, moreover, insofar as even the most thoroughly industrialized and spectacularized cultural productions are viewed as reflections of the flux they seek simultaneously to exploit and to arrest.

In this formulation, some readers will be quick to note that the importance of gender and class is upheld at the expense of a few arguably equally important social divides: those between "straights" and gays in a society organized around a still more or less compulsory heterosexuality, and between "whites" and African-Americans, Latinos, and other non-white populations in a nation whose psychic and economic boundaries are still cut, yet ever more crosshatched, along the "color line(s)." The emphasis here is, for better and for worse, symptomatic of what follows – but not precisely so. If the chapters ahead give most of their attention to the third word of the phrase "white straight masculinity" in relation to femininity and feminism, they are not devoid of attention to the processes by which the other two words are interrogated, placed in motion, put in question, and/or redefined in relation to those various oppressed and repressed Others on which they in turn depend. In such efforts I have been especially inspired and instructed by the work of a number of writers who receive little if any mention in the text, and therefore deserve it here. On the construction of "whiteness" and the racialized social formation in the US, I owe considerable debts to the pioneering works of David Roediger, Ruth Frankenberg, Alexander Saxton, and, above all, Michael Omi and David Winant;[9] while for my understanding of the power dynamics of straight/gay relations in general, and sensitivity to their formative presence in cultural texts, I am chiefly indebted to the equally groundbreaking work of Jeffrey Weeks, Eve Kosofsky Sedgwick, and Alexander Doty.[10]

Still, insofar as this book's primary axis is that of gender, my greatest intellectual obligation is to two works in gender studies whose contribution outstrips by far my most optimistic hopes for this one. The footnotes scattered throughout this text citing Lynne Segal's *Slow Motion* and R.W. Connell's *Gender and Power* hardly do justice to the formative influence of their works on my own.[11] Connell's synthesis of nearly two decades of feminist analysis and an even longer tradition of sociological approaches to gender reformulates the field even as it maps it, and opens up whole new ways of thinking through the levels of the social on which the brutal games of gender are played, from state policy to face-to-face interaction, and from the discursive reworkings of dominant ideology to the bedroom and the street; while Segal's work on contemporary masculinities – gay and straight, alternative and dominant, "black" and "white," to choose only a few – the ideologies that re-present them, and the other deter-minations that bang up against or fit together with each and all of them, truly set the standard for my research and my thinking, and brilliantly articulated the left-feminist principles on which both have been based. To say that the present work falls short of that standard, and that I am by no means convinced either Connell or Segal would endorse the positions taken up in it, is a profound understatement. To add that I would be happy if the only effect of this book were to provoke more readers to go off and read their works comes closer, but still does not adequately express the obligation these pages owe them.

Nor can I do more here than tip my hat to a few of the people around me who have helped me think and write my way through this book. On the way to doing so, let me first acknowledge the enormous help I got in terms of time, space, and collegiality from the year-long residential fellowship I received from the Center for the Humanities at Oregon State University for academic year 1991–92. It was during this stay in Corvallis that most of the reading for and conceptualization of the present work was done, under conditions that could not have been more conducive to it, and in the company of a wonderful group of people – Peter Copek, the Director, Wendy Madar, the late Patty Paulson, my old friends Laura Rice and Rich and Kris Daniels, and my new friend and co-Fellow Mart Stewart, among others – whose warmth and kindness I will not soon forget.

I benefitted as well from the opportunity to present a version of Chapter 1 of the present text at the OSU Center, as well as at the 1991 Summer Institute of the Marxist Literary Group, and at the University of Michigan. A slightly different version of this chapter eventually appeared in *Socialist Review* 23, 2 (1993). But my chief thanks go to Jerry Watts, Farah Griffin, and Jim Miller, each and all of whom were instrumental in helping me focus my thinking on these "male rampage" films back in the early summer of 1990 – and to Ann Augustine, who on a rainy night in our basement apartment in Seattle in November of that year, helped me get the Greimas square right!

For Chapter 3, on rock masculinities in general, and Bruce Springsteen and Axl Rose in particular, I'm indebted to Andrew Goodwin for a few minutes of intense conversation and his fine presentation at Wesleyan's Center for the Humanities later on that same night in the fall of 1992; to Barbara Benedict, Mark Miller, and Henry Abelove for an extremely useful, if slightly drunken, evening-long dialogue, and to Barbara and Mark again for their helpful comments on the first draft; to Jim Kavanagh and Jim O'Hara for their smart comments and criticisms on a version of this chapter delivered as a talk at Wesleyan's Center in the winter of 1994; to Dick Ohmann and the other folks working at the Center, who invited me in to give it and discuss it afterwards; and to Laurence Goldstein and the *Michigan Quarterly Review*, where yet another version of this chapter was published in vol. 22, no. 4 (Fall 1993).

Henry Abelove deserves more than a passing salute for the help he gave me with the project that became Chapter 4, on contemporary detective fiction by straight white men. Talking over the subject with him clarified my choice of three of the four writers I had already tentatively chosen to discuss; and strolling through the bookstore under his guidance brought me to the fourth and best of them all, the K.C. Constantine that Henry rightly imagined I would like. But I also received important book loans, vital information, and sound advice along the way from Ron Thomas and Jan Cohn — so to them, too, many thanks for the lift.

I have a lot of people to thank for their help with Chapter 5, on the "men's movement" of the late 1980s and early 1990s; but I don't know their names in many cases, and in others have pledged not to use them. The unnamed are, of course, those men I talked with, listened to, or — I might as well confess it — overheard, who regarded themselves as enthusiastic participants in that movement; and for some of them I am afraid mere thanks may not be enough. Let me say here, then, that wherever it seemed necessary to alter a story told in confidence, I have done so, while attempting to preserve its basic substance; and let me apologize, too, for any confidences I may nonetheless unintentionally have betrayed. Aside from these debts, though, there are others to which I can attach some names: so thanks to Ted Swedenburg for accompanying me into the lair of the "Wisdom Councils" as a second set of reality-checking eyes and ears; to Michael Seaver for serving as a one-man clipping service of "movement" publications and newsclips in the Bay Area; and to both of them for good listening, better advice, and many evenings of excellent attitude adjustment all through my Seattle time, and ever since. And a very special thanks to Judith Newton, for reading this chapter over when it was even more a sprawling mess than it is now, and giving me invaluable advice on how it might be cleaned up and improved.

Finally, I should also mention my gratitude to Tom Moylan and all the folks in the newly formed Cultural Studies Program at George Mason University, for inviting me down to give the talk on *In the Line of Fire* on which some pages of this book's Conclusion are based, as others are drawn from a Coda added to the aforementioned essay on the *Lethal Weapon* and *Die Hard* films in *Socialist Review* when that journal had held back the essay from publication so long as to require the update. For some last-minute help with statistics, thanks to Doug Henwood and the indispensable *Left Business Observer*, and for the tip on the New World Order sociology of "postmodernists" Jerald Hage and Charles Powers, which I invoke in the course of my reading of *In the Line of Fire*, I am indebted to my dear friend Tony Vogt.

With the mention of Tony's name, though, I also begin to turn away from those to whom I owe specific intellectual debts, and towards those whose chief gift to this book has been the companionship and affection they have held out to its author. Among them are many whose names, like Tony's, have already appeared above, but here are some others. With John McClure and Mary Lawler, I have discussed practically everything else but this book, and thank God for that! Lisa Gonzales's passion for justice and suspicion of white liberal versions of feminism have long since made me an ardent listener when she is around; and Modhumita Roy and Mike Sprinker have both remained steadfast comrades, despite a stretch of hard time.

But the person to whom I owe the greatest load of gratitude and for whom I have the deepest appreciation is my partner Ann Augustine. Throughout the term of this project, she has serenely borne the anxieties I have carried along with it, and put up with the neurotic behaviors I developed or resumed to deal with them. Moreover, as these chapters have come out, draft by draft, she has read every line as my first and most trustworthy reader. This book is immeasurably better for her suggestions on smoothing out sentences, cutting or clarifying passages, tempering my argument here and punching it up there. This is not to say that she agrees with every argument posed and each position trotted out here, but rather that even those with which she continues to take issue have been rendered more precise and plausible by her attention to them. Finally, too, what almost goes without saying is perhaps what most needs to be said: that my first and most trustworthy reader is also my most beloved, whose daily presence in my life is the one true miracle that life knows.

But I began this introduction by saying that the book that follows had been delayed by two fears and a weight of grief; so allow me to conclude it by saying for whom that grief is felt. I felt and go on feeling it for Anne Elizabeth Krosby and for Harriet Marie Herriman Pfeil – the first an extraordinary artist, dear friend, and former lover; the second my mother – who died between the fall of 1992 and the spring of 1993. For a considerable interval of time around each of their deaths, I was so consumed by the fact of their absence from the world in which I continue that I was incapable of working on this book, or doing much of anything else; and even now there is not a day when I am not freshly rendered breathless by the fact that they are gone. This, of course, is hardly a fact that needs to matter to anyone else, and certainly not intellectually or politically even if so. Yet it has mattered a great deal with regard to the writing of this book, and I'll bet not only in terms of delay. So, because it has mattered so much and goes on mattering, in ways I know and others I don't, and for all the incongruity or even inappropriateness that might seem attached to the act, I would dedicate, not so much this book as whatever in it might turn out to have been worth writing or thinking about, to the memory of these two women I so miss and so love.

NOTES

1. Faye Ginsberg and Anna L. Tsing, eds., *Uncertain Terms: Negotiating Gender in American Culture* (Boston: Beacon Press, 1990), p. 2.

2. Rowena Chapman and Jonathan Rutherford, "The Forward March of Man Halted," in Chapman and Rutherford, eds., *Male Order: Unwrapping Masculinity* (London: Lawrence & Wishart, 1988), p. 11.

3. Ibid., p. 18.

4. As Jane Flax puts it, in a formulation as admirable as the point of view it expresses is rare: "men and women are both prisoners of gender, although in highly differentiated but interrelated ways. That men appear to be and in many cases are the wardens, or at least the trustees ... should not blind us to the extent to which they too are governed by the rules of gender. However ... this does not mean that men and women occupy a fundamentally equivalent status ... gender relations, at least as they have been organized so far, are (variable) forms of domination" (*Thinking Fragments: Psychoanalysis, Feminism, and Postmodernism in the Contemporary West* [Berkeley: University of California Press, 1990], p. 139).

5. Stephen Heath, "Male Feminism," in Alice Jardine and Paul Smith, eds., *Men in Feminism* (New York and London: Methuen, 1987), p. 1.

6. See Janice Radway, *Reading the Romance: Women, Patriarchy, and Popular Literature* (Chapel Hill: University of North Carolina Press, 1984), and "Identifying Ideological Seams: Mass Culture, Analytical Method, and Political Practice," *Communication*, 9, 1 (1986), pp. 93–123; Susan Jeffords, *The Remasculinization of America: Gender and the Vietnam War* (Bloomington: Indiana University Press, 1989), and *Hard Bodies: Hollywood Masculinity in the Reagan Era* (New Brunswick, NJ: Rutgers University Press, 1994); and Andrew Ross, *No Respect: Intellectuals and Popular Culture* (New York and London: Routledge, 1989) and *Strange Weather: Culture, Science and Technology in the Age of Limits* (London and New York: Verso, 1991).

7. Tania Modleski, *Feminism Without Women: Culture and Criticism in a "Postfeminist" Age* (New York and London: Routledge, 1991); Constance Penley and Sharon Willis, eds., *Male Trouble* (Minneapolis: University of Minnesota Press, 1993).

8. Modleski, pp. 141–145 (for *Lethal Weapon*); Jeffords, *Hard Bodies*, pp. 54–58 (for *Lethal Weapon*), pp. 58–63 (for *Die Hard*).

9. David Roediger, *The Wages of Whiteness: Race and the Making of the American Working Class* (London and New York: Verso, 1991); Ruth Frankenberg, *White Women, Race Matters: The Social Construction of Whiteness* (Minneapolis: University of Minnesota Press, 1993); Alexander Saxton, *The Rise and Fall of the White Republic: Class Politics and Mass Culture in Nineteenth-Century America* (London and New York: Verso, 1990); and Michael Omi and Howard Winant, *Racial Formations in the United States: From the 1960s to the 1980s* (New York: Routledge and Kegan Paul, 1986).

10. Jeffrey Weeks, *Sexuality* (London: Routledge, Chapman and Hall, 1986), and *Sexuality and Its Discontents* (New York and London: Routledge, 1985); Eve Kosofsky Sedgwick, *Between Men: English Literature and Male Homosocial Desire* (New York: Columbia University Press, 1985), and *Epistemology of the Closet* (Berkeley: University of California Press, 1990); Alexander Doty, *Making Things Perfectly Queer: Interpreting Mass Culture* (Minneapolis: University of Minnesota Press, 1993). But see also that mine of contentious riches compiled by editors Henry Abelove, Michèle Aina Barale, and David M. Halperin, *The Lesbian and Gay Studies Reader* (New York and London: Routledge, 1993).

11. R. W. Connell, *Gender and Power: Society, the Person and Sexual Politics* (Stanford, CA: Stanford University Press, 1987); and "Towards a New Sociology of Masculinity," co-authored with Tim Carrigan and John Lee, in *Theory and Society* 14 (1985), pp. 551–604. Lynne Segal, *Slow Motion: Changing Masculinities, Changing Men* (New Brunswick, NJ: Rutgers University Press, 1990), and *Is the Future Female? Troubled Thoughts on Contemporary Feminism* (London: Virago, 1987).

CHAPTER ONE

FROM PILLAR TO POSTMODERN: RACE, CLASS, AND GENDER IN THE MALE RAMPAGE FILM

1. DIS-LOCATING REDEFINITIONS, FAMILY TIES

Lethal Weapon (1987), *Die Hard* (1988), *Lethal Weapon 2* (1989), *Die Hard 2: Die Harder* (1990): produced or co-produced by Joel Silver for Warners and Fox with the regularity of the seasons themselves, these films showed up at the rate of one per summer in the late 1980s and early '90s, marching from air-conditioned mall cineplexes all across the land to the list of top-ten grossers for the year.[1] Each film, moreover, followed the same basic narrative formula: a white male protagonist, portrayed by an actor of proven sex appeal, triumphs over an evil conspiracy of monstrous pro-portions by eschewing the support and regulation of inept and/or craven law-enforcement institutions, ignoring established procedure and running "wild" instead, albeit with the aid of a more domesticated semi-bystanding sidekick.

Thus summarized, the films seem to hew too close to the wearisome pathways laid down in frankly reactionary 1970s films like *Dirty Harry* or *Death Wish* to be worth any prolonged study in their own right. We might simply wish to note, with a chill, the convergence of their narrative project with what Andrew Ross has called "the desperate attempts, under Reagan, to reconstruct the institution of national heroism, more often than not in the form of white male rogue outlaws for whom the liberal solution of 'soft' state-regulated law enforcement was presented as having failed," and then pass on;[2] or, as Susan Jeffords does, to linger only to explore and condemn the Reaganite rhyme.[3] Yet if the basic formula of all four films is genealogically derived from "right-cycle" Hollywood films of the 1970s, and fueled by the Reagan-era *ressentiment* of the besieged racist-sexist "little man," what I want to explore here in some detail are the specific ways in which that formula is worked out in film after film. For it seems to me that both these operations, and the *mise-en-scène* of their enactment, react back on the formula to reveal each of our films and all of them together as a peculiarly hybridized, overdetermined, multivalent "dreamwork of the social":[4] one, moreover, that has at least as much to tell us about the irresolutions, anxieties, and contradictions sawing away at each other within the constructs and discourses of straight white masculinity as it has to say about the newest ruse of patriarchal power.

We might begin our look at these unsettled and unsettling features of our four "male rampage" films by noting those formal elements within them that are, when we take them out and look at them, rather surprisingly postmodernist. True, the straightforward plots of *Lethal Weapon* and *Die Hard* I and II have little in common with the loopy surprises and multiple thematics of a *Brazil* or *My Beautiful Launderette*: their formula is simply to enact the amusing yet brutal struggle of a white male protagonist trying to get his anguished head straight while defeating a criminal conspiracy of monstrous proportions. But on the more formal levels of cinematic style, narrative structure, and constitutive space-time, our fast-paced smash-em-ups have a lot more in common with certified Pomo art-films like, say, *Diva*, than you might think:

- *stylistically*, the *Lethal Weapon* and *Die Hard* films project a particular "urban look," their palettes shifting between bleached or even washed-out pastels and dark metallic blues and greys, with an occasional burst of apocalyptically lurid orange, managing as a *Variety* reviewer noted, "to be gritty and glamorous at the same time."[5]

- *chronotopically* (to invoke Bakhtin's useful term for the constitutive space–time of a given narrative realm), leaving aside, for the moment, the domestic space of home in the *Lethal Weapon* films, they contrast two different spaces: the spanking new high-rise office building, penthouse suite, or airport terminal versus the functioning viscera, oily and steaming, beneath the polished façades and abandoned industrial landscapes now grown gothic and obscure. The freighter's massive hold at the end of *Lethal Weapon 2*, the ventilation ducts and elevator shafts of the Nakatomi office tower in *Die Hard*, are surprisingly close kin to the cool post-industrial ruins of *Diva*. Similarly, spatial relations in all five films are perplexing: neither the cop heroes of the *Die Hard* and *Lethal*

Weapon films nor the Jules and Gorodish of *Diva* seem to go anywhere (or, alternately, in the *Die Hard* films we could say that John McClane always has to go somewhere, but, as with Jameson's famous postmodern subject lost in the hotel, we never really know where he is/we are). The action is simply taking place *here* – and *here* – and *here* – in spaces whose distance from one another is not mappable as distance so much as it is measurable in differences of attitude and intensity.

- *narratively*, too, an older model of plot development, moving from a state of stasis S1 through destabilization and development to a new and more fully resolved stasis S2, is largely superseded in all five films by the amnesiac succession of self-contained bits and spectacular bursts. There does remain a difference between the *jouissance* offered us in *Diva* – between, say, the delightfully twisted bits of aphasic narrative trash Gorodish's Vietnamese lover tells Jules in *Diva* as he bleeds away in the telephone booth in the video arcade – and the brutal industrialized thrills of the Hollywood films, whose narrative logic and rhythm are so eloquently described by rampage hero and *auteur* Sylvester Stallone: "It's chop-chop-chop-chop, chop-chop-chop-chop. It's almost like a diced salad. You have to keep it going."[6] Still, such a salad is quite different from the meat and potatoes of *The Maltese Falcon* or *High Noon*.

We will return to that difference, which for now I evoke merely as one more instance of these films' discontinuity with classical Hollywood cinema, a formal aspect of their "postmodernity." Yet the mention of Stallone also begins to remind us of how much the *Lethal Weapon* and *Die Hard* films have in common with other Hollywood productions past and present – in terms, that is, both of temporal continuities and lateral affiliations. For starters, one has only to think of the central icon of both sets of films, that is, the taut, torn, upper torso of the white star brandishing his lethal weapons (giant pistol, machine gun, deadly martial-arts skilled hands) in perfect readiness for whatever comes next, despite the wounds, burnmarks and other signs of mortification marring the muscle-rippled skin we can see through the rags of his clothes. The locus classicus of this image is, of course, that of Rambo himself[7] – yet less the Rambo of the block-buster hit *First Blood II*, the one who fights and wins a second Vietnam war all by himself in the terrible year of Reagan's re-election, than the one who, in 1982's *First Blood*, finds himself humiliated and hunted by an obsessed local sheriff on whose small mountain town Rambo, goaded beyond endurance, ultimately unleashes the sad and terrible violence he must otherwise, as a post-traumatic-stress-syndrome-ridden Vietnam vet, carry always within himself.

Thus the importance of this earlier film as precursor of the ones we shall be examining: as the movie that introduced the image and theme of the wounded warrior alone in the wilds, deserted and even abused by the authorities who ought to have appreciated and supported him, and that, through that figuration, offered US audiences a new synthesis of what Robert Ray has called the "left and right cycle" films of the 1970s. According to Ray, the mass audience for Hollywood product was in the 1970s offered a choice between two kinds of anti-establishment film: a "left" version, in which the protagonist uncovers an evil conspiracy of power elites, and is usually defeated and killed before he can publicize or contest it in any effective way (*Chinatown*, *The Parallax View*); and a "right" version, in which the established authorities are so corrupt and/or impotent that they leave the hero no choice but to wage his own war against the scum who threaten him, his family, and/or All That Is Decent from below (*Dirty Harry*, *Walking Tall*).[8] If so, *Rambo: First Blood* was one of the first movies of the 1980s to dream these two sides or cycles together, and thus to offer us the sight of a downscale, de-authorized figure going native (Stallone as canny proto-Indian "savage" in the long central section of the film, tracking and killing his human and non-human quarry without resort to rifle or gun) against those irrational authorities who oppose, misunderstand and/or abuse him again and again.

This new synthesis presents us, in turn, with more ideological semes than we have time to follow out in anything like their full historical detail. There is, just for starters, the Vietnam trope itself, used here, as in *The Deer Hunter* and elsewhere, as a perfectly ambivalent emblem of a certain kind of sado-masochistic fantasy/experience: that is, signifying not so much that the US–Vietnam war was either evil (left-populist) or incompetently and faintheartedly waged (right-populist), as that it was *both* a place where white guys learned to practice a lot of especially mean and violent techniques, to "go wild" in short (Rambo, we learn, picked up his forest survival skills "over there"), *and* where they suffered horrible physical and psychological trauma.[9] There is the "wild man;" the white man gone native/wild, which thanks to Ronald Takaki, Richard Drinnon, and Herman Melville, we could track back to the mythic history of John Moredock; the white man who lives to kill the Indians who massacred his family, and who lives like an Indian to kill them.[10] And Rambo's misunderstood, abused and embattled goodness contains a trace of yet another old, and quintessentially American, popular narrative of white masculinity: that of the heroically strong and honest worker who fights the greedy, corrupt, and powerful for the benefit of all, and whose concealed elite or aristocratic origins, Mike Denning has argued in his study of nineteenth-century dime novels, function as a sign of his allegorical status as a figure of the rightful American republic, in whose special virtues we (white males) all presumably may share.[11]

The function of the privileged origins in our dime-novel narrative would then, in the *Rambo*, *Lethal Weapon*, and *Die Hard* films, be nicely taken up by the star system itself. Mel Gibson and Bruce Willis, the already-established white stars of the latter two sets of films, both offer themselves as figures of the common (white) working man, and allow us (white men) to be flattered by that image with which we identify. Yet, especially in view of the blockbuster audiences hauled in by our four films, it is also worth pointing out that the stardom Gibson and Willis bring to these films is to some extent a crossover phenomenon, both having some measure of proven box-office appeal to women – and perhaps to somewhat upscale women at that: Gibson as the heart-throb and/or beefcake of *The Year of Living Dangerously* and any number of other Australian (ergo, in this country, somewhat classy) films, and Willis as co-star with Cybill Shepherd of the long-running television series *Moonlighting*, much-favored site of "TV-slumming" for thirty-something white professionals in the mid-to-late years of the last decade. Moreover, as we shall see, their definition in these male rampage films is precisely, indeed crucially, that of *wild yet sensitive* (deeply caring yet killing) guys – which mutation, moreover, is braided together with that other "non-racist" liberal trope, running back from *I Spy* and the interracial buddy film all the way to *The Adventures of Huckleberry Finn*, that makes the white guy and his black pal both supposedly equal, brothers-in-arms, yet domesticates the latter while keeping the former out there, wild, on the edge.

But with these observations we have already begun to change the direction of our gaze from the vertical toward the horizontal, from genealogy to affiliation. Given the erosion of generic boundaries in contemporary film and TV production, after all, and their replacement with the new, polymorphous logic of bricolage, we can see bits of our four films scattered all about the terrain of mainstream Hollywood film in the 1980s. Does the interracial partnership of Riggs (Gibson) and Murtaugh (Danny Glover) in the *Lethal Weapon* films owe more to the foul-mouthed madcap duo of Eddie Murphy and Nick Nolte in *48 Hours* (1982) or impulsive, anti-authoritarian Richard Gere and rigid disciplinarian Lou Gossett in *An Officer and a Gentleman* (1982) – or, indeed, is it some recombinant blend of the two? For that matter, is the partnership of urban professional FBI man Sidney Poitier and Northwest mountain man Tom Berenger in *Shoot to Kill* (1988) a relatively inert variant of the complementary roles played by Glover and Gibson, and the scene in which, wisecracking steadily, the former duo lie cheek to cheek on top of one another in a snow cave, a knockoff of the latter's homo-social play? Or how about those closing moments in both the initial *Die Hard* and *Lethal Weapon* films when the monstrously strong, skilled, and monomaniacal double/Other we thought our hero had vanquished stages one final, terrible, impossible reappearance: are they – aren't they? – spin-offs of the thing's last attack on Sigourney Weaver in the original *Alien* (1979), or, *a fortiori*, of the robo-killer's last attempt to destroy *The Terminator*'s (1984) female protagonist?

Such lines of influence, like all metonymic shifts, stop nowhere – and, indeed, could be made to run backwards in time as well as sideways (for example, *Die Hard* as bastard offspring of an unholy union between Chuck Norris action films and the disaster flicks – *The Towering Inferno, Airport* – of the 1970s). And no doubt a full reading of our four films would require, for each and all of the films' many interwoven semes, *shticks*, and motifs, a labor of genetic reconstruction that is far beyond my powers here. The point of my hasty sketch of our films' antecedents and travelling companions has rather been, first of all, to situate them, albeit roughly, where they come from and go within the stream of industrial-popular cultural production in this country in general, and film production in particular; and, secondly, to suggest something of just how highly condensed, overdetermined, and *nodal* – to borrow some psychoanalytic terms – these action films really are.

Finally, though, alongside these aesthetic mutations and generic syntheses, we should also keep in mind another, equally widespread but far less fun kind of shift: the long changeover, very much still in progress here, from "Fordism" to "post-Fordism" that is the economic context in which these films and their national reception both take place. In the USA in particular, in the de-industrializing 1980s, this "squeeze in the middle of the labour market" was accompanied by a small increase in the number of skilled technical or professional positions and a veritable explosion of low-paying jobs in service industries and small-scale production sites, with people of color and women especially targeted for such low-wage employment, if indeed they were "lucky" enough to find work at all.[12] A deepening gulf in the divison of labor, then, *within* what had been called the working class, and doubly so: that is, *both* in terms of the distance between those with enough luck and training to reach the lower strata of the PMC and those pumping gas, flipping ratburgers, or sewing up slacks in a sweatshop at piecework rates down at the bottom, *and* in terms of the faultlines of gender, race, and ethnicity, simultaneously deepening and crosshatching that larger divide. All this, as we shall see, is not only the backdrop against which the newest crop of mainstream rampagers must be seen, but in very real ways their subject matter as well; for out of just such distances, disappearances, and convergences, and within an ever more generalized postmodern culture, the new subaltern subjects of domestic post-Fordism construct and receive various narrative versions of their own uneasy dreams.

2. CRUISING THE SQUARE

But now, let us home in on the *Die Hard/Lethal Weapon* films themselves, starting where they do: with two convergent yet distinct problems per film, one private or personal and the other public, even international, and their resolution through the violent action of a white male protagonist – Mel Gibson as Riggs, Bruce Willis as McClane – working outside the system, and aided by a much tamer sidekick who happens to be black.[13] In the *Lethal Weapon* films, Danny Glover portrays middle-aged family man Roger Murtaugh, the cautious yet nurturant soul who seeks in vain to curb Martin Riggs's daredevil tendencies; in *Die Hard*, Reginald VelJohnson gives us plump, good-natured Al Powell, the cop with a pregnant wife waiting for him back home, who functions via walkie-talkie as our hero John McClane's only tie to the outside world. Moreover, the stable satisfactions of Al and Rog's domestic lives stand in stark contrast to those of Riggs and McClane: the latter confused about his professional wife (Bonnie Bedelia), a rising executive in a Japanese multinational; the former trapped in a shabby trailer with a blaring TV, a few photos of his dead wife, and a pistol to suck on experimentally when the pain is at its worst.

Failing or defunct marriages thus constitute the personal problems of the *Die Hard* and *Lethal Weapon* films; criminal conspiracies by mercenaries, drug lords, evil South African ministers, and European technovillains, the public concerns. Yet these conspiracies themselves take two different forms, each with its own type of arch-villain, and our two sets of films present us, neatly enough, with two examples of each. In the first *Lethal Weapon* film and *Die Hard 2*, the bad guys are either American mercenaries or paramilitary who, usually with some foreign ties or foreign help, are either running a heroin network out of Laos back to the States (*Lethal Weapon*) or attempting to spring a Latin American druglord-general in the process of his extradition back to the States (*Die Hard 2*). In the original *Die Hard* and in *Lethal Weapon 2*, on the other hand, the evil ones are less military and more upscale in their general profile. Arjen Rudd, the wicked Minister of Diplomatic Affairs for the government of South Africa and his grey-suited henchmen are running a triangular trade in drugs, American money, and South African Krugerrand gold (the precise logic of which, by the way, is never all that clear, but what the hell) in *Lethal 2*; while, in *Die Hard*, a mostly European group of skilled technicians headed by suave, impeccably well-tailored ex-terrorist Hans Gruber, take over the spanking new office tower in which McClane's wife's Japanese corporation has its American HQ, passing themselves off as real terrorists to buy the time they need to computer-hack their way into the vault in which their real goal, some $640 million in negotiable bearer bonds, lies stashed.

It goes without saying, of course, that our heroes and their buddies ultimately triumph over both these flavors of dastardliness; but not thanks to normal law enforcement procedures and/or officials, whose guidance and aid invariably prove to be irrelevant, ineffectual or worse. In the first *Die Hard* film, the official efforts of the LAPD, presided over by a chronically irascible buffoon of a lieutenant, are both belated and easily crushed; and the subsequent involvement of the FBI nearly proves fatal to both the corporate hostages and McClane himself. Likewise, in *Lethal Weapon 2*, when the South African conspirators begin an assassination campaign against the police department in retaliation for the harassment they have received, the department appears powerless to predict or prevent the attacks, especially given the evil minister's invocation of diplomatic immunity as his ultimate line of defense. And in *Die Hard 2*, we are in for yet worse: though McClane does receive some grudging help from the local airport police at Dulles who dismissed him at first, the crack anti-terrorist military team sent in to defeat the paramilitary plotters and recapture the Latin American general turns out to be in league with its presumed antagonists. Only in the first *Lethal Weapon* are enforcement officials other than our heroes and their non-white companions depicted as anything other than explicitly disabled, incompetent, or corrupt; yet even in this

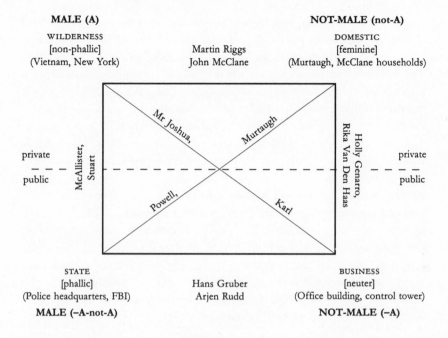

MALE (A)

WILDERNESS
[non-phallic]
(Vietnam, New York)

Martin Riggs
John McClane

NOT-MALE (not-A)

DOMESTIC
[feminine]
(Murtaugh, McClane households)

Mr. Joshua,

Murtaugh

private

public

McAllister, Stuart

Holly Genarro,
Rika Van Den Haas

private

public

Powell,

Karl

STATE
[phallic]
(Police headquarters, FBI)
MALE (–A-not-A)

Hans Gruber
Arjen Rudd

BUSINESS
[neuter]
(Office building, control tower)
NOT-MALE (–A)

Figure 1

film, clear (albeit usually comic) signs are thrown off concerning the de-authorized slackness of the police department from which both Riggs and Murtaugh dissociate themselves anyway once the bad guys make off with Murtaugh's daughter Rianne.

From all this plot material, we can extract four basic nodes of opposition and difference from which these films generate their dramatic energies. I place them in Figure 1 in the familiar form of a Greimasian rectangle in which position (A) is the nameable yet never represented space of "the Wild" – the place the white protagonist has come from before he lands in LA, be it Vietnam (in *Lethal Weapon*) or, in *Die Hard*, that other well-known symbol of multiracial rot and riot, New York. The Other, or (not-A) of this space would then clearly be "Domesticity," the site of (heterosexual) life and family life. The Opposite (–A) in these films must be the place of Business or professional-technical work. And finally, filling the place of (–A-not-A), functioning as the inverse of the nurturant realm of hearth and home, we find the official space of law, authority and order, that is, the state.

Set up in this way, these positions permit some further subdivisions along two additional axes: one between private and public (or, perhaps more accurately, between individual and collective), given here as a dotted line bisecting our rectangle horizontally, and the other between gendered lines of force, here given as our two uprights. The left-hand "male" vertical connects what, loosely drawing upon Lacan and his feminist appropriators, I call the "phallic" State with what I will argue is a non-phallic "male-rampage" Wilderness; the right-hand vertical – not, significantly enough, so much "female" as *"not-male"* – lines up wife and mother in the "patriarchal-female" family home with the "non- or post-patriarchal neuter" professional in her/his office or (in *Die Hard 2*) control tower.

The structuralist *combinatoire* I have just sketched out is thus a road map merely, not the ground itself. The real significance of these films lies in the complex shifts, shadings, exchanges, and tensions that play upon the diagram's categories, in the relationships, for example, between the political/historical/newsworthy materials viewers are given as background to the public plots and the simple Manichean bad-guy/good-guy dualities they disturb. Take, for starters, the explanation that (typically) flies by in the original *Lethal Weapon* of how the evil paramilitaries of "Shadow Company," the Special Forces unit now turned vicious heroin cartel, got their start working with the CIA in Vietnam. It is simply sound business practice in the realm of mass cultural production to scramble your left-wing ideologemes (runaway CIA and paramilitary elements engaging in renegade criminal activities) together with some from the right. But it is equally the case that a kind of metonymic relay system of partial incorporations is being set up here, through whose operations the Other is not only resisted but partially, covertly taken in. In *Lethal Weapon*, to continue our example, if you recall that Riggs, the Mel Gibson protagonist, was also Special Forces in the War, and, indeed, bears the same tattoo upon his arm as the ruthless Mr Joshua (Gary Busey), that relay system in this case looks something like this: Viet Cong ⇔ Shadow Company ⇔ Riggs, where the relationship between each term and the next in the series is one of both opposition *and* identity. (As, by the way, the predominance of specifically "Asian" martial-arts techniques in the final *mano-a-mano* contest between Mr Joshua and Riggs also suggests.)

Something of the same type of antagonistic linkage is set up between the extradited Latin American general of *Die Hard 2*, the renegade paramilitary units, in and outside the government, who are trying to spring him loose, and our hero John McClane. Here again, the political explanation we are given is both fleeting and steeply ambivalent: General Esperanza, we are told, is a Central American officer whose flagrant human-rights abuses finally resulted in his fall from power (shades of the brutal autarchy of the US-backed Guatemalan and Salvadoran armed forces, ergo a "left" element even if, of course, no such officers in real life to date have been punished or removed for their crimes), *and* who then turned to cocaine smuggling (shades of Panamanian leader Manuel Noriega, a "right" element) after he was deposed. This burst of ideologically Janus-faced info, moreover, is given in the form of a TV news blip whose continuous sound and visual image also functions as the hinge of a straight cut from McClane, idly gazing at a screen inset in the central information booth in the main lobby of Dulles, to the paramilitary arch-villain we will soon come to know as Colonel Stuart, staring at the screen with cold contempt while he concludes his T'ai Chi, his musclebound nakedness enclosed by a motel room so stripped of all adornment and so drab olive green as to suggest some purely military space. The point here is not only the effective subordination of the scrambled ideological message to the exigencies of plot, but the blurring of that scramble with another similar linking of opposites, that is, of McClane with Stuart, insofar as on some level, despite the ominous music that strikes up around the latter, we recognize or suspect a certain kinship or brotherhood here – a sense that once McClane's topcoat and scarf are off, once he too gets stripped down for action, he's going to prove every bit as tough an hombre as this other guy. Later on, the film itself will spell out explicitly the implications of this covert affiliation, when McClane says to hard-bitten Major Grant, the head of the anti-terrorist team sent in to locate and defeat Stuart's unit, "Guess I was wrong about you – you're not such an asshole after all," and the Major replies, "No, you're right. I'm just *your* kind of asshole." And later still, when Grant is revealed to be one of the bad guys, he and McClane punctuate their final confrontation out on the wing of a taxiing 747 with the following exchange:

GRANT: Too bad, buddy; I kind of liked you.
McCLANE: Too bad, buddy. I got enough friends.

Such kinship in antagonism, simultaneously asserted and refused, flickers at the core of all four films, given their definition of heroes and villains alike as men highly skilled in pain- and death-dealing techniques, perfectly willing to commit virtually any act of outrageous violence to persons or property in pursuit of their ends. Thus the secret dream-sense and magical power of that ostensibly gratuitous moment in the first *Die Hard* film, just at the end of arch-villain Hans Gruber's victory speech to McClane, delivered in the mistaken belief that McClane is finally disarmed and destructible, and McClane's last-minute turning of the tables. The elegant, cosmopolitan pseudo-terrorist Gruber says, "What was it you said to me before? 'Yippi-ky-aye, motherfucker'" – throwing McClane's defiance, and the film's most famous line, back in his face, and laughing contemptuously. Then – and here the moment changes, the underside comes bubbling up – that laughter is joined, first by the big square-shouldered thug who is the only member of Gruber's gang remaining, and then by McClane himself, as his wife Holly, still literally in Gruber's clutches, stares around in shocked bewilderment: for that laughter of Gruber and the thug is no longer contemptuous, no more than McClane's seems merely strategic, but *exuberant*; for just that one scant second all three men, all three outlaws, compose a community no woman can enter, and share a joy no woman can know.

The current of pleasure and affiliation that radiates from this *Brudderbund* of rampagers thus runs across and against these films' structured oppositions – and not merely from the bad guys to the good. According to our grid, the African-American figures of Al Powell in *Die Hard* and Roger Murtaugh in (especially) the first *Lethal Weapon* film cross in opposition the line connecting frenzied wildness and professional competence that defines the pointedly Aryan figures of Karl (Alexander Godunov) and Mr Joshua. Powell and Murtaugh – mildly incompetent cops who play by the rules and unproblematically love their wives and families and who, it is worth noting, hardly threaten white audiences at all – are the perfect antitheses to their blond, blue-eyed white Others' combination of steely, square-jawed efficiency and perfect murderousness. Yet, for both these good guys, as for the white villains and heroes, where professional concerns give way to personal ones, the brotherhood of the wild begins. Shadow Company's kidnapping of Rog's daughter Rianne in *Lethal Weapon* seals his determination to go on the warpath after them. The shift is signalled quite nicely by the movement between two scenes and shots: the first, a tableau, in the russet Murtaugh home, of Rog being held and comforted on the staircase by his wife, standing a step above him and holding his head against her chest, while in the foreground, filling up most of the screen, Riggs's handsome psycho-loner lethal-weapon face and head, stiff with grim resolve, appear in close-up; the second, a two-shot of Roger and Riggs preparing for battle in the lurid orange light (whose ostensible source is, ironically, the lights of the family Christmas tree), two figures of equal strength and value now, Roger acknowledging with pressed lips and curt nods his acceptance of Riggs's rampager's code: "We do this my way – we shoot and shoot to kill. We're gonna get bloody on this one, Roger."

And so, of course, they do, up to and including that climactic moment when the vanquished Aryan warrior, having risen or reappeared from the ashes of his defeat, is put paid to at last by the black sidekick. Only *Die Hard 2*, which departs from its companion films in this regard by more or less "randomizing" race across its spectrum of male actants, fails to provide us with some such moment, which the original *Lethal Weapon* and *Die Hard* films deliver in all its bristlingly multivalent glory.[14] When in *Die Hard* Al Powell lifts his weapon to blow away wild-eyed, blood-spattered Karl when, miraculously undead, the latter shows up on the steps of the ravaged office tower from which McClane and Holly at long last are free, we know he has thus healed himself (with, one feels, the help of McClane's good example) of the sickly hue of irresolution that has rendered him impotent as a street officer ever since he mistakenly shot and killed a thirteen-year-old. Likewise, albeit less explicitly, when despite the terrible clobbering Mr Joshua of *Lethal Weapon* has just taken at the punching, chopping hands, high-kicking feet, and hard-squeezing thighs of Riggs, that bad guy too manages to slip yet one more gun into his wicked hands, and lift his head to aim and shoot one last time; though here both Riggs and Murtaugh manage to whip theirs out, and plug the Evil One together simultaneously, it is Murtaugh's shoot-to-kill reflex action that signifies most, given his frequent criticisms of Riggs's propensity, earlier in the film, to kill whatever he draws his gun on.

Yet this literally invigorating tale of cross-racial influence – in which, one cannot help but notice, the black man seems to receive from the white man's hands not only the capacity for effective violence, but something very like virility itself, both gifts the white male imaginary has often enough feared it might lack in comparison to blacks who might possess them in excess – is only half a story that also includes the equally proto-sexual healing of the white man by the black. Or, more accurately, *gendered* healing, *feminine* healing, insofar as Powell and Murtaugh manage to curb McClane and Riggs's worst, most excessively male tendencies towards self-destructive behavior by bringing them back to the pleasures of the hearth. Murtaugh lures Riggs in from the suicidal shoals by bringing him literally into the family, an action whose intended cure we realize is complete when, at the film's conclusion, Riggs hands the daughter whose life he and her father have saved the silver bullet (shades of the Lone Ranger!) he had once meant to use on himself; in *Lethal 2*, moreover, while working in their kitchen on a meal for the Murtaughs, Riggs can now at last tell Rog's wife Trish what happened on the day his wife was killed. And the self-recriminations that crowd Riggs's account of that fateful day on which he was too bound up with work to meet his doomed wife on time find their counterpart in McClane's confession of sins to Al over the walkie-talkie, at the Gethsemane-like moment in *Die Hard* when, hiding in a men's room, blood oozing from the glass in his feet, he begins to feel that perhaps he will not make it out alive after all. In this down mood, McClane calls for his friend; Al replies, "I'm here, John"; and McClane asks the only person in the world to whom he is both literally and affectionally connected to transmit the following rambling tearful message to his wife:

> tell her that – uhm – tell her it took me a while to figure out what a jerk I've been – when things started workin out for her I shoulda been supportive – shoulda been behind her more – tell her that she's the best thing that ever happened to a bum like me. She's heard me say I love you a thousand times, she's never heard me say I'm sorry – tell her that John said I was sorry…

The manifest motivation for this flurry of sensitive insights derives from the hoary narrative trope of the need to come clean in the face of impending death. But its latent suggestion is the sense, as in the *Lethal Weapon* films, that only thanks to the presence and influence of the nurturant, supportive, domestic black buddy can the white hero at last let himself be straightforwardly soft and sensitive too.

To sum up the last several paragraphs, we might say that one primary aspect of these films' ideological/entertainment project is the construction of a hot spot at the center of our diagram, a place where some of the bad guys as well as the good, and black guys as well as white, both care and kill – kill, indeed, *because* they care (even Karl of *Die Hard*, vile assassin that he is, knowing the pain of losing a brother, hisses when he at last gets his hands on McClane, "Ve are professionals; zis iss *personal*") – and where race doesn't really matter any more. Accordingly, our black side-kicks' execution of the Aryan bad guys functions not only as a clear sign of their enhanced potency, but as a sacramental emblem of their purgation of the inward equivalent of such testosterone-crazed thugs from our white protagonists' souls. Nor, in addition to this psychotherapeutic component, does this zone where quasi-emasculated blacks and thuggish whites trade domestication and *cojones* lack its own Eros as well. McClane and wife Holly may have just embraced, following the death of Gruber, in the light provided by the flaming building they're still in; but once they walk outside together, the movie's largest gush of romantic violins is reserved for that drawn-out moment when the two men, Al and John, at last come face to face, approach one another and fall into an embrace (followed, in its stead, by Al's prompt dispatch of Karl). Likewise, in the first *Lethal Weapon*, where Riggs's and Murtaugh's joint execution of Mr Joshua is capped by Riggs's backward collapse into Murtaugh's waiting arms: "I've got you, partner," Murtaugh says, and we go to dissolve, for the climax is complete. And at the end of the sequel, the same maternal-erotic charge is pushed beyond the point of parody: *Lethal Weapon 2*'s final image, before the helo-shot lifts us up and away, is of Riggs lying sprawled across Murtaugh's lap in a perfect Piéta, trading joke lines (despite the clip of bullets just emptied in Riggs by Afrikaaner arch-villain Arjen Rudd before – you guessed it – Murtaugh blows him away) whose main butt is the sensitive, health-conscious, "post-feminist" guy ("Hey Rog – anybody ever tell you you really are a beautiful guy?" followed by hilarious snorts and brays).

Hence the truth of the revelation laid by one of producer Joel Silver's friends on the *Vanity Fair* flak-writer profiling him: the one who, watching the widely promoted scene from *Lethal Weapon 2* in which Riggs shares with his friend Murtaugh the risk of death from the gravity bomb wired to the toilet Murtaugh's on, suddenly exclaimed, "'This movie's about *love*.'"[15] But now let us move on and turn our attention to those actants and sites that such erotic and comradely rites and festivals either leave on the sidelines or destroy: women and their supposed "natural habitat," that is, the family home. Our four films are, as we have seen, manifestly supportive of both; yet the underlying dream logic of the *Lethal Weapon* films in particular suggests a somewhat different attitude. Something of that attitude is implied, for example, in the very scene we have just mentioned, and surfaces as soon as we allow our minds to play with the montage-logic of its climax: Riggs and Murtaugh, hands firmly clasped, rising swiftly then toppling, embracing, in the bathtub, underneath the black bomb cloth – and we cut to the front lawn outside to see part of the Murtaugh house's second story blow up. Likewise with the Murtaugh family station wagon in the same film, which we see getting more and more battered with each action sequence, beginning with the opening chase scene – and even with the otherwise rather curious degree to which the full comic potential of this bit of *shtick* is left unrealized, given the tepid and occasional nature of Murtaugh's protests at this abuse.[16] And while we are talking about cars, homes, and families, how about that moment near the end of the first *Lethal Weapon*, just after the frenzied Mr Joshua blasts his way into the Murtaugh home, when suddenly an empty squad car careens through the front picture window, sent by our rampaging, no-holds-barred partners Murtaugh and Riggs?

Again, the manifest content here would have it that this action is a ploy to distract Mr Joshua so our boys can get the drop on him. Yet it seems at least as significant that our squad-car-gone-wild delivers a spectacular trump to the action on whose heels it lands: Mr Joshua's comic-demonic drilling of the TV set on which *The Christmas Carol*'s Scrooge has just enquired of a passerby what day it is. "Christmas Day!" the maddened Mr Joshua shrieks, pumping lead into the exploding set next to the bedecked Christmas tree – and then on top of that comes the squad car smashing through the walls. It is Christmas, the time, symbolically, mythologically, of maximally happy domesticity, in three out of four of these films (*Lethal Weapon 2* being the exception), all three of whose endings prominently feature an ironic play between the visions of domestic coziness conjured up by familiar renditions of canonical Christmas songs on the soundtrack, and the disordered or ravaged landscape presented to our eyes. According to co-producer Silver's friend in the *Vanity Fair* puff piece, Silver's response to the line on love quoted above is "'Why do you think I play so much Christmas music in these films?'"[17] But the visual contexts in which those corny old renditions occur – the wrenched, flaming rubble of the office tower at the close of *Die Hard* and the swirling tumult around the jet on the still-disabled airstrip of Dulles at the end of *Die Hard 2* (both shown against Vaughn Monroe purling out "Oh the weather outside is frightful/But the fire is so delightful/So as long as you love me so/Let it snow, let it snow, let it snow!"); and even the close of the first *Lethal Weapon*, as Riggs enters the Murtaugh home together with his dog, who immediately, though offscreen, takes off after the cat, so that over the strains of "I'll Be Home for Christmas" we hear the smashing objects, hissing snarls and barks – all invite us to enjoy a far more aggressive, even sadistic, and certainly anti-domestic holiday than that response implies.

If all four films, and the *Lethal Weapon* duo in particular, thus wring the full ambiguity out of the old domestic injunction to "keep the home fires burning," their depiction and deployment of women is also ambivalent at best. We have already described how these films translate racially coded actants into gender-coded ones. What bears emphasizing now is not only the culturally androgynous and complete killing-caring guys who result from this translation, but the perfect adequacy of this all-male couple and, accordingly, the relative superfluity of all those around who remain merely biologically female. We might come at this same point slightly differently by noting that the one secondary woman character in these movies who comes closest to embodying the old nuclear-patriarchal ideal – Roger Murtaugh's wife Trish – has, as her single character note, only her partial divergence from that very role: the running joke is what a terrible, incompetent cook she is after all. On the other hand, the definition of Holly Gennaro and Rika Van Den Haas, the official love interests of both *Die Hard*s and *Lethal Weapon 2*, respectively, presents the male protagonists of those films with a problem to resolve: both are business-suited, dress-for-success professionals pursuing careers that take them away from home.

So, in the first *Die Hard*, following the brisk exposition of his uncertain marital situation McClane gives to the young but sympathetic (that is, in these films, black) chauffeur who, courtesy of the corporation Holly works for, has him picked up on his arrival in LA, we watch his face frown as he looks in vain on the video-directory screen in the office tower's lobby for the listing under McClane, then crumple when he finds Holly under her maiden name, Gennaro – all, moreover, while still reacting to the guard-receptionist's mocking/menacing claim for the machine he's using ("if you have to take a leak, it'll even help you find your zipper"). Next, upon his arrival upstairs, where a posh yet casual corporate Christmas party is underway, he is immediately cruised by an attractive female employee, and kissed on the mouth by a male one. "California," he mutters with sour humor, thus suturing geographic region and multinational enterprise by finding them complicit in the same unseemly behavior. Such lax, unwholesome goings-on may be found even in his wife's own office, which as it happens Ellis, the glib, sleazy yuppie exec who we know was hitting on Holly just a few minutes ago, is presently using to stuff his nose with coke; yet Mr Tagaki, the company president who shows McClane into the office, merely issues a hushed warning to his mega-deal-making hot-shot employee ("Mr McClane," he says, "is a *policeman*") and leaves it at that.

Such is the amoral but sumptuous world for which Holly McClane née Gennaro has broken up her home with husband John. Yet it is clear from her breathy close-up when they too are at last together that he still excites her – not to mention that later moment when, as one of the hostages, she looks on at Karl's fit of rage, and sighs joyfully in the knowledge that her man is still alive and on the job: "Only John," she declares, "can drive somebody that crazy." Moreover, despite all these hints (or, just as accurately, thanks to them), we are not invited to vote openly against this professional woman's pursuit of a career. For one thing, McClane doesn't seem to know or credit what we know: that she's still a fully domesticated, family woman underneath, who rejects Ellis's invitation to "hot mulled wine, aged brie" and a fire in favor of her traditional Christmas vision of "families, stockings, chestnuts roasting, Rudolf and Frosty," even as she strides down the corridor to look at some spreadsheets. Moreover, in the couple's first and only scene together before the pseudo-terrorists bust in, we are given one moment whose intent is quite clearly to position us on Holly's side: when McClane, washing up in Holly's individual corporate washroom, converts the loving warmth in her eyes to blazing anger with a tirade, whose immaturity he will concede a minute later, on the perfidy of her use of her unmarried name.

Yet in other equally obvious ways, the film actively subverts its own lip service to this bourgeois feminist ideology, and the right it asserts for all women deemed qualified to have their own high-salaried jobs in tall buildings. For not only does it amply demonstrate the impotence of all these corporate professionals in the face of real danger – in which a fast-talking schmoozer like Ellis, for example, in his greasily unscrupulous attempts to "negotiate" a way out, simply gets himself blown away, and from which, wouldn't you know it, the suit types can only finally escape thanks to the efforts of a low-class, wisecracking yet inarticulate ordinary guy. The filmscript, indeed, even arranges things so that when the evil Gruber, shot by McClane, falls backward through the office tower window, he nonetheless manages to drag Holly, his final hostage, with him to the edge of death by holding on to the strap of the Rolex watch – the one Ellis pointed out to McClane earlier, back when the party was still on, as the Nakatomi Corporation's token of appreciation for a mega-deal well made – so that McClane must undo the strap of this trinket-turned-handcuff to free her from the evil that is literally attached to it, and thereby save her life.

The case of Rika Van Den Haas in *Lethal Weapon 2* is both similar to and far cruder than that of Holly Gennaro in *Die Hard*s 1 and 2 (in the latter of which, still a businesswoman, she must be rescued again, this time from a circling jet), so we need not linger on it long. Suffice it to say, first, that Rika, Riggs's only (briefly) living love interest, is also a business-suited employee of a major firm, albeit one headed by jowlishly sinister, pale-eyed Arjen Rudd, and dealing drugs, currency, and gold under its cover as embassy arm of the South African government. Second, beneath her grey suits it soon turns out she has all the giggling sexual good health of a Playboy Bunny, and so is immediately susceptible to Riggs's rather fumbling yet domineering moves. Third, on the other side of their one lovemaking bout, she first turns immediately domestic (as evidenced by her rescue of Riggs's dog from the bad guys, her immediate rejection of her job, and her prompt invitation to Riggs to move in with her) and then gets iced herself. Her death, in turn, will once again trigger Riggs's trauma and rage over his wife's death, all the more so since it turns out that the same wicked South Africans were to blame in both cases – and so, with him and Murtaugh, we are soon off on the rampage again. But meanwhile, the film's soft-porn characterization and perfunctory treatment of Rika merely underlines the double-bind brutality of all four films' traffic in women – dismissed or disappeared insofar as they settle for being love toys and/or domestic servants, they must have their noses rubbed in their lack of real capacity and power if they don't.

Finally, a slight yet revealing submotif of the *Lethal Weapon* films takes us to an unexpected stake within all four films' depictions and deployments of the gender divide. I refer to the female police psychiatrist whom we meet in the first *Lethal Weapon* film on her way down a corridor in police department headquarters, badgering the male, middle-aged lieutenant who oversees Murtaugh and Riggs on the subject of the latter's suicidal tendencies and resultant unfitness for duty. The lieutenant wants to dismiss her diagnosis and recommendation as just a "bunch of psych bullshit," but she so relentlessly dogs his trail that he has to duck into the nearest men's room to escape her. Subsequently, in *Lethal Weapon 2*, she reappears in the same setting just after Riggs has dislocated his shoulder then just as painfully put it back in, in order to escape unaided from a straitjacket and so win a bet with his fellow cops. With a sadly disapproving shake of the head, she tells the still-panting Riggs that the door to her office is always open. But Riggs's sarcastic reply is swift and devastating: "I think we ought to keep this on a professional level, don't you, Doctor?" And once again the female shrink is humiliated and cast aside by the invocation of sexual difference, this time accompanied by the sneering laughter of the crowd on the screen, as well as the audience looking on.

Now obviously the pleasure the films invite us to share at these moments is a sexist one – but not exclusively so. It is equally the pleasure of watching *a professional* get her comeuppance from a regular working guy, in organic relationship to other working folks, men and women alike, gathered round: and all the more so, we might say, insofar as in each case it is a reference to the crude fact of gendered embodiment that deflates her claims and brings her down. Correlatively, I have already hinted that no small part of the appeal of the *Die Hard* films for mass audiences of non-professional people (not to mention those subpersonalities within professional folks with an anti-corporate, anti-professional populist cast) might well lie in the fact that in both cases McClane literally brings his corporate-professional wife down to earth. In this sense, in these ways, just as these films' black-white racial code turns out to be transmitting messages that are as much about gender as they are about race, its woman-man code turns out to fuel its reactionary sexual politics with the high octane of anti-professional, anti-corporate *ressentiment*.

But this *ressentiment*, and the pleasures of venting it, come in a wide variety of forms. *Die Hard* alone offers them to us in such profusion that we could, if we liked, compile a list of all the actions in the film that offer us the glee of discharging such spleen, ordered in terms of what we might call their "degree of disavowability." The shockingly sudden, perfunctory, and, in terms of narrative time, *early* murder of Mr Tagaki, head of Nakatomi–US operations, by the suavely elegant Gruber would probably top this list: he seemed to be a nice enough guy when he was showing McClane around, McClane seemed to like him; plus when the bad guys take over the building and Gruber stalks the crowd of corporate execs for him, Mr Tagaki faces up to his nemesis with courageous dignity. On the other hand, though, he *did* make that smooth little crack, when he first met McClane at the Christmas party about the Japanese being "flexible – we couldn't get you at Pearl Harbor so we got you with tapedecks;" he did try to slide the fact of Ellis's coke-sniffing under the rug; he *is* a ruling-class capitalist manager of enormous power, wealth, and smugness, *and* a foreign one at that. So let's kill him anyway; or no, let's *have* him killed, but have Gruber do it; we'll even have McClane himself there, looking on from a hidden place, so that when Tagaki gets his, right in the center of the forehead, so close that the force of the shot knocks him straight back off his chair, we immediately cut to McClane's shocked and horrified reaction: that way we can enjoy the death at the same time we enjoy our disavowal of that enjoyment, in the form of a savory horror at the villainy of our new arch-villain and his crew.

The subsequent execution of yuppie cokehead Ellis provides us with another example of hostility simultaneously discharged and disavowed, of the mechanism which so clearly resembles the "double/Other-ing" whose spider web of likenesses/antagonisms spun from black sidekicks to white wild-guy protagonists to Aryan nasties we traced out a while ago. Yet in *Die Hard* the relation of the mobile functionality of Gruber and his bad guys to their assigned iconic value in our *combinatoire* on the one hand, and our audience pleasures on the other, soon becomes an even richer and more slippery subject. For starters, as the film's voice of (delegitimated) authority, LAPD Deputy Chief Duane Robinson is wont to point out to McClane's outside friend Al Powell, both the pseudo-terrorists *and* McClane are responsible for the destruction of the brand-new shiny office tower itself, whose wrenched and shattered form is, as we have already noted, surrounded by smoldering heaps of ruin as the Christmas music strikes up at the film's close. It is with places of business as with homes in these films, as, according to the American officer's notorious comment some twenty-odd years ago, it used to be with Vietnamese villages: one has to destroy them, apparently, in order to save them – and one does so virtually side by side with those villains from whom one is saving the particular space or site.

But all that is still really *only* for starters, since what truly complicates *Die Hard* and its preferred pleasures is the degree to which the Gruber gang's "double-Othering" is itself doubled: or, to speak more plainly, the extent to which they function as doubles for the corporate managers and professionals they have taken hostage in the film, *as well as* for the rampaging McClane (whose opposition to them becomes, accordingly, more resonantly multivalent still for those of us looking on). Clearly enough, the entire group of bad guys are specialist-technicians, each and all, in their respective fields: electronics, explosives, and, perhaps most of all, computer hacking, performed here by a brainy, witty, and rather likable black techno-twit named Theo, who not only keyboards himself past a battery of key-code gates protecting the boodle in the corporate vault, but presides over the destruction of the LAPD's crack anti-terrorist force and its most sophisticated weaponry with the wholesome élan of a brainy teen at video games (as a specialized armored car is struck by a rocket whose launch signal he has given and explodes, Theo shrieks in self-mocking delight, "Oh my god, the quarterback is *toast!*"). Except for Theo, more-over, who sports a rather collegial sweater, the group's sartorial taste runs to stylishly loose-fitting turtlenecks and baggy trousers, albeit in sombre hues of grey and black – really a kind of uniform of off-duty elegance for the casual yet industrious professional-managerial man of the 1980s, with a dash of European flair.

The group's leader Hans Gruber is, on the other hand, in another class altogether, if not quite a class of his own. As the head of his own international group of experts and specialists, he is befittingly garbed in a quietly expensive, custom-tailored grey wool suit. Indeed, on the way up to the chief executive's office and boardroom with Tagaki, Gruber, in between humming the "Deutschland uber Alles" theme he has picked up from the Haydn quartet that was being performed at the Christmas party when he and his boys first busted in, makes a point of telling Tagaki that he recognizes the Saville Row tailor of his suit, and in fact owns two of the same man's suits himself: "Rumor has it," he murmurs with a disarming insider's charm, "Arafat buys his there." Moreover, between the time of Tagaki's execution and the herding of the hostages up to the roof, Gruber presides over the hostage-employees of Nakatomi with a blend of casual grace and perfect firmness that is itself the mark of one to the manner born. Even the subtle relays of the film's soundtrack music, diegetic and not, from the Bach and Haydn the Tagaki/Nakatomi string quartet is playing at the party, through Gruber's humming, to the strains of Beethoven's "Ode to Joy" that pour forth as the vault finally opens up, underlines the extent to which Gruber and his band are continuous with their ruling-class and/or corporate-professional hostages: all those, that is, with the cultural capital to listen to classical music, like it, and know it as their own.[18] And that continuity, in turn, makes possible yet another double pleasure for the viewing audience to enjoy. Besides getting off on (while disavowing, if need be) the rush of seeing yuppie-professionals terrorized and office towers smashed to bits, we get to see surrogate yuppie professionals and one incredibly smooth ruling-class creep eat lead and die.

Again, as in the case of women, when we turn to the equivalent characters in the *Lethal Weapon* films, we find a bolder, cruder version of the same, this time in the person of Arjen Rudd and his well-coifed thugs in their uniformly formal silver-grey suits and ties. Yet Rudd and the bad boys of his South African syndicate remind us in turn of another aspect of all these proto-corporate figures of evil we have left unexplored until now, that is, their use of *politics as camouflage*. Gruber and his gang pose as political terrorists to lure the authorities into a series of helpful false moves; Rudd protects himself and his men with the invocation of "diplomatic immunity." In *Lethal Weapon 2*, even Riggs and Murtaugh get into the act, as Murtaugh fakes a political incident downstairs at the embassy then whips up the enthusiasm of the anti-apartheid lobby outside so that Riggs can slip into the building all the way to Rudd's inner office and tweak the devil's beard in his own den. What are we to make of this consistent – and, judging from the films' receptions, apparently consensual if not downright pleasurable – depiction of international politics as a ruse and a shuck?

On one level, the answer to this question coincides with another we have already given, on the overriding importance of the *personal* motive in our heroes' struggle against the evil people and powers they face. In *Lethal Weapon 2*, just before Riggs takes off in his truck to pull down singlehandedly the multimillion-dollar stilt house Rudd and his cronies live in, thereby handing us another jolt of left-populist eat-the-rich joy, he tells Murtaugh, "I'm not a cop tonight, Rog. It's personal." And in the film's final confrontation Rog, having taken the cue, will complete the sentence Arjen Rudd, having just gunned down Riggs, has begun – "Diplomatic immunity" – with "has just been revoked," and a bullet of his own. In the same way, an exchange between Tagaki and Gruber in *Die Hard* (Tagaki: "What kind of terrorists are you?"/Gruber: "Who said we were terrorists?") receives its rhyme in another that follows shortly between McClane and the first of Gruber's gang he kills (Bad guy: "You won't hurt me 'cause you're a policeman; there are rules for policemen."/McClane (as he kills him): "Yeah? That's what my captain keeps telling me."). Through such rhymes and echoes still another link in the chain of double/ Otherness is forged in the form of a tacit agreement between heroes and villains that state and legal institutions finally have nothing to do with what is really going on.

Clearly, this anti-institutionalist, anti-political seme offers its own populist pleasures; there are satisfactions for both left- and right-populist subalterns, after all, in depictions that suggest that underneath the level of politics and statecraft the media always babble about there is only naked greed, and, finally, that beyond all talk of government and law, it's up to us – and primarily us white men – to clean up the muck. Yet these films also hint at other, darker sentiments and forebodings concerning their own anti-institutional cast. We have only to recall the apparent helplessness of the LAPD in *Lethal Weapon 2* in the face of the offensive staged against their members by the South African cartel, or the spectacularly, disastrously ineffective shows of force mounted against the pseudo-terrorists of *Die Hard* by both the LAPD and FBI, to sense that there is anxiety as well as delight in the distrust of authority that all four films in some measure tap and display.

When we begin to look in these films for evidence of what precisely is amiss in the house of authority (loosely labelled "the State" in our *combinatoire*), we come up with an interestingly similar pattern of details. I'm thinking here once again of that scene from *Lethal Weapon* between the female psychiatrist and the male superior officer in which the latter must duck into the men's room to get away, and of the other scenes and details that surround it: of the shot of the female police officer conducting a blue-uniformed chorus of "Silent Night" with her nightstick that opens this whole sequence introducing us to police headquarters, and of her reappearance in a sort of Christmas mambo line of herself and her fellows just after the scene with the shrink – a laughing, singing collective whose ludic image provides the spatial suture between that scene and the next one in Murtaugh's office, between Rog and another, unnamed plainclothes cop delivering a jeeringly ironic rap on what a sensitive guy he is. Then, in *Lethal Weapon 2*, there is the scene in which Riggs and Murtaugh are taken off the case they're on, the one that leads to the South African cartel, and given state's witness Leo Getz to protect instead: these orders, which we pretty much already know they will largely ignore, all the more since Riggs even now is flaunting his refusal to respect the No Smoking sign that their superior officer, the same one badgered by the shrink in the original film, has posted in his office.

The amused contempt we are invited to feel for this officer in the *Lethal Weapon* films is thus quite close to that we come to have, with Powell and McClane, for blustering, ineffectual Deputy Chief Duane Robinson in the first *Die Hard* film, and even for the parodically hard-bitten FBI officers who ignore his presence and dimiss his authority as soon as they enter in turn – and for the same general reason. For soon enough in *Die Hard* we shall discover what the *Lethal Weapon* films have had, more insistently and explicitly, to tell us: that the underside of even the FBI guys' rulebound power trip (in a voice drenched in sarcasm and disgust, Powell tells McClane, "They got the Universal Terrorist Playbook, and they're running it step by step") is the outright *childishness* of white agent Johnson's creepy glee as their helicopters swing in toward the office tower roof on a disastrously ill-conceived mission of first picking up the hostages and then blowing the "terrorists" away. (White Johnson [following war-whoop]: "Just like Saigon, huh, Slick?"/Black Johnson [grinning with amused contempt]: "I was in junior high, dickhead.")

But there is an old joke from the US–Vietnam war itself that sums up what all these comic-disastrous examples of weakness in the site of institutional power have in common. "What's the difference between the US Marine Corps and the Boy Scouts?" the riddle goes; and the answer is, "The Boy Scouts have adult leadership." Or, more precisely, for our purposes at least, *male* adult leadership – by which I mean *phallic* power in the Lacanian sense of the term, stretching as it does from gender across formal social codes to law. To put it in other, more concrete terms, and to bring it back to our films, it is as if both the municipal and federal police departments were modelled on the pattern of Rog Murtaugh's family, in which the father – Rog himself, that is – is clearly loved yet equally clearly too much of an incompetent child himself, for all his bluster, to be seriously obeyed. In short, the site of the State in our diagram is weakened by both its *domestication* and by the *subversion of patriarchal-male authority* that contemporary domestication brings in its wake.[19]

If any further proof is needed that such a hollowing-out of Phallic authority is not only to be enjoyed as crypto-domestic sitcom but felt as a nagging problem as well, let us close our cruise around this Greimasian block with the briefest of glances at those genuinely patriarchal-Phallic figures of fully empowered male authority, Shadow Company leader Peter McAllister (in *Lethal Weapon*) and Colonel Stuart (in *Die Hard 2*) – or, more precisely, of the common iconography of their death. For if both these uniformly rigid, disciplined and disciplinary (ex-) military men must be finally defeated by our wild-guy heroes, it will not be before they have given us ample proof of their ability to command exceptional obedience from their men (think of Mr Joshua's roasting his own flesh at McAllister's command in *Lethal Weapon*), and to hand out punishments and executions with relentless swiftness to their enemies (the murder of Hunzacker in *Lethal Weapon* the moment he has spilled the Shadow Company beans, or, more impressively still, the catastrophic air disaster Stuart coolly stage-manages as object lesson in *Die Hard 2*): proof, that is, of the very ability to lay down the Law, be obeyed, and be effective that is woefully absent from the sites of legitimate state authority in these films. Nor, it is equally worth noting, will either of these evil yet authorized arch-villains be dispatched without literally trailing clouds of glory as he goes. McAllister's escape car, loaded with explosives and grenades, carries him off to hell in a giant fireball; Stuart vanishes in an even more spectacular explosion, literally on his ascent in the 747 jet that bursts in the night sky more gloriously than the most gorgeous fireworks. Is it too much to suggest that such grandiose demises give evidence of yet one more ambivalence they invite their audiences to indulge – toward the figure of a Patriarch who deserves to be honored in the very act by which He is cancelled or refused, in the form of the death/disincarnation of a god?

3. BODIES AND BUILDINGS, OPEN AND SHUT

diehard, adj. — stubborn in resistance; unwilling to give in. n. — a
stubborn or resistant person; especially, an extreme conservative.
Webster's New World Dictionary, College Edition (1966)

It's the only thing I was ever good at.
Martin Riggs, in *Lethal Weapon* (1987)

White, working, men: we have seen how these films define each of these crucial terms of race, class, and gender via a quite complex yet highly specific network of contrasts, codes, and correspondences; and we have studied how that network is in turn offered to the audience as an equally complex, multiply gratifying pleasure machine. But now, when we stand back from the network/machine we have articulated, what seems most deserving of contemplation is the indisputable ubiquity, and therefore the apparent centrality, of *gender* in all these operations of knowledge and naming and narrative pleasure: gender, that is, as these films' fundamental medium of exchange, even when the nominal point of the transaction is good guys versus bad guys, not to mention race and class.

Nor is it difficult to discern behind this general deployment of gender the shaping influence of recent shifts in the dominant sex/gender system, including those of which the ideologies and movements of feminism itself are either cause, effect, or both. The increased presence of women in professional positions in the national workforce; the erosion and decline of phallic-patriarchal power, in both the national state and the family home: these events and processes are clearly registered by our four films as *faits accomplis* that must be acknowledged and accepted, even as the anxieties and resentments they have provoked within the dominant male culture are rechanneled and released in a variety of directions and ways – via projection of gender code and homosocial bonding across racial lines, via the marginalization, humiliation, and rescue of (or revenge for) the *incapacitated* woman, and via the ambivalent pleasures of "keeping the home fires burning," to name only the most prominent of those we have seen.

Yet gender is even more deeply, consequentially present in these films than we have so far admitted, even as, at a certain level, what we have been calling gender begins to turn into – or to become also, and inextricably – something else. To find this level, though, we need to move away from narrative analysis per se, and back to those elements of dramatic rhythm and *mise-en-scène* which we touched on as aspects of these films' strictly *formal* postmodernity. For now, on the other side of our prolonged look at the network of relations and pleasures provided by our films' plots, it is possible to say a bit more about just what and how much those forms might signify.

Thinking back, to begin with, to the unsublimated energies of these films' dramatic forms, of their ready and indeed almost regular ("chop-chop-chop") gratifications of the desires they excite for graphic outbursts of violent action, we may now discern, despite and even through their industrialized regularities, a deep and as it were virtually "organic" connection between this formal aspect and our films' more explicit thematics of post-patriarchal male "wildness" – a breakdown and rejigging of the oedipal patterns of classical emplotment such that the slow-cooked and massively overdetermined climactic shootout is now dispersed into the rhizomatic form of one affiliated bit before and after another, each typically carrying its own relatively self-contained buzz or jolt. Yet it also seems that at precisely this deepest or at any rate least coded and most directly felt level of experience and pleasure the invocation of gender alone as an explanatory category becomes inadequate; or, to put it differently, that from here on- and in-ward, gender must be thought in conjunction with the traditionally Marxist concept of mode-of-production, even as the meanings and energies called up by the former concept are unleashed upon the latter, to transform it irrevocably.

For who, after all, could by the late 1980s fail to see the extent to which the present transformations of our national capitalist system (in conjunction with and athwart those of other national systems, and of multinational capital) are, subjectively and objectively, gender-coded and delineated through and through? Donna Haraway, in fact, has gone so far as to speak of the displacement and destruction of the old, semi-organized, male-dominant working class as constructed by centralized Fordist models of production and authority as, precisely, a "femininization" of work:

Work is being redefined as both literally female and feminized, whether performed by men or women. To be feminized means to be made extremely vulnerable; able to be disassembled, reassembled, exploited as a reserve labor force; seen less as workers than as servers; subjected to time arrangements on and off the paid job that make a mockery of a limited work day; leading an existence that always borders on being obscene, out of place, and reducible to sex.[20]

What, quoting Marxist geographer Edward Soja, we referred to earlier as the "squeeze in the middle of the labor market" is here rearticulated in a way that reveals a new gendered kinship stretching across the gulf left by the disappearance of the "First World" proletariat; for Haraway, post-Fordism and (post-)feminism are indissolubly connected processes, and the literal and symbolic feminization of professional-managerial layers and subproletariat alike relates to "the paradoxical intensification and erosion of gender itself" as both cause and effect.[21]

In the light of these formulations, the rhythms of excitation and satisfaction in these films – as well as those of their even more obnoxious cousins, for example, *Rambo II* and *Top Gun* – appear as expressions of this "paradoxical intensification and erosion," asserting male violence and/ or death-trip spectacle again and again even as their own speeded-up processes of gratification undermine any claim to male authority. Riggs's boastful yet plaintive disclosure of his talent as crack-shot assassin in Vietnam – "the only thing I was ever good at" – thus rhymes with "die-hard" John McClane's wisecracking New York street savvy. Both evoke, with various admixtures of pride, embarrassment, and wistfulness, the resonance of skills discounted or dismissed in the new late-capitalist Processed World of LA, within films that go on to reassert the ongoing value, even necessity, of such skills and savvy in the struggle against international criminal-commercial enterprise – as well as, paradoxically, in the triggering and justification of the desublimated, spectacularized pleasure of free-floating aggression casually, frequently released.

I am trying here to speak of the ultimate ground of these films, the reactive core of their overall imaginary, as a place where fantasies of class- and gender-based resistance to the advent of a post-feminist/post-Fordist world keep turning over, queasily, deliriously, into accommodations. "Who are you, then?" arch-Eurovillain Gruber demands via walkie-talkie of our hero; and John McClane, skipping nimbly from room to room across a corporate landscape that includes a stone statue of an Asian god framed by bonsai trees, says, "The fly in the ointment. The monkey in the wrench. The pain in the ass." And so he is, of course, in one sense; but in another less plotbound and verbal and more visual-iconographic sense, as guerrilla warrior in a new wild, foreign space, he fits right in. Likewise, our heroes' ability to move behind and through the skin of these new surfaces to the mechanisms and generators that run them – the beltways of Dulles Airport, the heating ducts of the Nakatomi tower, even those bizarre industrial backrooms of the heavy metal nightclub in *Lethal Weapon*, with their array of hooks, pulleys, and chains, from which Riggs and Murtaugh must make their escape – suggests not only their ability to get *behind* the surfaces of the new space, and to strike back at those surfaces from those forgotten and repressed undersides, but also their really quite uncanny familiarity with this whole new world, their weirdly intimate knowledge of their way around the very spaces they do so much, to our delight, to destroy.

These buildings/bodies, moreover, which literally in-corporate Fordist old and post-Fordist new, these sites or spaces both ruined and saved: do they not rhyme in turn, or even coincide, with the bodies of our oh-so-desirable heroes themselves, simultaneously displayed as beefcake and mortified as beef? In *Lethal Weapon 2*, recall how we first see Riggs dislocate his shoulder and smash it back into place on a bet, then see him do the same again when, tied and tossed into the water to drown, he comes face to face with the drowned body of his new lover Rika, killed by the same gang that earlier murdered his wife. In that second smashing of his shoulder to put it right, then, and in the howl he gives out, we feel and hear an amazing mélange of significance in which our dripping, sexy hero (at the moment of maximum pain and undress in these films, our heroes often come wet) demonstrates all at once his wildness and his sensitivity, his vulnerability to pain and his incredible ability to take it. And those torn but still beautifully exposed slick-muscled bodies, those bulging arms and firm springy pecs: how do we distinguish between their fierce (re)assertion of gendered difference and their submission to the camera – surely every bit as abjectly/potently complete as any by Hayworth or Monroe, in their own way – as objects of its gaze and our own? What, likewise, is the boundary line between the diehard assertion of rugged white male individualism and its simultaneous feminization and spec-tacularization?

I confess that I do not know the answers to these questions; indeed, I suspect that our four films and their protagonists have been constructed in just such a way as to make them unanswerable. Yet the tactics of confrontation and accommodation with a post-feminist, post-Fordist universe these films re-present, and the complex circuitries of pleasure they propose, are at least distinctly preferable to others deriving from the same imaginary, and doing at least as well at the box office as our four. Take *Batman* (1989), for example, a blockbuster film whose inner structure of desire and disavowal bears so many interesting similarities to that of the films we have been analyzing, and perhaps even more significant differences. I am thinking here, first and foremost, of the striking equivalent *Batman* offers to the white male populist rampagers heroized in the Silver films – and then of the fact that this equivalent character in *Batman* is Jack Nicholson's Joker, whom our hero, the aristocratic Bruce Wayne/ Batman, must vanquish for the picture to come out right. Only, oddly enough, that film does not really come out all that right. For one thing, the Joker's splashy violence, his openly tacky self-display, in contempt of all that is officially considered good taste and high culture – the populist charge of all this energy is soured by his sociopathic narcissism (though even here, a line like "Now, the moment when I relieve you, the little people, of the burden of your failed and useless lives," uttered just before the Joker releases poison gas on the Gotham City population, retains the faint aroma of a revolutionary utopian promise). For another, his enemy and our hero Batman is not only an oedipalized neurotic (his symptoms are classically repressed, whereas our Joker *acts out*) who shows little or no explicit concern for the public good; he is a stiff-faced, stiff-masked, stuffed-shirt drag as far as popular pleasures are concerned. Not for nothing does the film's climactic sequence display Batman in his rather dully hi-tech Batplane gliding in to snip the ties to the Joker's poisoned balloons, and not for nothing, in terms of our pleasure, does the Joker then pull out a ludicrously low-tech, long-barreled pistol and blow the plane to bits. What we notice and "connect with" in this film, aside from the spectacular East Coast/Fordist ruins of its *mise-en-scène*, is its bad guy, the rampager as anti-elitist arch-villain (and, as Andrew Ross observes in the essay previously cited, with a hint of African-American "blackness" in his soul, garb, and actions as well[22]), even as we disavow the very energies that are in the Silver films triumphantly affirmed.

Or, for yet another related but distinct set of meanings and pleasures, this one constructed across a number of ever-more-successful 1980s films, there is the stupefyingly overstuffed and intransigent figure of former bodybuilder Arnold Schwarzenegger. For Arnold, too, like McClane/Willis and Riggs/Gibson in the Silver films, is offered as an image of the new/ old white working man – insofar as his brawny, hard-shelled body, croaking out its monosyllabic lines while smashing whatever lies across its path, registers by now with us as *both* Barbarian (the *Conan* films of 1982 and

1984) and Cyborg (*The Terminator* [1984] and, less explicitly, *Running Man* [1987] and *Total Recall* [1990]). Yet, for all the overlap between most Schwarzenegger films and the *Lethal Weapon* and *Die Hard* series in terms of their desublimated, post-oedipal patterns of narrative pleasure, the fact remains that in many ways Arnold's appeal is virtually the opposite of Mel and Bruce's. Where they are mobile, he is stiff and unswerving; where they are sensitive, he is impervious; where they can think deviance and will the perverse,[23] he is involuntarily programmed (whether as law officer, terminator robot, or instinctive barbarian); where they float wisecracks, he drops gruesome puns (for example, after a decapitation, "He lost his head over me").

What marks Schwarzenegger most obviously as a specifically post-modern icon is, of course, our awareness of him as a monstrous mutation of the deadpan, dead-souled lineage of Bronson, Eastwood, and Chuck Norris. More generally, though, he also functions as figure of both past and future, by parodying the hard-working, industrious, compulsive white male worker he simultaneously represents – and not only onscreen. Indeed, one issue of *Time* from the closing days of 1990 artfully linked a story of Arnold's steady, self-willed rise to stardom, emphasizing his old-fashioned industriousness, tractability, strong will and good cheer, to its ensuing story, also slotted in the "Business" section, on American dominance in the global "Leisure Empire" – a dominance whose "most potent symbol" and "sword bearer" is, wackily yet appropriately enough, "an overgrown Austrian with a face and body out of a superhero comic."[24] If *Batman*'s regime of pleasure/power is thus, in accordance with the Gothic look of its urban industrial ruins, a primarily reactionary one in which transgressive social and libidinal desire runs free only insofar as it is stigmatized as Evil and defeated by the Good of Phallic Law,[25] the fun offered by Arnold, even in films like *The Terminator* and *Running Man* with superficially left-anarchist story lines, is something altogether more neo-conservative, inviting us to respond to his ridiculous implacability, obscene violence, and hulking insensitivity with a sneer that then permits the qualities sneered at to be embraced and enjoyed: as, in the decade just past, like many a young hip paper trader playing a financial system whose manifest absurdity and rottenness allowed him a measure of contemptuous detachment from his own avid participation;[26] or, for that matter, like Ollie North's Contragate minion Robert "Bo" Owen, in his smirking disapproval of those thuggish Contra leaders to whom he was, with the approval of the highest figures in the Reagan administration, nonetheless illegally funneling government funds for resupply in their war against the Nicaraguan revolutionary state.[27]

To slide back from such films and figurations to the wild, violent, mortified white male body at the center of the films we have been studying is to see that while the latter can hardly be taken as an icon of progressive movement, or even of its unambiguous possibility, by comparison with the bodies and regimes of pleasure that lie near or next it the permeability that comes along with that body's persistence, the sensitivity that accompanies its violence, the affiliations on the underside of its mechanisms of rejection and disavowal – all at least suggest a certain *comparatively* large and still negotiable space. Our films, as we have seen, depict a very specifically white/male/hetero/American capitalist dreamscape, inter- and/or multi-national at the top and multiracial at the bottom, in which the interracial is eroticized even as a sharp power line is reasserted between masculine and feminine, in which, indeed, all the old lines of force and division between races, classes, and genders are both transgressed and redrawn. If the results of all these constructions and operations are scarcely to be extolled as examples of radical or liberatory cultural production (and who would have ever thought they could be, given the economics and social relations of blockbuster film-making?), they nonetheless suggest a new and vertiginous psycho-social mobility, a moment of flux. In her brilliant study of the poetry of Rimbaud and the political culture of the Paris Commune, Kristin Ross tells us she has sought to counter those who approach the cultural productions of the past "uniquely from the perspective of the relentless 'it couldn't have been otherwise' logic of the commodity," by seeking to prise open a set of conjunctural politico-aesthetic possibilities that, virtually by definition, have long since been denigrated and lost.[28] My purpose here has been similar, though the "it couldn't have been otherwise" logic I seek to counter is less that of Frankfurt School or New Historicist cynics than of those within feminism and/or among the left who have come to take it for granted that the white male imaginary is not only Bad – racist, sexist, domineering, exploitative, individualistic, oedipal – by definition, but that it must be statically, monolithically so, and though the moment I speak of is the one we inhabit today. If, given the omnipresence of power relations and our being within historical time, no psycho-social body is ever finally closed, no imaginary ever complete or fully resolved, it is nonetheless possible – and, for radicals, arguably necessary – to be aware when certain bodies are mutating, and which social-symbolic imaginaries are disturbed and up for grabs. The *Lethal Weapon* and *Die Hard* films are at once a sign of opportunity – an indication that the sign white-straight-working-man is in flux and open to renegotiation – and a warning sign reminding us that if, as activists and theorists, we find ourselves uninterested in the task of seeking to manage, mine, and redefine that white-straight-working-man sign, other groups and forces will certainly be more than willing to shoulder the task for us, and in ways we are unlikely to approve.

NOTES

1. Some figures and ratings from *Variety*: *Lethal Weapon* earned rentals for its distributors of $29.5 million from March to December 1987, and was the number 10 top-grossing film of the year; *Die Hard* earned rentals of $35 million from July to December 1988, and was the number 7 top-grossing film of 1988; *Lethal Weapon 2*, with $79.5 million in domestic rental earnings, was the number 3 film of 1989; and *Die Hard 2* earned $66.5 million in rentals, and came in as the number 7 top-grossing film of 1990. Needless to say, these figures are only a rough gauge of our films' overall popularity at best, not least because the income they measure derives only from rentals and ticket sales in theatrical outlets, and does not include videocassette rentals and purchases – in many cases, including those of these films, a source of sales and profits large enough to be quite as significant a measure of mass popularity as traditional theatrical rentals and sales.

2. Andrew Ross, "Ballots, Bullets, or Batman: Can Cultural Studies Do the Right Thing?," *Screen* 31, 1 (Spring 1990), p. 33.

3. Jeffords's effortless and untroubled conflation of these films, and virtually all the others she discusses, as straightforward expressions of the masculinist-misogynist Will-to-Power in the Age of Reagan may be found in her *Hard Bodies: Hollywood Masculinity in the Reagan Era* (New Brunswick, NJ: Rutgers University Press, 1994).

4. The phrase comes from Michael Denning, *Mechanic Accents* (London: Verso, 1987).

5. Quoted from the review by "Jagr." in *Variety*, 4 March 1987, p. 24.

6. Quoted in Pat H. Broeske's critical summary of Stallone's *Rambo: First Blood* Part II, in *Magill's Cinema Annual 1986*, edited by Frank N. Magill (Englewood Cliffs, NJ: Salem Press), p. 323.

7. I can imagine some argument on this point from others who would insist that the real progenitor of Riggs and McClane is not Stallone/Rambo but Chuck Norris (in, for example, *Invasion U.S.A.* [1985] or *Delta Force* [1986]) – and, I suppose, before him, Charles Bronson and Bruce Lee. And of course these figures, and the brutally violent, explicitly reactionary and/or jingoistic subgenre in which they appear, have their role in the genealogy of the films we are studying here. However, I would maintain that Rambo is nonetheless the most immediate and direct forebear of Riggs and McClane and their respective films, insofar as the characters they portray and the bodies they display are defined by their sensitivity, suffering, and mortification, as well and as much as by their lethal strength and competence.

8. Robert B. Ray, *A Certain Tendency in Hollywood Film 1930–1980* (Princeton: Princeton University Press, 1985).

9. Of course I do not mean to deny the validity of this account of the US-Vietnam war insofar as it corresponds to the experience of any number of veterans still suffering from the effects of their participation in it. What is at stake here is, rather, Hollywood's projection of this traumatized individual perspective as *the Truth* of the War. Such a "therapeuticization" of our country's genocidal and imperialist aggression is, of course, most flagrantly ideological precisely in its offer to sidestep larger questions of policy, outcome, and responsibility. Yet my concern here is, as will soon become clear, less with the political utility of this narrative "ideologeme" for dominant elites or within mainstream culture than with the gender- and race-specific fears and desires which it runs on and expresses. For a provocative, insightful (if somewhat monological) analysis of the Vietnam narrative(s) which links up such desires and anxieties to a project of ideological retrenchment, see Susan Jeffords's *The Remasculinization of America: Gender and the Vietnam War* (Bloomington: Indiana University Press, 1989).

10. For profiles of Moredock, and analyses of the symptomaticity and spread of his behavior, see Ronald Takaki, *Iron Cages: Race and Culture in Nineteenth-Century America* (New York: Knopf, 1979); Richard Drinnon, *Facing West: The Metaphysics of Indian-hating and Empire-building* (Minneapolis: University of Minnesota Press, 1980), and Herman Melville, *The Confidence-Man: His Masquerade*, chs 25–27 (first published 1857; many editions available today). More generally, the standard work on the historical construction of American masculinity as a synthesis or negotiation between violent "savagery" and "civilized" behavior and belonging, is Richard Slotkin, *Regeneration Through Violence: The Myth of the American Frontier, 1600–1860* (Middletown, CT: Wesleyan University Press, 1973).

11. Denning, *Mechanic Accents*.

12. The quoted phrase is taken from Edward Soja, *Postmodern Geographies* (London and New York: Verso, 1989), p. 187; but see also *The State of Working America* (Washington, D.C.: Economic Policy Institute, 1990), and the guided tour of post-Fordism offered in *Socialist Review* 21, 1 (January–March 1991).

13. I use the term "black" here and throughout the analysis that follows, rather than the politically preferable "African-American," insofar as the films themselves construct this main line or axis of racial difference as precisely a "black/white" affair.

14. In *Die Hard 2*, Al Powell makes only a token appearance, while McClane encounters other Blacks (or should we now, in this context, say "African-Americans" again?) in the persons of the paramilitary thug he fights but fails to capture in the first action scene of the film, Barnes (Art Evans) as a sympathetic and helpful control tower technician, and, of course, the good–evil character of Major Grant (John Amos). I owe to my statistics-hip partner Ann Augustine the wonderful insight that "If you want to discount a variable, randomize it" – along with many other insights and editing suggestions along the way.

15. Jesse Kornbluth, "*Die Hard* Blowhard," *Vanity Fair* 53, 8 (August 1990), p. 66.

16. This may be the place to note the shift in the characterization of Roger Murtaugh himself in the follow-up film – or, rather, the sense in which that shift picks Murtaugh up as he is at the end of the first *Lethal Weapon* film, a more or less unhesitating partner and accomplice of wild-man Riggs. In structural terms, then, the position Murtaugh

occupies in our *combinatoire*, and in the first *Lethal Weapon*, is given to a new sidekick for them, in the comic personage of Leo Getz (Joe Pesci), the money launderer turned prosecution witness they are supposed to be guarding, who is pointedly depicted as being even more hysterically inept and comically domestic (he dons an apron and wields a vacuum cleaner in a vain attempt to clean up Rigg's bachelor-pad trailor) than Murtaugh ever was.

17. Kornbluth, p. 66.

18. There is more to this musical seme and its meanings than I have space to develop here. For one thing, the classical music whose presence is introduced at the Nakatomi Christmas party is in striking contrast to the Christmas rap music Argyle the chauffeur has just been playing for McClane on his way in from the airport, prompting McClane to ask, "Aintcha got any Christmas music?" The suggestion here, then, would be that neither Argyle's nor the corporate folks' music is genuine (white) people's Christmas music: *that* is up to McClane to produce or make possible himself, as, by the end of the movie, he does. Yet on the other hand, when his victory and the happy end of the film finally prompts such tunes to purl out on the closing soundtrack, the images of ruin they play against give them a rather ironic lilt, as we have seen.

And there is also the interesting and no doubt significant sense in which it is important that the classical music is identifiable with "Europeanness" – which in turn attaches itself easily enough to Gruber and his cronies, but has interesting implications for the ideological resonance of Japanese corporate figures Tagaki/Nakatomi. But I'm sure most readers will agree that the present reading is already sufficiently detailed and lengthy that I need not delve further into these matters here.

19. Here again there are some curious echoes of the Rambo films, and especially of *First Blood*, in which the local sheriff (Brian Dennehy) behaves as a hysterically punitive yet ultimately impotent paternal/institutional power, in contrast to the authorized *and* ultimately nurturant figure of Rambo's former commanding officer (Richard Crenna) from – where else? – his Special Forces days back in Vietnam. Yet, as the whole world now knows from *Rambo II*, this latter father will ultimately be shown to be less than fully supportive and empowered, leaving our hero to suffer and rampage through the wilds all on his own. For an interesting feminist-psychoanalytic speculation on all that may be represented and at stake here, see Jessica Benjamin, "The Oedipal Riddle: Authority, Autonomy, and the New Narcissism," in John Diggins and Mark Kann, eds, *The Problem of Authority in America* (Philadelphia, PA: Temple University Press, 1981).

20. "A Manifesto for Cyborgs: Science, Technology, and Socialist Feminism in the 1980s," first published in *Socialist Review* 80 (1985); here quoted from Linda Nicholson, ed., *Feminism/Postmodernism* (New York: Routledge, 1990), p. 208.

21. Ibid., p. 209.

22. See Ross, "Ballots, Bullets, or Batman."

23. One of the many reasons why *Total Recall* (1990) is such an unsatisfing film lies in its impossible premiss: that Arnold is a government-business operative turned dissident, a rebel who has joined in solidarity with the mutant Martian proletariat.

24. See "Box-Office Brawn" and "The Leisure Empire" in the 24 December 1990 issue of *Time*, which also knits the pieces together visually by using the same logo at the beginning of both articles: a headless United States standing on top of the globe on muscle-bulging legs, flexing its even more bulging arms, and thereby rhyming as well

with the "Box-Office Brawn's" main photo of Arnold holding a globe up on his hypertrophic shoulder and grinning out at us ... which photograph in turn is reproduced, in miniature and beside the title "America's Box-Office Muscle" on the issue's cover, over the image of a figure in business shirt, tie, and Arab robe and headdress, whose blank face is instead filled in with the cover-story headline "WHAT IS KUWAIT? And is it worth dying for?" Truly, as Henry James said, relations stop nowhere. (The quoted material in the main text, incidentally, may be found on p. 53 of this issue of *Time*.)

25. See Rosemary Jackson, *Fantasy: The Literature of Subversion* (London and New York: Methuen, 1981). And let me note here as well my own recognition that the contrast I am making between *Batman* and Schwarzenegger is a bit too neatly schematic; after all, many viewers will feel that *Batman* also winks out at us every now and then while restaging its reactionary script.

26. See, for a near-perfect example of this type, Michael Lewis's egregious but symptomatically self-congratulatory memoir *Liar's Poker: Rising through the Wreckage on Wall Street* (New York: Norton, 1989).

27. "Nice bunch of guys we're working with," Owens commented sardonically of the Contra leaders in a note to his boss Oliver North, whose main purpose was to report on how that – blatantly illegal but now, thanks to the cooperation of the legislative and judicial branches of "our" government with the executive, happily dismissed – work was going.

28. Kristin Ross, *The Emergence of Social Space: Rimbaud and the Paris Commune* (Minneapolis: University of Minnesota Press, 1988), p. 61.

CHAPTER TWO

THE YEAR OF LIVING

SENSITIVELY

In a film industry whose "classical" era of vertical concentration and studio production lies far in the past, and whose deal-driven craziness in the present exemplifies the speculative, and spectacular, frenzy of post-industrial economic life at the big-money end of the scale, the rampage films I have just been considering probably come as close as any bunch of movies can nowadays to comprising a film genre. Such is hardly the case, however, with the next group of films I want to discuss, whose generic referents (insofar as we and they have any left) range from Western and slapstick comedy across melodrama to fantasy and children's film. What nonetheless allows me to think of them together is, first of all, the convergence of their thematic agendas, which are all explicitly concerned with the redemption and conversion of their white male protagonists from one or another variant of closed-down, alienated boor to an opened-up, sensitive guy; and, second, the rather striking fact that all of them were released in the same year. It may or may not be the case that what we get from those entertainment industries whose business it is to secrete narratives to us are increasingly so many serialized *seasons* rather than genres; in any event, 1991, the year that gave us *City Slickers, Regarding Henry, The Doctor, The Fisher King*, and, as its boffo finale, the redoubtable *Hook*, must be considered, at least in film, as The Year of Living Sensitively.

We will come back later to poke at the question of how the political and ideological climate of the moment was able to sprout this particular clump of mushrooms. For now, I would like instead to take a closer look at the most telling features of the rhizomatic growth itself, beginning with some further elaboration of the thematic claim just lodged above. For not only does each of our several protagonists undergo conversion to sensitivity in the course of his film; each does so as the culmination of a passage through trials and suffering, on the other side of various terrifying and redemptive encounters with sundry Others, and, correspondingly, via so many humiliating and purgative abjections of the Self. In *City Slickers*, Mitch's education and mortification at the hands of Jack Palance's parodically leather-faced trail boss and through the exigencies of the trail are, of course, played mainly for laughs – or, perhaps it would be more accurate to say, using laughs as the lubricant with whose aid the redemptionist paradigm of *Regarding Henry* and *The Doctor* may be spread outward and downward from the upper reaches of the professional class. In these latter and in *The Fisher King*, movies made if not with a professional-managerial target audience in mind, at least with invitations to their audiences to imagine professional-managerial lifestyles as standard or even normative features of life, the same basic story and message are delivered wrapped in color schemes, framings, compositions and musical scores that openly insist their films' burdens of seriousness. The cattle drive in *City Slickers* is set up as a greenhorn's fantasy, a kind of Baudrillardian simulation that then gradually turns into a real life-threatening test; by contrast, *The Doctor* and *Regarding Henry* straightforwardly place their respective protagonists in danger of death early on, and *The Fisher King* begins by fixing its antihero with the responsibility for an innocent woman's senseless murder and her husband's consequent madness. Still, for all these differences in strategy (and, presumably, intended audience), the basic movement in all these films, and *Hook* besides, is from an initial state of alienation, through trial and suffering, to reconnection to family and cosmos, up to and including that final triumphant gesture of inclusion/resolution, the elaborate crane or helo-shot that draws back and (usually) up from our protagonist with his loved ones into an extreme long shot that reinserts them back into the world.

In effect, then, these sensitive-guy films might almost be considered the obverse and complement to the rampagers of the last chapter, ordinate to the latter's abscissa. Where the *Lethal Weapon* and *Die Hard* films stage contemporary versions of what Nina Baym has called the "melodramas of beset manhood" in nineteenth-century American fiction, struggling "horizontally" against and with kindred spirits by and against which they are metonymically defined, the films that configure the Year of Living Sensitively function to represent a proto-religious process rather than to stage a social agon, with protagonists who do not fight back nearly so much as they lift off. So too with the form and meaning of the typical endings of our two types of film: if, as we have seen, the rampagers end the many various and complex symbolic exchanges that comprise them with what amounts, for all the hyperviolence, to a shakily negotiated settlement – if, indeed, the violence *itself* is in some respects a symptom of the difficulty and instability of the final result – the transcendence of the hero makes it doubly impossible to imagine what might come after the ending of films like *Regarding Henry* or *The Doctor*: impossible, that is, to imagine a sequel *and* impossible to imagine in what ways and by what means the main character and his family are to live.

But it is time to ground some of these general claims in a descriptive analysis of a particular film. I choose Mike Nichols's *Regarding Henry*, since, for reasons I hope will become clear, it seems the most complete and ur-sensitive of all the films I want to discuss here. Its basic plot is easily summarized: Henry Carter (Harrison Ford), an amorally brilliant and ambitious corporate lawyer, is wrenched out of his career path and his increasingly loveless, selfish relationships with his wife and child when he is shot down in the course of a Mom-and-Pop store robbery in his posh New York City neighborhood. His near-lethal wound leaves him dispossessed of most of his memory and a conveniently unspecified amount of intelligence, so that, in effect, he becomes more or less literally a child. But with his regression comes a new (or should we say restored?) emotional vulnerability to joy and sorrow alike, and a compassionate sensitivity he brings in turn back to both his family and his former vocation. By the end of the film and as the conclusion of a series of heart-warming realizations and reappraisals, the new Henry walks his high-paying job in the cold-hearted law firm where he used to work, and, together with the wife whose love and passion for him he has rekindled, rescues his equally doting daughter from the harsh private school to which his wife and the girl's mother had mistakenly sent her – so that the final shot of the film, that extreme-long shot I mentioned before, gives us the lovingly reunited family strolling across the autumnal, leaf-strewn green of the school grounds, away from the white chapel that both consecrates this reunion and, more subtly, represents the class-bound repression from which all three, but especially Henry, are now delivered at last.

The double duty of this final landscape is as tellingly typical as the connotations of its color scheme, whose golds, russets and rich greens oppose their triumphant organicity to the dull, bleached pastel blues and greys and whites of the previous Henry's former spaces at home and at the office. (One thinks here of that notorious, fashion-setting, early-eighties assertion by producer–director Michael Mann that the secret of his success with *Miami Vice* was "No earth tones" – and then of the aggressive arborealism of his *Last of the Mohicans* in the early nineties.) Yet for all this contrast of textures and hues, and the apparent vociferousness of Henry's refusals, the organic-pastoral New England vision that encloses him and his family at the end also offers its own reassuring suggestion that by bowing out Henry has not at all ceased to belong to the privileged WASP world of his kind; having given up nothing worth keeping, he has now merely gained access to a corner of that world that is more beautiful, comfy, and life-affirming than the one the earlier, less worthy Henry inhabited.

There is more to say about how this closing scene manages to let Henry, and the audience who cheers for him, have it both ways; but to see and say it we will need to note a few key features of the earlier, developmental sections of the film. I'll start with what might seem to be in and of itself an inconsequential detail: the shot that gives us the moment at which the fallen Henry comes out of the coma in which he has been adrift. Henry's impeccably svelte, yet properly loving wife Sarah has been tearfully and ineffectually trying to draw him out; but now, just as she leaves the hospital room, the camera picks up the black nurse still in attendance and tracks her from medium-long to extreme close-up as, moving towards the camera, she also moves towards, and so blocks out, the still figure of Henry on the bed. Thus, at the climax of the shot we have an extreme close shot of her shoulder, a patch of white tunic emphasizing all the more the blackness of what we can see of her neck and hair – and then, when she moves back toward screen right, we see that Henry's eyes are now suddenly, miraculously, open at last.

I might be less justified in arguing that it is as though Henry had been delivered at this moment by the healing power of Blackness itself were it not for the central significance the film soon lends to yet another African-American character, Bradley, the sensitive, caring, yet fully masculine physical therapist who gets our damaged and bewildered Henry up and running again. Significantly enough, Bradley's first success comes when, on one of his first visits with Henry, he starts tossing the old heterosexist banter around, telling Henry of one passing nurse, "Got to get me some of that," and of another, "Already had me some of that" – and Henry responds by tracking after these women with his own dull, blank eyes. So the two men, child Henry and nurturant Bradley, are sealed and certified simultaneously as men and as brothers by a sexism that few identifying with the film's ostensibly liberal-PMC point of view will want to condemn in a Black man (cultural difference, you know). Moreover, Bradley's hyper-heterosexuality will be backed up by his later confession that he too once lived a former life – as a hot-shot college football player hoping and expecting to make it to the pros. These two bits of character detail are neither innocent nor random; together, they function to reassure potentially skittish viewers that far from being either sexually ambiguous or in-adequately masculine, this Black man is for all *his* sensitivity exactly enough of a mutha' to *be* a mother to our newly born, born-again child-man.

Following his wound, then, and through contact with a genially bene-ficent Blackness, Henry comes back into the world a new kind of White Man. Yet the main business of *Regarding Henry* will be to negotiate and define this new White masculinity in a way that will not upset those still invested in the present norms of patriarchal domesticity; or rather, it will be to titillate and alarm us with the possibility of disturbing those norms, only to restore them in a refreshed and reinvigorated form by the end of the film. Not at all accidentally, such possibilities arise as soon as Henry is released from Bradley's care to his wife Sarah's. The episodic plot that follows his return home presents us with two types of incident: one composed of Henry's encounters with his former circle of colleagues and friends, in which his present innocence and honesty expose their cynicism, cruelty, venality and viciousness, and his own in his former life; and another in which his childish ignorance and naiveté lead to amusing and/or touching results. The didactic function of the first type of incident is tediously obvious, but its lessons are complicated by at least some of the other scenes, whose sentimental surface fails to smooth over their poten-tially disturbing implications.

I am thinking here particularly of a series of episodes, counterpointed with those of the first type, in which Henry and his grade-school-age daughter Rachel interact as equals, or with Rachel as mentor: as when she teaches him to read, or when they sit on her bed together comparing scars. The climax of this series is a scene whose script and editing alike seem designed to articulate the danger to the whole family of Henry's remaining too much of a child, even as it follows a lunch scene between Henry and his former legal-team partners that lays bare their turpitude in the case we saw Henry himself summing up at the beginning of the film. "What we did was wrong," says the new Henry to them: to which his partner Bruce replies, "What we did was pay for our lunch." Here, obviously enough, we are urged to agree with Henry's judgement, and in so doing to find the childlike innocence from which it issues unambiguously worthy of emulation. But then this scene follows: we open with a shot of Sarah on the phone in the office in which she presumably is now working. "So everything's okay? Still love me?" she asks. And the reverse shot, against our expectations, gives us not Henry but Rachel on the other end of the line. She assures Sarah that everything's fine and asks when she will be home; Sarah tells her and warns Rachel not to spoil her dinner. Rachel agrees and hangs up, but then the camera follows her over to where Henry is standing over a cookbook and a cookie recipe he is audibly struggling to read.

The scene thus far suggests a mainly comic topsy-turviness in which the Wife–Mother plays Husband–Father, the Kid plays Wife–Mother, and the Husband–Father plays Kid. But the comedy curdles in what follows, first in the remainder of this scene, then in the subsequent one. For Rachel now introduces her father, the Kid, to the fact that she is supposed to leave home soon for an exclusive private school. Reluctant and frightened to leave, she asks him if he still wants her to go. "I don't want you to go anywhere," Henry replies, his voice atremble, "but I'm not sure it's up to me. Is it up to me?" The question follows him directly into the next scene, set that night in the bedroom he shares with Sarah, who, sitting over him as he lies clutching his pillow to his face, gently insists that, in general, she must be able to count on carrying through on some of the decisions they made together before Henry was shot, and that specifically this is one she feels they should hold to. In effect, the abdication and incapacity of the present Henry, for all his incipient wisdom, charm, and sensitivity, nonetheless leave Sarah perforce holding the Phallus of the former Man of the House: a double problem, insofar as it's both a mistake for Rachel to be sent away, and, by implication, a dangerous, destabilizing idea for a woman to hold that kind of decision-making power. (An idea, moreover, whose dangerousness is both simultaneously expressed and disavowed by Sarah's unambiguously upper-class position; so that we can say, if we like, that it's not really so much that we find women having power dangerous as that this *particular* woman's class identity leads her to error...)

Accordingly, the problem the rest of the film fitfully tries to work out is that of how the born-again, sensitized White Guy can keep the wisdom of his new-found or reborn childishness without dropping the reins of his power. Fitfully, I say, because it seems so tough a problem that *Regarding*

Henry cannot consistently admit, let alone satisfactorily resolve it. Nonetheless, the dilemma does inflect what remains of the film with some rather surprising, if not outright incongruous, accents. For example, in the scene that opens the morning after Sarah and the new Henry have at last made love, she regales him with the story of how she met and fell in love with the man he used to be: the one who stood before her and announced "'I'm Henry'," who knew where the best blowfish in the City could be ordered and eaten, a man of "such confidence," she says, still rapt in the memory, "it drew me in." While the scenes that follow for the most part return to the growing gulf between the new Henry and the world of the old one, from this point on it is as though the new Henry must now, paradoxically, reach back to the repertoire of his former self for some of that confidence and power, if only to make that break with his earlier self.

To effect this tricky transplant, the film will once more call on Black mother-man Bradley, who reappears carrying the classically American-individualist-masculinist message of autonomous self-declaration: "Don't listen to nobody tryin' to tell you who you are." Armed with such instruction, the new Henry will at last be able to provide the claimants the first Henry opposed with the evidence they will need to reverse the earlier judgement he had won; to sever his remaining ties to the evil law firm; and to come back home to take his rightful place at the head of the family as husband and father with a speech that sutures the confident strength of his former self with the childlike moral purity and direct access to his own wants and needs of his new one. "I know this great blowfish place," he recites to Sarah:

> I don't like my clothes. Maybe they used to be my favorites, but I don't feel comfortable with them any more.... I don't like eggs or steak. And Sarah – I hate being a lawyer.... I want us to be a family – for as long as we can...

To which Sarah, in *her* place again as the properly subservient wife, replies "Whatever you want is fine."

With all these negotiations and balancing acts in mind, we can turn to the film's closing scene; for here they are all woven together and concentrated into Henry's encounter with one final figure of repressive authority. Nor should it be surprising, given all we have seen so far, to find that that figure too is incarnated in a woman's shape – albeit yet another woman who melts and folds under the simultaneously liberating yet strongly assertive influence of our now triumphant man-child. I am speaking, of course, of the headmistress whose stern voice we hear as soon as the film straight-cuts from Henry's clinch with Sarah to the coldly white chapel of the private school to which the unhappy Rachel has been exiled under Sarah's well-meaning but off-kilter command. From the pulpit of this austere chamber, the headmistress is in the midst of laying down the very Law above which our Henry has risen:

> Now you're all learning what that means when you ask yourself, "Why do I push myself? Why do I strive to be a harder worker, a better listener?" Well, look around you: there are the answers to those questions. *Competition.* Everyone close your eyes. Repeat to yourself silently: "I will work harder; I will be a better listener..."

The message here may seem a little mixed at first, in its injunction to advance oneself in opposition to others to whom one must nonetheless fervently attend. But all this, of course, is precisely what our renovated man-child has learned and chosen *not* to do: neither, that is, to engage any longer in the quintessentially capitalist drive to advance oneself at the expense of others, nor to attend to others' perspectives at the expense of one's own wants and needs. It is this dual discourse that the now restored, regressed and yet transcendent Henry interrupts and ends with the fetchingly simple, direct statement of what *his* needs are: "I missed her first eleven years and ... and, I don't want to miss any more" – a statement whose miraculous transformational effect is all the greater for being uttered even as the camera is shooting our hero from the level of the headmistress's pulpit, at a downward angle normally used to suggest or emphasize a character's lack of power. For the headmistress, too, elevated as she may be in a literal sense, is immediately put in her place vis-à-vis our leading man, when his passionate sincerity reduces her to patting his hand and murmuring her last line: "It's good to see you doing so well, Mr Turner."

So now at last we return to our final long shot: what it means is that our Henry, our real, right, updated White Guy, can both be and have it all. He can be a child *and* a proper husband and father; indeed, he *should* be a child precisely because that is the right way to be both the latter as well. Yet the film also makes clear that knowledge of this profound yet simple wisdom does not come easy to today's White Men, who may well be so driven and so steeped in error that for all practical purposes they must die and be born again to come to it. They will at least need a temporary assist from another male figure who comes in from a different, less empowered or authorized (and therefore less damaged) position to lend a hand, and then discreetly disappears. And even with this help,

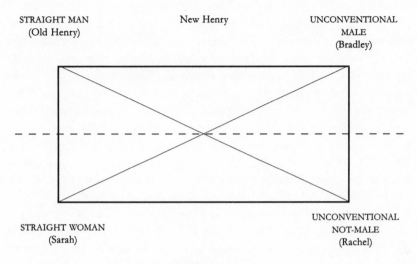

STRAIGHT MAN (Old Henry)   New Henry   UNCONVENTIONAL MALE (Bradley)

STRAIGHT WOMAN (Sarah)   UNCONVENTIONAL NOT-MALE (Rachel)

Figure 2

before coming to the new and higher selfhood our heroes will also have to spend some purgatorial time in the virtually powerless position of a child – but time that has its own instructional value, insofar as it re-connects our heroes to the simple truths and immediate pleasures of living in the moment and acting spontaneously and directly, out of the heart-truths of what they really feel. And he will probably also need some help from the last *and* least of our transforming presences: that, of course, of the good (that is, supportive, sympathetic, unquestioningly loving) wife or partner figure. She can't always understand what's going on, but she's in our hero's corner all the same, and all the way.

So close does this summary of *Regarding Henry*'s thematic and narrative material come to serving as a template or formula for this spate of films that we can put it in something like Greimasian rectangular form (see Figure 2). Something like it, yes, but quite different, too, from the usual model in which each corner represents one position in a field charged by a double set of structured oppositions. For here, the ideal or utopian figure of the new Henry is a *synthesis* of his recovered child-self with selected aspects of what he has learned from Bradley *and* some of the manly authority and confidence of his first, empowered yet insensitive self – a three-way fusion, in effect. Likewise, in these films we find no specific evil or dystopian figure combining the worst features of "conventional" and "unconventional not-male" and set in direct, antagonistic opposition to our hero's ideal self – or not quite. The masculinized, conventional woman in the form of the stern headmistress at the end of the film might seem to come close to being an absolute villain; but she would hardly represent the kind of vile negative synthesis of bottom-line qualities and figurations that Arjen Rudd and Hans Gruber did in our rampage films; nor is she comprehensible as a synthesis of the categories defining them. Rather, insofar as there must be a negative, stigmatized or dystopian subject to be expelled or warded off in these films, it is there in the form of a *relationship* rather than a character: that between a man who has gotten stuck in the child's position and a woman who may therefore have to take on the power and inflict the repression the man possessed and inflicted back in his conventional former life, when he was both in power and out of touch with his true self. The dream, in cheap Lacanian shorthand, is that men may recover and retain access to the free flow of the Imaginary, thanks to help from a few children and subaltern adults, and yet not have to let go of the Phallus. The nightmare, so terrible that it can only be hinted at, can only exist as a trace element at the margins of these texts, is that they will be unable to embrace the "inner child" that lies within each of them crying for expression, and hold onto their sceptres at the same time – so that adult women will have to step out of place, grab those sceptres, and for the best of misguided reasons institute an Age of Terrible Misrule.

The real test of this sloppy Greimas, though, must be how well it helps us locate, summarize, and comprehend the basic themes and relationships structuring the other sensitive-guy films I have promised to discuss. So let us move on to another one: *The Doctor*, directed by Randa Haines and released the same summer as the Nichols film. *The Doctor* stars William Hurt as Jack MacKee, a callous, arrogant and alienated surgeon who is brought low and transformed by his experiences in the same hospital where he works, once he is diagnosed with a potentially lethal cancer. And what is most immediately striking about this film compared to *Regarding Henry* is, on the one hand, the care with which it distributes racial and gender differences on both the side of the angels and within the ranks of the fallen and corrupt, and, on the other, the degree to which this liberal evenhandedness then functions as a context in which the nightmare just described can come that much closer to center stage. When callous, conventional Jack is horsing around in surgery in the film's opening scene, he is joined and egged on by the white guys on his team; only the Black woman who is his operating nurse refuses to enter into the cruel fun.

Likewise, on rounds with his residents, his lecture on the necessity of detachment is received enthusiastically by the two young white guys in the bunch, but critically interrogated by the Asian-American man and young white woman. Yet *The Doctor* will take care to turn these tables later on: we will, before we're out of the film, meet a pretty unsympathetic Black male radiologist; a real sweetie of a white-guy surgeon, Eli Bloomfield, a.k.a. the Rabbi; and, most important of all, Dr Abbott, the *female* eye, ear and throat doctor who takes his case, and turns out to be – surprise! – more brutally indifferent to suffering than even Jack himself.

The most intensely alarming moments in *The Doctor* are, in fact, those that confront the viewer with precisely the dreaded relationship we described above as the dystopian pole of our *combinatoire* – as, for example, in the scene of Jack's first appointment with Dr Abbott in which, having dismissed his joking banter, and poking around in his throat with her scope, she notes with cold indifference, "This won't be pleasant," then bluntly declares, "Doctor, you have a growth." The film's iconography and editing, here and in later scenes, underline the point by alternating between two kinds of shots. In the first, a two-shot in which Abbott appears sitting in medium long shot, screen right, looking coldly out at both us and Jack, who sits with his back to us in medium close-up, we can only tell his expression from the wall monitors at screen left, still recording what the office scopes and cameras pick up; his real self and true feelings have been literally detached. In the second, we cut back and forth in a standard shot/reverse-shot pattern between medium close-ups of the briskly businesslike Dr Abbott and our visibly shaken hero; but the message is conveyed in the contrast of their backgrounds – the warm butterscotch-colored blinds and greenery behind him, the cold sterile white shading off into metallic blue behind her – and it is in their expressions themselves. The man is vulnerable and helpless; the woman is in control, wielding the very kind of power he had formerly arrogated to himself. The point is not only that there is something wrong with this kind of power wielded in this way, but something wrong, or more wrong yet, with the idea of any woman wielding it over any helpless man.

Accordingly, the movie's climax is probably the moment when, counseled and strengthened by his "strange angel" June, Jack walks back into a hospital now bathed in that ominous blue and demands to see Dr Abbott in order to inform her he is taking her off his case. The decision, of course, paves the way for him to choose the caring "Rabbi" for his upcoming surgery instead, and to break with his cynical and criminally negligent partner (carefully cast as and played by, let us note, a counter-balancing Jew). But who is this "June" in the helping position I have already implicitly slotted under the category of the "Unconventional *Male*"? First of all she is another patient whom he first meets, both literally and figuratively, at the bottom of the hospital, in the lobby of the radiology lab where they both are under treatment. Secondly, though she is obviously not a man, the film works hard to make it almost equally obvious that she is not quite a woman either. The brain tumor that will kill her within the film supplies the pretext for the decentering operation that produces her as an ambiguously gendered – or perhaps more accurately, *de*-gendered – helper-subject, positioned, in terms of our grid, halfway between "Unconventional Male" (or not-woman) and "Not-Male," and composed of important elements of both. For most of the film, she appears cloaked in black with her bald skull swathed in exotic russet scarves and topped by a black bowler hat, a costume that itself renders her gender in equal measure ambiguous and irrelevant, while serving simultaneously as an icon of her unconventionality. So too with the (Asian) Indian scarves, the (American) Indian blanket on her bed, and the interest she expresses in the American Indian Dance Troupe. Finally, her bald head, when revealed, emphasizes the wide-eyed roundness of actress Elizabeth Perkins's face, in so doing both further effacing her gender and extending our sense of her as a wise yet infantile (wise because infantile? infantile because wise?) cherub.

All of these meanings will of course be carried along into and borne out by the wisdom this wise angelic baby hands on to Jack before her death conveniently takes her away. June's message to Jack is like Bradley's to Henry insofar as both insist on the value of honesty, even when painful or impolitic. But it is unlike Bradley's, and more like the truth Henry receives from both his daughter and his wound, in June's insistence on following out one's spontaneous impulses and living always in the moment. When Jack arranges for the two of them to fly to Nevada to catch a performance of the Indian Dance Troupe, she has him halt the car he's rented and pull it off into the desert, where they dance and spin in ecstasy to Laurie Anderson's "Strange Angels" in the golden twilight. And her beyond-the-grave benediction and injunction via letter to "let down your arms" – the arms, that is, that Jack has held up to keep others safely at a distance – "and we'll all come to you," comes as something like Jack's reward for letting down his guard and opening his heart as much as he has, and as the last line of the film.

We will come back to look at what we are shown as we hear these words in just a moment; but first we should observe what little there is to say about the wife's – that is, the "Conventional Woman's" – position and function. *The Doctor* does have a wife named Ann, and at times it makes some efforts to bring her into the rest of its plot. The problem there, we are told and shown, is that Jack has held his arms up too long in his marriage, too, even when he is diagnosed with cancer. Thus, at the climax of the argument whose reconciliation winds up this subplot, his hurt and furious wife throws the pain of her rejection in his face with the line, "I was there for you, and you didn't need me!" The implication, here and throughout Jack's other scenes with Ann – that being needed is the sole desire, and standing by your man the only function, of a good wife – might be more offensive if the film were more concerned to make this point. But even within this climactic scene, it turns out not to be: ultimately, Ann will melt, weeping with laughter at the sight of Jack doing the ec-static spin-of-life he first executed with June out in the Nevada desert, becoming as she does so far less the classically co-dependent wife who does her husband's feelings for him than the infinitely approving Mom gazing with pure delight at her kid's newest neat trick.

It should not surprise us, then, to find at the end of *The Doctor* a Jack whose newfound sensitivity and spontaneity seem to have left him even more on top of things than he was before. For so he appears, quite literally, in the film's final frames: on top of the hospital, centered between the shadows of the towers on either side of him, and shot from below so as to be a towering figure himself as he chuckles with delight at the ghostly presence of June hovering about him in the form of her words and the fluttering, chortling pigeons on the ledge. The painful wisdom Jack MacKee has had to learn has not reduced his power; on the contrary, it has made him an even better doctor than he was before, not to mention that much more justified in ordering his resident staff around (for example, forcing them to don patient tunics and be treated for a weekend as patients themselves). Once again, as in *Regarding Henry*, the point is not finally to give up power, but to emerge from a temporary, tonic power shortage as someone more deserving of its possession and more compassionate in its exercise. Accordingly, both the narrative operations and their underlying themes would seem to preclude an equal distribution of power and sensi-tivity across the genders and between man and wife by constructing a process of regeneration from which at least mainstream women are excluded, and by positing an outcome in which their emotional needs are met through the same operations by which they themselves are rendered virtually superfluous.

No film comes closer than *The Fisher King* to tipping its hand where this latter operation is concerned. For in its closing frames, just as the reconciliation between yet another Jack and Ann is effected, the camera straight-cuts from the wall down which the two lovers have just slid in their joyous embrace, and, across the cut, seemingly continues its descent, only now through the moonlit sky beneath which Jack is lying nude in Central Park alongside – his naked friend Perry! Or perhaps I am wrong, and the prize should go instead to *City Slickers*, whose main character discovers that his proper work, and the "one thing" in life he should stick to, is actually ... *mothering*! But these two movies have more in common than merely the explicitness with which men, and relations between them, effectively hip-check women out of the picture. Both offer us as their protagonists men whose careers place them below or at least off to the side of the solidly upscale professionals we've been studying so far; and both use elements of straight comedy and their own kinds of self-mocking fantasy as a screen behind which openly social anxieties can be raised and through which they are filtered into something we can take in and calmly accept.

Perhaps, then, we might reconnoiter the two of them together, back to back, taking up first the problems with which each begins. The dilemma for *City Slickers'* Mitch (Billy Crystal) is that, at the end of his thirties, he is trapped in a demeaningly pointless job without a future, selling radio airtime to advertisers. ("Where's my work?" he laments. "It's air – I sell air!") The problem for *The Fisher King's* Jack (Jeff Bridges), a highly successful and abrasive talk-show host, is that the glib diatribes he tosses off against eighties yuppies have prompted an unbalanced caller to burst into an upscale restaurant and open fire on a roomful of them. Jack is immobilized with guilt over the results of his amoral, self-centered ambition; Mitch gags on the vacuity of his life. Yet the motivating problems they are given have so much overlap that they might almost be said to be the same: to be, that is, the old crisis of meaning and value, particularly in public life and the workplace, in a relentlessly secular and individualist society in which feral ambition and soulless rationalization ceaselessly function as each other's flip side.

To the extent that these films' diagnoses of what's wrong with Jack and Mitch lead us beyond the eighties stereotype of the callous male yuppie to some of the deeper and more fundamentally disturbing pressures of late capitalist life, their narratives will have that much more and/or differ-ent work to do to come out right: that is, as we have come to understand, to bring our heroes out to a place where they have all they started with, and are better, more sensitive guys to boot. Hence the necessity for the particular blends of comedy and fantasy each film comes up with to fuel the journey of its respective protagonist, who might well otherwise be unable to reach that final destination running on the lower-octane fuel of straight melodrama; and hence, as well, the queasy instability of each mix. *City Slickers*, as we have already noted, takes Mitch, his buddies, and the audience on a cattle drive that starts out as a tourist attraction but ends up a serious, sure-enough trial – and so into a generic Western narrative whose hoary tropes and truths are simultaneously debunked and embraced. Curly (Jack Palance), the drive's hypermacho cowboy boss, is played as a parody of an outmoded stereotype, at the same time as we are asked to take him seriously as *City Slickers'* equivalent of *Regarding Henry's* Bradley, that is, as the unconventional enabling male whose "one-thing" speech and resolute example give Mitch the wisdom and the model that he needs. Likewise in *The Fisher King*, with the fantastic allegorical-chivalric land-scape perceived by Perry (Robin Williams), former academic turned home-less loony by a senseless murder – of Jack's wife, it turns out – that Jack's heedless comments unintentionally provoked; we are invited, and Jack must learn, to perceive that landscape, too, simultaneously as evidence – comic and pathetic by turns – of Perry's madness, and to take it seriously as a magically redemptive narrative for Perry and himself. The social and/or therapeutic narrative suggested by the guilt-racked wish Jack expressed with such pathos earlier in the film, that "there were some way I could just pay the fine and come home," is thus transmuted, through the alchemy of Perry's fantasy, into the romance narrative of the quest. So the climax of *The Fisher King* will be Jack's theft of a "Holy Grail" that turns out to be an old trophy cup, yet does seem to bring Perry back to himself (that is, to the delightful mixture of his old professional self and his new, playful one that we might well be coming to expect to find at the end of all these films). In both cases, our protagonists must in effect be steeled into heroic mold by the *faux*-adventures they undertake, even as they are schooled in a softening compassion all the while.

Finally, too, behind each film's strategy for mining and mocking its own masculine adventure narrative a strategy of displacement is in effect. Though *The Fisher King* invites us to revile the TV producer who wants Jack to star in a new sit-com called *Home Free*, "'all about the joy of living'" among the homeless, it does the very thing it purportedly despises when it depicts street and squat alike as sites of a spectacular pageant in motley, and uses Perry's cracked vision to convert the serialized passage of indifferent commuters past the homeless in the lobby of Grand Central into a dazzling, swirling waltz of all with all. By contrast, in moving the action from New York out West, *City Slickers'* displacement is, of course, even more literal, its disjunction from the secular reality of Mitch's every-day life arguably more honestly acknowledged. At least that is how I understand the absurd comedy of its final image. In the extreme-long shot we have come to expect, we see the minivan carrying Mitch, his wife, and his newly expanded family, now including Norman the calf, over the Triboro Bridge to the Bronx, with the blue skyscape of Manhattan standing in for that of the Rockies, the Western music on the soundtrack only emphasizing how far we are from that other landscape of heroic quest and fulfillment, and how ludicrous it is to expect either for Norman to survive or for Mitch's new-found mothering vocation to re-enchant his life here.

Precisely to the degree to which these films depict the dilemmas and anxieties of their protagonists as problems arising from the culture of contemporary capitalism rather than as the effects of bad lifestyle choices, they are forced to reach for more desperately strained, if not pathetically fanciful, stratagems for resolving and allaying them – in which respect, we may note, they are not unlike the "men's movement" that was achieving the zenith of its reach and popularity around the time they came out. And I suppose they are also akin to the men's movement in the way they depict, deal with and use the women within their texts. I have already pointed out how in both films, as in a good deal of the men's movement and its literature, women are removed from the picture, and how the protagonist's education/feminization in nurturance, empathy and joy comes at the hands of an enabling but culturally marginalized male figure. Yet at more or less the same time both films, and most of the movement, take pains to offer respect to the women they shunt to the side and off-stage, to invite sympathy for their situations and agreement with their assessments of what's wrong. The point is not that there is anything *wrong* with Mitch's wife Barbara in *City Slickers*, or with Jack's girlfriend Ann in *The Fisher King*, the former is right to send him on his way to the cattle drive, after all, just as the latter is right to rage at Jack for his failure to commit. Rather, despite all the indubitable goodness and insight of women, it still takes a man (or, in *The Doctor*, at least a not-woman) to soften up and save a man.

By this point, the internal circuitry of the sensitive-guy film ought to be clear enough that we can move on to the question I promised to address at the beginning of this chapter: why 1991? Or, better still – since the question of Why can never be fully answered without resort to one form or another of idealist or materialist reductionism – *together* with what else, *symptomatic* of what, in 1991?

Let us start with the former line of inquiry, recalling for a moment what the most noted films of the summer, and arguably of the year, were. I refer, of course, to James Cameron's *Terminator II: Judgement Day* and Ridley Scott's *Thelma and Louise*, two films that play an interesting counterpoint to our *sensitivos*, insofar as each is quite obviously carrying its own mail concerning what the current gender order is and ought to be. On one level, both films seem to construct and endorse a literally empowered womanhood, in the persons of *T2*'s buff warrior-mom Sarah Connor, and the gun-toting outlaws of the latter film's title, in free-spirited revolt against patriarchy wherever they find it, at home or on the road, in the state apparatus or the country-western bar. Both, moreover, take pains to suggest that perfidious male domination pervades and governs social space at virtually every level of mainstream, "straight" society. Yet each film also places limits on the effectivity of women's newfound power, and hedges on its blanket opposition to the rule of men. *Terminator II*'s Sarah finds she is unable to defeat that ultimate expression of testosterone-poisoned instrumental rationality, the dreaded T–1000, without the help of another man-machine, the one played, of course, by our Arnold, who is simultaneously softened and sensitized into a man who can both kill *and* care.[1] Similarly, even as *Thelma and Louise*'s on-the-lam narrative through-line pumps the message that there is no way out, so that even two women with as much moxie and insight as our heroines are inevitably doomed, a sidebar subplot works overtime to convince us that within the veritable belly of the patriarchal beast there is a Harvey Keitel cop who understands and sympathizes with our women, and tries in vain to pull them back from the abyss into which they will plunge to their deaths.

Now it would be easy enough to dismiss such contradictions and equivocations as simply a reflex of Hollywood's desire to gather in the largest possible audience by having it, ideologically speaking, as many different ways as it can – and not only easy but accurate enough, so far as it goes. But I am not convinced such a judgement does go far enough; and I am especially suspicious insofar as it assumes an unproblematic 1:1 relationship between ideologeme and viewer constituency, and an additive approach to the question of audience. Even in the case of Keitel's Hal in *Thelma and Louise* – a manifestly trumped-up characterization if there ever was one – I am less persuaded that the main effect of such an insertion is simply to pull in another sector of the film audience who might otherwise have stayed away, than that even such a seemingly tacked-on figure speaks to and resonates with certain contradictions, aporias, and impasses spread so widely through the mass audience that they may be said to be part of contemporary "common sense" itself. Granted, executives, producers, and writers do sit around at meetings and discuss plots and characterizations in just such "additive" terms as I am contesting; granted also that Hollywood film is institutionally disposed by its very nature towards inflecting, tilting and hedging popular desires and anxieties towards fundamentally conservative ends. Yet I still wish to insist there is something left over to say, even after these concessions, about a mass audience who not only flocked to the widely touted *Terminator II* and the widely discussed *Thelma and Louise* but also to the little-noted and generally panned *Regarding Henry* and *The Doctor* in the summer of 1991 – and who found in these films, for all their differences, a similar operation on the field of gender: one in which the female is simultaneously vindicated and doomed or thrust aside, while the male is simultaneously feminized and re-empowered.

There is, of course, a classic Adornian-elitist slip in the last paragraph wherever the phrase "mass audience" appears; but I would like to think its redress only lends that much more weight to my main argument. Admittedly it is a mistake to suppose that the audience for *T2* is the same as that for *Thelma and Louise*, or the latter identical to that for either *Regarding Henry*, *The Doctor*, or any other film of their ilk. But I invite you to bear in mind the following considerations, ranging from verifiable fact to impressionistic anecdote. First: There is no one "minding the store" anywhere within or on the sidelines of the film industry (for example, in *Variety*) as far as audience demographics is concerned. Aside from some attention to first- and second-run theatrical bookings, all that counts, or gets counted, is gross domestic revenues. Accordingly, both film industry "players" in their meetings and we in our humbler offices and studies can only guess at the actual breakdown of a given film's audience in terms of race, class, gender or any other variable, at best extrapolating and projecting from our own necessarily limited observations and experiences. Second: When *Terminator II* was released, it was estimated that merely to make its production and release costs back on its first domestic run each member of the existing American audience for film would, on average, have to see the movie twice; but the film went on rather quickly to earn back these costs and more. Third: In the final figures for the domestic theatrical grosses of films released in 1991 published in *Variety*, *T2* came in first (unsurprising) and *City Slickers* third; but *Regarding Henry*, despite all the withering press it received, came in at twenty-seventh, and shared the spot with the much more widely touted and officially controversial *Thelma and Louise* – and *The Doctor*, at thirty-fourth, came in only slightly less well.[2] Fourth: my own contribution to cultural critique via unbridled extrapolation from the personal. I saw, and know of, a lot more men who went to see *Thelma and Louise* than bought a ticket for either *Regarding Henry*, *The Doctor*, or *The Fisher King*. Accordingly, on this flimsy basis, I suspect (but will never be able to prove) that the audience for at least the first two titles was composed of far more women than men.

With these admittedly shaky warrants behind me, I want to put forward two overlapping claims: first, that the audience for each of the films we have been discussing was at least (that is, in the case of *T2*) gender-mixed, and perhaps, for some of the sensitive-guy films as well as *Thelma and Louise*, composed predominantly of women; and second, that therefore something more is involved and at stake in the sensitive-guy films than simply the newest ruse of patriarchal power (or, if you will, *in addition to* the newest ruse). Of course, it is possible to write off those women who I am supposing not only attended but enjoyed these films as just so many dupes of patriarchy. But what happens if we try to imagine the pleasures they are offered by these films and take from them as evidence of a symptomatic *ir*resolution, one of those "morbid symptoms" that occurs when, as Gramsci said, "the old is dying and the new cannot be born," rather than as a sign that the new fix is in?[3]

What sense, in other words, do these films make if their workings are taken as a distorted indicator of the effectivities and aporias of everyday white, middle-class, proto-*feminist* consciousness at the end of the eighties and the beginning of a new decade? To ask the question is, of course, first and foremost to wrench us immediately back to the dreary horrors of twelve years of Reagan–Bush, a nightmare era which, from the point of view of any feminist, might more accurately be dated from the first passage of the Hyde Amendment in 1977 to Bush's veto of even a pitifully watered-down Family Leave Bill in 1991, and from which the Clinton administration often seems only just barely to have emerged. But to answer it at all adequately also requires us to shake off the chill of that awful sense-memory and demand of ourselves a sober account of the fortunes of feminism, as well as of the vicissitudes of the dominant gender order, during this same time.

Here, of course, I can only offer the sketchiest and most summary of accounts, drawing on the best and most comprehensive feminist assessments I have been able to find. I begin by quoting, from an extraordinarily informative essay, Johanna Brenner's judicious formulation of the main thrust of second-wave feminism in the USA over the past two decades: "to make women fully free sellers of our own labour power, by substantially dismantling the legal and normative edifice which had mandated women's subservience in marriage, denied us rights in our bodies and reproductive capacity, and legitimated our economic marginalization."[4] Brenner's argument is neither that this goal is unworthy nor that it has been unequivocally reached in every, or for that matter any, social sphere. Rather, she is first of all concerned to document where and to what extent it has been secured, even in the course of the Reagan–Bush eighties, when, under the pressure of an ever-more deregulated capitalism on a political and ideological killing spree, "feminist demands for equality have been increasingly institutionalized and culturally incorporated as women's right to compete and contract free from limitations imposed on account of her sex."[5] Only when such gains have been properly weighed does she turn her attention to the extent to which such liberal-individualist goals, even if posed outside or after the high tide of Reaganism, necessarily lead to benefits that will, at best, be unequally distributed amongst women of different races and classes, and, at worst, be catastrophically divisive of that very unity in whose name the struggles for these liberal feminist "market reforms" are waged. Thus, for example, "reproductive rights" has become ever more narrowly construed as each individual woman's right to an abortion, although

> for most women *real choice* about childbearing requires much more than the right to make decisions about carrying a pregnancy to term.... [F]or working-class women, poor women, and women of colour, the right to be mothers is also under attack. Lack of quality healthcare and childcare, homelessness, low wages, the social isolation and poverty of single parents, pressures on women in the welfare and public health-care system to get sterilized, all deny many women the material conditions necessary to have children and to raise their children in dignity and health.[6]

So too with the issue of jobs and incomes in general, where only the most market-friendly discourses of a watered-down affirmative action have been able to survive. And likewise with the averaging out of both women's and men's wages and salaries in liberal feminist discourse, which has obscured the gains middle-class, college-educated white women have been able to make it in the professions, both absolutely and in relation to the stagnation and/or outright decline in poor and non-white women's income, and, indeed, in relation to a more than decade-long *decline* in men's incomes (except, that is, for the top tenth, whose incomes predictably soared).

Some of the same statistics, and much the same differentiated economic profile, are set forth in Kathleen Gerson's *No Man's Land: Men's Changing Commitments to Family and Work*.[7] Here, however, Gerson is concerned not only to note the massive entrance of women into all levels of the workforce, and to document the long decline of the male "family wage," but to emphasize the ways both correlate with contemporary shifts and instabilities in working-class, middle-class, and/or professional men's attitudes towards, and degrees of involvement with, their jobs and careers versus their families and personal relationships. Like Brenner, Gerson insists that the "expansion of women's legal rights, employment opportunities, sources of economic support, and capacity to live independently" – that is, the achievements of liberal feminism – have "undermined men's ability to control them, as wives or as workers."[8] And she also notes those recent surveys that suggest a real, albeit uneven correlation between women's increasing numbers and economic power as waged and salaried workers, on the one hand, and the growing (though still unequal) contributions of men to domestic labor and child care, on the other. But her main interest lies in capturing the full extent of men's multivalent attitudes toward and reactions to this creeping subversion of the gender order. "The decline of the male breadwinner," she writes,

> has prompted confusion and discomfort because it calls into question many of our most deeply held beliefs about manhood and masculinity. If men no longer share a distinctive identity based on their economic role as family providers, then what is a man? If men can no longer claim special rights and privileges based on their unique responsibilities and contributions, then how can they justify their power? If men can no longer assert patriarchal control by being the heads of their households, then what kind of relationships will they establish with women and children?[9]

Gerson groups the (predominantly white) working- and middle-class men she interviewed into three broad, and roughly equal, categories: those who remain primarily invested in the "breadwinner ethic," defining themselves and their relations to partners and children on the basis of their economic contributions; those who identify with and are committed to "participation in domestic work, especially child rearing;" and those who for a variety of reasons identify with neither definition of their primary role. But her most important findings arguably concern the degree to which each and all of these three possible positions, even the most conventional, is now formed and ingrained with, under and against the pressure and limits of the economic and political currents that bear liberal feminism along as well. Thus, for example, most of the "breadwinners" Gerson interviewed confessed that their commitment to that ethic came as the *effect* of a stable, well-paying job (and, usually, a domestic partner with conventional views regarding the woman's primary role in child care), something that, given present economic trends, they had not really expected to get. Similarly, many men in her "autonomous" group cite as their reasons for remaining aloof from women and children their doubts that their wages would be able to support a family, even with another, lesser income, and their fears of being required to work a "double day," of full-time work in the public sphere followed by a stint of domestic chores and child care. Finally, even among those men who have consciously chosen to involve themselves in domestic life and child care, and who identify with that choice, Gerson notes, and expresses some sympathy with, a strain of ambivalence, regret and, at times, thinly veiled resistance – not just because these men have had as a result to give up their traditional patriarchal power. "Although full-time domesticity," she writes, "has declined as an option for women, it has not emerged as an option for men." This is so not only, and perhaps not even primarily, insofar as the remaining "gender gap between men's and women's incomes [makes] it impractical and, indeed, impossible for most men to consider staying home while their wives went to work," but also insofar as for both men and women alike, now "the social value of public pursuits outstrips the power and prestige of private ones."[10] Insofar, that is, as the overriding goal of mainstream feminism has been, as Brenner puts it, "to make women fully free sellers of our own labour power," the effect has been to shunt child rearing off to the side as an "undervalued, isolating, and largely invisible accomplishment for *all* parents," and thus to encourage "women's flight from domesticity" while simultaneously depressing "men's motivation to choose it."[11]

But liberal, market-based feminism has not been the only flavor generally available over the past decade and a half. Both Gerson and Brenner also acknowledge the swelling popularity throughout the eighties of the quite different strain of feminist doctrine that Brenner, following Alice Echols, terms "cultural feminism."[12] All three are harshly critical of what we may properly call this "discourse" (for it does have its own institutional and social fields, its bookstores, tapes, organizations, and speaker series, albeit largely within alternative subcultural circles); but Brenner's lapidary formulation of both its influence and drawbacks is especially useful here:

> "Cultural feminism" has replaced radical feminism as the hegemonic worldview in what remains of the autonomous women's community.... The polarization of "male" to "female" ways of being, knowing, feeling and thinking that is fundamental to cultural feminism encourages a politics of salvation through womanly virtue that leaves little room for the pragmatic, limited, ambivalent, and conflictual political practice of coalition-building among women divided by race, ethnicity, sexual orientation, not to mention with organizations of working-class and oppressed people which include men.[13]

All I would add to this admirable definition and critique is the connection *between* liberal (or "equality") feminism and cultural (or "difference") feminism that is already implicit in Brenner, and that, in what I hope is already a classic polemic, Katha Pollitt characteristically hangs out on the line for all to see. Citing both the achievements and impasses of liberal feminism's market reforms, Pollitt argues that "difference feminism is essentially a way for women both to take advantage of equality feminism's success and to accommodate themselves to its limits."[14] In fact, I am tempted to argue that in this way, cultural or "difference" feminism functions precisely as the dialectical obverse and complement to liberal or "equality" feminism, both within individual feminist women and across feminist communities, including and especially white middle- and/or professional-class individuals and groups. The possible – and visible – combinations and permutations of the two ideologies are legion. It is possible for women who are making careers in traditionally male professions like business or law to shrug off any sense of complicity with what is, after all, the gender-blind amorality of everyday capitalist career-building, by keeping an inner candle lit to the shrine of their virtuous inner feminine selves. It is possible for women who have not been able, or willing, to achieve such mainstream success to console themselves at the same shrine for their "failures," while simultaneously accepting and condemning their male partners' efforts to keep up their breadwinning predominance in the public realm, at the cost of their comparative absence and detachment from home. It is possible to finesse the tensions and hostilities between white middle-class feminists on the one hand, and poor women and women of color on the other, by holding fast to a faith in the moral superiority of women to men that includes as its corollary a corresponding (though perhaps lesser) superiority of non-white to white, indigenous tribal to urban secular, lesbian-gay (or perhaps just lesbian) to straight, and so on, thus in practice obviating any need for actual contact, discussion, or political negotiation with any of these ideally Othered groups. And, of course, perhaps above all it is possible, during an era in which the chances of achieving any straightforward political progress in the cause of women's liberation were, on the federal level anyway, virtually nonexistent, to fall back on cultural feminism's "empowering" assurances as inner compensation for all the external, enabling power it seemed impossible to win.

In all these ways and more, cultural feminism has commingled with liberal feminism through the 1980s and into the 1990s, the former insisting on the very autonomy the latter's successes erode, and the two together functioning both to warrant whatever progress women have been able to make and to valorize or conceal whatever impasses in public and private life in which they find themselves enmired. In fact, it is just this protean mélange of ideologies that in all its flexibility forms the preeminent "common sense" of US feminism through the past decade – especially, though hardly exclusively, outside the academy.[15] And so it is from the perspective of this feminist "common sense" that I would now like to return to our sensitive-guy films. The point here is not to deny the extent to which the films may be read (and enjoyed) as I have for the most part read them so far, that is, as so many clever episodes in a concerted attempt simultaneously to renovate, modulate, and extend male dominance – one, moreover, that seems all too congruent with then-President Bush's own schizzier and clumsier attempts from the late eighties to the early nineties to call for a "kinder, gentler" nation while brandishing his saber in Panama and the Persian Gulf and slashing away at social programs at home. What I wish to think about now, instead and as well, is just *how else* these films might *also* have been enjoyed by just those Reagan- and Bush-reviling middle-class and professional women (and men) who identify with and are interpellated by this "common-sense" feminism I have been trying to describe.

What pleasures are there for such audiences in narratives that, as we have seen, enact a critique of the callous selfishness of dominant modes of white straight masculinity, and endorse the traditionally feminine attributes of sensitivity, compassion, nurturance and emotional fluency, yet leave their women characters short of power and their male protagonists reinvigorated in their predominance? Here are some of the possible, albeit perverse, satisfactions I can see. Let us not forget, first of all, that these men are not educated or worked over by any particular political struggles, in the course of any particular social processes. The example of Henry Carter in *Regarding Henry* is especially telling here. At the beginning of the film, before he is shot down, this cynical corporate lawyer and domestic shitheel is clearly ineducable; he must be killed, his present being destroyed, in order to be born again. So too with *The Doctor*'s and *The Fisher King*'s two Jacks, redeemed and transfigured only at the end of so many dark nights of the soul and brushes with real or symbolic death. It requires little ingenuity to suggest that it might be a pleasure for feminist or proto-feminist women to watch men going through hell for their insensitivity; but the fact that these men nearly have to die to be saved, and that they are saved rather than transformed, or for that matter even defeated in struggle, does invite us to consider the question of how much room exists in the liberal/essentialist imaginary of mainstream middle-class feminism to imagine men changing, or being changed, in this latter way – how much room, and how much desire. For if white straight men cannot be changed short of shooting them, there is not much use pressing them to do so; nor, since their terrible behavior comes so naturally to them it might as well be rooted in the blood, is there much risk of turning into one of them if you happen to be a woman.

It is even possible to see how, for putative gender progressives of this type, the two seemingly most objectionable features of these films might be somewhat enjoyable, or at least unobjectionable in their own peculiar way. I refer to the shunting aside of women, even as educative agents, and the re-empowerment of men that seems wired into these films' endings. I picture Harrison Ford's Henry Carter being helped to become a whole new person through the agency of a white woman instead of by Bradley, and can hear the clamor of "common-sense" objections that would have been hurled at the screen. From the perspective of this liberal/essentialist feminism, it is not for women to transform men any more than it is for people of color to cure whites of their racism; yet if white straight masculinity is nothing but evil by definition, the task of self-transformation is more or less out of the question as well. Hence the necessity for white straight men to get the help they must have from representatives of some *other* subaltern group (Blacks, homeless people, sexless dying angels, children – or, what the hell, even cowboys, that ridiculous vanished breed), but *not* from women, who have cleaned up the messes men make, and are, quite long enough. The education of our reborn heroes can only be carried out by agents who are secondary Others to the main event of (white, middle-class) men versus (white, middle-class) women, who, if they inhabit the political imaginary I have described, might well enjoy both the pleasures of this education *and* the satisfaction of carping at it, as I have, for leaving women out. So, too, with our films' endings, whose visions of a sensitized yet shored up male power may be sneeringly enjoyed in something like the same ways: look, the guys are still in power, women are still screwed in the end; and/but, who wants to play their rotten games anyway?

What is missing from all these movies, of course, and from the mainstream feminist common-sense perspective from which I have been arguing they may be enjoyed, is above all any adequately political sense of gender as a set of historically constructed and maintained power relations, and thus of domination as both a structural and social fact. Without such a sense, the defects and shortcomings of white men can only be understood as either so many individual flaws or as the inherent evil of all those in a group; just as a feminism deprived of this sense is condemned to oscillate between arguments and actions against "discrimination" in the name of liberal-individualist equality, and other arguments launched and actions undertaken precisely to cordon off, honor, and protect women's superior virtue and wisdom from the depredations of their evil Others. *With* such a sense, on the other hand, as both Gerson and Brenner argue, it might be possible to put together multiracial and cross-class coalitions of women (and perhaps even some men) which would struggle for the political and economic policies that we must have in place if we are to topple the last redoubts of the old gender order (which the new economic order of transnational, "flexible" capitalism is making over anyhow from without), and to put a more comprehensively liberatory gender order in its place. I have already quoted Brenner on what demands a fully feminist radical reproductive rights program ought to include, and so will add here only one more example of the kinds of issues she and Gerson believe a properly radical feminism should once again and/or for the first time engage. Gerson cites convincing evidence of an increasing willingness, even in some cases desire, among men across class lines to take up more of the burdens of domestic work and child care. But she also insists that both the degree of willingness and the number of those willing can only increase to the extent that new family-support policies are wrested from business and the state: ones that guarantee equal opportunity and pay for all women, flexitime and paid family leave for all employees, and a work week reduction to thirty hours or less, and publicly funded yet effectively decentralized, locally controlled child care and medical services.

To change men further and free more women more, then, both Gerson and Brenner insist that feminists must broaden the scope of their institutional politics beyond its present limits in individualist, rights-based discourse to embrace issues of collective rights, powers, and opportunities in ways that cut across racial boundaries and class lines. That obviously is my point here as well: to argue, first and foremost, for the adoption of such a purpose and the widest possible dissemination of such a perspective. Beyond that, of course, it is hardly my intention here to tack up a new feminist agenda; nor am I the right person to read off, even in quotation, items thrown up on the list. They will come up in any case only after and insofar as the *radicalism* of the cultural feminism in present-day feminist "common sense" is *politicized*, and the *politics* of liberal feminism is *radicalized*. The chances for such a self-transformation in the present moment are not great; on the other hand, they are distinctly better than they were during the Reagan–Bush years here, when it must be admitted that every side and aspect of our home-grown, revolutionary-utopian imaginations were stunted and deformed for lack of air and hope. But without the construction and mobilization of some such new feminist imaginary, some campaign to make it the new common sense of those who think themselves "progressive on gender," I am afraid we may well and justly be condemned *at best* – for example, even assuming that the Christian Right and the Republican Party are miraculously rolled back to the nether reaches of this country's cultural and political life – to consume and deplore, deplore and consume even more, and even more offensively inadequate, sensitive white-guy films than those released in the summer of 1991.

After all, the film that brought this particular cycle of sensitive-guy films to its end at the close of 1991 was surely from any progressive perspective the most disgusting of them all. Steven Spielberg's *Hook*, released to great fanfare as a "family entertainment film" over the 1991 Christmas holiday season, tells the story of how yet another ambitious workaholic professional – a corporate executive with a very eighties specialty in raiding and acquiring other companies, no less – recovers the playful, loving self he has lost along the way. He is guided through this process, moreover, by a combination of an unstraight Other (Tinker Bell,

our Unconventional Not-Male) and a whole flock of children (the Lost
Boys, our Unconventional Males). Once his transformation/restoration is
complete, moreover, he returns to and reunites his family, including the
conventional wife and mother who warned him of the error of his former
ways but was herself predictably powerless to effect the change she now
adores, along with the kids who clump together with her around Dad as
the camera pulls back one more time into that obligatory long shot.

At this level of general summary, *Hook* seems no more or less offensive
to the everyday sensibilities of white middle-class gender progressives than
any of the other films we have been studying. But it differs significantly
from them in its emphases, concerns and proposed resolutions, all of
which are by several degrees both more egregious and more manifestly
desperate than anything the other films dredged up. To sketch out how
this is so, I must begin by mentioning what practically anyone on the
planet in 1991 had to know was the clever "hook" of *Hook*: that the
"Peter" (Robin Williams) who is *Hook*'s protagonist is, unbeknown to
himself, actually the adult version of the real Peter Pan, whose perspective
and powers he must reassume in order to rescue his children when they
are captured by Captain Hook and taken off to Never-Never Land. The
task of this protagonist is thus from the beginning more classically heroic
than that put forward in any of our other films: Peter must not only find/
redeem his true, playful, opened-up self, but also find within that self the
power to save his kids.

In *Hook*, then, the connection between sensitizing the reformed white
male self and re-empowering it could hardly be more explicitly drawn; nor
could it be any more clear that the struggle for power is a struggle over
masculinity, to be conducted perforce on an exclusively male terrain. Never-
Never Land is constituted by its division between the (in the film, un-
mistakably phallic) island kingdom of the Lost Boys, and the pirate ship
and port town, entirely male as well except for a few stray, blowsy doxies:
scarcely a woman in sight, then, and certainly nothing resembling domestic
space. A key scene in Peter's reawakening/re-education is, in fact, an anti-
domestic mock-dinner scene that urges us to rejoice with Peter and the
Boys in his rediscovered power to hurl, first, gross insults, then imaginary
food in Play-Doh colors across the table at his new/old adversarial pals.
When he excels at both, and throws his head back in triumph, a cock
crows in the distance to cap off the scene; just as later, when Rufio, the
lead Boy before Peter's return, acknowledges the superiority of Peter's
child-self regained, the shot catches him literally framed between Peter's

legs, kneeling down and surrendering his sword, as he utters the ritual obeisance, "You are the Pan."

If, to put it schematically, Act One in Never-Never Land is about our protagonist's recovery of his *real* Peter, the resumption of a Boy-self that, paradoxically, makes him into Pan "The *Man*," *Hook*'s second act consists of a confrontation between two versions of *fatherdom*. For, as Peter has been rediscovering himself on the island of the Lost Boys, Captain Hook has been attempting to steal his children away from him psychologically as well as physically. With the children as his literally captive audience, Hook emphasizes Peter's paternal weaknesses and deficiencies in his former life as a harried, absent, chronically anxious business executive, and proposes himself as a better model. Peter's daughter Maggie – necessarily and reassuringly, from this film's wholly masculinist point of view – resists this seduction from the start, and so is trundled off to the edge of the boat deck to sing the song of maternal omnipresence ("when you're alone/ you're … not really alone") her mother sang to her, while dropping obligingly, like a good girl, out of the plot. But even before the trip to Never-Never Land, she and her affection were never really at stake; throughout *Hook* what counts most is whether or not Peter will be able to win his son Jack's (yes, yet again) love *and respect*.

The two contending versions of fatherhood *Hook* models for us are, moreover, all the more ideological for their contradictory overlapping. Captain Hook offers Jack one that consists of three not altogether consistent elements: a starkly honest, if one-sided, account of the negative aspects of parenthood (parents read you stories at night "to shut you up"; before your birth, "your parents were happy") and acknowledgement of the mutilating pain involved in taking on the Father's Name (on the verge of piercing Jack's earlobe to give him an earring like his own, he advises Jack to "Brace yourself, lad – 'cause this is really going to hurt"); responsibility and faithfulness to Jack's concerns and well-being (attending the ballgame he sets up for Jack, and rooting for him, unlike the former Peter, who let his business commitments override his promises to be there for Jack); and, curiously enough, a denial of the inevitability of biological time and mortality, as evidenced by Hook's phobic war against all timepieces, and the scene in which he gleefully incites Jack to pour out his hatred against his father by smashing the dead clocks he has gathered up and shut away. Against all this, the reinvigorated Peter offers Jack, and us of course, a fatherhood defined first of all as pure joy – the very "happy thought" that enabled him to fly again, as he informs the delighted

Jack, is that "I'm a Daddy!" – which is why, we are also told, he decided to shed his perpetual boyhood in the first place. But this fatherhood is also paradoxically defined precisely *by* its boyish playfulness, which the entire movie labors to convince us will last for ever more, now that it has been regained. Peter, we are told, entered into the time-stream and allowed himself to become an adult in order to become a father; yet the whole film works to permit us to imagine that the best fathers both can and should remain kids. Indeed, it is Hook himself who at the end of his climactic battle with Peter is revealed to be susceptible to the ravages of time, first when his black wig falls off to reveal a bald pate, and finally when he is crushed and devoured by the giant crocodile and clock face that crashes down on him. Peter, on the other hand, demonstrates his reliability and irrepressibly playful youthfulness at the same time and as the same thing, by rescuing his children with the rest of his Lost Boy crew in such a fun, adventurous way, with so many neat tricks and flying loop-the-loops. In so doing, he holds out the promise or ideal of a masculinity whose arrested development and deliberate regression are the guarantee of its power and its right to rule.

It is hard not to see both the relatively trouble-free process Peter goes through on his way to incarnating this ideal (surely his rediscovery of his true Pan nature constitutes the most painless, unmortifying conversion process in all the films we have studied) and that ideal itself as fantasies designed to fit the experience and please the tastes of all those greying baby-boomer dads who are having trouble, not only with squaring the old demands of career with the newer ones of domestic life, but dealing with the long slide through middle age as well. Its resolution of the first set of problems is essentially the same as *Regarding Henry*'s, and so might well prompt the same stupid practical question. Now that Peter's back with the kids from his redemptive adventure, now that he's thrown his dealmaker's cellular telephone out into the snow, do these acts of liberation mean that his wife Moira will now have to go out to work instead? It scarcely needs adding that the film does not deign to answer this question, any more than it resolves the problems boomer men might be having with the advent of middle age.

But on the latter score, *Hook* does hint at a symptomatic difference between its ideal man and its idealized women, who are endowed in it with a form of eternal life quite different from Peter's childish immortality. To get a whiff of what it is, we might recall that bit of cinematic exposition in which we learn that when the prelapsarian Peter's original girlfriend Wendy grew old and became Maggie Smith with some extra wrinkles, he simply turned his attention to her granddaughter Moira, whose daughter Maggie in turn finds herself on the same deck of the same pirate ship on which her great-grandmother was once a captive, singing the same consoling lullaby her mother sang to her. One way of thinking through the implications of this difference, then, might be to point out that if Peter is going to remain young while Moira grows old, once his child Maggie nears the age of twelve someone ought to alert Child Services. Another way might be simply to note that whereas for men the project is to save themselves from age – to hold on deliberately, desperately, to the power of childhood – for girls and women the goal is to submit to mortality, while each and all embodying from start to finish the same utterly traditional patriarchal femininity, like a genotype whose DNA code consists of three letters instead of four – Little Girl, Lover, Mother, all of whom will always love our Peter Pan.

Finally, something needs to be said about the particular noxiousness of *Hook*'s racial politics. We have already drawn attention to the grotesquely explicit, quasi-authoritarian phallicism fueling Peter's re-emergence as the Lost Boy's true and natural leader; but we have not yet linked this message up with the fact that the troupe of Boys who first re-educate then bow down to this "Pan the Man" are a distinctly multi-culti bunch. There's the spindly Black boy who, stroking Peter's face and looking deep into his eyes, declares to the others that perhaps the true Peter might be in there after all; the roly-poly "Thudbutt," yet another African-American child, who befriends Peter virtually from the start; and, inevitably, the racially hybrid, Mohawk-headed Rufio, up-to-the-minute hip head of the tribe. The former two sympathetic and physically non-threatening troupe members are singled out for many a radiant close-up; and fat-boy Thudbutt, least threatening of all, receives from his master the Pan the sword of leadership when Peter prepares to leave Never-Never Land for home. Rufio, on the other hand, even though he has submitted to the Pan and fights alongside him, ends up being the one member of the Lost Boys tribe to be killed in the final encounter. Peter leaves him to be run through by Captain Hook as he flits off to protect his own child Maggie instead, returning just in time to catch the poor punked-up mixed-blood's final words: "I wish I had a dad – like you." The offensiveness of such racist liberalism, which rewards the weak and obsequious for their dog-like devotion while gleefully fantasizing the deathbed subjection of those uppity non-white Others who resist and refuse to be led, should require no further comment. But within the newer overarching thematic of power-through-playfulness, could not both these familiar racist operations and their outcome be understood in a new light as well: namely, as perhaps *also* the fantasy of the white middle-class male self's supremacy within "postindustrial" economic life as natural (because most powerful, most powerful because most creative) leader of the multicultural, if not outright transnational, Creative Work Group of the future, out there on the cutting edge?[16]

Of all the films from this brief season at which we have looked, *Hook* is surely the most top-heavy in terms of the size and the heaped-up unwieldiness of the ideological load it is made to carry. So it would be possible to sort through and throw down off that load any number of additional examples of the lessons in gender, race, and sexuality I have enumerated, and, indeed, find any number of secondary supporting lessons as well. But I trust I have managed to locate and articulate enough of the film's central operations and preoccupations both to see their likenesses to those of the other sensitive-guy films, and the extra payload of selfish desperation in this one. So perhaps I can close out this reading and conclude this chapter by turning to what is known of the film's reception instead. For starters, it seems worth noting and musing on the fact that many of *Hook*'s initial reviewers noted its thematic kinship with the earlier films (one reviewer suggesting it might better have been titled *Regarding Peter*) and commented, usually sarcastically, on the strangeness of dis-covering such preoccupations in what seemed at the same time to have been designed at grotesque expense to be the blockbuster of the 1991 Christmas season.[17] But such jibes and speculations rapidly took second place to the central question raised by *Hook*: could Spielberg's newest possibly turn a buck despite the dual burden of its shrilly masculinist agenda and its monstrously swollen budget? The question itself became a kind of narrative premiss, in a culture in which we are more and more often invited to enjoy the second-degree pleasure of tracking the process and degree of our own subjection to whatever the newest spectacular production is to slide down through the tubes, and to take that pleasure not aside from but in addition to, or even as the pretext for, the first-degree one of buying a copy of or a ticket to the production itself: some-thing like an intellectual equivalent, for culturally upscale types, of all the other spin-off products, like the Hook go-cups you could now buy at the fast-food franchises, or the Hook shirts and caps at the big chain discount stores.

At any rate, by dint of such hoopla and other techniques, and with who knows what motivations or desires in mind, large numbers of who knows what demographically sortable groups of Americans must have made it to their local theatres to see *Hook*, which, despite its late release date in mid-December, had already finished at year's end 1991 as the twelfth top-grossing film.[18] With how much pleasure, in what ideological interactions with what forms of gendered coded and/or racialized common sense, who could possibly say with any confidence, really? All we may hazard here in closing is the hopeful, fearful historical speculation that with this soured summa, and perhaps all the more so with the dismal box-office failure of both *City of Joy* and *Grand Canyon* in 1992,[19] it seemed that The Year of Living Sensitively was over; and that it was, and arguably remains, time for something else to start, or to resume.

NOTES

1. For more on the gender politics of this film, see my "Home Fires Burning: Family *Noir* in *Blue Velvet* and *Terminator 2*," in Joan Copjec, ed., *Shades of Noir: A Reader* (London and New York: Verso, 1993), pp. 227–60.

2. "Top Rental Films for 1991," *Variety*, 6 January 1992.

3. Antonio Gramsci, *Selections from the Prison Notebooks* [trans. Quintin Hoare and Geoffrey Nowell-Smith] (London: Lawrence & Wishart, 1971), p. 276.

4. Johanna Brenner, "The Best of Times, The Worst of Times: US Feminism Today," *New Left Review* 200 (July–August 1993), p. 104.

5. Ibid., p. 102.

6. Ibid., p. 135.

7. Kathleen Gerson, *No Man's Land: Men's Changing Commitments to Family and Work* (New York: Basic Books, 1993), pp. 3–22, and 268–72. Among other trends, Gerson points out that "between 1979 and 1989, when men's average wages were falling, women's were *rising* an average of 6.7 percent" (pp. 270–71, my emphasis).

8. Ibid., p. 266.

9. Ibid., p. 260.

10. Ibid., pp. 245, 249.

11. Ibid., p. 248.

12. See Alice Echols, *Daring to Be Bad: A History of the Radical Feminist Movement in America, 1967–1975* (Minneapolis: University of Minnesota Press, 1990). Gerson's remarks on the popularity of cultural feminism may be found in *No Man's Land* on pp. 12–13, and p. 295 n. 37.

13. Brenner, p. 153.

14. Katha Pollitt's "Are Women Morally Superior to Men?" appeared first in *The Nation* (28 December 1992). I am quoting here from its reprinting in *Utne Reader* 59 (September/October 1993), p. 108. The latter publication, the *Reader's Digest* of the alternative press, and thus of alternative culture, is a valuable resource for anyone

interested in studying the role, influence, and multiple effects of "difference feminism" in alternative, and perhaps especially New Age, subcultures.

15. The quotation marks are there to direct the reader to the Gramscian definition of the term, made widely available to the English-speaking left throughout the past decade in the lectures and essays of Stuart Hall. For Hall and Gramsci, the "common sense" of a subaltern individual or community is apt to be in any given conjuncture a fusion of radical energy and insight, on the one hand, and deep ideological subjection to the dominant, on the other, which it is the business of the radical cultural worker to disarticulate, realign and activate as a force for progressive structural change. See Gramsci, pp. 321–43; and Stuart Hall's *The Hard Road to Renewal: Thatcherism and the Crisis of the Left* (London and New York: Verso, 1988), especially pp. 123–49 and 161–95.

16. In the Conclusion to this book, I argue that something like the same new work selves and relationships are modeled, yet processed and judged quite differently, in *In the Line of Fire*.

17. The reviewer mentioned parenthetically here is Peter Travers, whose review of *Hook* appeared in the 9 January 1992 issue of *Rolling Stone*, pp. 54–5. Other reviewers – all, it is worth noting, white men, most of whom also panned at least one other *sensitivo* that same year – include Richard Schickel in *Time*, vol. 134 (16 December 1992); David Ansen in *Newsweek*, vol. 118 (16 December 1991); David Denby in *New York*, vol. 25 (6 January 1992); and Terence Rafferty in *The New Yorker*, vol. 67 (30 December 1991).

18. "Top Rental Films for 1991," *Variety*, 6 January 1992.

19. In "Top Rental Films for 1992," *Variety*, 11 January 1993, *Grand Canyon* is listed as finishing up in forty-sixth place, despite having been in theatrical release for the entire calendar year, while *City of Joy*, released in April 1992, made an even more dismal showing, coming in at ninetieth, with a paltry domestic gross of $6 million. Moreover, while *City of Joy* did not receive many positive reviews, *Grand Canyon* did poorly in spite of generally favorable notices, including plugs from several reviewers who had generally scorned the sensitive-guy films of the previous year. See, for example, the reviews by Schickel in *Time*, vol. 138 (30 December 1991), Denby in *New York*, vol. 25 (13 January 1992), and Peter Travers in *Rolling Stone* (23 January 1992).

CHAPTER THREE

ROCK INCORPORATED: PLUGGING IN TO AXL AND BRUCE

Those bodies displayed beneath the throbbing lights, those rock stars shrieking and stomping, writhing and wailing away – one Bruce, the other Axl, arguably the two foremost rock superstars of the late 1980s, in the USA anyhow – what could be more immediately, more intensely True than the sight of either or each of them up there doing his own particular corporeal-musical thing? Why not just go to the videos or fanmag photos, bear down on a few representative shots and paradigmatic poses, read their reality straight off the surface where its charge lies waiting to be picked up and run through us as well?

Here is the basic, not-so-simple reason why not: because rock stars, *especially* in their most apparently immediate forms and visages, have a nest of assumptions and histories packed inside them, a complexity that the seeming directness of their respective physicalities belies and thus the more effectively insinuates.[1] Or, to put it the other way around, because we are already so primed for those bodies before we even see them, given what we already know, cannot help knowing, of rock-and-roll as social relations, popular culture, capitalist industry and musical form – because, as that old fascist expert in yearning Martin Heidegger might say, we come to such bodies "so belatedly," no matter how fresh or originary they might feel.

Later on, we will return to belatedness as a motif of at least one of the bodies we will read. What needs to be emphasized here, though, is the resemblance of both the body called Bruce and the other named Axl in the practice of rock-and-roll to the commodity as described by Marx in the practice of capitalist economic life: both apparently simple things whose

71

sheer obdurate, naturalized *quidditas* elides their backstage histories and futures as particular moments within a mammoth, ongoing process of production, consumption and unequal exchange; therefore, both ensembles of social praxes and desires whose real specificities can only be understood by way of a whole series of general relations and determinations, rising as we narrow towards the concrete.

Not – not quite – that the rocker's body is itself a commodity. Rather, like the movie star's body it so resembles, it is precisely that which is permanently withheld from circulation, unapproachable and unpurchasable except in terms of those products that yield us partial, mediated access to it: the fan-mag interviews and photos, the album, the concert video, and of course the live concert itself. Thus the rocker's body, a production that never quite becomes the product, stands behind every rock commodity like its unmoved mover, guaranteeing its integrity yet untainted by its sale. On our slow zoom-in to close-ups of Axl and Bruce in the flesh, we'll be trying to articulate other background assumptions and definitions: some, like the one just noted, of long standing, rooted in our common sense of "rock"; others, closer to our imaginary playmates, reflecting newer and more volatile attempts to display, resolve, and/or transmogrify into the stuff of pleasure some more recent and more conjunctural social processes and contradictions. But all of them, emerging through the sights and words and music, with something to tell us about how the codes and values and exchanges of sex and gender, race and class, work in this culture, how they trade off and double up and stand in for each other, working difference into domination and domination into difference, keeping us dancing in the dark.

1. AUTHENTICITY/HISTORY

"This is *not* about Michael Jackson."
Axl Rose, upon accepting the Michael Jackson Video
Vanguard award at the 1992 MTV Music Video Awards

Questions of what constitutes rock and how to assess its meaning-effects vex all but the most simple-minded and/or hype-ridden accounts of its origins and effects. McClary and Walser, speaking of popular music in general, point out both how many more or less purely musical signals are sent and codes evoked by even the most basic pop single, and how impoverished and impressionistic are the languages we use to describe their combinations and effects.[2] (Case in point: how to describe in formalist musical terms the blend of pitch, pulse, emphasis and melisma at work in the young Michael Jackson's first entrance – "uh-*unh*-uh-unh-*UH*" – in that masterpiece of 1970s bubble gum "ABC"?) And Andrew Goodwin reminds us of the exponential surge in complexity and indeterminacy that wells up as soon as we move from a strict musicological analysis to the kinds and combinations of "iconographies stored in popular cultural memory" that any given cut might call up:

(a) personal imagery deriving from the individual memories associated with the song; (b) images associated purely with the music itself … which may work through either metaphor or metonymy; (c) images of the musicians/performers; (d) visual signifiers deriving from national-popular iconography, perhaps related to geographical associations prompted by the performers [for example, images of Irishness associated with the Pogues]; and (e) deeply anchored popular cultural signs associated with rock music that often link rock with a mythologized "America" (cars, freeways, beer, beaches, parties).[3]

The polysemousness of pop music thus comes as both blessing and curse to culture critics – including this one, I confess – whose readings are licensed and privileges leveled in the same multivalent breath. Yet, notwithstanding the sprawling complexity of pop in general, it is still possible to limn out a few of the borderlines and defining traits of the realm of rock that lies within it. A few of these topographical markings are musical in nature, even if their diacritical distinctiveness must shift with the times just to stay in the same dissident relation to the ever-changing practices of pop. If Buddy Holly were alive today, for example, and "Peggy Sue" were a brand-new release, it would probably not be considered rock-and-roll, given its bouncy beat, teenybop lyric, and Buddy Holly's cheery warble. What set it off from other pop music in its time is, however, what still differentially sets off rock from pop in our own: that is, the *relative* centrality and foregroundedness of electric guitar and drums, together with the *relatively* aggressive insistence of the "driving" 4/4 rhythms they make and keep; all that, in combination with the *relative* "rawness" of the R&B-tinged sound it offers its white mainstream audience.

The socio-musical emergence of rock-and-roll in the 1950s and 1960s as a fusion of rhythm-and-blues and/or rockabilly with various formal, timbral and structural elements from mainstream pop, is a story that has been told in a variety of ways, each with its own axe to grind: neutrally, as a paradigmatic instance of the interplay of subcultural or, in some accounts, folk practices with mass culture;[4] negatively, as another instance of racist and/or capitalist appropriation and exploitation;[5] and, positively, as a romantic narrative of the rise to popularity and acclaim of a music of unquenchable energy, passion, and truth, the "music that will set you free," as The Lovin' Spoonful said. This last is, unsurprisingly, the favored narrative of the music industry itself, from the smallest fanzine and one-band promoter to the upper reaches of Geffen Records and *Rolling Stone*, and for obvious reasons: it helps to sell product while obscuring process, for music consumers and for many an industry insider as well, for whom the myth of rock-and-roll ennobles what would otherwise be just another way to make a buck. Yet while this triumphalist narrative should hardly be taken as gospel, neither should it be dismissed as sheer mystification. The ideology of rock-and-roll works – and goes on working, however tenuously – because whatever else it does, it has also, and from its inception, always worked on and within a much larger, ongoing social and ideological project: the social placement and definition of white male youth, from the first of the baby-boomers back in the 1950s to the youngest of their sons today.

Once we take rock's romantic ideology in as an aspect of this larger historic project, we can see how its heroic narrative of emergence and triumph actually includes the other, less flattering narratives at least as much as it effaces them. After all, on the one hand rock-and-roll is a branch or category of popular music; on the other, as a wide variety of critics have argued for years,[6] it has since its inception been coextensive with a host of other practices used *by* and *on* kids, especially young white guys, to say who they are. So, for example, working on early rock music and 1950s mass culture, Harris Frieberg has traced out the complicated dialectic that a tune like Elvis's "Hound Dog" has to dance between a free sexuality still at least partly coded "Black," and the scrambling into near incoherence of Big Mama Thornton's country-blues lyrics and smoothing-down of her "raw," throat-tearing vocal style into a sufficiently tamed and whitened product so as to be fit for mass consumption. Yet Frieberg goes on to remind us that despite such bowdlerizing and for all the bottom-line repressiveness of many if not most lyrics, early rock was rightly viewed with suspicion and hostility by American cultural and political conservatives, insofar as the "ideology of the beat" it proposed and the "speech of the body" it invited were "not compromised."[7]

Frieberg's account of fifties rock is still more nuanced than my summary here can suggest. But I want to add yet another layer to it, before moving

Dockers pants-tag: "Inspired by the comfortable
well worn clothes of the working man."

Two versions of post-industrial:
Bruce as white worker cancelled yet preserved...

...and Axl as the one that doesn't work.

Wild outside, sensitive within: neo-native "rituals"
of the white guys' tribe.

on to Mark 2 of this brief social history, by suggesting more emphatically than Freiberg does that what is constructed vis-à-vis the compromise formations he explores is not only a space within the music industry for a new kind of product aimed at that new social subject, the "teenager," but also and more specifically the definition of a new version of "teen" (that is, adolescent white) *masculinity* as well – a masculinity, moreover, with the well-nigh irresistable attraction of being almost exactly as transgressive as it is normative. So, to return to our example, the new masculinity defined by the white male rocker of the fifties includes, for starters, a different kind of *Whiteness*, one that comes with access to the musical-libidinal resources of Blackness, but unlike Mailer's fantasized hipster-ideal, with no additional risk or requirement to become a "white Negro" oneself;[8] the same domestication of Black country blues styles and idioms Freiberg describes in commercial terms as a prerequisite for mass (re)production here reappears as the comforting sense, for those who get it, that no matter how much friendly shakin' is goin' on there is no doubt who is ultimately in control.

Something of the same is true as well of the new masculinity proposed by fifties rock in terms of gender. Shumway rightly reminds us that for much of white America in the fifties what was most shocking about Elvis was his offering of himself, that is, his *male* body, as a sexual object for (mainly) *women* to gaze at and enjoy.[9] But this reversal of direction and field in sexual objectification was hedged in a variety of ways; and in any case, in and of itself, it never amounted simply to feminization. Rather, in Elvis's person and music the smooth composure of the tepidly hip white male crooner (Perry Como, Dean Martin, Frank Sinatra) erupted into two virtually opposed attitudes, perhaps best expressed by the young Elvis's two most characteristic *moues* – the baby-faced pout, to be held for publicity shots and while singing "But I Can't Help Falling in Love with You," and the sideways sneer for rocking out. If the first suggests a new emotional vulnerability or even, along with songs like "Can't Help Falling in Love" or "Love Me Tender," a childlike near-subjection to the adored and empowered female love, the open sexuality of the second only appears accompanied by a striking blend of narcissistic arrogance: as his famous hips gyrate, Elvis tosses his head with eyes closed in self-satisfaction, then looks out at the screaming crowd of girls with a gleeful jeer.

"To an unusual degree," Middleton writes, "Presley offered an individual body, unique, untranslatable, outside the familiar cultural framework, exciting and dangerous."[10] We know that body was indeed an affront to white middle-class norms of what masculinity should be. But Middleton also reminds us that the other side of whatever seems to us to be the most uncoded behavior is the very code from which it seems to have escaped, that the "nature" of any "*jouissance* ... varies in relation to the positioning of the semiotically constructed subject who is 'lost.'"[11] Accordingly, what may strike us now from our position within a moment governed by somewhat different codes is not so much the scandalous invitation issued by the figure of Elvis for young men to open up their constrained bodies and unbind their sexual energies, as the lines of power and definition that continue to be drawn between white and Black, men and women, even within the new dispensation. The new masculinity proposed for young white men by the voices and bodies of 1950s rock-and-roll may have been "downwardly mobile" in a variety of ways (including classwise, though we have not here dwelt on that fact), even "wild" in Connell's sense of the term;[12] but it was hardly an oppositional one even so.

Yet in Mark 2 of the story I want to tell here, the white masculinity proposed by rock-and-roll does take on a broadly political hue. Or, perhaps more accurately, it participates in and derives some part of its energy from a widely shared fantasy of a political project. I'm speaking, of course, of the 1960s (meaning, as we usually do, mainly the years between 1966 and 1974), when rock-and-roll was taken to be in cultural practice what the so-called "youth movement" was perceived to be in politics: to fans and detractors alike, an organic expression of a generation of white American youth whose size, affluence, and consequent influence in political and buying power were unprecedented. For these "baby-boomers," the idioms and energies appropriated from Black music, together with the sexual flaunting of bourgeois norms, seemed "naturally" affiliated with sympathies for Blacks and other oppressed people at home and abroad, and a hostility towards the corporate boardroom, the military-industrial complex, and the state. What brought rock and white youth movement politics together was their mutual opposition to everything "straight."

At this moment, then, rock-and-roll took on the same sort of resonance for and relationship to its social audience of white baby-boomers that the English novel did for its bourgeoisie a century or so earlier, so much so that we might speak of it as the equivalent of the earlier form's moment of "organic realism." At the same time, fueled by industry hype, the consensual definition of rock stretched to the widest limit of its loose unity, ranging from the extended obbligato figurations of blues-based psychedelic music (for example, Cream or Jefferson Airplane) across now-traditional rock forms (Creedence Clearwater Revival) to include a variety of eclectic transactions with older idioms of popular music (for example, the Beatles and the music-hall sing-along tune). It even briefly expanded to include a few women as bona fide rockers – Grace Slick and Janis Joplin – and, along its most countercultural edge, one African-American, Jimi Hendrix, as crossover flower child. Yet the body to be found at the epicenter of the moment characterized in our romantic narrative as *the* Triumph of Rock-and-Roll, is, inevitably, still that of a white man, Mick Jagger, lead singer of the Rolling Stones.

The Stones' music, especially in the years 1968–72, played across the spectrum we have just described, yet all the while continued to develop and refine its appropriated home in R & B into an edgier, grungier yet more amped-up sound that even today serves as the North Star of Rock. Moreover, on an album like *Beggars' Banquet*, the Stones' bad attitude slid easily from solidarity with the oppressed ("The Salt of the Earth") to a gleeful Nietzschean identification with power ("Sympathy for the Devil"). But the clincher here is the way Jagger's body looked, sounded and performed throughout the late 1960s and into the 1970s: doing "Sympathy" in his American flag suit and cape, prancing through "Jumpin' Jack Flash" or lashing the mike cord like a whip for "Gimme Shelter," wrapping his fat lips around the mike for the verses of "Satisfaction" then snarling out the choruses, as his skinny hips jerked and pumped. Just as the Stones consolidated rock's paradigmatic sound, Jagger's body re-enacted and extended its Mark 1 version of white masculinity. His pasty-white Britishness gave him license to steal stage moves from soul stars like James Brown and their reviews more brazenly than any fifties rocker ripped off any Black R & B performer; he could do all the blues dips, growls and slides he liked, knock off any number of – usually uncredited – Robert Johnson tunes, since his every attempt to do a Black English drawl (the way he does his "my"s, say, in "Under My Thumb") was doomed to succeed exactly as much as it failed. Moreover, like many a hippie's or New Left activist's, Jagger's lissome frame appeared before us not only fully sexualized, but in marked distinction from – indeed, in virtual opposition to – that fully armored body image of (especially) working-class masculinity whose "muscle tensions, posture, ... feel and texture" traditionally enforce both a hierarchical order within masculinity and the domination of women, by "allowing belief in the superiority of men, and the oppressive practices that flow from it, to be sustained by men who in other respects have very little power."[13] But, as with the misogynous New Left men so brilliantly anatomized in *The Mermaid and the Minotaur*,[14] the counterweight to all Mick's dabbling in androgynous and/or feminine qualities and imagery was a taunting sexualized viciousness towards women in the songs themselves, from "Under My Thumb" to the notorious *Black and Blue* album and slogan (the battered woman on the billboard proclaiming "I'm Black and Blue from the Rolling Stones and I love it!"), with many stops in between.

In a pair of valuable essays on rock, sexual identity and commercialism whose narrative tracks run close to mine here, Jon Savage and Mary Harron both maintain that in the 1970s the radical impulses and energies that fueled rock culture and the youth movements of the 1960s hit the skids, as the murky left-libertarianism of the latter evaporated into so many lifestyle choices, and "artists and fans who wanted to express themselves rather than simply be entertained" turned into a pack of consumers to be manipulated by "record companies ... making their biggest profits ever by *regulating* the urge to be different that had once given rock music its reason to live."[15] Yet, according to Savage, the "consumer society based on the teenage sensibility" that survives "is still dominated by that brief but explosive period in the mid-sixties whose implications (and detritus) live with us still."[16] But for all their valuable attempts to take stock of commercial motives (Harron) and the confusion of political commitment and consumerist lifestyle (Savage), such accounts are distorted by their complicity with the very romanticism they seek to resist. After all, it is not so much that rock-and-roll lost its soul in the seventies and eighties as that various forms of rock-and-roll practice, and various audiences, claimed they had it and the others didn't; not so much that the music industry once had to run as fast as it could to keep up with rock "authenticity" but now needs only pump out its simulacra, as that the "urge to be different" has itself become differentiated within rock-and-roll and so demands further product differentiation in turn.

The specific historical point here may be extrapolated into something of a categorical observation on what the social project of rock "authenticity" has been about from the get-go. Rock critics have generally agreed that "[t]he rock aesthetic depends, crucially, on an argument about authenticity";[17] and even that this "myth of authenticity" is the spinning flywheel of the rock imagination, Maxwell's Demon of the industry, insofar as the "desire for the original and the authentic exists alongside the recognition that there can never be such a thing."[18] But no one, so far as I know, has pointed out just how thoroughly this desire for a break with commercial culture and a disavowal of the commodity status of rock – to be opposed to "pop" from within, by dint of an "organic" relationship with the music, its traditions and its audience – is imbricated with the desire to construct, maintain and emulate an alternative white masculinity. Rock, Harron writes, "wants deep emotion and catharsis and truth ... has a religious element that pop does not ... believes in originality and self-expression in defiance of crass commercialism."[19] But all these terms, true enough in themselves, read as an allegory of racial and sexual positioning as well. Decoded in this way, what rock authenticity means is not just freedom from commerce and opposition to all straight authority, combined with deep vocational allegiance to the music, but being a free agent with ready access to the resources of femininity and Blackness yet with no obligations to either women or Blacks.

Rock, then, is a cultural practice that defines itself – musically, socially, and perhaps most of all, physically – in diacritical distinction from Blackness, opposition to official authority and mainstream rectitude, and a combination of diacritical difference and charged opposition to women. The coexistence and historical development of these factors is both cause and effect of the fact that at any given moment almost all rock stars are white men; or, to put it the other way around, why so little music by women or non-white bands (with, generally, single exceptions at best – today, Living Colour and Los Lobos) is ever considered rock, by promoters, critics, fans, or for that matter the bands themselves; why the most Michael Jackson can ever aspire to is the self-proclaimed title "The King of Pop"; and why it is so important for so many reasons that Axl Rose insist his band's award for best new video is "not about Michael Jackson" at all.

2. THE "GET IN THE RING" TOUR: BODIES AND MASCULINITIES

When in the 1970s and 1980s contending rock bands, genres, and audiences vied for rock lineage and natural title, what was then at stake in the opposition of their musical idioms, mythical histories, and social behaviors was not a merely musical issue, much less just a matter of marketing and profits. The question of who is the hardest, realest rocker will above all be a matter of which alternative white masculinity is to be affirmed and approved over all other options. The place where such choices show up in their most condensed and visible form is the rocker's body itself: the space where, as Shumway puts it, "the various codes and media in which rock-and-roll finds expression all contribute to the production of the performer,"[20] the figure in which the polysemousness of rock music and its claims to authenticity find their anchor and *omphalos*.

The problem is, though, that the closer we approach such nodal figures, the more seductive their Siren songs of authenticity tend to become. How else to understand no less astute a commentator than Simon Frith falling prey to the authenticity trope – or, more likely, to the whole complex of rock meanings and effects known as Bruce Springsteen – when he tries to make the two into a genre he seems to think, and want us to think, was there the whole time? An "interesting way of approaching genres," writes Frith,

> is to classify them according to their ideological effects, the way they sell them-
> selves as art, community or emotion. There is, at present, for example, clearly
> a form of rock we call "authentic." It is represented by Bruce Springsteen and
> defines itself according to the rock aesthetic of authenticity.... The whole point
> of this genre is to develop musical conventions which are, in themselves,
> measures of "truth." As listeners we are drawn into a certain sort of reality; this
> is what it is like to live in America, this is what it is like to love or hurt.[21]

Here, in the slippage between rock in general and one rock star in particular, the whole conceptual level of genre is elided. Nor is this the only place in Frith's oeuvre where he lets his categories slide for Bruce's sake. In an essay-review of the live box-set issue, *Bruce Springsteen and the E Street Band Live*, ominously entitled "The Real Thing – Bruce Springsteen," Frith tells us that "what matters in this post-modern era is not whether Bruce Springsteen *is* the real, but how he sustains the belief that there are somehow, somewhere, real things to *be*."[22]

What is wrong – astonishingly wrong, really – with such pronounce-ments is not only that it is, of course, possible to think in much more specific generic terms about the kind of music Springsteen makes than Frith is willing to acknowledge, but that there are any number of other rock stars and bands working other idioms in such a way as to sustain "the belief that there are somehow, somewhere, real things to be" – albeit for other rock audiences of whose existence Frith is momentarily unaware. Perhaps foremost among these other audiences in the seventies and eighties, as Deena Weinstein argues so well and Guns N' Roses' shot to the top of the charts has made so plain, is that for heavy metal.[23] And just because Axl Rose sustains the belief that there are real things to be in a way that's different from Bruce's doesn't make Axl's "Real" any more or less constructed than the Boss's; it simply means that there are two different *constructions* here, of the Real, of rock authenticity, and of alternative "wild" white-guy masculinity, one that went supernova back in 1985–86, and the other on its heels at the cusp of the eighties just past, a timing sequence that suggests something happening to the place and image of white guys, something legible in the contrast between these stars.

Genre in rock is in fact nothing more than the way such differences – in claims for authenticity, definitions of the real, visions of masculinity, and audiences willing to swallow or at least enjoy them all – group themselves around a given sound and all its associations, inherited and constructed. It exists in roughly the same co-constructive relationship with the figure of the rock star as film genre does to the movie star. In both cases, the star condenses "values felt to be under threat or in flux at a particular moment in time,"[24] and does so from a peculiarly intermediary position between the "personal" – the star's "offstage personality" and "private life" given to us through an array of interviews on TV, in magazines, and so on – and the generic pool of meanings and values with which their performances are associated.[25] What most distinguishes rock from film culture in this respect is, however, the consistency and coherence rock fans expect from their stars in terms of just this relationship between rock genre and "offstage" personality profile. In the late 1940s and early '50s, for example, Humphrey Bogart's star image was a contrapuntal construction, existential tough-guy loner on the generic side thanks to *Casablanca* and film noir, happy family man with loving wife Lauren Bacall in private life. Rock performers, on the other hand, tend to pay a price for such inconsistencies – as heavy metal's Ozzy Osbourne found out when he went clean and sober, and as Bruce himself, the former New Jersey rocker now happily ensconced in his Beverley Hills mansion with his lovely wife and kids, may be learning from the slump in sales receipts for the two albums he put out in 1992.

Such surmises may be found in any music or entertainment guide that covers rock;[26] and in any case, I'd rather ponder the more interesting possibility that what those disappointing sales figures mean, combined with the monster success of GN'R, is that Bruce's auratic power as a rock star was fading as Axl's (at least up through the close of 1992) was blazing ever brighter.[27] But to explore this possibility, we'll have to shuttle back and forth between star image and rock genre for both Bruce and Axl without either buying or dismissing either's claim to authenticity –

and repeatedly, inevitably, find ourselves stumbling over their bodies as we do.

Axl and heavy metal, then, Bruce and – and what? The problem of locating Springsteen generically is an interesting and complicated one, partly because the generic claims he and his music make have always been so syncretic, and partly because of the way those claims have accreted and altered over time. The through-line, though, is a mythologized biography dwelling on, and so reinforcing, a pre-given set of associations in rock culture: the white working-class kid from a working-class family in a blue-collar town in New Jersey, no less, who grows up first loving then playing rock-and-roll, and pays his dues by playing it year after year in his own area, building a following among kids like him, playing the joints and developing a name. Eventually, thanks to his devotion to the music/his culture/the kids, this kid miraculously gets signed by the most prestigious producer in 1960s rock, the guy who signed Dylan, no less. But even then he just keeps on putting in his time, working on his albums but still giving everything he's got up on stage, putting himself and the music out there on the line until eventually, in 1984, he cuts this album and goes on this tour and *everybody* gets it, *everybody* identifies. But even that doesn't change him: he's still the same Bruce, the same hard-rockin' working-class guy.[28]

The basic image, then, through which Bruce's authenticity-effect is secured is that of unbroken organic affiliation and continuity: Bruce = rock-and-roll = the sound of passion, excitement, and rebellion in industrial working-class life. Hence, too, Bruce's physical image, even offstage, in jeans and sleeveless t-shirt with a day's growth of stubble on his face, not to mention the guy with his back to us and his baseball cap in his back pocket on the front of *Born in the USA*. But before going on to explore this image further, it's worth pointing out just how gradually and, at least at first, uncertainly it was built up over the course of Bruce's recording career. Take, for example, the earliest and most "organic" performance collected in *Bruce Springsteen: Video Anthology 1978–1987*: Bruce and his E Street Band rocking out on "Rosalita" in what looks vaguely like a mid-sized auditorium, with the crowd so near and the security so lax that through much of the performance he is assailed by adoring young women leaping onto the stage. Here we seem to be watching a Bruce before superstardom, back when his fame was still mainly regional, not that far from the Asbury Park days; yet already we see the distinguishing marks of his later live performances. The joyful and capricious interactions with the other members of the band, especially Black saxophonist

Clarence Clemons, the "Big Man," filling stage left to Bruce's stage right; the playful yet sincere, parodic yet enthusiastic rock moves of aiming the guitar neck out at the crowd as the riff is "fired off," of stalking the stage or dashing across it to skid to his knees as the song's excitement mounts, of tossing himself up back-down on the lid of the piano in the sheer delight of his own guitar riffs: all these gestures and behaviors testify not only to the raw excitement and ecstatic pleasure of the music, but combined with Bruce's near constant eye contact with his audience and eager smile (except when he is singing – that, as we shall see, is something else), they equally evince his need to offer these same pleasures to his audience, to include them – his desire, in short, to *please*.

So runs the now-familiar rhetoric of joyful populist sincerity in the Springsteen performance. Yet at least as interesting and significant as the continuity of this behavioral communication are the disjunctive elements in Springsteen's image at this point. Disjunctive, that is, with the more emphatically blue-collar imagery that will eventually become official, even regulative, aspects of Bruce-ness once he goes mega: for this earlier Bruce is a guy with a smooth face, tousled longish curly hair, some kind of a silk or polyester shirt unbuttoned to the waist underneath a box-shouldered *sportcoat* – Bruce actually *dressed up*. This dressed-up quality, ironically enough, may supply further warrant for the organic nature of Bruce's relationship with working-class milieux and audiences at this point, for those who know how much such folks tend to appreciate the performer who suits up a little for them. Moreover, this attire harks back to the time and image of such fifties "dreamboats" as Fabian, Frankie Avalon, and the "pop"-ularized Presley himself, all stars plucked from white working-class backgrounds and molded into visual and musical shapes designed to attract young white working-class women most of all.

This retro image appears more explicitly in the live performance that follows "Rosalita" on the video anthology, a version of "The River" Bruce delivers decked out in a baby-blue sportcoat with his hair in a D.A.-ed pompadour. But here it is refined, complicated, and updated even as it is emphasized by the rapt attentiveness with which the camera holds Bruce in close-up through the song, except for a few slow zooms in and out. This still concentration, along with the quiet intensity of Bruce's delivery, not only helps pin our sense of Bruce's sincerity to the lyrics' narrative of male working-class experience ("For my nineteenth birthday, I got a union card and a wedding coat") and its dissatisfactions ("Is a dream a lie if it don't come true/Or is it something worse?"), but invites us to regard those words as somehow more artful and more deeply true than the usual rock lyric, just as Bruce's curly locks in the "Rosalita" video and the *Born to Run* record cover, backed of course by his occasional Dylanesque use of the mouth harp, are conversely meant to say "Rock *Poet*" to us.

This image of Springsteen as working-class *artist* will, later in his career, be de-emphasized but never revoked. (And if one knows, or remembers, the story of how Bruce Springsteen was introduced as "the next Dylan" to John Hammond, the man who first signed him for Columbia, so much the better.) Even for those whose fandom began twelve years later, when *Born in the USA* hit the racks, its faint yet precious penumbra of cultural cachet stands behind and backs the later image as swaggering, solidly muscled working-class rocker, legitimating backdrop for what the foreground seems to authenticate. In this sense the packed lines and homegrown metaphors in Springsteen's lyrics and the raspy clenched coarseness of his singing voice from the beginning complement and justify one another. Taken together, moreover, they serve still another function: that of obscuring the dubious (from a rock perspective, that is) genealogies of many of the musical idioms Springsteen has tapped for his songs. Of the two most famous songs from what we can now call the "early" period of Springsteen's fame, for example, "Rosalita" stripped of Springsteen's gritty delivery sounds more like "Only in America" or some similar piece of mid-sixties pop by a group like Jay and the Americans than any rock-and-roll, while the overwrought "epic" structure of "Born to Run," minus the edge of the electric guitars and Bruce's voice, seems suspiciously close to the near-forgotten pop pretensions of Richard Harris's "MacArthur Park."

Something of the same "stirring" film-soundtrack sonority runs through "Born in the USA" as well, in a similar pattern of instrumental repetition of the song's main phrase as the lead-in to each verse. Here again, the trick is to ennoble what the voice authenticates via the sound's marriage to the gritty shout – so "close to the heart" and "true to life" it is hardly even singing, one might feel – of Bruce's monotonously emphatic stamping out of the lyrics, a "singing" that functions in turn as a metonymy for the monotonous oppression of male working-class life the lyrics narrate from hometown to Vietnam and back. But before delving any further into this particular song and its associated body-image, I want to close off this no doubt incomplete tour of musical idioms by noting the regular, indeed well-nigh constitutive presence in much of Springsteen's output of yet one more strand: rockabilly and country-western. You can, of course, at times hear in Bruce – say, in a song like *Tunnel of Love*'s "Spare Parts" – a little

Chuck Berry; but then Chuck Berry has his own complicated relationship to white rockabilly sound. At any rate, the main point here is how relatively little Bruce's music owes to Black-centered blues and R & B, how much to the traditionally white idioms of country blues and ballads. Such influences show up practically everywhere in his music: in the western Frankie Laine or Jimmie Rodgers-style yodeling he trails off the end of a song like "I'm on Fire"; in the ballad structure of "Spare Parts" and other songs; in the pulse of the rhythm, timbre and drawl of his voice in a first-person love-trouble tune like "One Step Up," to name only a few.

The "Whiteness" of these musical influences contributes to the construction of Bruce's image in a variety of ways, even as they are inflected by other elements of the Springsteen complex. Circumscribed and to some degree masked by Bruce's "tougher-than-the-rest" voice, and elevated sonically, visually, and/or verbally by the various strategies of ennoblement described above, they nonetheless function to *dis*affiliate Springsteen's rocking from rock's traditionally uneasy, energetic, and exploitative relationship with "Blackness." At the same time, and as part of the same process, they help to reconnect the notion of rock and authenticity to the class signifier to which they were first attached in Mark 1 of our narrative: the white *working-class* rocker, albeit shorn here of any musical attachment to Blacks. In so doing, moreover, we might say that the image of this ennobled yet class-specific rocker simply leaps back over and "forgets" the 1960s moment when rock largely lost its class accents to become the music of "its" generation, that is, of college- and draft-age baby-boomers as volatile political subjects and target-rich consumer group: a moment when, as we have seen, rock masculinity draws closer to "femininity" and "Blackness" alike, while remaining distinct from each.

Nor are these elements the only ones lost in this great leap backward; we need to take into account the effect of the leap itself as well. At a moment in the Reagan eighties characterized by the decline of traditional manufacturing sectors and the loss of those jobs, Bruce's reconstruction of the rocker as organic white working-class hero might – on the surface, as it were – seem a potentially volatile and energetic figure capable of condensing and reflecting, if not actually galvanizing, a progressive class-based political will. Yet as all but Bruce's most indefatigable boosters have acknowledged, Bruce has been "read" as a progressive left-liberal figure mainly, if not exclusively, by intellectual and/or professional baby-boomers who've retained some vestige of radicalism from the sixties. Otherwise, he has proved notoriously enjoyable, not only but especially in his most explicitly proletarian poses in *Born in the USA*, by a predominantly Reaganite generation of middle-class white youth, and even appropriable, during the 1984 campaign, by Reagan himself.[29]

How, then, to explain this lack of danger or threat in Bruce's white working-class image, especially given the "organic" linkage (re)articulated between that image and the discontents his songs explicitly name? For starters, I want to say it has something to do with the sheer overdetermined "pastness" – or "belatedness" as I referred to it earlier – of the working-class image constructed in Springsteen's music and words. So many of those songs themselves – "Atlantic City," "Glory Days," and "My Hometown," to name only a few – and the video clips that accompany them, speak of industrial working-class life and its entertainments in the past tense, as it were. These themes of disappearance and attenuation, moreover, are both complicated and at least partially canceled out when put alongside songs like "The River" that balladize the frustrations of working-class life *with* a job, or "Born to Run," which dreams of escape from that life. But the confusion we might feel as to whether blue-collar white working-class life and masculinity are worth saving, whether we should mourn or celebrate their passing away, is obviated both by the aestheticizing strategies described above, and by the sanitizing "back-to-the-future" jump over the 1960s Springsteen's rock makes in terms of the idioms from which it most commonly draws. The way Springsteen works in the mid-eighties is thus the opposite of how Harris Frieberg tells us Elvis and Chuck Berry worked in the 1950s. In their cases, the pulse and energy and provenance of the musical idiom, combined with the sight of the rocker, belied and overcame the conservative containment strategies embedded in the songs' lyrics; in the case of Bruce, thanks to both the whiteness and the belatedness of the musical idioms involved, it is the other way around.

Bruce, then, could be massively enjoyed as working-class hero precisely insofar as the working-class life he portrayed came across as aesthetically and historically distanced from the lives of those taking him in as an *authentic artifact*. Even the nickname "The Boss," affixed to him at that moment of his greatest success, bespeaks this sense of distance, insofar as underneath its obvious implication that Springsteen is the champion of rock-and-roll lies the pleasant reminder his star image offers its audience of an earlier moment in industrial culture when there were, directly above your head, *visible* bosses owning and running the plant; only that moment is so far gone and so fuzzy that a white guy dressed sort of like a worker sort of makes you think of that.[30] By the same token, Bruce's claim to be

"Tougher Than the Rest," in the song of that title (where its meaning is, basically, more capable of a mature, responsible, hetero relationship), can even take on a vaguely progressive hue for those with liberal gender politics without quite losing the piquant, residual *frisson* of white working-class swagger – just, and just as easily, as what's left of that swagger can, regardless of the lyrics, be folded into the reactionary flag-waving on which so many Reaganites battened, young and old. For that matter, the Bruce body that showed up in 1984 – that scruffy-whiskered, sideburned, thickly-muscled, bare-armed one in jeans jacket or a sleeveless T or both – also fed into the climate of Reaganite reaction simply by appearing, on the album cover, in concert, and on MTV, against the background of the flag. For, as Connell reminds us, such images are already conjoined in patriarchal reaction, insofar as "working-class milieus that emphasize physical toughness" have long since come to function within the industrialized world as crucial allies of male dominance in the upper reaches of the economy and the state.

Yet now, returning from all these histories and determinations to this parodic paradigm of the heavy-duty white male worker, this body-become-superstar, it is time to note one final respect in which the meanings of Springsteen – virtually all the meanings, reactionary as well as progressive – are held in by that body's performative behavior, by the extent to which this Bruce's singing and movement speak of energies *confined*. Here again, the locus classicus is probably the concert footage from "Born in the USA," though other examples from the same period are not hard to find. Watch the way he delivers the song, starting with the way his head and shoulders jolt in time with the rimshots squarely keeping up the hard 4/4 beat. The camera gives us much of his singing in close-up – the intensity effect, remember? – yet there is something special and specific about the rigid quivering of that face as it shouts out the lyrics, about the tightness with which the eyes are clamped shut as the head bends down and the right arm stiffens in a clenched-fist salute. Or think how, in the video clip of his cover of Edwin Starr's "War" (coincidentally, probably the "Blackest" song in his repertoire), the hard-working, bicep-bulging body in black vest over a sleeveless red T is over and over so heavily taken by the "woah-oah-oah-oah"'s of the choruses that they bunch him up and bend him over like a man with some serious abdominal pain. Otherwise, in both clips the body basically stays still and stiff: no wiggling or thrusting here from inside those jeans; nothing more than the hammer-like heel of the right boot clumping out the beat.

For me at least, in the context of all Bruce's other meaning-effects and in conjunction with his white worker image, such rock-and-roll behavior glimmers with resonance. For starters, it insists that he ain't anywhere *close* to being Black, which fact, together with how rigidly *straight* it also appears, helps to balance off or mitigate the effect of having an actual Black man up there to play off from, and sometimes even flirt with, on the front of the stage.[31] Moreover, the power of the burly white working-class signifier is at one and the same time made *available to* young and yuppie Reaganite economic reactionaries and "gender progressives" alike (if you'll pardon the phrase), and *safe for* both groups, thanks to the visible bottling up and strained containment of its potentially alarming force for class mobilization and/or oppression of women, good and/or ill. The constricted self-binding of rock energy in The Boss's performances thus bespeaks neither aggression nor rebellion, but *ressentiment* in its classic Nietzschean sense, as "impotent hatred, envy, repressed feelings of revenge, the inability to act out antagonistic impulses in open conflict."[32] The degree to which that pain and anger and sheer energy are held in, squared off, bottled up – exactly as much, we might say, as his body is built up – is part and parcel of the way, in other aspects of Bruce's music and beyond it, that a certain kind of white working-class masculinity associated with Fordist regimes of mass production and capital accumulation is being rendered artifactual. Bruce's worker's body circa 1984–86 pins down and neutralizes all the other meanings in his music by becoming, finally, an object of nostalgia, a social emotion suitably defined for us by the great American socialist poet Thomas McGrath as "failed dynamite."

With the appearance of Axl Rose, though, and in accordance with changing times as well as musical idioms, the mythic narrative departs from those reassuring continuities with which the story of Springsteen's "authenticity" is invested. What's real about Axl is founded not in continuities but in breaks, in both senses of the term: not being a good crowd-pleasing boy even in rebellion, like Bruce, but being offensive even – indeed, especially – in success.

To understand the viability of Axl's distinctive story and body requires us to review the dynamic of authenticity that story and body must engage. As Axl himself has described it for *Rolling Stone*, the "basic root" of the Guns N' Roses' music "is hard rock, a bit heavier than the Stones, more in a vein like Aerosmith, Draw-the-Line type stuff." The formulation, though circumlocutory, is accurate: the term Rose's description of GN'R's socio-musical practice walks around is, of course, heavy metal, mutated offshoot of 1960s rock. We need to turn, then, to where that sound comes from, who it reaches, what body images it calls for and calls up, and what all that has tended historically to mean.

Heavy metal, not at all coincidentally, picks up at the tail end of the moment Bruce's music leaves out, that is, with the rock of the late 1960s.[33] Both culturally and musically, it derives from "acid" or psychedelic rock of the late 1960s and the white boomer-based counterculture that claimed that music as its own. In bands like The Jimi Hendrix Experience, Big Brother and the Holding Company, and Cream, acid rock used a base provided by Black blues, especially the industrialized, electrified "Chicago" sound of Muddy Waters, Willie Dixon and B.B. King, as launching pad for ever more extended, free-form guitar improvizations, and similarly emphasized the instrumental-expressive qualities of the voice over its tune-carrying, lyric-delivering capability. Led Zeppelin, widely considered the premier heavy-metal band, was in the early seventies one of the first to inflect this mix in a "heavier" direction, by mixing a miked-up drum kit and bass drum – metal's so-called "bottom sound" – into a thicker, louder, and more steady-rocking impasto of boogeying guitars lending low-pitched blues figures an insistence both monotonous and menacing. Likewise, extended guitar solos became yet more aggressively chromatic, at points of maximum intensity crossing over from musical to acoustic event to express the guitarist's artistry and deep emotion, just as the abrupt movement of the singer's vocals from tender lyricism to gruff roars or falsetto screams suggested equally arbitrary shifts from the "soft" emotions of love and sorrow to the sharp edges of anger, fear, and pain.

Such musical developments coincide and, for most commentators, are correlated with the large-scale social and cultural shifts in the rock audience sketched out in the first part of this essay.[34] As the white youth movements of the sixties foundered on their own contradictions, and the counterculture broke into a scattering of lifestyle options and fads, heavy metal became the homeboy sound, in Weinstein's words, "where lower-middle-class and working-class whites were more likely to be found ... in the large cities of the American Midwest, as well as in medium-sized cities and blue-collar suburbs,"[35] and so inflected the gender and generational connotations of sixties rock with fresh accents of uncertainty and rage. Metal's attitude problem, Weinstein argues, is a function of the downward mobility that young white lower-class and/or working-class men have suffered in the seventies and eighties, as their sense of racial and gender superiority, perhaps especially *within* what was left of 1960s youth culture, has come under assault from women, Blacks and other non-white peoples seeking power, justice and redress, at the same time that their economic prospects, at the end of the Fordist era of mass production and in the age of Reagan, have dried up and blown away. Hence the complicated circuitry of politics and pleasure involved in finding this music "real" and using it to authenticate and legitimate your own life.

Take what Weinstein calls "the essential sonic element in heavy metal" – "power, expressed as sheer volume,"[36] together with the regular rhythmic forward snapping of head ("headbanging") and upraised arm that are the classic metalhead audience's response to that power's exhibition in live performance. One common enough reading of these behaviors would have it that the metalheads' actions constitute a straightforwardly proto-fascist identification with white male power in its most nakedly direct and violent forms. But surely this is too univalent and reductive. It is more likely that such identifications are only one moment of a much more mobile response, in which the sonic force of the music oscillates among various guises and affective relationships to the metal fan: as oppositional or subversive power with which the metalhead identifies; as hegemonic authorized power against which his responses beat their oppositional time; as an overwhelming life force he joins; and as an inexorably destructive, apocalyptic fury he both welcomes and fears – to name only the most likely alternative possibilities. Of course it matters that the members of the band putting out that deafening sound and swathed in an equally enormous spectacle of smoke and light are the same sex and color as yourself, wear the same regalia and sport the same long hair – or, for that matter, like Alice Cooper or Kiss, two of the longest running and most successful, look and act even more socially out of it than you are, and celebrate the fact. On balance, though, the fan's response to performance and scene is as multiform and multivalent as is any enjoying subject's dazed and blurry decoding of an experience whose foremost effect is simply to overwhelm – any experience, that is, of the romantic sublime.

Along with this multivalence toward a multiply defined power, moreover, the genre of metal as a set of rock-and-roll practices from production to reception and back has tended to insist on an equally definitive set of exclusions and negations. Women as a group tend to be marginalized by the deliberately aggressive and/or ugly loud sound of metal, and are frequently evoked in metal songs as sex objects, "bitches," or some combination of the two. And the portentous *Sturm und Drang* into which metal converts its blues figurations stiffens and bleaches the Blackness out of them, helping to produce heavy metal as, in effect, the equivalent of rap for downscale young white men. Finally, in spite of the very long and often teased-up hair, and what Weinstein describes as "the S&M paraphenalia of segments of the gay subculture"[37] – or because of it – the practice of metal hardly commends any softening or femininization as part of the alternate "wild" masculinity it models, much less any blurring or breakdown of the lines separating gay from straight. Such distinguishing practices seem designed, rather, to increase and emphasize the distance of metal music, bands, and fans from the straight world, while reinforcing what Eve Kosofsky Sedgwick has taught us to call a strictly "homosocial" fraternity of defiant, socially and politically incorrect rejects for whom the social stigmatization of being "out of it" culturally, economically, and politically has been rendered via metal a heroic, even transcendent fate.[38]

But before these generalizations congeal any further, they ought to be quickened with a more detailed sense of metal history. First, it is important to note what every metalhead knows and practically every metal-hater doesn't, that is, that all metal bands are not and have never been the same. Nor are the differences between, say, Aerosmith, Motley Crue and Metallica merely sonic and/or musical in nature (even though they are always also that); there are also, within the general outline and description, important distinctions in temperament and emphasis. Aerosmith blends some Stones into the standard metal mix, not only in terms of its relatively bright and polished sound or the visual homage Steve Tyler's face, coiffure and wardrobe render to Mick, but in the band's ongoing preoccupation – expressed in video clips and interviews as well as in the songs themselves – with specifically sexual (though always heterosexual) forms of naughtiness and transgression. Motley Crüe, coifed in teased hair and semi-clothed in black leather, gives us a rougher, more classically metal sound, trading in a squarely conventionalized language of social transgression and apocalypse. One of its signature songs, "Dr Feelgood," effaces all allusions to good sex and/or Blackness in general and Aretha in particular in favor of a jeering vocal and a driving manic energy, that sheer "sonic power" as the fuel of the song. And Metallica – to take one last example – combines some of the thickest bottom sound and most gravelly vocals in all metal with an attitude compounded of equal parts of its most romantically despairing self-exaltation and the principled anarchist suspicion associated with its more culturally upscale cousin, hardcore.

Moreover, as metal's audience has grown in the 1980s, that audience and what it calls metal have further diversified as well. Thanks in no small part to the influence of MTV, which in the first part of the decade gave it very extensive coverage,[39] one of metal's edges has softened its sound and look and moved towards the mainstream and a more female-admixed audience (for example, that for Jon Bon Jovi); while another, in response to this dilution, has hardened its sound, quickened its tempos and borrowed from hardcore to come up with an altogether more hostile and nihilistic mix (for example, Anthrax or Suicidal Tendencies).[40] Towards the end of the decade, then, within and across this diversified field, Guns N' Roses will become superstars both in range and in presumption. The band's range extends from the "power ballads" of so-called "lite metal," defined by Weinstein as "songs with just enough metal sound (the bass) to be heard as metal, but not so much … that they will be detested by those who are turned off by traditional heavy metal music"[41] (GN'R's hit "Yesterdays" is a good example here), all the way out to the distended Moody Blues-style shlock of "November Rain." Likewise, along metal's harder shores they can shift from the classic hysteria of "Welcome to the Jungle" and the paranoia of "Out ta Get Me" on the band's debut album *Appetite for Destruction* (1987), to the manic thrash rhythms and energies of "So Fine" on *Use Your Illusion II* (1991). Their level of presumption is already suggested by Axl's choice of "hard rock" rather than "heavy metal" to describe this range to his *Rolling Stone* interviewer, a rhetorical power play whose implicit aim is to redefine the broader field of rock on terms favorable to declaring GN'R Heavyweight Champion of it. (Their 1992 World Tour, and one of *Use Your Illusion*'s tracks, is titled "Get in the Ring.")

But this struggle over the signifier of rock is hardly the limit, or even the most decisive instance, of GN'R's audacity, which also extends to the speed and manner in which they broke themselves, and were broken, as a "national" act in the first place. The dues-paying component of most rock mythologies has traditionally been more sternly required in the province of metal than in any other rock genre, given the stigmatized outsider status of the classic metal fan. Yet far from touring for years to build credibility and a following, Guns N' Roses was signed to Geffen Records in 1986 a mere nine months or so after its formation, by a guy who'd been brought in from Elektra expressly to bring Geffen its own version of Motley Crüe. The following year the band's first album, *Appetite for Destruction*, was released and chalked up steady but not earth-shaking sales (it took ten months to crack *Billboard*'s Top 100), until such time as the video clip for "Welcome to the Jungle" was released and played extensively on MTV. And the rest, as they say, is history: by the end of 1992, with some seventeen million sales worldwide, *Appetite* was the best-selling debut album of all time, while Geffen let it be known that as part of its strategy for marketing the double album *Use Your Illusion* I and II, it intended to stretch out its release of singles from the album over a three-year period, 1991–94.

The full eccentricity of such a narrative compared to that conventionally required of metal-band success lies, moreover, not just in these details themselves but in their dissemination as part of the GN'R mystique.[42] The massive anonymous crowds of GN'R's first full-length performance video, "Paradise City," are there to make a point virtually the opposite of that made in the footage of Bruce doing "Rosalita": here it's not about the moment of intimate regional renown, but about what a monster band they are right off the gun.[43] Such a freely confessed market strategy dovetails nicely with lead singer Axl Rose's unabashed interest in making money and achieving commercial success – as in the first of his *two* interviews in *Rolling Stone*, the one attendant on the runaway success of *Appetite* in which he counsels "any kid in high school" no matter "what else you're gonna do," to "take business classes," and proudly asserts that in the making of *Appetite*, "Everything was directed at trying to achieve the sales without sacrificing the credibility of our music…"[44]

There are a couple of important points to make about how such an avowedly complicit hustle gets squared with – and thereby redefines – the cardinal rock-and-roll value of authenticity, both of them relevant to the way we take in Axl's body and the meanings we take out of it. But on our way to them it is worth pausing to note a contradiction around Bruce's body image and its exchange value that stands in direct opposition to Axl's stance. This contradiction is suggested by a possibly apocryphal bit of Springsteeniana. The story goes that a spokesman for Levi's, when asked whether the company had tried to engage Springsteen's services for its ads, replied that he could not imagine how Bruce could help them any more than he already was.[45] Thanks to his intransigent refusal to compromise or cash in his authentically burly working-class masculinity, in other words, it is with Bruce as with the sailors and/or longshoremen on the tags attached to those Dockers pants marketed to mid-level professional-managerial-class boomers like myself. In these images, drawn and colored in a faux-thirties style for the nostalgia of the thing, the working man is invariably depicted as an idler whose strapping shape and proletarian style draw the erotic gaze of the swanky, well-dressed woman being drawn past him on the dock or at the train station by the oblivious, dun-suited, upper-class man to whose arm she is attached. Obviously enough, the allure of the workman for the woman in the illustration and, *a fortiori*, for us, is inextricable from the purity and unbridgeability of his distance from her, from us, and from the system of gazes to which he is nonetheless linked; just as that relay of gazes, the woman's exposed and ours hidden, creates the space of a new desire for, and a new definition of, an intermediary masculinity between the stiff orthodoxy of the empowered, normative ruling-class male and the superseded, rough-hewn worker – the space of the sensitive yet still sort-of-rough guy who buys and wears Dockers and appreciates Bruce.

If the very distance the Bruce image seems to take from commerce and commodification only serves to render it more serviceable to both, the complicity displayed by Axl and GN'R follows out a perverse counter-logic whereby one is exactly as much *"in"* as "out of it," and the only possibility for authenticity involves flaunting just how unapologetically dirty you are. Such repositioning and such shocking pleasure are exactly what happens and matters in the video clip of "Welcome to the Jungle," widely considered to have launched *Appetite*'s flight to the stratosphere of sales and GN'R's ascension to rock superstars. Musically, the song is a classic metal blues-boogie graced by one of Axl's most extensive displays of hysterically shifting chops, from a grated snarl through most of the verses, to high rips and overwrought stutters on every chorus, and falsetto taunting through the instrumental bridge. Lyrically and dramatically, as the title suggests, it's a celebration – ironic, oppositional, and straightforwardly sincere, like most of metal's evocations of power – of the contemporary social landscape as a terrain of utter savagery: "Welcome to the jungle, it gets worse here every day ... You can get anything you want, but you better not take it from me ... I'm gonna watch you bleed/scream," and so on. The video clip wraps a basic before-and-after narrative around this sado-masochistic circuitry, a narrative both punctuated and punctured by the performing Axl at its center. As the video (but not the song) begins, the first Axl we see is the ballcapped hayseed chewing a stalk of green wheat as he steps off the bus onto the mean streets of the city. He gawks at the figure of a passing woman, then turns his dazed and overstimulated gaze to a display window full of TVs, all broadcasting an extreme close-up of You-Know-Who snarling and writhing with a leather strap across his head. At this point the song's blues-bottom figure kicks in, as the video straight-cuts from this TV image to yet another Axl, this one wearing virtually the same expression in performance on stage, switching thin hips poured into tight black leathers and sporting a nimbus of teased blonde hair as he tears into the opening verse.

There are more Axls waiting for us in the remainder of the clip: a very glammed-up one in the first instrumental break, shown watching a group of TVs in a softly lit, peach-colored living room together with a few other men and/or women as sexually ambiguous as himself (this, by the way, following the only verse that explicitly addresses the subject of the song's taunting appeal as a "very sexy *girl* [my emphasis] ... very hard to please"); a straight-haired pre- or post-decadent Axl strapped to a chair à la *Clockwork Orange* in the second break and forced to watch two banks of four TVs apiece pulsing out the same images of riot, police and military repression, and lush female bodies on display as the last Axl was watching in the living room; and finally, at the song's end, a near version of Axl-on-stage back out on the street shaking his head in sad disgust at the display window's stacked close-ups of the televised tortured Axl we started with, and walking away. But the video's main image is clearly that of the demiurge who both generates and grows out of all the others, the Axl who delivers the song. In a Springsteen clip – say, "Glory Days" – that plays with narrative as much as this one does, the Springsteen performing the song up on the cramped stage with his bar-band is continuous with all the other Bruces we see in the course of the video, first practicing his own pitching, then finally tossing a few to his own kid: wherever the performing Bruce belongs temporally, however we order him into the narrative, the point is that he *fits*. But the relationship of the performing Axl to the proto-narrative suggested by the "Welcome" video is by no means so smoothly accommodating. Alternately taunting and whimpering, strutting and collapsing, his long hair, bangles and tattoos both placing him monstrously beyond any system of pleasure and repression and positing him, effeminized, overinscribed and abased, at the bottom of its vortex, this performing body reflects, exceeds, screams back at, submits to and masters every other image in the video, including and especially any and all other images of himself.

The struggle, then, to make GN'R's metal-based rock into the definition of Rock is thus condensable into the struggle to posit Axl as the figure of a new (or newly modulated) wild rocking masculinity, to move beyond merely serving as an organic figure for other young, culturally and economically subordinate white men; and, conversely, the task of this redefinition overlaps with that of remaking rock authenticity itself. Axl may be a kid from a downscale family in a small Rustbelt city on the skids, and may advertise that fact when he plays his Indiana hometown: "I know what the fuck's goin' on out here and this band's one of the only things these kids got."[46] But the more distinctive stage attitude of GN'R is not identification with the audience but suspicion, hostility, and even contempt for it, manifested in a wide array of notorious behaviors: short sets and chronic lateness; abrupt cancellations whenever Axl's throat is giving him trouble; Axl's walking off the stage if the technical arrangements or security is not up to scratch; or even, in one famous case, Axl's jumping offstage and, still resplendent in white feather boa, personally smacking up one unruly fan. We began our exploration of Bruce onstage by noting how he aimed to please; here, as Axl's mid-concert sermon to the crowd in New Orleans demonstrates, it's a question of the fans being worthy of the gift.

> O.K.? How much did you pay for this show? … I'll tell you what I'll do – I'll pay you back because this just isn't going to work. It's hard to be up here giving like this with all you people sitting there taking a f—ing nap. Yeah, yeah, I know, there he goes begging for attention again. My therapist always says, 'You crave attention.' And I go, 'No s—.'[47]

Such displays of narcissistic need and aggression are consistent with another aspect of the band's mythical profile we have left unmentioned until now: their advanced reputation, even among other metal-based bands, for dissipation in general and heavy drug and alcohol use in particular. According to this heavily promoted legend, most of GN'R's advance on their first album went out to the LA street to service old debts and score new stuff; heroin addiction cost GN'R's first drummer his job eventually, and conspicuous consumption of smack is even said to have strained relations between Axl and his half-black lead guitarist Slash.[48] Such well-circulated stories, together with tales of wrecked hotel rooms and casual sex, and the virtually obligatory presence of some Jack Daniels, Jim Beam, or at least a Bud in the hand in every fan-mag photo, provide further evidence of GN'R's poor impulse control in such a way as to redefine and legitimate their leap over the dues-paying moment. Not for these boys the hard work of establishing a presence, connecting with the audience, coming up slow; they're way too greedy, bored and pissed off for that.

Such fables and photos of advanced dissipation, along with the tales of stage misbehavior and performance breakdown, thus serve to counterweight as well as justify the band's commercial success, reassuring us that their complicity with the Powers That Be does not constitute acceptance, that you can have a career and be a Bad Boy after all: this is arguably a message whose comfort is at least equal to that given off by Bruce to those going or staying upscale in "post-industrial," post-working-class America, albeit quite different in kind. So also with GN'R's and Axl's easy avowal of degrees of homophobia, racism, and xenophobia that even most metal bands and their fans keep under wraps, not to mention near-parodic levels of misogyny in others (for example, "Back Off Bitch"). When asked to comment on the open expression of the first set of thuggish attitudes in a song called "One in a Million," Axl's reply provides a beautiful instance of the dissolution of any sense of difference or community in an ocean of undifferentiated self. "The thing with 'One in a Million,'" he said, "is, basically, we're all one in a million, we're all here on this earth. We're one fish in a sea. Let's quit fucking with each other, fucking with me."[49]

If, as we saw, Bruce's contained and emblematically working-class body was racked and choked by the classically oedipal-neurotic reactions of guilt, disappointment, and dreams of escape, Axl's nakedly exposed, multiply-tattooed body *acts out* its rebel masculinity and rock authenticity as a fitful, flailing rage. Rock's newest wild white boy is, as he likes to tell us himself nowadays, the offspring of a dysfunctional family; and up there on stage he behaves as if he were still in one, the way he stalks obliviously past the other band members' widely scattered positions, or randomly dashes from ramp to ramp or wing to wing, or stands stage center leaning forward from the waist, staring blankly past the crowd as his voice shrieks intensity and his outstretched stiffened arm quivers in disjunct convulsion, his actions and gestures as alienated from whatever song he may be singing as he is from both his audience and the rest of his band, each of them in his own particular trance: no community here, neither onstage nor beyond it, only one damaged fish in the sea. Likewise, while Bruce appears offstage in the same working-guy t-shirts and jeans, seamlessly continuous with his history and himself, the clothing signifiers pinned to Axl's chronically unstable body keep altering their random concatenations throughout his show in the "Get in the Ring" tour: from tartan skirt to spandex shorts, buckskins to frogged and epauletted officer's coat, a t-shirt with Manson's image to one reading NOBODY KNOWS I'M A LESBIAN. This is rock authenticity as pure pre-oedipal fury and appetite, "wild" masculinity in the unbounded and amoral form of what Lacan wittily called the "l'hommelette," the body that eats and rages, whines and snarls, grabs and flails; the loose-limbed asexual body whose pronounced racism, homophobia, misogyny are only so many paranoid reflexes of its un-bounded narcissistic self; perhaps above all the unproductive, overinscribed, spastic body that, although complicit, is nonetheless scandalously un-available to appropriation because it *doesn't work*.

3. THE KIDS MIGHT BE ALL RIGHT; OR, MASCULINITIES IN BLOOM

Obviously, I have not written this piece to plump for either Axl's or Bruce's version of rock masculinity. Rather, I have tried to show how each carries complex messages of racial and sexual differentiation; how Bruce's moral authenticity is part and parcel of the nostalgia that contains it; how Axl's sincere instability, complicity, and snarling viciousness are one and the same; and how their rock bodies deliver all these messages in each case. On the other hand, I am also very far from arguing that the commodification of whatever synaesthetic body-center cluster of sounds, words, and images constitutes rock-and-roll at any given moment must be in and of itself the sign the fix is in re white straight masculinity or anything else, given the ongoing power of popular music to condense, idealize and disseminate new models of being and behaving far beyond their initial moment, site, and audience, together with the industry's hard-wired hunger for dissent.[50] Rather than argue for one body over the other, the artifact of modernity or the postmodern basket case, as incarnation of a white straight masculinity worth pursuit and affirmation, I want to end here with an evocation of a rock masculinity – that is to say, still virtually by definition, of a white straight masculinity – that seems to me to have more potential than either Bruce's or Axl's, to hint at something more and something else.

You can see it, or I hope you can, in the video clip of "In Bloom" performed by Nirvana, the flannel-shirted, tattered-jeaned all-white male group from Seattle whose "grunge" album (think a dirge-like fusion of punk and metal, those of you who haven't heard it) to everyone's astonish-ment went platinum in 1992. The clip ironizes that fame, and takes a Brechtian distance on MTV and rock bodies alike, by referring to a moment in rock history that prefigures both their presents. It opens with a shot of another, older TV set on which an Ed Sullivan-style host, in grainy early-sixties black-and-white, has just come back on camera at the end of a performance by the unseen but "world famous Dancing Poodles" to introduce "three fine young men from Seattle ... thoroughly all right and decent fellows" to the screaming crowd. The basic through-line of the rest of the video consists of crosscuts from this bland-faced band, a time-warped Nirvana in matching striped sport coats and Beatle-length hair duly combed down and back, cheerfully bobbing as they strum their instruments and "sing" slightly out of sync, and group shots of a hysterically wrought-up, shrieking crowd of mainly junior-high girls circa 1963 – only every so often, especially around the chorus, something happens like a reception problem, or swishpan, or both, and we get instead an image of the same band on the same set but looking quite different and hardly playing the same song at all. Instead, as the chorus thuds blearily, drearily along –

> He's the one
> who knows all our pretty songs
> and he likes to sing along
> and he likes to show his gun
> but he
> knows not what it means
> knows not what it means

– the band members lurch around in the frocks they're wearing now, at one moment pushing over the flats of arches that framed them, at another haplessly watching the drum-set topple down. Lead singer Kurt Cobain tries a couple of goony airplane spins with arms outstretched; engages in a mock duel during the instrumental bridge with his co-guitarist, who falls to his knees and leans back in his dress as Cobain shuffles astraddle him with his guitar; tries whipping his guitar by its strap around his waist only to have it slip and fly offstage; and mimes a moment of great intensity by hobbling forward with his knees pressed together and his hands crushing his dress against his groin, as if suffering from either menstrual pain or a kick in the nuts. And all the while we keep cutting away to that screaming audience, swishing back to that straight band of really decent guys, until the song is done and the host comes back out to shake their hands and declare, through the girls' screams, that these guys are "gonna be *really big stars.*"

What this clip is about for me has more to do with the rock masculinities it mocks and refuses than with any it might be said to recommend. I appreciate the way it posits the band's anarchist shenanigans as the end of a line that began with the hysterical sexualization and careful counter-regulation of the white male rocker's body; and I like the way they wear and use those dresses, not to increase and ambiguate their sexual allure, but to include gender breakdown as part of the confusion and revolt they recommend. These are male bodies that refuse to be sexually fetishized, but not in the usual way: not by being too stiff, too drably or officially suited, too repressed and covered up. And when in their dresses they mimic the homosocial moment of "cock-rock" communion through dueling guitars, it cracks me up.

Last but not least, I like the way all these dissident behaviors are explicitly linked by the lyrics I have quoted, with a sneering refusal of a conventional identification between white male band and white male fan, an alliance in which knowing the words to the songs is felt to be equivalent to having and showing a gun, a possession that's about phallic mastery. Such a refusal breaks with all those other rock masculinities we have seen that pay the price of difference from hegemonic masculinity with the coin of emphatic "Whiteness" and/or hyper-hetero-misogyny. If the mutation in this rock tradition named Bruce finally signifies the depletion and vacuousness of his white working-guy image, as well as of the class-centered, racist-masculinist left populism that once buoyed that image up, and the counter-image of unbound Axl, extension of this tradition, warns us against embracing a newer psycho-politics of dispersion and desiring-flow, Nirvana's ability to hold onto its insistent, bored anger while individually and collectively "refusing to be a man"[51] hints at a politics and definition of white men that just might be a big improvement over what we've made and got so far, within rock and outside it – not to mention a bunch of kids out there who, with some luck and some tough coalition-building, still might be all right.

POSTSCRIPT: Cobain's suicide in May 1994 obviously throws a wet blanket over the hope expressed in the sentences above, written in the spring of 1993. Indeed, I would argue that, for some Nirvana fans at least, what was shocking about the death was our understanding, our complicit familiarity and even, in that sense, our agreement with some of the motives that seemed to lie behind it. For aside from Cobain's strictly personal difficulties, what his last communications seem designed to express was his sense of the terrible difficulty and psycho-emotional cost of attempting to sustain such a counter-logic from within the mainstream, in the face of commodity culture's apparently limitless power to deflect and absorb. For those of us to whom Nirvana and Cobain suggested the possibility that the conventional romantic-resistance effects built into rock-and-roll could be deconstructed from within, via the right blend of rage and abjection, the death of this explicitly anti-masculinist, anti-homophobic 27-year-old *lumpenprole* carries a special chill, here in the middle of what was supposed to be the beginning of the end of the Reagan–Bush time, when there is still far too little peace or justice or even decently paid work around. The "star-text" Cobain incarnated brought many of us a jolt of hope and joyful recognition, by articulating that old radical-individualist resistance with a freely admitted self-loathing, complicating the arrogantly assertive desire to break on through with the vulnerably self-effacing urge to nod out. The suicide that short-circuited that text brings us the arguably even more salutary message that performances like his are an almost impossibly hard act to pull off all by yourself – even, and perhaps especially, when that ever more isolated and commodified performance becomes, despite your best intentions, only an act.

NOTES

1. For further elaboration of this point, see Lawrence Grossberg, "Teaching the Popular," in Cary Nelson, ed., *Theory in the Classroom* (Champaign-Urbana, IL: University of Illinois Press, 1986), pp. 177–200.

2. Susan McClary and Robert Walser, "Start Making Sense! Musicology Wrestles with Rock," in Simon Frith and Andrew Goodwin, eds., *On Record: Rock, Pop, and the Written Word* (New York: Pantheon Books, 1990), pp. 277–92.

3. Andrew Goodwin, *Dancing in the Distraction Factory: Music Television and Popular Culture* (Minneapolis: University of Minnesota Press, 1992), p. 56.

4. Such neutrality at its best – that is, as the result of a complicated dialectical balancing act of contradictory determinations – characterizes Harris Frieberg's "Hang Up My Rock & Roll Shoes," a lecture delivered at the Center for the Humanities, Wesleyan University, Middletown, Connecticut, 15 November 1992.

5. See, for example, Nelson George, *The Death of Rhythm & Blues* (New York: Pantheon Books, 1988).

6. For a relatively early but still cogent version of this general argument, see Simon Frith, *Sound Effects: Youth, Leisure, and the Politics of Rock'n'Roll* (New York: Pantheon Books, 1981); and for a smart piece on rock *as* a set of practices, see David R. Shumway, "Rock & Roll as a Cultural Practice," *South Atlantic Quarterly* 90, 4 (Fall 1991), pp. 753–69.

7. Frieberg, "Hang Up My Rock & Roll Shoes."

8. "The White Negro," in Norman Mailer, *Advertisements for Myself* (New York: G.P. Putnam's Sons, 1959), pp. 337–58.

9. Shumway, p. 763.

10. Richard Middleton, *Studying Popular Music* (Philadelphia, PA: Milton Keynes, 1990), p. 263.

11. Ibid., p. 266.

12. Connell refers to "wild" masculinities as those complementary, subordinate, and fitfully oppositional masculinities that rest "on impulses or practices excluded from the increasingly rationalized and integrated world of business and bureaucracy" as that world and its hegemonic forms of masculinity have emerged and consolidated themselves in the nineteenth and twentieth century. See R.W. Connell, *Gender and Power: Society, the Person and Sexual Politics* (Stanford, CA: Stanford University Press, 1987), p. 151.

13. Connell, p. 85.

14. Dorothy Dinnerstein, *The Mermaid and the Minotaur: Sexual Arrangements and Human Malaise* (New York: Harper and Row, 1976), pp. 265–8.

15. Mary Harron, "McRock: Pop as a Commodity," in Simon Frith, ed., *Facing the Music* (New York: Pantheon Books, 1988), p. 193.

16. Jon Savage, "The Enemy Within: Sex, Rock and Identity," in ibid., p. 163.

17. Simon Frith, "Towards an Aesthetic of Popular Music," in Richard Leppert and Susan McClary, eds., *Music and Society: The Politics of Composition, Performance and Reception* (New York: Cambridge University Press, 1987), p. 136.

18. Steve Connor, "The Flag on the Road: Bruce Springsteen and the Live," *New Formations* 3 (Winter 1987), p. 134.

19. Harron, p. 210.

20. Shumway, p. 768.

21. Frith, "Towards an Aesthetic of Popular Music," p. 147.

22. *Music for Pleasure* (New York: Routledge, Chapman and Hall, 1988), p. 95.

23. Deena Weinstein, *Heavy Metal: A Cultural Sociology* (New York: Lexington Books, 1991).

24. Christine Gledhill, "Signs of Melodrama," in Gledhill, ed., *Stardom: Industry of Desire* (New York: Routledge, 1991), p. 217.

25. Richard Dyer writes of this process in "*A Star Is Born* and the Construction of Authenticity," in Gledhill, ed., *Stardom*, pp. 132–40.

26. See, for example, Greg Sandow, "Who's the Boss?", cover story for the 5 June 1992 issue of *Entertainment Weekly* (no. 121), pp. 12–18.

27. In all fairness, I must also note here that the relationship of the actually existing individual Bruce Springsteen to the Springsteen image has its own complex history – albeit one that it is not my present business to recover. The analysis that follows is concerned to explore the construction and consumption of the Springsteen image in the hour of its hegemony within rock-and-roll, that is, roughly during the years 1984–87. There is ample evidence that even off and on during that time, the individual Bruce Springsteen came to hold his own reservations both as to how and where that image was circulated and what it came to mean. See, for example, Jim Kavanagh's pages on Springsteen's attempts to wrest that image back from the 1984 Reagan re-election campaign in his "Ideology," in Frank Lentricchia and Thomas McLaughlin, eds., *Critical Terms for Literary Study* (Chicago: University of Chicago, 1990), pp. 318 ff. Likewise, Jim O'Hara of Wesleyan University has provided me with a wealth of anecdotal evidence from performances, videos, and interviews from the late 1980s and early 1990s, all of which reinforce and confirm my sense that for the past several years Springsteen has been explicitly attempting to use his musical performances and public appearances to modify and even to critique the image of rock masculinity that put him over as a

superstar. A study of how effective these admirable efforts have been, and, not least, what relationship if any they bear to the slow decline in sales of Springsteen's recorded music is surely in order. But once again, such a study is not my project here.

28. For the fullest elaboration of this perspective and mythic narrative, see Dave Marsh's adulatory *Glory Days: Bruce Springsteen in the 1980s* (New York: Pantheon Books, 1987).

29. In the waning days of his crushingly successful re-election campaign and, it must be said, in blissful ignorance of the content of Springsteen's songs, Reagan saluted the "American spirit" of Springsteen's music for whatever the evocation might yield in the way of a few extra votes.

30. My friend Mark Miller rightly points out that "Boss" is also "roady-stagehand lingo gone public": a fact that complements the genealogy I have been laying out in the main text without contradicting it, at least as far as I'm concerned.

31. In "Sexual Mobilities in Bruce Springsteen: Performance as Commentary," *South Atlantic Quarterly* 90, 4 (Fall 1991), pp. 833–54, Martha Nell Smith argues that Springsteen in performance often flirts with and even at times transgresses the boundaries of conventional masculinity and heterosexuality. "Homoeroticism permeates his performances," she claims, "assumption of the feminine is one of his repeated artistic maneuvers, and, though he writes and sings about Adam, he finally seems much more like Eve in his approach to knowledge" (p. 849). But I would argue both that such flirtations and provocations are far less frequent than Smith suggests, and, more importantly, that the emphatically masculine, heterosexual signal Bruce's image sends out is so strong and insistent as to render such potentially transgressive divergences practically unnoticeable even when they do occur.

32. Lewis Coser, Introduction to Max Scheler, *Ressentiment* (New York: Free Press, 1961), p. 21.

33. Here and below, my account of heavy metal draws from Weinstein's *Heavy Metal* and is much indebted to it.

34. In addition to Weinstein, see, for example, Grossberg's comments on heavy metal in "Teaching the Popular"; Will Straw's "Characterizing Rock Music Culture: The Case of Heavy Metal," in Frith and Goodwin, eds., *On Record*, pp. 97–110; and Dan Rubey's gloss on metal music and music videos in "Voguing at the Carnival: Desire and Pleasure on MTV," *South Atlantic Quarterly* 90, 4 (Fall 1991), pp. 879–84. Another useful text is Robert Walser's *Running with the Devil: Power, Gender, and Madness in Metal Music* (Hanover, NH: Wesleyan University/University Press of New England, 1993), whose strong suit, despite its subtitle, is actually its close musical analyses.

35. Weinstein, p. 118.

36. Ibid., p. 23.

37. Ibid., p. 106.

38. The word and concept of the "homosocial" as a concept contiguous to yet diacritically distinct from, and often opposed to, "homosexual," comes to us of course from Eve Kosofsky Sedgwick's *Between Men: English Literature and Male Homosocial Desire* (New York: Columbia University Press, 1985).

39. For a quick sketch of the marketing considerations that dictated such a strategy in the early days of MTV, see Goodwin, pp. 135–6.

40. Again I am indebted to Deena Weinstein for this insight; see *Heavy Metal*, pp. 45–53.

41. Ibid., pp. 46–47.

42. Most of the story I've just told above, for example, is taken from Daniel Sugerman, *Appetite for Destruction: The Days of Guns N' Roses* (New York: St Martin's Press, 1991), a quickie band-bio knocked out in time to catch the upswell of the release of *Use Your Illusion* I and II in spring 1991. The exception is the detail concerning Geffen's plan to "time-release" the singles from those two albums; that is taken from Deborah Frost's "Wimps 'R Us," in *The Village Voice*, 1 October 1991, pp. 77–8 – though presumably it comes originally from a Geffen press release designed to fuel the hype.

43. A shrewdly calculated falsehood, by the way: actually, unbeknownst to MTV viewers, the crowd was there for Aerosmith, the band GN'R was opening for. And typically, this sleight of hand too is openly admitted by the company that made the video for GN'R and Geffen: see the quote by the head of video production and surrounding explanation in Goodwin, pp. 106–7.

44. Del James, "Axl Rose: The Rolling Stone Interview," in *Rolling Stone*, 10 August 1989, p. 44.

45. Connor, "The Flag on the Road," p. 135.

46. Quoted in Dean Kuipers, "Guns N' Neurosis," *Spin*, October 1991, p. 74.

47. Quoted in Jeanne Marie Laskas, "On the Road with Guns N' Roses," *Life*, 1 December 1992, p. 108.

48. Again, it is symptomatic that I have been able to collect these stories from the Sugarman band-bio mentioned above, as well as such fan mags as the "special collector's item" issue of *Wow!* for summer 1991, devoted to Guns N' Roses and Skid Row, and complete with "backstage exclusives" and an even more special section: "The 'Lost' Interviews 1987–89: Guns N' Roses' Wildest Tour Stories!"

49. Quoted in James, p. 44. And James also recites the relevant lines from "One in a Million": "Police and niggers, that's right / Get outta my way / Don't need to buy none / Of your gold chains today"; and the following verse, "Immigrants and faggots / They make no sense to me / They come to our country / And think they'll do as they please / Like start some mini-Iran or spread some fuckin' disease."

50. On this last, see Goodwin's *Dancing in the Distraction Factory*, passim, but especially pp. 131–54; or, if you are white and listen to popular music, think how many times you heard and/or watched the video of Arrested Development doing either "Tennessee" or "Revolution" in the summer and fall of 1992, and what meaning-effects you have made out of that.

51. The phrase in quotes is a rip-off of the title of Dworkinite feminist John Stoltenberg's latest book, *Refusing to Be a Man: Essays on Sex and Justice* (New York: Signet/New American Library, 1990) – though I think it safe to say that Stoltenberg is far too suspicious of any physical or sensory pleasure or license, especially any enjoyed or enjoyable by actually existing men, to approve of Nirvana's antics here.

CHAPTER FOUR

SOFT-BOILED DICKS

In the book industry, as practically everyone knows, for some years now the trend has been towards vastly increased economic concentration on the publishing end – indeed, as in the case of Warner's media empire, to the verge of its virtual disappearance as a separate activity – and on the retail side as well, from what we might think of by now as the older generation of "McBook" stores like B. Dalton's and Barnes & Noble to such younger and would-be tonier upstarts as that culture-hungry child of K-Mart, Borders. Likewise, in terms of what gets published: as in the film industry, more and more money (in the form of advances, sales of rights and subsidiaries, promotional budgets, and so on) now drives an ever-smaller number of titles, especially in fiction, while outside a small bantustan of bona fide names with long-established reputations, the Toni Morrisons, John Irvings, and E.L. Doctorows, the field of "quality lit" is left to shrivel in the sun of its neglect.

However, if we turn our eyes away from quality lit and towards all those genres that together comprise popular fiction, a quite different picture presents itself. For here, within the genres, the trend is towards proliferation, with each new subspecies seeking its own market niche. So, for example, the groundbreaking insights of Tania Modleski, Ann Snitow, and Janice Radway into the circuits of pleasure running between romance novels and their female readers need further specification, now that it is possible to select from and amongst series that specialize in upscale professional women and/or offer a much greater sexual explicitness than their relatively muted and univocal foremothers did, and continue to do.[1] The same is true within the province of detective fiction, one small corner of which I will be exploring here. For starters, you do not have to choose any longer between LA and New York City or San Francisco as the Sodom whose iniquities the detective will plumb; now you can pick and choose from any number of mean-streeted towns, from Seattle (Earl Emerson's series, among others) to New Orleans (James Lee Burke) to tiny Rocksburg, Pennsylvania, a small ex-industrial city somewhere north of Pittsburgh. Nor need your detective be a man, as the V.I. Warshawski series and the alphabet novels of Sue Grafton among many others have proved. Nor, as Walter Mosley's widely touted Easy Rawlins series testifies, need he be white; nor straight, for that matter, as Sandra Scoppetone's lesbian PI and Joseph Hansen's gay male claims investigator demonstrate. Indeed, as Earl Emerson's fireman hero, Joseph Hansen's claims adjustor and Jonathan Kellerman's child psychologist Alex Delaware demonstrate, our detective-protagonist need not even be a police-person or private investigator at all.

The overall picture of the book business today is thus a paradigm of that interaction of giant and far-flung economic structures with the marketing logic of product differentiation that McKenzie Wark has urged us to stop calling "post-Fordist" and start thinking of as *Sonyist*: cartelized, transnational systems of production and distribution offering consumers "a stylized glut of semiotic objects" within each generalized, generic rut of industrialized taste.[2] Yet within each genre generally, and the detective genre in particular, I would still insist that each generic mutant must derive no small part of the sense and enjoyment it provides from its relation to its more monolithic forebears. Part of the pleasure of reading the newest adventures of V.I. Warshawski, that is, derives from seeing (or perhaps more accurately, sensing) what it's like for a *woman* to pull the same moves Sam Spade and Philip Marlowe used to get to the bottom of things – and/or, *a fortiori*, how she does so differently. This is equally so, moreover, for those contemporary detective novels whose protagonists are men; indeed, one central component of their interest for us must lie in the distances they take and the differences they make between themselves and the classic hard-boiled dicks of the past.

Hence, a full reading of today's white straight male detective-hero and of the versions of masculinity he models would place him and them in both lateral and vertical contexts. He would be read, that is, alongside and in the context of his non-white, unstraight, and/or female comrades in arms, as well as in relation to his forefathers. What follows here, however, falls far short of such a reading, which would require a whole book of its own – and, I confess, a lot more literal reading than I am willing, or have time, to put into the effort. What I offer instead, as a preliminary contribution toward this larger project, are, first, some notes on the construction of the hard-boiled detective as a masculinity – in fact, as *two* complementary masculinit*ies* – in the work of Raymond Chandler and Dashiell Hammett; and, second, a series of schematic observations on the work of four contemporary writers, and their detectives, who taken together seem to me to constellate something like the field or spectrum of contemporary play within the segment of detective fiction that is still centered on white straight men.

Kellerman and his child psychologist, Robert Parker and his long-running hit detective Spenser, James Lee Burke and Cajun detective Dave Robicheaux, K.C. Constantine and his dumpy Serbo-Italian cop Mario Balzic: we will deal them out separately and shuffle them together to see what games can now be dealt, in the wake of the tough guys and games that came before them. We will look at how the rules have changed and stayed the same, at how the style of play has maintained or transformed itself, at who gets to play alongside our heroes and whom they play against, at what gets served up along with the action, and at what kind of world – within the novels and outside of them – delimits for us the kind of masculinity we find ourselves enjoying and detesting here and now, within the sex/gender system and the socioeconomic regime of "late," or "senile," or "Sonyist" capitalism, however it is named, which latter sets the rules and will accordingly have to be consciously and collectively changed if we are to play something else more to our liking. That, at any rate, is the side bet this chapter wants to place and play out.

1. STRAIGHT STUD:
TWO STYLES OF FORDIST PLAY

[D]own these mean streets a man must go who is not himself mean,
who is neither tarnished nor afraid. The detective in this kind of story
must be such a man. He is the hero; he is everything. He must be a
complete man and a common man and yet an unusual man. He must
be ... a man of honor – by instinct, by inevitability, without thought
of it, and certainly without saying it. He must be the best man in his
world and a good enough man for any world.

Raymond Chandler[3]

> I see him ... a little man going forward day after day through mud
> and blood and death and deceit – as callous and brutal and cynical
> as necessary – toward a dim goal, with nothing to push or pull him
> to it except he's been hired to reach it.
>
> Dashiell Hammett[4]

But first, some rehearsal of the defining features of hard-boiled fiction is in order. Thanks to the efforts of John Cawelti, among others,[5] it is by now well known that such fiction made its first appearance in the 1920s, chiefly in a pulp magazine called *Black Mask*, to which Hammett himself was an early contributor. Hammett's novels, published in the brief stretch between 1929 and 1934, established the generic baseline that all subsequent hard-boiled detective writing, including that of Raymond Chandler ten years later, would follow out, and the bases it would have to tag.

These generic features can be quickly summarized. In the first place, and again following Cawelti's analysis, we should note the decisive substantial and formal breaks that separate hard-boiled writing from what is now called the "classical detective fiction" that preceded it. Whereas the classical detective, still familiar to many readers through his/her past and present incarnations in (especially) the English popular novel, typically depends on brilliant ratiocination to solve the enigma of the crime-puzzle, the hard-boiled American detective gets to the bottom of things and restores order by revving up the disorder he finds around him, and by hurling himself into it, often violently. As Hammett's Continental Op (that is, Operative) puts it in *Red Harvest*, on the verge of an orgy of gangland violence he has deliberately fomented, "sometimes just stirring things up is all right – if you're tough enough to survive, and keep your eyes open so you'll see what you want when it comes to the top."[6]

We will return in a moment to consider further the meaning of toughness and the nature of our detective's gimlet-eyed acumen. For now, it is enough to note the close relation between the detective's involvement in the disorder he investigates and one of the genre's constitutive stylistic elements: that is, the frequent employment of the first-person *recit* to recount the tale. All of Chandler's fiction is governed by Philip Marlowe's narration, just as Hammett's first two books are narrated by his Continental Op; and even when, in such later novels as *The Maltese Falcon*, the narration is third person, the relationship between its terse, camera-eye objectivity and detective Sam Spade's clipped utterances is so close as to seem continuous with his point of view. Such narration serves to amplify our sense of the detective-protagonist's close involvement, indeed his complicity with the events he recounts, just as the more distanced accounts of classical detective fiction, employing either third-person narration or, as in the Sherlock Holmes stories, the use of a sidekick *ficelle*, serve to increase both our own more cerebral detachment from events, and the classical detective's.

But the detective's first-person narration is only half of the stylistic innovation that established the hard-boiled genre; the other half is the hard-boiled style itself. David Geherin describes that style as "a carefully controlled blend of colloquialisms, terse understatement, objective descriptions, all narrated in a detached tone";[7] Frank Krutnik characterizes it as an "idiom" that is "'tough,' cynical, epigrammatic, controlled," and adds that its "defining characteristic is perhaps the 'tough wisecrack.'"[8] We shall return to consider these properties later in this section; here, let us note only the extent to which they are offered to readers as an attraction in themselves, as in these two famous opening passages from Hammett's and Chandler's respective first books:

> I first heard Personville called Poisonville by a red-haired mucker named Hickey Dewey in the Big Ship in Butte. He also called his shirt a shoit. I didn't think anything of what he had done to the city's name. Later I heard men who could manage their r's give it the same pronunciation. I still didn't see anything in it but the meaningless sort of humor that used to make richardsnary the thieves' word for dictionary. A few years later I went to Personville and learned better.
>
> Using one of the phones in the station, I called the *Herald*, asked for Donald Willsson, and told him I had arrived.[9]

> It was about eleven o'clock in the morning, mid October, with the sun not shining and a look of hard wet rain in the clearness of the foothills. I was wearing my powder-blue suit, with dark blue shirt, tie and display handkerchief, black brogues, black wool socks with dark blue clocks on them. I was neat, clean, shaved and sober, and I didn't care who knew it. I was everything the well-dressed private detective ought to be. I was calling on four million dollars.[10]

There are some important differences here in tone and emphasis that we will eventually want to explore. What matters now, though, is what these openings have in common: their plain, additive sentence structures and shorn and sober facticity; their flat, laconic declarativeness combined with an air of somewhat cynical or world-weary knowledge; and the smooth abruptness with which both swerve into action as soon as they have sketched a minimal background for themselves.

Finally, we should add a few words about the world such a style constructs and confronts, and the nature of both crime and the detective within it. Here again, the contrast with the *socius* of classical detective fiction is sharp. In the latter, whether set in a rural village, a country estate, or within the city itself, the world is posited as a rational, knowable space, whose inhabitants occupy fixed roles, and whose authorized officials and authority structures are finally not in doubt. Crime in such a world is a localized disruption caused by specific individuals whose identity it is the business of the detective to track down through the use of his/her superior reasoning skills. Hard-boiled detective fiction, by contrast, presents us with an altogether darker and more morally ambiguous universe. Its typically urban space is like that of Brecht's phantasmic American jungle of cities, or, perhaps more to the point, that of the popular "mystery" novels of George Lippard and others in the 1840s and '50s, derived in their turn from Eugène Sue's serialized blockbuster *Les Mystères de Paris* (1842–43): an unknowably divided and disarticulated class society in which corrupt elites have joined in unholy alliance with the thugs, goons, and scum at the bottom, and in which official authority itself is either helpless or suborned.[11] To undertake a job, then, is for the detective to entangle himself in this sprawling spiderweb of limitless iniquity; to go into this morass, "stir it up," with violence if necessary, until it yields him up the resolution he seeks; yet all the while to brush its sticky corruption off him, and maintain his integrity as best he can.

To plunge into the sewer without getting wet: the nature of the mission does much to help us understand the tight-lipped self-control of the narrating voice, and its characteristic admixture of immediacy and detachment. So too with the "tough wisecracks" the detective so often employs in both his narration and his dialogue, which signal to other characters and the reader alike the detective's fluency in a wide variety of sociolects, and his masterful detachment from and disregard for them all. More generally, though, such observations also open the way for us to think more broadly about the social implications of the gratifications provided by this new brand of popular fiction. Perhaps most obviously, one such pleasure must be that of imaginative identification with a phantasmal space that is both on and outside the class map. Chandler's Marlowe and Hammett's Sam Spade are both, in effect, petty-bourgeois entrepreneurs, Hammett's Continental Op an employee of a Pinkerton-type detective agency, albeit one with a generous amount of autonomy. Insofar as they begin and return to such fixed positions and oppose themselves to the vicious and decadent intermingling of those above and below them, such figures sound a faint and sour echo of an older ideological tune, that of the moral uprightness and decent productivity (especially in fiction that offers us nary a glimpse of production as such, industrial or otherwise) of the middle-class Republic, here seen as overwhelmingly beset and nearly swallowed up by corruption from all sides.[12] Their narrow triumphs over those overwhelming forces thus invite us into a complex circuit of class-coded pleasures: we get to walk on the wild side, and, as Marc Vernet has pointed out, to ogle at "the splendours of power and money ... only as a preparation for their condemnation in the name both of humble, ordinary folk, and of an egalitarian morality."[13]

Yet this pleasure is both augmented and further complicated by a fantasy of *dis*-location and separation, in the form of the same narrator-protagonists' outsider status and virtually untrammeled social mobility. On this point, I could not hope to improve on Dean MacCannell's description, which, if anything, applies even more exactly to hard-boiled fiction than to his subject, the *films noirs* that fiction helped to inspire. "The hero," he writes,

> moves through any and every situation liminally as a kind of cipher of the unrealized possibility of the coexistence of democratic openness and capitalistic closure. The hero abjures regular, ordinary routine, normal, for-profit pursuits, does not have an evident class perspective, operates within the law only when it is convenient for him to do so, and has few institutional attachments or obligations.... The hero demands a paradoxical combination of rights: to be completely detached from society *and* at the same time to be allowed total access to every part of it.... He holds himself external to and above specific class, domestic and institutional relations in order not to be marked by any specificity. He is thus free to enter into everything. If some heavy attempts to block his entry into a club ... he shoves the guy aside. Philip Marlowe walks freely through the mean streets of the city's underside in one scene and, in the next, strides with the same nonchalance across the oriental carpets of the hot-house billionaire General Sternwood. In its most positive manifestation, *film noir* [and, all the more so, hard-boiled detective fiction] affirms the right of Democratic Everyman to go anywhere as a matter of principle.[14]

In this sense, the detective, far from occupying a fixed location, hovers outside and above all fixed social space. The bare seediness of Marlowe's or Sam Spade's office is less a sign of the bleak fortunes of a disenchanted and nearly defeated petty bourgeoisie than a symptom of the literally utopian liminality of the detective's perfectly free-enterprise space

– "utopia," that is, in its original sense, as *no-place*. Existing nowhere, he can go anywhere and be just as alienated and just as at home; needed and employed by rich, by *lumpen*, and by middle-class alike, he remains disdainfully free from all their neuroses and constraints, a knowing *flâneur* of a mass culture he disdains, Zen master of a capitalist morass he is in but not of.

But to all these pleasures there is still another dimension, one we must now discover by reading over and rewriting all we have just said. For the gratifications of socioeconomic and sociopolitical fantasy in these fictions are redoubled by their equally complex operations around the definition of heterosexual masculinity and its Others in the gender Imaginary. From this perspective, and just for starters, the contradictory blend of placement and location, of native fluency and inviolate disaffiliation we have just discussed as an ideologeme of class reappears as a particular ideological construction of *masculinity* – one, moreover, whose historic throughline back to the indicatively male Hegelian Subject is almost embarrassingly clear.[15] Yet as Subjects of the histories they recount, these narrating detectives enjoy, and offer us *as* enjoyment, a distinctively troubled type of mastery, by enacting on the molecular level of style and the molar level of plot alike a distinctively intensified and vertiginous dialectic of dirtiness and purity, complicit involvement and pristine detachment.

Let us reconsider first the gender coding at work in these fictions' depictions of the world their protagonists encounter. We have said that the world is characterized by the collusion of elites at the top and thugs at the bottom, and by the incapacity or unwillingness of those officially authorized to keep the law. In the poisoned Personville of Hammett's *Red Harvest*, for example, old man Willsson, owner of the town's mines, has himself brought in the gangs that are tearing the town apart as he helplessly looks on, and the police themselves have become part of the problem; while in the southern California of Chandler's *The Big Sleep*, it is the sociopathic and viciously amoral daughter of immensely rich General Sternwood who, in the company of various sordid blackmailers and criminals, has run amok. This last example reminds us, in turn, of another feature of these fictions we have left unmentioned until now: the frequency with which we find that the person situated at the nodal point or relay station between the high and the low is a woman, whether she herself is revealed to be the chief instigator of the plague of evils now released upon the land (Carmen Sternwood in *The Big Sleep*, Velma Grayle in *Farewell, My Lovely*) or not (Dinah Brand in *Red Harvest*, Gabrielle Dain in *The Dain Curse*).

Insofar as – following Freud, Lacan, and their various feminist appropriators – we understand the fixity of the social-symbolic as a meaning-effect of the Law of the Father and submission to the power of the Phallus, such a world appears as nothing less than a nightmarish breakdown of that Oedipal Law and a fearful erosion of phallic power. And accordingly, the detective's lonely opposition to such fearful intermingling now reappears as a singularly desperate and embattled attempt to rescue masculinity and restore male-dominant order to this implicitly or explicitly feminine and pre-oedipal morass. As Frank Krutnik puts it,

> the "tough" thriller pivots around challenges to and problems in the regimes of the masculine (both in the ordering of masculine subjectivity and the masculine regimentation of the social/cultural order). Problems of law ... become specifically figured in terms of problems besetting masculinity (crime becoming associated with the destabilisation of masculine identity and authority).[16]

Likewise, just as the detective's isolation emphatically signifies his masculine singularity and integrity, his lack of biography, especially of any family background of his own, suggests the extent to which he is, and must remain, Father to himself alone, holding himself together by dint of private conviction and sheer, solitary will.

Thus, too, the overriding importance of our protagonists' toughness in language and in action alike. Not that the two are in practice all that easy to disengage, as Krutnik notes when he observes the frequency with which, in confrontations with others and even in more or less casual banter, the detective uses language in the form of the tough wisecrack "as a weapon" and as much or more "a measure of the hero's prowess than the use of guns and other more tangible aids to violence."[17] Even within the narration itself, the notoriously tight-lipped facticity and deadpan tone testify to the detective's relentless need and ability to hold at a distance the swirl of actions and relations into which he must enter to reach a resolution. Moreover, as the detective lips off to gangsters, women, police chiefs and the like, his dialogue asserts itself into and against the intended flow of conversation, just as his violent interventions interrupt, expose, and ultimately put a local and temporary end to the awful dissolutions and comminglings he discovers wherever he goes.

But such detachment, such holding back, only tells half the story of the gender-coded satisfactions of this fiction. The other half involves precisely the opposite pleasure, that of yielding to and immersing oneself in the very morass that must finally be resisted and tamed. Perhaps the most obvious instance of such dipping in is, indeed, our detectives' use of violence itself: by eschewing rational deduction in favor of pulling the gun, and "stirring things up," they enter into and at least temporarily increase the disorder they investigate. In doing so, moreover, they fall prey to the temptations of that disorder: the gang war the Continental Op touches off in *Red Harvest* brings him close to the edge of becoming "blood-simple," as drunk on violence as the rest of the town, just as surely as the necking that Chandler's Marlowe slides into with Mrs Grayle threatens to trap him in her web of deceit in *Farewell, My Lovely*. Nor are the pleasures of yielding to this no-man's land confined to the protagonists. For the male or male-identified reader as well, a large part of the pleasure of these texts must be the invitation they issue to dally with a violent yet carnivalesque world of dissolving distinctions and eroded authority that – though held at bay throughout, as we have seen, through the operations of the style itself – need only in the last instance, at the climactic moment of resolution, be firmly disavowed.

If hard-boiled detective fiction can thus be characterized, from a feminist perspective, as a cultural production structured around an urgent tension within early-twentieth-century American masculinity between the desire to go with the flow and the need to stigmatize, demonize, and oppose oneself to it, it is also true that just here, around the degrees and kinds of temptations and the nature of the resistances put up to it, a significant and equally constitutive difference appears between Hammett and Chandler. In the work of the later author, much as he portrayed it as continuous with that of his progenitor,[18] the temptation to yield is everywhere more marked and more indulged. We can begin to pry open this divergence by noting the stylistic difference in the opening paragraphs quoted above, from *Red Harvest* and *The Big Sleep*, respectively. There, the tone of Hammett's Op is impeccably deadpan, his emphasis on hard empirical fact. Its only play, on Personville/Poisonville, is subjected to various testable hypotheses – one of which tests, we are promised, the one that is to be confirmed, comprises the impending action of the book. Within the general ambience of the hard-boiled idiom, then, Chandler's prose establishes a feeling tone and set of emphases in marked contrast to those in Hammett. Perhaps most obviously, the jazzy rhythms of sentences 2–5, nicely underscored by their repeating "I was" lead-ins, combine with the narrator's self-mocking yet real narcissistic attention to his presentation, to establish a sense of self-regarding stylishness wholly foreign to Hammett's work. But I would also want to take note of the latent lyricism of the prepositional phrase that tails out of the end of the primary clause of the first sentence, and leads away from its Hammett-like statement of bare fact to give us the landscape around the detective as, in effect, a moral and aesthetic atmosphere: the sun present under erasure, as it were, and the "clearness of the foothills" similarly coexistent with and neutralized by the "look of hard wet rain."

"Where Hammett's descriptions measure things coolly by size, weight, color, and shape," Cawelti writes, "Marlowe's perceptions are charged with strained and blocked emotion. Objects manifest themselves by their impact on the narrator's oversensitive nerves."[19] The formulation is perhaps even more telling than it was intended to be; in the slippage it enacts between Hammett-as-author and Marlowe-as-author/character, it suggests the enormous difference between the quasi-Cartesian transparency of the former's neutrally narrating protagonists and the richly distinct subjectivity that Chandler's prose must compulsively exhibit and restrain. That same contrast becomes even more striking at decisive turning points in the action. Let us take a look at two such moments, when our detectives discover some bodies – Chandler first this time, then Hammett:

> He lay smeared to the ground, on his back, at the base of a bush, in that bag-of-clothes position that always means the same thing. His face was a face I had never seen before. His hair was dark with blood, the beautiful blond ledges were tangled with blood and some thick grayish ooze, like primeval slime.
>
> The girl behind me breathed hard, but she didn't speak. I held the light on his face. He had been beaten to a pulp. One of his hands was flung out in a frozen gesture, the fingers curled. His overcoat was half twisted under him, as though he had rolled as he fell. His legs were crossed. There was a trickle as black as dirty oil at the corner of his mouth.[20]

> I was lying face down on the dining room floor, my head resting on my left forearm. My right arm was stretched straight out. My right hand held the round blue and white handle of Dinah Brand's ice pick. The pick's six-inch needle-sharp blade was buried in Dinah Brand's left breast.
>
> She was lying on her back, dead. Her long muscular legs were stretched out toward the kitchen door. There was a run down the front of her right stocking.[21]

Clearly enough, the Continental Op's situation gives him by far the greater warrant for vivid and/or emotional expression. A dead woman he has known fairly well is lying immediately next to him, and their bodies are arranged so that it looks as though he is her murderer. Yet here and throughout the ensuing paragraphs, as our detective methodically investigates the surrounding circumstances and effaces all evidence of his presence, the writing goes on assuring us not so much that he is keeping a lid on his emotions as that he has no particular reaction at all to this event. When Chandler's Philip Marlowe finds the body of an unknown man, however, that discovery provides the occasion for the production of at least three types or registers of writing: one, like Hammett's, that renders the body to us as a precise, objective *fact* (overcoat half twisted, legs crossed); one constructing both the murder itself ("smeared," "beaten to a pulp") and the experience of viewing the body that act has produced ("that bag-of-clothes position," "his hair ... dark with blood") as vividly brutal and immediate *sensation*; and a third that uses the first two as a springboard for some gruesomely witty linguistic *play*, most notably in the similes that bring each paragraph to a close.

On the molecular level of sentence production itself, it would seem that despite their shared refusal to ascribe any affective or emotional response directly to their heroes, who presumably both go on functioning without feeling, there is a substantial difference between our two writers here. Chandler again and again risks losing himself, his detectives, and his readers in yielding to precisely those plot-retarding elements of narrative – immediate sensation, lyricism, language play – that Roland Barthes has taught us to think of as the semic, and whose punctual pleasures interrupt and delay the imperatives of the proairetic (that is, of the plot whose goal is to link up events in a narrative chain that swiftly and surely "comes out" in the end) and the hermeneutic (that is, the underlying, all-encompassing sense, patterned theme, or knowledge-effect of the work – including, and perhaps especially, that of who-done-it). Inversely, Hammett's prose is quite singularly devoted to the latter two registers at the price of the near-extinction of the first. But this is as much as to say that Chandler's work is far more prey to the temptations of what a patriarchal-oedipal culture encodes as the feminine – sensation, disorder, and play – than Hammett's. By implication, then, the relentlessly single-minded drive of Hammett's detectives and the sentences they ostensibly produce to de-mystify (the "Dain Curse," which turns out to be a cover; the "Maltese Falcon," which turns out to be made of lead) by forging and forcing a chain of factual cause-effect relations both through the narrative and around its actions, is nothing more or less than the expression (or production, if you will) of a rigidly dominant and dominating, instrumentalizing and objectifying masculinity whose everyday business it is to drain the swamp and squeeze the juice out of the world.

Such a difference will in turn do much to explain why on the surface at least, Chandler's work is so much more politically problematic than Hammett's: why, that is, in Fredric Jameson's words, "Chandler faithfully gives vent to everything racist, sexist, homophobic, and otherwise socially resentful and reactionary in the American collective unconscious."[22] It is not enough (though true enough, as far as it goes) to speak here of the latent and violently repressed homosexual desire charging his writing, or even more generally of its homosociality. Rather, the fear that obsessively links women, Blacks, overt homosexuals, and doctors within the same underworld through a complex chain of equivalences and affinities in Chandler's work must be understood as the flip side of a desire to yield to and to be penetrated by the infernally disordering and dissolving force they serve and represent, to suffer and enjoy the violation of precisely that hard-shell masculinity which must be defended at all cost. Here I can only remind readers in passing of the number of times in Chandler's work the lethal yet seductive woman's tongue, in kissing or in speech, darts like a snake; of his deadly fear of doctors' injections; of the number of times his detective loses consciousness, and, indeed, of the scarcely concealed sensual pleasure encoded in Chandler's descriptions of passing out.[23]

In this respect, then, the fearful and desiring imagination that underlies and energizes Chandler's writing is less akin to Hammett's than to that collective psyche Klaus Theweleit limns out for us so brilliantly in the first chapter of *Male Fantasies*: the psyche, that is, of those officers of the Freikorps, nerve center of the Nazi movement to come.[24] Chandler's writings, like the Freikorps novels, letters, poems, and diaries Theweleit quotes, compulsively construct and oppose themselves to a feminized and mongrelized mass in unholy collusion with various members of a decadent elite, and just as routinely imagine for themselves climactic moments of resistance and triumph that are marbled through with intimations of ec-static abjection to the demonically destructive element they so vehemently oppose.

> I went back towards her around the sump. When I was about ten feet from her, at the edge of the sump, she showed me all her sharp little teeth and brought the gun up and started to hiss.
>
> I stopped dead, the sump water stagnant and stinking at my back.
>
> "Stand there, you son of a bitch," she said.
>
> The gun pointed at my chest. Her hand seemed to be quite steady. The hissing sound grew louder and her face had the scraped bone look. Aged, deteriorated, become animal, and not a nice animal.

I laughed at her. I started to walk towards her. I saw her small finger tighten on the trigger and grow white at the tip. I was about six feet away from her when she started to shoot.

The sound of the gun made a sharp slap, without body, a brittle crack in the sunlight. I didn't see any smoke. I stopped again and grinned at her.

She fired twice more, very quickly. I don't think any of the shots would have missed. There were five in the little gun. She had fired four. I rushed her.

I didn't want the last one in my face, so I swerved to one side. She gave it to me quite carefully, not worried at all. I think I felt the hot breath of the powder blast a little.

I straightened up. "My, but you're cute," I said.

Her hand holding the empty gun began to shake violently. The gun fell out of it. Her mouth began to shake. Her whole face went to pieces. Then her head screwed up towards her left ear and froth showed on her lips. Her breath made a whining sound. She swayed.

I caught her as she fell...[25]

Summing up a wide variety of late-nineteenth and early-twentieth-century anti-modern European discourses, Andreas Huyssen speaks of how, within them, "[t]he haunting specter of a loss of power combines with the fear of losing one's fortified and stable ego boundaries, which represent the *sine qua non* of male psychology in that bourgeois order."[26] But this passage from Chandler's first novel (which by this point, I would like to think, hardly requires any exegetical effort on my part), and indeed Chandler's whole *oeuvre*, reminds us that wherever that dreaded specter appears it is apt to be all the more terrifying to the white male bourgeois (or petty-bourgeois) imagination for its seductive power. Nor does such fear and such desire, together with the specter they co-construct, show up within high or modernist culture alone.

Yet the last point I wish to make in this background sketch of the matrices of hard-boiled detective fiction returns to Hammett, and to something closer to the sociopolitical Imaginary we explored some time ago. Here is another famous passage, and another moment involving the detective's apprehension of a criminal woman: from Sam Spade's speech to Brigid O'Shaughnessy in *The Maltese Falcon*, his explanation of why, despite all her seductive appeal, he is going to turn her in.

"Listen. When a man's partner is killed he's supposed to do something about it. It doesn't make any difference what you thought of him. He was your partner and you're supposed to do something about it. Then it happens we were in the detective business. Well, when one of your organization gets killed it's bad for business to let the killer get away with it. It's bad all around – bad for that one organization, bad for every detective everywhere. Third, I'm a detective and expecting me to run criminals down and then let them go free is like asking a dog to catch a rabbit and let it go. It can be done, all right, and sometimes it is done, but it's not the natural thing."[27]

I do not want to gainsay what in the light of the preceding paragraphs must now seem most obvious about the self-positioning of Hammett's detective here: namely, the absence of any desire to succumb to the seductions of the criminal-feminine; or, if you will, its unalloyed and un-troubled subjection to the overriding Symbolic, the Law(s) of male-domi-nant morality, professionalism, and good business sense. Without leaving this meaning behind, though, I would draw attention to what is in some sense its opposite – to the *dis*-connection, to the gap that separates Spade here from the Symbolic creed(s) on whose behalf he simultaneously professes to act.

That, at any rate, is how I read the repetition of "supposed to," the detective's comparison of himself to a dog, the air of weary detachment that wafts through this entire scene: as symptoms not of repressed and rebellious emotion, but of an imploded hollowness and blankness suggestive in their turn of the all-but-complete evacuation of the space in which an individual personality might dwell. This desolate emptiness is in Hammett precisely the self-cancelling space of the detective, just as the unremitting demystification of all that seems at first sight to be lurid, sensational, or mysterious into instrumental means and objective fact is the definition of his job. As the Op's interlocutor and arch-criminal antagonist Fitzstephan says to and of him in *The Dain Curse*, "'It's fellows like you that take all the color out of life.'"[28] – color that, in the form of possible love interests, Maltese Falcons, and Dain Curses alike, must be accordingly injected into the plots of Hammett's novels precisely so that his sentences and protagonists can drain it away.

Insofar, then, as this is our protagonist's job description and identity, I would also want to maintain that they have a meaning for us in addi-tion to and through their production of an idealized, normatively hard-shelled American masculinity composed of equal parts of Hegelian man and Hawkeye. To get to that meaning, though, it may help to reach all the way back to the beginning of our survey, and take one last look at the quotations from Hammett and Chandler that opened it. What the two most obviously have in common is a consensus on the meanness and deceitfulness of the fallen world; but beyond that, the opposition implicit in their respective general portraits of the detective forms a strange and telling complementarity. Chandler's hero is "a man of honor", Hammett's a "little man" doing a job, moving toward resolution "with nothing to push or pull him to it except he's been hired to reach it." Chandler's hero is "neither tarnished nor afraid"; Hammett's little man for hire, demystifying mystery and passion for the sake of an order he neither believes in nor disbelieves, is practically nothing at all. Likewise, as we have seen, the style machines of our two writers are almost diametrically opposed, one functioning to pump color and expressivity into the landscape and the action, the other reducing human action to Hobbesian scrabbling and the world to a virtually Cartesian plane. When I consider the complementarity of these opposed elements – not, once again, beyond the masculinity they co-produce in the sense of above so much as *through* it – I am led to think in terms of the systems logic of capitalism itself, and particularly in terms of that regime of capitalist accumulation we have come to call Fordism: the regime that brought us mass production and mass culture, consumer society and the corporatist convergence of interests (backed, of course, by oligopolistic economic power and the coercive apparatuses of the state) between the institutions of the working class, capital, and the state.[29] One of the chief effects of, and challenges to be managed within, such a regime was clearly the ever more incommensurable division between the increasingly alienated, regimented and rationalized realm of production, on the one hand, and the miraculous, glittering, magically transformative qualities of the goods it produced and advertised for all, on the other: between social operations devoted to a ruthless and unceasing *de*mystification, *de*territorializing, *de*coding of all inputs to production (labor and raw material, fixed and variable capital) into abstract and interchangeable units of exchange-value, and those just as frenziedly devoted to the *re*sacralization, *re*territorialization, and mystical *en*coding of the items produced in their luminously mystified form in advertisements, on the showroom floor, or within the grocery-store display.[30] In this sense, then, the difference between Chandler and Hammett is not only to be measured as that between a masculinity deadly sure of its adherence to the oedipal–patriarchal Law of the Symbolic, and another, more dangerously insecure and divided one, but as the two sides of a Janus-faced coin circulated throughout American culture in its Fordist heyday: heads, Chandler's flashing, gleaming, pumped-up prose and detective-as-knight; tails, the flattened-out speedup of Hammett's colorless language, tonelessly uttered by a hero who is "just a body doing a job."[31]

2. WILD-CARD GAMES: MASCULINITIES FOR SONYISM

Our task now is to explore what has happened to this whole nest of meanings and definitions, and to their complex and overdetermined relations of convergence, opposition and complementarity, within the historical moment we presently inhabit: a moment marked by the complex interaction of feminism and its more recent companion of the eighties and nineties, what Judith Stacey calls "post-feminism"[32] – with that seismic shift and restructuring still in process for which we are trying out the name "Sonyism." I have chosen the series works of Robert Parker, James Lee Burke, Jonathan Kellerman, and K.C. Constantine, not only because each offers its own working definition of contemporary white straight masculinity, but because together those definitions suggest a set of themes and issues bound up with such identities, constellating a symptomatic field or terrain of operation for masculinity in our moment, just as Chandler's and Hammett's did in theirs. The increased number of writers and works compared here, moreover, illustrates something else besides the phenomenon of that proliferation within genres of popular writing which I began by describing. Indeed, it suggests the running theme of the pages that follow – namely, that of the smashing and diffusion of the conventions and definition of normative straight white Fordist masculinity in our day, like a single atom hitting the wall at the end of a particle accelerator, and the proliferation, transformation, and eccentric recombination of the subatomic particles released.

All the more reason, then, to take this part of the chapter by the numbers, and even to risk a certain amount of schematic reduction. What follows issues from my reading of fourteen of the twenty Spenser novels by Robert Parker published between 1973 and 1993; nine of the ten Mario Balzic novels by the pseudonymous K.C. Constantine published in the years 1972 through 1993; five of the six Alex Delawares by Jonathan Kellerman, whose publication dates run from 1985 through 1993; and all six novels in James Lee Burke's Dave Robicheaux series, published between 1988 and 1993.[33] To shape all this material and my reflections on it into some sort of order, I have arranged the aggregate reading that follows into a number of topical groupings, each of which seems at least analytically separate, however much it inevitably leaks over into and links up with all the others. My hope is that this arrangement will not only clarify the ideologically distinct differences between the various masculinities modeled in these fictions, but will illuminate their overall relationship to and difference from their Fordist forefathers as well.

Perhaps the clearest, most immediately discernible such difference concerns the greater degree of connection and interrelation the new generation of detectives has with other characters and, in most cases, the social worlds they inhabit. In this regard, it is worth pointing out that only one of our protagonists *is* a private detective. Kellerman's Alex Delaware is, as already noted, a child psychologist by training; but after years of workaholic frenzy, and thanks to a series of smart investments (two sure markers, by the way, separately and in conjunction, of this hero's credentials to yuppiedom in Reagan's high-flying 1980s), he has retired young to the hills north of Los Angeles, and now only takes consultations from lawyers, judges, and his police detective friend and gay sidekick Milo Sturgis. James Lee Burke's Dave Robicheaux is also in a kind of retirement, in this case from the New Orleans police force, where, in the first novel of the series, he still served as a detective; these days, he temporarily signs on to do detective work in the New Iberia parish where he was born and raised, and where he now runs a bait, boat, and barbeque establishment. Likewise, K.C. Constantine's Serbo-Italian hero Mario Balzic is employed as the constantly beset chief of police in a small hardscrabble city of working-class ethnic whites and African-Americans somewhere north of Pittsburgh, where he too was born and raised. And much has been made in these latter two sets of works, as we shall see, of our detectives' familiarity with and love for the social worlds in which they do their work.

Even the one professional detective we have, Robert Parker's Boston-based Spenser, is less a loner than Chandler's Marlowe or Hammett's Op – though much more akin to them than our other heroes are, in this and several other respects. In his first-person narration and actions alike, Spenser is depicted as a tough guy, first and foremost. He works out of a classically seedy and threadbare downtown office, lives alone in an apartment for the most part, observes the world around him with impeccably skeptical detachment, and smarts off on nearly every occasion to clients, leads, underworld kingpins and their goons alike. In terms of physical strength and gun-toting ability, moreover, he is if anything more single-handedly potent than his predecessors. In book after book in the series, we are reminded of Spenser's past training in boxing, his daily regimen of weightlifting or work on the heavy bag, followed or preceded by a long run, to keep his massively strong body in shape so he can flatten his opponents whenever and wherever they come after him. Yet the purity of Spenser's separateness and self-sufficiency is hemmed in and mitigated in several respects. Indeed, the feature of these books that has brought them the greatest attention is precisely the long-running relationship Spenser has, from the second novel on with Susan Silverman, first a guidance counselor and therapist at the suburban high school of a teenage boy Spenser has been hired to find, and ultimately a psych Ph.D. who functions as much as a partner or consultant as lover to our man.

Though for Spenser the stunningly savvy and beautiful Susan is almost from the start the love of his life, the course of this true love does not run smooth. At times Susan's feminist impulses and principles trouble the surface of her boundless regard for him. More commonly, though, she contents herself (and, *a fortiori*, Spenser himself) with something like this:

> "Spenser," she said. "You are a classic case for the feminist movement. A captive of the male mystique, and all that. And I want to say, for god's sake, you fool, outgrow all that Hemingwayesque nonsense. And yet..." She leaned her head against my shoulder as she spoke. "And yet I'm not sure you're wrong. I'm not sure but what you are exactly what you ought to be. What I am sure of is I'd care for you less if killing those people didn't bother you." (*Mortal Stakes*, p. 171)

For one stretch of several books published in the first half of the 1980s, Susan does undertake a trial separation from our man, in part to pursue further clinical training, but mainly to get away from what she has come to find the oppressive dominating strength of his clear-cut convictions and solid identity. (We need scarcely point out how such a "critique" only casts our hero's emphatically self-sufficient masculine singularity in all the more laudable and exemplary a light.) Eventually, in *A Catskill Eagle* (1985), Susan must be rescued, at the cost of much violence, from the consequences of her straying, but not without insisting that Spenser hear the most trenchant insights into the dynamics of his idealized love for her she will ever have to make ("'You projected your strength and love onto me and used it to feel better. In a sense I never knew if you loved me or merely loved the projection of yourself'" [*A Catskill Eagle*, p. 182]). From then on, however, their *modus vivendi* is fixed. The new, simultaneously strengthened and chastened Susan now assists Spenser in many of his cases, offering a therapeutic ear to damaged victims (for example, in *Pale Kings and Princes* [1987]) and therapeutic insights (for example, in *Stardust* [1990]) to help him on his way; and now she seems entitled and empowered to extract information from our hero on his background (it turns out – surprise! – that he was raised by three tough, loving men, his father and two uncles). In return, though, she leaves both him and Parker, as it were, free to ease back into the same mode of implicitly self-congratulatory idealization she once criticized:

> I sat on the bed and watched her. I loved to watch her. I loved to watch the bend of her arm, the attitude of her head as she paused to consider something. I loved the way she looked with everything just right. Her clothes fit just right, her makeup was flawless, her thick dark hair fell against her neck the way hair is supposed to fall…. Watching her was timeless. Sound seemed to stop. Light seemed clearer. (*Pale Kings and Princes* [1987], p. 73)

Conversely, Susan too is even more freed up, now that she understands him that much better, to admire Spenser as he deserves, as at the close of one of the more recent novels:

> "You're probably peerless, there's a kind of purity you maintain. Everything is inner-directed."
> "Except the part about you," I said. (*Pasttime* [1991], p. 220)

One does not even have to be a feminist to find this portrait of a supposedly ideal adult heterosexual relationship so risibly flattering to its fantasy of virile, omnipotent masculinity as to be hardly worth the breath it would take to condemn it. But to laugh or deplore and stop there would be to miss the extent to which even Parker's texts have had to clear some sort of space for the feminine, to grant it and professional woman Susan some sort of autonomy, and, however slightly, to compromise the autonomy of his hero in order to bring him into a continuing relationship with it. Nor is Spenser's love-partnership with Susan Silverman the only relationship developed in these books. As that relationship evolves, not at all coincidentally another ongoing character makes his appearance as helper and sidekick. Hawk, the Black enforcer with whom Spenser works out at the gym, and with whom he partners up whenever the level of mayhem rises too high for him to handle alone, is altogether tougher, colder, and more heavily armored, both literally and emotionally, than Spenser himself. Unlike Spenser, Hawk does not hesitate to sleep with an emotionally disturbed, masochistic former terrorist when she offers herself to both of them (in *The Judas Goat* [1978]), or to shoot a bad guy in the middle of the forehead when he's down (in *Early Autumn* [1981]). And unlike the Spenser of the later books in particular, he is completely unforthcoming as to where he comes from or what he feels, leaving Spenser, in effect, to explain him to Susan and others just as Susan had to explain and justify the ways of Spenser to others a decade or so earlier, for example, in *Looking for Rachel Wallace* (1980):

> "You have a sense of who you are," I [Spenser] said. "And you're determined to keep on being who you are, and maybe the only way you can keep on being who you are is to go inside, to be inaccessible. Especially, I would think, if you're a black man. And more especially, if you do the kind of work Hawk does." (*Double Deuce* [1992], p. 181)

It is not hard to spot the displacement and projection at work here. To the extent that Parker is willing to admit a critique of the traditional amorality, psychic armor, and propensity to violence of his leading man, those qualities in their purest form are shifted onto another figure, who is given an extra twist by being coded and explained as a Black man. We will see the same sort of literally self-serving liberalism at work in Jonathan Kellerman's construction and deployment of Milo Sturgis, whose gayness operates in the Alex Delaware series to excuse and distract us from his function as back-up enforcer for our sensitive hero. And this same triadic constellation of character functions – one female character to, we will say, the "left" of the hero, encouraging his impulses towards emotional sensitivity, non-violence, and, in some cases, non-involvement; another male character on his "right," encouraging and assisting our hero whenever he wants or needs to "go into the lion's den and spit in the lion's mouth," as Dave Robicheaux's white low-class sidekick Cletus Purcell puts it (*A Stained White Radiance* [1992], p. 64) – is a constitutive feature of the Parker, Kellerman, and Burke series alike.

Our new breed of detective is thus distinguishable from his forebears in the extent to which his masculinity is openly and positively defined as an ongoing negotiation between what we are led to think of as his feminine and his hypermale sides. Moreover, these new detectives are also set apart from their fiercely solitary progenitors by their positions within various familial or proto-familial constellations. Even Spenser, the most traditionally hard-nosed detective of the bunch, has something like his own child in Paul, the listless, apathetic boy he rescues from shallow, narcissistic parents in *Early Autumn* (1981), and whom, with a secondary assist now and then from Susan, he so successfully inducts into proper manhood that Paul is allowed to make his return every now and then (for example, in *The Widening Gyre* [1983], *Valediction* [1984], and *Pasttime* [1991]) for further aid, and as a demonstration of what a good job Spenser has done. Likewise, though significantly more distantly, the shades of familial relations float over the Alex Delaware books as well, in which Delaware's involvement with the case is typically triggered by his concern for a damaged child towards whom, in his professional capacity, he acts as the good, sensitive parent the boy or girl has lacked, and with whom, in two books (*Over the Edge* [1987] and *Private Eyes* [1992]) he already has a prior relationship when the action begins. And in the course of James Lee Burke's series, Dave Robicheaux takes two wives, one of whom is murdered, and adopts the child Alafair, a Salvadoran girl whose mother is killed in the small-plane crash that opens *Heaven's Prisoners* (1988).

If our contemporary detective's negotiation between a woman's way of knowing and acting and that of a hypermasculine man bears the impress of feminism's critique of normative American masculinity, his proto-familial relationships with women and children reflect a more general and widespread turn away from its ideal of isolated mastery towards a post-oedipal sense of interrelationship and connection. Such a shift is all the more evident inasmuch as the degree of explicitness and completeness of the family relation in these books is almost precisely equivalent to the degree of their heroes' involvement in and allegiance to the worlds they inhabit. So Burke's Dave Robicheaux, a Cajun who has been to modernity in the shape of the Vietnam War, who loves and hates the provincialism of the bayou country he is from, and reviles even more its vitiation and corruption by the developers, corporate powers and gangsters who have now moved in, *almost* has a real, natural family (albeit one he scarcely attends to all that much). And so too the one hero to have a biological family – wife, two girls and an old, wise, and censorious Italian mother – whose interactions and arguments with him are given their own ongoing space in these books, is K.C. Constantine's Mario Balzic, the protagonist who is most fully, indeed constitutively, a member of the community that surrounds, supports, infuriates, and nearly overwhelms him in every book.

Here, though, both the overlap and the differences between Mario's relationship to his wife Ruth and those between our other detectives and their women are worth noting. On the one hand, over the course of the Constantine novels the perpetually overworked and harassed police chief becomes increasingly sensitive to the extent to which he has left his wife to make do with the company of his mother, and left them both to bring up his daughters without him, while Ruth grows correspondingly more and more angry at his absence, his emotional stuntedness, and his reliance on her to keep him and their home afloat. On the other hand, there is in Constantine's works no equivalent of the hypermasculine, super-tough guy as counterweight to the feminine pressures exerted from the home front – pressures, we might well add, stemming from grievances that are throughout implicitly granted legitimacy, becoming, by *Bottom-Liner Blues* (1993), one of the chief areas of interest and concern. In its place, we might say, there is the all-male world of Muscotti's bar, where Balzic repairs again and again to drink his wine, muse on his frustrations, and kibitz with the likes of Father Marazzo, lawyer Panagios Valcanas, Vinnie the barkeep, and Iron City Steve, each of whom has his own obsessions and frustrations to vent. But even in this bar, masculinity appears less an allegiance to some great official and oedipal Symbolic backed by violence than an identity ceaselessly dissolved, qualified, and only partially re-constituted, like the novels' own plots and resolutions, by an ongoing barroom babble of ambiguous, cranky stories and crazy-quilt codes. Similarly, as with the help, and sometimes hindrance, of his own townspeople, local police, and the state troopers, Balzic careens his way through the action, cobbling together whatever solutions seem most right and least wrong, he is far more open and indeed prey to his own emotions than our other detectives. From *The Rocksburg Railway Murders* (1972), when their weight topples him over so that he falls down on the grass one moment and takes a minute out to go to the john and cry in the next, to *Joey's Case* (1988) in which his anxieties over a bout of impotence make him grouchy and inattentive, and for all the emotional and domestic deficiencies Ruth rightly finds in him, Balzic appears as an unprecedented figure in detective fiction – a white straight sleuth who lives in, feels, acknowledges and acts on a welter of emotions that can either steer him straight or lead him astray.

With all these distinctions in degree and type of interrelation in mind, along with their overriding difference from the Fordist detective's exemplary detachment, we can move on to a second feature of that generational difference. Let us begin by thinking of it in terms of the licensing in these texts of certain types of sensuality, even hedonism, for the reader and detective alike. Take food, for a crude starter: who remembers, or cares, what Sam Spade or Philip Marlowe has to eat, or how their whiskey tastes to them? But in Kellerman's *Private Eyes* (1992), we can accompany Alex

Delaware twice to a new little restaurant called La Mystique, across the street from a therapist's office he has under occasional surveillance, and learn that on his first visit he has a delicious espresso and some spectacular strawberries, on the second a superb poached bass, with some Grolsch beer to wash it down. All fans of Parker's Spenser know that in addition to being a super-strong he-man, he is also a gourmet cook, capable of intermixing even his most cold-blooded deliberations on the case with delicate improvisation at the stove ("If I killed him I'd have to kill the Hog. Maybe a little red wine..." [*Mortal Stakes* (1975), p. 121]). So too in the Robicheaux series, throughout which our Dave alternates his heavy-duty workouts with any number of shrimp boils, po'boy sandwiches, piles of shrimp étoufée and the like; while for Mario Balzic (who never works out, by the way) the greatest pleasures, constantly specified and elaborated by coldness, quality, and taste, are those of the grape.

Nor is food by any means the only item offered for our, and our detectives', delectation. The vicarious pleasures of clothes, culture, land-scape, and furnishings alike are on display for us as well in most of these books. In praise of the first Dave Robicheaux novel, the *Washington Post Book World* reviewer accurately enough conveys the near-equivalence of some of these pleasures in a phrase later pulled for one of the paperback puff-quotes: "setting ... so vivid you can feel the heaviness in the air, see the heat lightning, and taste the sauce piquante" (inside cover, *The Neon Rain* [1987]). Indeed, each Robicheaux comes complete with any number of swatches of "gorgeous" landscape writing to be consumed by readers with something close to a gustatory delight:

> The day was warm, the ground swells long and gentle and rolling, so that when they crested the wave broke into a thin froth and blew in the wind. I kept the bow into the wind and idled through the swells while Alafair set the rods into the sockets, spun out the lines behind us so the lures bounced in our wake, clicked on the drags, and threw chum overboard as if she were flinging shot. High up against the blue dome of sky, brown pelicans drifted in formation on the wind stream. Then suddenly their wings would collapse, cock into their sides like fins, and they would plummet with the speed of an aerial bomb into the water and rise from the foam with a menhaden or flying fish dripping from their pouched beak. (*A Morning for Flamingos* [1990], p. 42)

There is no attempt here to adjust the idle of the full-throttle prose, to qualify or restrain its enthusiasm for the landscape and itself; here and in countless other passages throughout Burke's work, the guilty pleasures

Chandler's performative yet tough-lipped writing simultaneously offered and repressed are, in effect, desublimated and openly displayed. In Kellerman, however, the proffered pleasures of the senses are apt to have less to do with plush style (though at times he does try) and more with upscale objects and furnishings. Alex Delaware spends a great deal of time around the pool of Japanese fish that his lover Robin has had put in for him in the yard of the yuppie pad he owns up in the hills, so we often get to hear about those fish. But he also goes out to eat with both Robin and, later on, when he and Robin are having a rough time, with a possible replacement for her; and we get to go along with them and learn what they eat when they do. So, too, when Alex, sensitive guy that he is, realizes "I'd been so wrapped up in the case ... that I'd neglected her [that is, Robin], using her as a sounding board without considering that she might need some attention herself":

> Determined to make amends, I made a three-point turn at a gas station on Fountain, drove south to Wilshire, and headed west, into Beverly Hills. There was about an hour left before the shops closed, and after parking in a city lot on Beverly Drive, I spent it like a gameshow winner on a spree, buying an antique lace blouse at a boutique on Cañon, perfume and bath soap at Giorgio, a quart of Frusen Gladje raspberry chocolate ice cream, an enormous gourmet basket at Jurgensons, the copper skillet she'd wanted at Davis Sonoma, a dozen coral roses arranged with leather fern and baby's breath. It was no solution, just a start in the right direction. (*Over the Edge* [1987], p. 271)

Nice of him to know that, of course; just as the "gameshow winner" simile supplies a discerning fillip of faint disavowal. Likewise, when Delaware enters the halls and inner sanctums of the fabulously wealthy, as he does in virtually every Kellerman novel, the pleasures of looking around will be all the more enhanced by our awareness that the people in these places have serious problems – an awareness, that is, left to hover off to the side of a luxuriously detailed visual wallowing that remains utterly untroubled by it:

> *Around* was a vast space crammed with treasures – an entry hall big enough for croquet, and at its rear a sinuous green marble staircase. Beyond the stairs, cavernous room after cavernous room – galleries built for display, vast and silent, indistinguishable from one another in terms of function. Cathedral and coffered ceilings, mirror-sheen paneling, tapestries, stained-glass sky lights, kaleidoscopic Oriental and Aubusson rugs over floors of inlaid marble and

hand-painted tile and French walnut parquet. So much sheen and opulence that my senses overloaded and I felt myself losing equilibrium. (*Private Eyes* [1992], p. 126)

We have come a long way from General Sternwood's claustrophobic hothouse in *The Big Sleep*. In Kellerman's novels, the sublime spectacle of such luxury will typically only be problematized by the revealed truth of the dysfunction and/or corruption of those who inhabit it *after* it has first been thoroughly, unambiguously enjoyed.

Adequately detailed description of such scenes obviously requires the narrator to possess enough *savoir faire* to name those Aubusson rugs for what they are; nor is Alex Delaware the only one of our detectives who has it. Our other top contender for the Most Cultural Capital Award is Parker's Spenser, who spends less time describing the objects of his taste and discernment but flaunts his credentials over a much wider field. In addition to his cooking skills, he is also, for example, a sharp dresser in accord with the fashions and name-brands of the time:

I put on jeans, a white Levi shirt, and white Adidas Roms with blue stripes.... I got a black woven-leather shoulder rig out of the suitcase and slipped into it. They aren't as comfortable as hip holsters, but I wanted to wear a short Levi jacket and the hip holster would show. I put my gun in the holster and put on the Levi jacket, and left it unbuttoned. It was dark blue corduroy. I looked at myself in the mirror over the bureau. I turned the collar. Elegant. Clean-shaven, fresh-showered, with a recent haircut. I was the image of the international adventurer. (*The Judas Goat* [1978], p. 42)

Moreover, the education in comprehensive masculinity he gives to his proto-son Paul includes a proper introduction – once again, with proper names and even price tags attached – to the finer things in life:

We had dinner at the Four Seasons, in the pool room, under the high ceiling near a window on the Fifty-third Street side. Paul had pheasant, among other things, and paid close attention to everything Susan and I did. We had some wine, and the bill came to $182.37. I have bought cars for less. The next day we went to the Metropolitan Museum in the afternoon and in the evening we took Paul up to Riverside Church to see Alvin Ailey and his group dance. (*Early Autumn* [1981]), p. 200)

Indeed, so precise and all-encompassing is our big guy's discernment that he and Parker are capable of deploying it to point up the vain shallowness of, for example, the pathetic, egregiously hip mother from whom Spenser rescues Paul, and her newest beau:

> Patty Giacomin came out and stood by the Bronco. Pale green slacks, lavender shirt, white blazer. Big sunglasses, bright lipstick. Stephan was with her. He was as beautiful as she – jeans with a Pierre Cardin patch on them, Frye boots, a half-buttoned tailored collarless shirt in vertical blue-on-blue stripes, a gray sharkskin vest, unbuttoned. His dark maroon Pontiac Firebird was parked in the Giacomin driveway.
> "The Firebird's not right," I said. "It doesn't go with the rest of the look."
> (*Early Autumn* [1981], p. 100)

And last but far from least, there is that impressive range of literary and cultural references sprinkled through Spenser's activities, dialogue and narration, coexisting in such delightful incongruity with his all-male toughness and strength. For example, on the job in London in *The Judas Goat*, he peruses Richard Slotkin's *Regeneration Through Violence* in his leisure moments; and on his way to some time-out sex with Susan, he blithely quotes modern American poetry and alludes to Christopher Marlowe and the Greeks:

> "Complacencies of the peignoir," I said, "and late coffee and oranges in a sunny chair."
> "Eliot?" Susan said.
> "Stevens," I said, and put my arms around her. "And the green freedom of a cockatoo upon a rug."
> "I never heard it called that," Susan murmured, and kissed me and leaned away and jerked her head toward the bedroom and smiled the smile she had that would launch a thousand ships. (*Pale Kings and Princes* [1987], pp. 164–65)

As the *B. Dalton Merchandise Bulletin* puts it in its hype, "Spenser has the shortsighted, large-fisted punch-now-pay-later philosophy of all our private eyes.... the difference is a literacy and panache the others lack" (inside cover, *Ceremony* [1982]).

How are we to understand and judge such open advertisements of the unfettered sensuality and vaunted cultural capital of this new breed of detective-heroes? One way would be to read their difference from their Fordist forefathers as one indication of the degree to which the sex/gender system of Sonyist culture in the First World metropole has been de-oedipalized. In plainer terms, the old version of normative masculinity, so emphatically characterized in first-generation detective fiction by its stern renunciations (and, in Chandler, covert and stigmatized indulgences) and strict adherences to what a properly principled man's gotta do, has now been substantially relaxed. Just as our new man may and even must to some degree be involved in relationships with others, so too they may, even must, to some degree enjoy the life-worlds they are in.

But here I am less inclined to ascribe this particular shift to the effects of feminism so much as to the tendential pressures inherent in the vast expansion of what in Fordist culture had been coded as the feminine province of consumer desire and commodified choice. Now, as anyone in this culture knows, the dance of a thousand commodities, including hair- and body-care products, clothes, and perfume, is staged just as much and as aggressively to win the hearts and minds of men as for women. The freeing up of the male sensorium and revolt against renunciation that arguably began in the countercultures of the 1960s has by now been fully appropriated and brought into the mainstream by the marketing genius of Sonyist capitalism, which no longer bothers to argue "For all you do, this Bud's for you," but instead that "The night belongs to Michelob" and that this rock concert is brought to you by Bud (or by Ice-Bud, or Lite Bud, or Real Draft).

Viewed in this light, the consumer skills and modalities of enjoyment that play such a large part in our heroes' respective characterizations can be graphed together with the degree and character of their domestic and/ or romantic relationships with women and children as a comparative measure of the outright male narcissism in these books. Highest ratings here go, obviously enough, to Kellerman's sensitive shrink Alex Delaware, whose largely unintegrated, tepidly pursued dinner-date romances with custom-guitar-maker Robin and school principal Linda link up in turn with his equally sensitive yet strictly professional involvement with children, and happily conjoin with the connoisseur's eye and power-shopping talents he brings to his yuppie single's lifestyle. But Parker's Spenser, with a proto-son and lover who are both more or less explicitly only advertisements for himself, and his impeccable displays of sartorial, culinary, and high-brow cultural tastes, is not far behind. Altogether farther back in the pack, Burke's Dave Robicheaux's less market-oriented appetite for indigenous cooking and landscape is just as neatly correlated with his explicitly familial relationship with two successive wives and adopted daughter, as well as his complex emotional investment in the land of his home. But even in these novels, some trace of narcissism remains in both the idealized and largely non-functional characterizations of woman and child – present in these books exclusively as figures of static purity, capable of being called in only to provide sweet succor when our hero is down or innocent targets for the bad guys on the prowl – and the analogously static, consumable display swatches of sensual prose served up with formulaic regularity for our pleasure.

Here, however, we might also take passing note of the compensatory measures undertaken in this fiction to insist that, however much our newly indulgent heroes may be wallowing in their pleasures, they are nonetheless emphatically not soft. Even Alex Delaware, our most officially sensitive hero, has his credentials in karate; while, if anything, Burke's Robicheaux and Parker's Spenser are bigger and stronger and more violent than their predecessors, as both their much more frequent recourse to horrific levels of violence and their frequently described physical regimens alike testify again and again.[34] We will have occasion later on to consider the extent to which the former, as in Chandler but even more so now, represents an indulgent surrender to the lawless disorder as much as a last-ditch stand against it. For now it is enough for us to note the degree to which something of the same is true for all the lavishly described weightlifting, jogging runs, and workouts too – how much, that is, they too license and measure a new level of narcissistic male self-regard and self-tending, even as they stridently hold the line against any undue softening of muscle tone.

Barbara Ehrenreich was perhaps the first to call attention to this historically distinct mode of masculinity, which opens the gates to sensual pleasure while keeping men hedged against equal partnership and full emotional intimacy with women, and responsibility for children: "[i]n the seventies' cluster of middle-class male values," she wrote more than ten years ago, "health was linked to class status, and both in turn were linked to a movement away from the rigidity of the breadwinner's role."[35] More recently, Kathleen Gerson has surveyed the diffusion across class lines of the compromise formation she designates as the "autonomous" option for contemporary men. Interestingly enough, however, in her analysis of in-depth interviews with a number of "autonomously-oriented" men, she plays down the "feminizing" consumerization of the male subject, and emphasizes instead her subjects' felt sense of being caught between declining economic power on the job, and rising expectations on the home front – that is, the ongoing pressure, in a job market severely skewed by the decreasing but still sizable gap between women's and men's earning power, for the man to bring home the breadwinner's check, combined with new demands for equal domestic partnership.[36] But we need hardly choose between Ehrenreich's harsh judgement of this new man's consumerized narcissism and the more sympathetic understanding of the performance pressures governing his choice of an "autonomous orientation"; each explains, covers up for, and rewards its flip side in the loosened-up yet tough-enough masculinity that results, both in our novels and in the outside world.

Finally, what is most striking in this regard about the Mario Balzic novels of K.C. Constantine is precisely the absence of just this "autonomous" or "narcissistic" model of masculinity, and the very different sensual pleasures of their texts. First of all, as we have already seen, Mario himself is caught and constituted by the increasing tension between his roles as a protector-provider to the community at large, and loving partner to his wife, mother, and children. Likewise, the pleasures of the wine he drinks and the food he eats are as briefly, flatly stated as the descriptions we receive through his eyes of the increasingly battered urban landscape he patrols. What sensual pleasures are then extolled and offered to us for our pleasurable consumption in these books, aside from their plots, if not those of eating, shopping, attire, and/or exercise regimes?

Every reader of Constantine knows the answer to this question: the pleasure of socializing, of talk itself, for which the crimes or mysteries to be resolved in his novels merely provide the occasions and tenuous through-lines off which the dialogue can be strung. One indicator of the extent to which a truly Bakhtinian dialogics of the social is both the main content and subject of these novels is the fact that Balzic himself appears in them through third-person limited narration. Though we have access to his thoughts and feelings, his perspective falls far short of governing and controlling the actions and conversations the text recounts as the first-person recitals of our other detectives do – so much so that Mario's own voice often becomes merely another in the text's ceaseless babble of tongues. Indeed, so fully are these books given over to the medley of voices within them that a full demonstration of this characteristic is practically impossible in any reasonably contained space. I can only choose one voice from the welter, that of Frances Romanelli, working-class daughter of a fiercely repressive Italian patriarch and wife to an unemployed husband who now seems to have run off – and even then, I am excerpting from a much longer and more free-ranging dialogue. I begin in the middle of her complaint over how both her old father and her young husband Jimmy have frozen her out. Mario has reminded her that she has just told him that her father did pay for her to go back to school. "'Oh, he did,'" Frances answers, and steams ahead:

> "But he never thought that was gonna mean that I'd wind up getting a job. Going to the community college was just in case. And the 'just in case' was never supposed to happen. I mean, women don't work. Not jobs work. House work. That's all. He's been mad at me ever since I couldn't have kids. And now he thinks that the real reason I couldn't have kids – no, *didn't* have kids – was so I could eventually get a job. So now he thinks I lied to him about not being able to have kids. Honest to God, between Jimmy and my father, I can't win. I can't do anything right!
>
> "I mean, here are the only two men in my life – no, not just men – the only two people in the whole world I care about and neither one of 'em'll talk to me and if Jimmy hadn't lost his job I'd've never found that out. I mean, imagine that! If that mine had never shut down and Jimmy would've never lost his job, I'd've never found out what my father and my husband are really like.
>
> "When I think of that, it drives me crazy. Sometimes I wake up in the middle of the night and I'm terrified, scared stiff, I can't get my breath – everything – and it's because I think not only my husband but my father liked me a whole hell of a lot better when I was pretty much just a maid and a cook and a day worker. And I think, boy, they really thought a whole lot of me, didn't they? And these aren't some strangers, some people off the street, some perverts, these are my father and my husband. My father for thirty-six years. My husband for eighteen years.
>
> "And in the last year, for all practical purposes, they both quit talking to me."
> (*The Man Who Liked Slow Tomatoes* [1982], pp. 44–5)

What is unbound here and throughout the Balzic series is not the sensuality of the exemplary male detective but the *socius* itself, with which his own voice mixes in with as much or more than it governs or controls; what is sensitive here, on the part of both author and hero alike, is not their taste but their sympathetic and pitch-perfect ears, constantly (albeit, on Mario's part, imperfectly) attentive to every register and gradation of devious manipulation, direct and displaced or projected grievance, and stunted joy, and from all ethnic and racial varieties and ages of men and women alike.

Such thoroughly communal pleasures, in turn, are in striking contrast to what in several books by two of our authors appears as nothing less than a distinct hostility towards communality itself, especially whenever it shows up in any countercultural and/or collectivized form. Such a revulsion is evident in Parker's very first Spenser novel, *The Godwulf Manuscript* (1973), where it is linked to an open animosity towards student radicalism. Student leaders of a campus movement have stolen a precious illuminated manuscript from the university that hires Spenser, and are dealing hard drugs as well, under the guidance of a wispy, inadequately masculinized (of course), fanatical professor. Then, when one of the drug-dealing radicals is murdered and his confused and overprivileged upper-middle-class girlfriend framed for the crime, Spenser tracks her down to the pagan commune, the "Ceremony of Moloch," where, happily, he busts into the communal lair just in time to rescue her from a diabolical initiation ceremony in which she is about to be penetrated by the "high priest's" phallic club. In the next novel, *God Save the Child* (1974), Spenser is hired by another messed-up *nouveau riche* suburban couple like the girlfriend's parents in *Godwulf*, only this pair wants Spenser to find their missing son, who has defected to another commune, this one headed up by a hyper-muscled, weightlifting homosexual bully whom Spenser has to beat up in order to win the inadequately masculinized son back to (in every sense, one assumes) "straight" life, and who is, it turns out, in cahoots with the town's police chief to peddle porno and prostitutes to the good people of the town. A few books later, though, in *The Judas Goat* (1978), the commune / radical youth group is refigured as a fanatical *right-wing* terrorist organization that engages in kinky sado-masochistic sex and assassination plots, and is headed by the vicious Paul and his monstrously strong sidekick Zachary, whose bludgeoning requires a dual effort by Spenser and his Black sidekick Hawk.

At that point, at least in the Spenser novels I have read, the demonized and stigmatized figure of the radical/countercultural commune disappears; in its place, where collective conspiracies are afoot, we typically find instead so many right-wing organizations and groups pressing into the body politic, as it were, from above. Moreover, in both *Looking for Rachel Wallace* (1980) and *A Catskill Eagle* (1985), when Spenser penetrates (as it were) to the bottom of the organization – in the first, a group called RAM (Restore American Morality); in the second, a right-wing transnational paramilitary corporation, headed by a family whose son has taken Susan as his hostage-lover – he finds its corrupt power source is not the well-heeled front man who seemed to be the fount of evil, but the vicious old woman who is that man's mother or wife.[37] In a sense, though, despite the change in focus and overt political ideology, such shifts illuminate the underlying rule: all collectives are either false fronts or sick, or both; and at the root of them all are botched masculinities, inadequate men putting up false fronts. So, in the one eighties novel in which the commune as such re-emerges, in the bizarre form of "the Bullies," a militant Christian sect that has swallowed up a woman Spenser is hired to find, we can pretty much guess how the story goes. They too will turn out to be a front, this time for a drug-running and laundering operation; and the vociferously masculine appearance and aggressive assertiveness of their leader, Bullard Winston, belie a weakness that turns out to be no match for Sherry Spellman, the confused and pathetic but ultimately evil woman who takes over from him.

It is perhaps not surprising to find such an inverse relationship between a narcissistically self-regarding, self-sufficient masculinity coded good and an alternative or radical communality coded evil in popular fiction written in the 1970s, a decade during whose latter years the first was promoted in white middle-class culture precisely insofar as the latter was demonized and on the decline. But in that case, it is all the more surprising to find much the same relationship pervading and constituting so much of the warp and woof of Jonathan Kellerman's Alex Delaware series, whose first title appears in 1985. In the second Delaware novel, *Blood Test* (1986), the New Age-tinged commune "The Touch" is neither the epicenter of the novel's plot nor the ultimate source of the evil Alex explores and exposes; but its members are quite bad enough. Located in a remote location in the Southern California desert, and headed by a former Beverly Hills lawyer turned spiritual avatar named Matthias, they purport to be, in Matthias's words,

> "refugees from a former life. We've chosen a new life that emphasizes purity and industry. We avoid environmental poisons and seek self-sufficiency. We believe that by changing ourselves we increase the positive energy in the world."
> (*Blood Test*, p. 158)

Here too, as in Parker's fiction, the high ideals are merely a front behind which decadent converts engage in Boschian coke-besotted sex orgies under Matthias's authoritarian direction, and Matthias himself smuggles in and deals out massive amounts of coke. In the baroque plot that winds itself out in *Time Bomb* (1990), moreover, a radical commune does come center-stage as something close to the source of all evil, albeit in a strained and hedged-about way. Here at the end of the enigma, as the source of the evil that bursts out at the novel's opening in the highly topical form of a shooting in a schoolyard, we learn that years ago, back at the end of the 1960s, a group of radical-left hippies moved out to Idaho, there to form an interracial utopian commune called "New Walden"; but their efforts to do so were hijacked by an ultra-right-wing racist populist, the neo-fascist Ahlward, who enlists weak-minded opportunist Gordon Latch to help him murder most of the group, and set himself up as a smooth-talking left-liberal politician – a thinly disguised version of Tom Hayden, in fact, complete with a prominent actress as his glossy wife – to further the ultimate project of "Wannsee Two," whose ultimate goal is the geno-cidal extermination of all non-whites and the construction of a racially pure Nazi USA.

Under the manifold mattresses of convoluted background story here we can just barely feel a dried pea of sympathy for a genuine left-utopian project. Nor, I suppose, is it insignificant that *Time Bomb*'s typically enor-mous cast of characters includes two survivors of that project's wreck, Old Left stalwart Sophie Gruenwald and her mixed-race grandson, Ike Novato, child of an interracial New Left couple murdered in Idaho. But surely it is at least equally significant that these characters are literally hidden away and presumed dead for most of the novel, and only briefly rendered in its closing pages, just as the utopian-communalist project can only be figured in Delaware's text at the moment and in the form of its vicious negation. It is the same, or something close to it, with the two more mainstream, middle-class-approved alternative institutions with whose corruption the action of Kellerman's first novel *When the Bough Breaks* (1985) is concerned: the day-care center of its back-story; and La Casa de los Niños, a non-profit community for homeless children, on its front end, where the action ends up. The former – once again, quite topically – turns out, despite the good intentions of the woman running it, to be a playground for her child-molesting husband; the second, the feeding ground for a network of like-minded, well-heeled white male perverts.

In Kellerman's universe, then, virtually all progressive or even charitably intended collective enterprises either appear under the sign of their sub-ornation, or are revealed to have been an evil conspiracy from the start. And, as in Parker's fiction, the appearance of the ostensibly perfectly assembled man is always belied in the end by the exposure of his weakness and complicity with the malign powers. In Kellerman, though, this man is typically figured as a professional colleague and competitor, that is, as a prescription-writing psychiatrist to his therapeutically sensitive psycholo-gist, like Dr Mainwaring in *Over the Edge* (1987) or Dr Lionel W. Towle in *When the Bough Breaks*, characters so similar in appearance and function that a single description, this one of the latter, will serve to capture both:

He was tall, at least six-three, and lean, with the kind of features bad novels label as chiseled. He was one of the most handsome middle-aged men I had ever seen. His face was noble – a strong chin bisected by a perfect cleft, the nose of a Roman senator, and twinkling eyes the color of a clear sky. His thick, snow-white hair hung down over his forehead, Carl Sandburg style. His eyebrows were twin white clouds. (*When the Bough Breaks*, p. 50)

This paradigmatically handsome and seemingly fully empowered older man appears to be running wholly under his own steam as he fluently spouts his false medical certainties. But just as his equivalents in Parker's fiction are run by the pathetic and dangerous women behind them, he too is merely a pawn in the hands of the monstrously corrupt: weak-minded Dr Towles, of the Black pseudo-minister Augustus McCaffery and his network of child abusers; weak-willed Dr Mainwaring, of the evil Heather Cadmus, who with the assistance of her attorney-lover Horace Souza and several others has conspired both to drug her nephew into psychosis and to frame him for a series of murders she herself has ordered up to look as though they had been committed by a self-loathing gay madman.

Buttressed by Kellerman's regretful suspicion and/or demonizing antagonism towards any collective project, these characterizations not only function to extoll a properly humane psychology over the false god of psychiatric medicine, but to endorse Alex's supplely sensitive, tousle-haired, loosened-up masculinity over the chiseled, whited sepulchres of the oedipal-patriarchal Father. Yet Kellerman's work in this regard is not wholly assimilable to Parker's; or rather, there is something else in Kellerman's novels that accompanies the valorization of the new narcissistic masculinity modeled within them, and that will be worth the time it takes to extract it from the rhizomatic sprawl of these long, fat books. One way to catch a glimpse of it is to note what at first might seem to be an odd discrepancy between, on the one hand, the allegiance the books profess to a humanistic psychology whose sensitive probings and insights are more or less explicitly deemed ethically and practically superior to the smug prescriptions of psychiatric medicine and, on the other hand, the techno-medical explanations that we find again and again at the foundation of the mystery to be solved. In *Over the Edge* (1987), *Silent Partner* (1989), and *Private Eyes* (1992), Alex shares his professional knowledge with us for pages on end, as he sorts through his psychological wisdom for a diagnosis of why the suffering, victimized people he cares about have behaved as they do. What lies in the dark abysses of the mind and its memories that has taken young, gay Jamey Cadmus over the line from eccentric brilliance to murderous psychosis; what terrible past experiences have prompted Sharon Ransom to fence off her psyche into a set of multiple personalities; what terrible fear or return of the repressed has led agoraphobic Gina Dickinson to vanish from the fabulous estate where she had hidden from the world for nearly the past fifteen years?

So diffuse and labyrinthine are the manifold windings of these novels, so insistent are their invitations to speculate with Alex in just this way, and so byzantinely complex their final explanations, that even many of Kellerman's readers may not fully realize by the end of these books that the basic answer to each and all these questions is Nothing. The psychotic symptoms Jamey exhibits in *Over the Edge* are the result of a psychotropic drug his evil aunt brought back with her from her anthropological field work in the Amazon. In *Silent Partner*, the features of multiple personality disorder in goody-goody Sharon Ransom's behavior are explained by the fact that she has an evil, libidinous twin sister, and that these two, plus another, pitifully deformed, blind, deaf and paralyzed third daughter, are in turn the result of hormonal treatments administered to their mother through the machinations of her no-good brother, in the hope of snaring the Howard Hughes-like multimillionaire whose first lieutenant and business associate hired her to introduce his friend to sex. Nor, as it turns out in *Private Eyes*, is Gina Dickinson's disappearance an action undertaken out of any psychic distress. She has been abducted by the violently homophobic behaviorist Leo Gabney, who has discovered the affair she has been conducting under the cover of therapy with the colleague and wife he thought "cured" of her lesbian proclivities by the sadistic electric tortures he applies and justifies as aversion-therapy.

Finally, something of the same is true even of Nona Swope, the dangerously disturbed nymphomaniac who, together with her equally dysfunctional boyfriend, is ultimately found to be at the root of the main-stage murder and havoc in *Blood Test* (1986). For Kellerman both has Delaware work her case up as a classic – though, once again, wildly byzantine[38] – example of the effects of father–daughter incest, and pins her down as the result of yet another instance of vicious meddling with nature. Nona is the Eve in her father's Bizzaro-world Garden of Eden, final term of a whole set of demented horticultural experiments undertaken in his "fascination with the grotesque, the stillborn, and the deadly" (p. 207), the ultimate product of his "stinking repulsive nightmare factory" out of which he has also manufactured

[a]crid smelling oranges and lemons, pruned and twisted to nothingness. An apple tree laden with grotesquely misshapen tumors masquerading as fruit. A pomegranate bush slimy with mucoid jelly. Flesh-colored plums harboring colonies of gyrating worms. Mounds of fruit rotted on the ground. (*Blood Test*, p. 203)

I quote this description because it seems to rhyme with so many other passages of ecstatic disgust in Kellerman's work: like "the filth" that "pour[s] out" of Sharon Ransom in Alex's last meeting with her in *Silent Partner*, followed by a "gurgling roaring sound" like "a cesspool over-flowing" (p. 389); or the feel and look of evil August McCaffery's black body atop Alex's at the climax of *When the Bough Breaks*, panting "his sour breath on me, the lumpy face crimson, the fish eyes swallowed by fleshy folds, squeezing," until he is shot from above, so that the "kinky hair explod[es]" and "blood, bright and fresh," comes "pouring out of his nose, his ears, his mouth" (pp. 344–5); or, for that matter, like Alex's memories in *Over the Edge* of Haight-Ashbury in the sixties, as

a crazy quilt of social outcasts living on the edge: baby-faced bikers, whores, pimps, and other assorted jackals. A broth seasoned with unstable ingredients that boiled over frequently into violence, the talk of peace and love a dope-inspired illusion. (pp. 266–67)

The work of Klaus Theweleit on the Freikorps and Stallybrass and White on the psychic construction of the bourgeois universe readily hands us one way of reading such passages.[39] Obviously enough, they are an expanded, contemporary form of the same lurid, desiring fascination we saw in Chandler's work with a monstrously disordered, feminized, animal-ized and/or racialized Other whose liquid being must be demonized and cast out for the male bourgeois Self to assert and maintain its integrity. But in Kellerman's version of this self-defining operation, the same circuitry is also implicitly thematized as an antagonism to all forms of intervention, modeling, and medical or social engineering – an antagonism whose flip side is nothing less than an adamant (if not necessarily conscious) cham-pioning of the "natural" sorting processes of capitalist life. Those who intervene, who meddle and experiment, create only monsters; indeed, most of those who do, *intend* to do so, serving evil in their attempts. The only right course of action is to behave as our sensitive *laissez faire* hero does: make some shrewd investments with the money you earn so that you can enjoy consumer life and pick your shots in your work; understand and sympathize with those in psychic distress; and express an occasional sigh at the manifold sorrows of the world, while repulsing and denouncing all misbegotten attempts to intervene in the way things naturally are.

The particular admixture in the deep structure of Kellerman's work of all these ideologies of class, race, and gender into a single, overdetermined circuitry of desire, identity, and political affiliation is, in turn, in striking but not altogether distinct contrast to what we find in James Lee Burke. For his Robicheaux novels are, if anything, even more explicitly and extensively marbled through with the seductive horror of the monstrous than Kellerman's are. One place to look for the monstrous in Burke is in the bad guys themselves, who come in three basic varieties. One is the grotesque and/or pug-ugly figure of the low-life indigenous scumbag. *A Stained White Radiance* (1992) gives us no fewer than three versions of this type: a virulently racist dwarf with the Dickensian name of Fluck, a cohort named Raintree who has "a face full of bone" (p. 38), and a third goon with "a mouth full of metal fillings" (p. 40) named Jack Gates. But at least one such monstrous criminal-lumpen redneck is described in perversely loving detail in every book. Here, for example, is a typically vibrant description of the vicious Eddie Keats, whose face, Robicheaux says, "I had never seen before," although "its details had the familiarity of a forgotten dream":

> His head was big, the neck as thick as a stump, the eyes green and full of energy; a piece of cartilage behind the jawbone flexed while he ground peanuts between his back teeth. The tanned skin around his mouth was so taut that it looked as if you could strike a kitchen match on it. His hands were big, too – the fingers like sausages, the wrists corded with vein. (*Heaven's Prisoners* [1988], p. 107)

The second deformed evil figure is that of the regional crime boss, usually though not always a man whose power rests on the trade in drugs and sex, and most often an Italian. Didi Gee in *The Neon Rain* (1987), Sally Dio in *Black Cherry Blues* (1989), Tony Cardo in *A Morning for Flamingos* (1990), Joey Gouza in *A Stained White Radiance* (1992), and my favorite, Julie "Baby Feet" Balboa of *In the Electric Mist with Confederate Dead* (1993) – all are either geeks or monsters. Tony Cardo, for example,

> was truly a strange-looking man. His head was long and narrow, his ears tiny and pressed tightly against his scalp as though part of them had been surgically pared away. His hair grew in gray and black ringlets that were tapered on the back of his neck like the flange of a helmet. His smile exposed his long white

teeth, and his chest hair was black and slick with perspiration. (*A Morning for Flamingos*, p. 120)

Or there is *The Neon Rain*'s Didi Gee, who, with a "waistline and stomach" that "had the contours of three inner tubes stacked on top of each other," and "hands as big as skillets," a "neck as thick as a fire hydrant," and a "curly black head as round and hard as a cannonball" (p. 66), is even more, and more typically, grotesque.

Finally, in his most recent novels Burke has added a third figure to this rogues' gallery. Vic Benson of *A Stained White Radiance* and Murphy Doucet of *In the Electric Mist with Confederate Dead* are local types, like the low-life creeps-for-hire described above. But they are older than the other two types of bad guy; and they incarnate a distinct type of cold-blooded evil, an appalling fiendishness that seems to exist for its own sake. *A Stained White Radiance*'s Vic Benson, whose "destroyed face" stares implacably out from the squad car after his last violent act "as though the invisible forces that had driven him all his life had gathered at this place, in this moment, to finally and irrevocably have their way with him," is actually the filiocidal father of a character who grew up with Robicheaux, served in the Vietnam War as he did, and now attempts to negotiate the growing gap between the Old and New Souths just as he does. And Murphy Doucet, the serial sex killer of *In the Electric Mist*'s present, with his "white eyebrows, jittering ... eyeballs ... myriad lines in his skin," and "slit of a mouth" (p. 298), turns out to be the same man Robicheaux spotted from a distance in his youth, murdering a black man for sleeping with an Old South middle-class white man's wife.

Linked to our hero's past and representing the "invisible forces" of psychic deprivation, economic blight, and chronic racism that are the flip side of Burke's depiction of the Old South culture of southern Louisiana as "a quiet and gentle place" where "life was a party to be enjoyed with the same pleasure and certainty as the evening breeze" (*A Stained White Radiance*, p. 65), these evil fathers embody the inherent viciousness that lurks within that vanishing culture. Together, they constitute one position on a charged allegorical field that throughout Burke's fiction is elaborated as both the psychological and political landscape defining and determining Robicheaux. After all, Dave himself comes out of the hardscrabble side of Southern culture, as we learn from the stark flashbacks and passages of brooding memory entangled with the present actions of these books; like the damaged Sonniers of *A Stained White Radiance*, he too is the product of a broken home, the son of an oil worker (like the Sonniers' evil father, Vic Benson) and a mother whose sexual hungers led her to abandon her family and destroy herself.

Nor is Dave Robicheaux a stranger to the same currents of wild, lurid violence that teem through the veins of our first type of bad guy, those monstrous lowlifes towards whom, with the encouragement and assistance of his alter ego, Cletus Purcell, he often ends up indulging in the same orgasmic releases of lethal passion they have inflicted, or threatened to inflict, on himself and/or his loved ones. Here, for example, is the zesty description of how he lets it go on Eddie Keats, the thug I described above, who has previously visited a vicious beating on him:

> I held the pool cue by the tapered end with both hands and whipped it sideways through the air as I would a baseball bat, with the same force and energy and snap of the wrists, and broke the weighted end across his left eye and the bridge of his nose. I felt the wood knock into bone, saw the skin split, saw the green eye almost come out of its socket, heard him clatter against the bar and go down on the brass rail with his hands cupped to his nose and the blood roaring between his fingers. (*Heaven's Prisoners* [1988], pp. 108–9)

We have seen by now that such delicious indulgences in the whirlpool of violence are a staple feature of the detective genre, and their release and restraint alike a constitutive feature of the masculinities it models. But what makes Burke's fiction unique in this regard is precisely the degree to which it explicitly thematizes and problematizes our hero's relationship to the violence it renders so vividly. In *Heaven's Prisoners*, Robicheaux gives vent to his desire for brutal revenge against the urgent pleading of his new wife Annie to leave things alone; moreover, in taking that revenge, he "stirs the pot" (as, you will recall, Hammett's Continental Op put it) so vigorously as to bring about her brutal murder in return – and so be forced in its aftermath to acknowledge the monstrousness inside himself:

> Annie was dead because I couldn't leave things alone. I had quit the New Orleans police department, the bourbon-scented knight-errant who said he couldn't abide any longer the political hypocrisy and the addictive, brutal ugliness of metropolitan law enforcement, but the truth was that I enjoyed it, that I got high on my knowledge of man's iniquity, that I disdained the boredom and predictability of the normal world as much as my strange alcoholic metabolism loved the adrenaline rush of danger and my feeling of power over an evil world that in many ways was mirrored in microcosm in my own soul. (p. 139)

Here, and throughout the series, Robicheaux's desire to drown himself in alcohol is so insistently linked with his urge to release himself in violence that the two become virtually identical. To catch the full significance of Robicheaux/Burke's confessional mode, moreover, it is worth comparing it to the treatment of the hero's violence offered us by another of our writers. Since Kellerman's Alex Delaware rarely indulges, leaving it for the most part to Milo and his other acquaintances among the police, let us take Parker and his Spenser instead. In one sense, Parker's treatment of his hero's violence is quite similar to Burke's: in the degree to which his hero and his Black buddy Hawk indulge in it, and to which those indulgences are served up as pungently as Parker's limited writing skills will allow. Here is a portion of one such episode, from the middle of the mêlée Spenser and Hawk have caused by busting into the middle of an orgy of sex and porn in the arch-criminal's Back Bay house in *Ceremony* (1982):

> We had roiled through the hall and into the sunken living room, going down the three steps as if riding a wave. A small man with a goatee was picked up and thrown against a wall and I was beside Hawk. He moved as if he were dancing, with a kind of joyful and vicious rhythm. The sweat rolled down his face. His bald head gleamed. There was a cut on his cheek and blood mixed pinkish with the sweat. His arms swelled and relaxed inside the sleeves of his gray flannel jacket. (p. 199)

It is hardly necessary to point out how much this intervention, though nominally opposed to the orgy in progress, in fact merely constitutes its continuation, albeit now as violence; yet this affiliation is constructed not for the sake of some future insight or critique, but for our straightforward pleasure in the here and now. Our access to that pleasure is arguably made all the more unselfconsciously direct and untroubled by the degree to which it is displaced onto Hawk, who becomes in effect both object and subject of the erotic brutality on display here, as he dances away in that "joyful and vicious rhythm," the sweat breaks and mixes with blood, and his arms swell and relax. By contrast, Robicheaux's former partner and ongoing sidekick Cletus Purcell is less a convenient dumping ground for pleasures the texts want simultaneously to offer and to disavow than a doubling mirror of his own spotted soul, the sign of his inextricable complicity in the evil he pursues. On the one hand, with his face that "looked like it was made from boiled pigskin, except there were stitch scars across the bridge of his nose and through one eyebrow" (*The Neon Rain* [1987], p. 9), and his ever-fattening body, which "always looked too big for his clothes" (*A Morning for Flamingos* [1990], p. 67), he bears a clear resemblance to the low-life goons and the gangsters – and, at a few points in these books, behaves like the former in hiring himself out to the latter. On the other hand, in several respects, including and aside from his far less conflicted tendency to "stir the pot," he is just as emphatically depicted as an only slightly more soiled and self-indulgent version of Robicheaux himself, from his eating and drinking habits to his exercise regime:

> He loved pizza, poor-boy sandwiches, deep-fried shrimp and oysters, dirty rice, *beignets*, ice cream, which he would eat with a tablespoon by the half gallon. He was convinced that he could control his weight by pumping iron every other night in his garage, and limit his ulcer damage by smoking Lucky Strikes through a cigarette filter and drinking his scotch with milk. (*A Morning for Flamingos*, p. 68)

If in Parker's Spenser series, Hawk's racial difference effectively functions as the dumpster into which both author and hero alike can toss all the text's most brutal pleasures, in Burke's novels Cletus performs an almost opposite function: in his very sleaziness, this white straight guy incarnates the connection between Robicheaux and his enemies, and the irresolvable instability of his position on the slippery continuum that binds him to them. So, for that matter, does local drug boss Tony Cardo in the very novel from which we have been quoting. For Tony too, like Robicheaux, is both unstrung by his memories of his time in Vietnam, and devoted to the child he seeks to protect at all costs. Before the book is done, Robicheaux will have listened to his confession of what he did over there, and provided him and his crippled son with an escape from both the big-time regional crime bosses up above him and the law.

Dave Robicheaux's sensitivity is thus a very different and a more complex aspect of his character than that displayed by either Kellerman's Alex Delaware or Parker's Spenser, despite the various celebrations of freed-up hedonistic consumption to be found in all the books in which the three of them appear. Where Delaware's and Spenser's sensitivity is both unproblematically positive and narcissistically self-regarding, Robicheaux's is openly riven by ambivalence, troubled by complicit desires and doubts, and obsessed with its old, unhealable wounds; where theirs are self-enclosed, his is explicitly defined by its connective affiliations to and with a continuum of others, from the various white male monsters whose terrible appetites he finds within himself, to the innocent vulnerability of those morally pure women, child, and Blacks he saves and protects.[40] Where their masculinities are paradigmatic ideal-projections of the new narcissistic and/or autonomous man, his is that of a man caught and constituted by the ceaseless tension between a Victorian paternalist-patriarchal idealism and its dialectical Other, the urge to get down with the rampaging monsters and go with the flow, and with the open acting-out of this tension in virtually every book.

The openly elaborated and conflicted sensitivity of our hero-in-recovery is, moreover, mapped over and overdetermined by a political allegory as well, one we may enter by noticing first of all what forces and figures are persistently referenced in Burke's novels without ever finding explicit figuration there. One, interestingly enough, in the novels of the late 1980s, is composed of those working for justice and human rights in El Salvador and Nicaragua, particularly North American religious workers, like the priest whose body Robicheaux finds at the beginning of *Heaven's Prisoners* (1988) in the cockpit of the submerged plane, together with the dead Salvadoran mother who sought escape from what the text plainly depicts as the genocidal violence being visited by the US-supported government on its helpless and innocent citizenry, and from whose arms Robicheaux manages to rescue the child Alafair. The parallel between such a depiction of the innocent Salvadoran people and Burke's paternalist characterizations of good women and Blacks is, I hope, too obvious to require more than a mention – as, I would also like to think, are the political limitations of a paternalist liberalism that recognizes only the moral superiority of those it deems "heaven's prisoners," that is, those victims "of greed and violence and political insanity" (p. 187) who do not possess, and who, implicitly, must not tarnish themselves by struggling to get, the collective power to defend themselves. Nonetheless, Burke deserves some credit for the moral sympathy his detective-hero extends to the oppressed, and the moral condemnation and distrust he expresses for the butchers in power in Washington and Central America alike.

All the more so, indeed, insofar as the latter are explicitly linked with the equally unseen criminal powers with whom they are in cahoots, to run drugs and guns back and forth from Central America, infiltrate the sanctuary movement, and provide aid to the Nicaraguan Contras. In *Heaven's Prisoners* these are the outside forces, for example, that Robicheaux discovers are backing Claudette, the wife of local Cajun kingpin Bubba Rocque, yet another brutal and brutalized poor-boy-gone-bad from Robicheaux's childhood, and, in *A Morning for Flamingos*, the boys from out of Houston who put out a hit on yet another of Robicheaux's mixed doubles, dirty damaged Tony Cardo. The malevolent effects of these evil powers are linked throughout Burke's fiction to those outside forces of capitalist development for which they serve as the chief instance:

> Over the years I had seen all the dark players get to southern Louisiana in one form or another: the oil and chemical companies who drained and polluted the wetlands; the developers who could turn sugarcane acreage and pecan orchards into miles of tract homes and shopping malls that had the aesthetic qualities of a sewer works; and the Mafia, who operated out of New Orleans and brought us prostitution, slot machines, control of at least two big labor unions, and finally narcotics. (*A Stained White Radiance* [1992], p. 32)

Present yet absent, working their effects on these novel's plots without ever appearing in them, the unseen big boys of organized crime serve precisely in their distance from the immediate scene and their lack of explicit figuration or incarnation as the synecdoche for the vast impersonal powers of late capitalism, systematically despoiling the land and corrupting the people Robicheaux loves. Indeed, Burke and his detective-hero even evince an awareness of the extent to which their preoccupation with the local low-lifes – a preoccupation that, as we have seen, is fueled by both the external dynamics of the plot and by Robicheaux's inner psychic contradictions – deflects attention from the real bad guys. Consider the following passage from *A Stained White Radiance* in which Robicheaux meditates on the typological significance of Eddie Raintree and the evil dwarf Fluck:

> Both men belonged to the great body of psychologically misshapen people that I refer to as the Pool. Members of the Pool leave behind warehouses of paperwork as evidence that they have occupied the planet for a certain period of time. Their names are entered early on in welfare case histories, child-abuse investigations, clinic admissions for rat bites and malnutrition. Later on these same people provide jobs for an army of truant officers, psychologists, public defenders, juvenile probation officers, ambulance attendants, emergency-room personnel, street cops, prosecutors, jailers, prison guards, alcohol- and drug-treatment counselors, bail bondsmen, adult parole authorities, and the county morticians who put the final punctuation mark in their files.
>
> The irony is that without The Pool we would probably have to justify our jobs by refocusing our attention and turning the key on slumlords, industrial polluters, and the coalition of defense contractors and militarists who look upon the national treasury as a personal slush fund. (p. 76)

But the irony is larger than that. After all, it is not just the exigencies of Robicheaux's job that keep his and our attention focused on these types, but the energy of Robicheaux's and Burke's psychic investment and interconnection with them, as external projections of subpersonalities at war within the riven man-in-recovery whose ongoing *psychomachia* is as much the subject of these books as the twists and turns of the external plots. In this sense, we could even go so far as to say that Robicheaux's wish to get to and attack the underlying forces of capitalist despoliation is not altogether sincere: such forces and Burke/Robicheaux's left-liberal condemnations of them *must* be held back on the outlying horizons of these novels precisely so that the defining and energizing psychic drama of yielding to violent impulse and upholding the Law, in a titanic struggle of intermingled, mutually constitutive Victorian superego and dirty-demon id, can be restaged yet again. We must repeat what we cannot master, as Doctor Freud said; if Robicheaux ever were to transcend his internal divisions and resolve his wounded ambivalence towards the viciousness and beauty of the Old South so that he could take up battle with the New, what alternative fuel source would have to charge the novels up, what new interests would propel us to read on?

Presently, I will turn to K.C. Constantine's work as one possible answer to this question; but before I do, it is time for a little summing-up of what we have discovered in our other three writers' works so far. First, we have seen that the types of masculine-as-mastery modeled in this fiction are distinctively different from those of the old Fordist model of the hard-boiled detective. Where the latter was premissed on the detective-hero's pristinely isolated distance from other characters and the *socius* in general, and from any hint of the feminine in particular, the new detective fiction of post-Fordist or Sonyist (or, just as significantly, post-oedipal and post-feminist) America tends to define the ideal masculinity of its heroes as an ongoing negotiation between the feminine and what we might say has now become the "hypermasculine": between sensitivity and enforcement, emotional openness and an even more brutal violence than that in which their forefathers indulged. Likewise, all three of our new-breed heroes enjoy a greater degree of connection and interrelation to the worlds they inhabit, through the relationships with significant others that are developed in the course of their series, and through a new indulgence that allows and even extolls their consumerized connoiseurship of the world as a type of sensual mastery in its own right.

This openly negotiated mastery-in-relation also obviously entails a more open engagement and interconnection with the social itself. Yet the second thematic under whose canvas we can heap up the results of our explorations must be that of the diminution and subordination of the *socius* in all these works. In Hammett's writings, the social is constructed as a vast Hobbesian landscape of grim functionaries and desperate scrabblers; in Chandler's, as a vast swirling whirlpool of temptations and dangers against which his lone heroic detective must stand tall. But in the work of these newer writers, despite echoes and intimations of these older constructions (for example, in the similarity of Hammett's world to that constructed by Parker, or Chandler's to those of Kellerman and Burke), the social appears primarily as a subset or accoutrement of the detective-hero himself. In Parker's novels, the world exists mainly as the thinly sketched setting for Spenser's various feats of prowess, as sensitive, emotionally discerning guy, tough mutha, and cultivated but unsnobbish connoisseur by turns – so thinly, in fact, that the appropriation of his main character as hero of a relatively successful network-TV series, *Spenser For Hire*, makes perfect sense. So too with Kellerman's far more lavishly described Southern California, which appears, as we have seen, mainly as a *laissez faire* playground for our yuppie-professional hero, and which, while benefitting from his sensitive therapeutic insights, must not be intervened in or manipulated, lest true evil be loosed on the land. And the liminal allusions to a left-liberal political perspective on the social in the novels of James Lee Burke are consistently marginalized by and subordinated to the construction of the social landscape as the projection of our Dave's tumultuous, riven psyche, outer mapping of all those investments, revulsions and resistances within his tortured mind.

Such transformations of the social in turn lead us to reflect on that operation by which they are most often warranted and effected within these books: that is, by what I want to call the therapization of both the hero and the *socius* alike. Burke's books provide the prime example of the recasting of the detective and his world as an intra-psychic field that must be ceaselessly renegotiated and remastered. But in Parker and Kellerman as well, the hero's concern for the social appears almost exclusively in the form of a discerning attention to the psychological and emotional disturbances of the client-victims whose causes they take up, and of the dysfunctional families that have deformed them; likewise, in both authors' works, virtually all attempts to intervene in or transform social conditions are stigmatized as a cover for the evil work of psychologically twisted, monstrous masterminds.

Here, then, is an aggregated ideal-type of the new man modeled in and promulgated by contemporary "soft-boiled" detective fiction: softened up and sensitized emotionally, freed-up sensually, and embedded to varying degrees within a psychologized *socius* to which he is therapeutically related, yet over which he still presides, despite his blockages and blemishes, and for all his occasional fallibility, by dint of his expanded expertise. To see how much the masculinity he models is akin to other white straight masculinities we have seen so far – in Axl Rose's acting-out, say, or in the rampaging sprees of Mel Gibson's Riggs and Bruce Willis's John McClane – we need hardly add that this new man is in many respects allowed to be all the more brutal than his forebears in the violence he inflicts, insofar as his impulses no longer need to be repressed. Similarly, we will see much the same intermingling of wildness and sensitivity under the sign and dispensation of the psychological when we move on to explore the subcultural intricacies of the "men's movement" that exploded on the scene a few years back. Moreover, in both these preceding chapters, this one, and the long one to follow, we have perhaps spent enough time reflecting on the ways such new masculinities have been formed under the pressure of feminist critique (backed, of course, by the massive entry of women into every sphere of public life), by the seismic social shifts attendant upon the ongoing transformation of the regime of capitalist accumulation from Fordism to post-Fordism or Sonyism, and by the flux and turmoil in the sex/gender systems of white middle-class America that both the former have provoked.

So, rather than expanding on these relations yet again, I will content myself with one brief foray into them. To return one last time to this thematic of therapization, and specifically to the way in which through its operations the new white straight masculinity is embedded in a de-politicized sociality that has been made safe for and subordinated to it: can we not hear in such transformations a weird echo of that slogan so fiercely held by and empowering to the women's movement of the late 1960s and early 1970s, and so culminative of all the New Left and countercultural movements of that time? I refer, of course, to "The Personal *Is* the Political" – a line to whose original "good sense" I still subscribe, and do still feel myself, together with the other folks with whom I work and live most closely, trying to live out. Yet, just as the Gramscian good sense inherent in the critique and renunciation of rigid oedipal models of masculinity and their stern delimitation of all that had been coded as too soft or sensitive for a full-fledged man to indulge has showed itself to be eminently open to hijacking by and into a newly expanded universe of commodified pleasures now open to all men and women with the jack to buy them, so too the good sense of "The Personal Is the Political" has been reworked and distorted under the torsions of Sonyist capitalism to make its logic run in reverse.

Hence even as I write these lines, and no doubt as you read them, an overworked and underpaid army of social workers and psychologists struggles to cope with a far larger population of "displaced" – that is, under- and unemployed – workers, all of whom seem to have contracted a variety of anxiety and substance-abuse disorders as their livelihoods are lost, their homes are threatened, and their neighborhoods give way to drugs, guns, gangs, and crime – in many places, including my own home town, the only growth industries around. (I need hardly add that the only check on the expansion of this newly dysfunctional client population is provided by a constant shrinkage in out- and in-patient insurance benefits attendant on the rise to power of the cost-cutting Health Maintenance Organization, and the ceaseless cutting of the social budget at the hands of our ever-vigilant state and federal governments.) For that matter, the USA itself is now governed by a President who himself is billed as the product of a dysfunctional family, and who is noted for his compassionate ability to feel our pain, even as he allows job programs to slide off the board, and considers various mean-spirited proposals to "reform welfare as we know it." And so, too, we white middle-class and professional folks are encouraged to enlist the kindred spirits of all our non-white and/or non-Western kin in the project of discovering and tapping into the empowering psychic energies of our deep, "essential" masculine or feminine selves, the twains of which we are now led to understand may draw nigh one another via various carefully regulated therapeutic rituals of shared drumming and the like, but which can neither know each other nor truly meet. Here and elsewhere, across the whole social landscape we inhabit, the discursive regime of the therapeutic is hard at work converting the new and old power relations alike to so many private, individual dysfunctions, the exploited and oppressed into so many pathologized deviants and victims; sensitizing us to cultural differences in lifestyle while inviting us to forget politics, opt for personal over collective empowerment or redistribution of power, and suspect the twisted motives of all those who still attempt to change the unchangeable way things are.[41]

In such a refigured, depoliticized universe, all three of the detectives we have concentrated on so far are fully at home; indeed, in such a world their opened up, sensitized masculinities are proffered, with all their psychic instabilities, sensual licenses, and relationships with others, as models of how today's white straight men may through negotiation still achieve and maintain a kind of mastery in relation to various non-white and/or non-male Others and within the *socius* itself. But what about our fourth hero, K.C. Constantine's Mario Balzic: to what extent does he model either this or some other, less hegemonic masculinity, and in what type of world and to what extent is he at home? I have already spoken of his main character's full immersion in the social, and of the carnivalesque and dialogic pleasure that is the main attraction of his books. To bring this chapter to a close, then, I will provide additional evidence of these features and bring them into conjunction with other distinctive aspects and elements of Constantine's work, primarily by describing two of his best works in some detail.

The two I have in mind, *The Man Who Liked Slow Tomatoes* (1982) and *Always a Body to Trade* (1983), are somewhat atypical of Constantine's work, insofar as in both our hero's involvement with a single case is allowed to proceed with relatively few interruptions or digressions. Constantine's next book, *Upon Some Midnights Clear* (1985), would be pretty much devoid of any narrative "through-line" whatsoever, its plot consisting instead of Mario's attempts to deal with various acute or slowly simmering crises here and there across his gradually disintegrating town and in his home life through the Christmas holidays. In most of the other Balzic books, the central case and Mario's pursuit of a solution to it has to pinball its way around and past a host of other flare-ups and aggravations that force themselves on this perpetually aggrieved and overworked police chief's attention and our own. In *Slow Tomatoes*, though, Mario has only a few other fires to put out, and so is able to devote himself more or less singlemindedly to the problem of what has happened to Jimmy Romanelli, the unemployed young coal miner who is Frances's husband and patriarch Mike Fiori's son-in-law, and who now seems to have disappeared without a trace. And in *Always a Body to Trade*, too, Mario is left pretty well free to pursue the question of who the young woman was who participated in a pair of break-ins into two cross-town apartments and the abduction of their occupant-of-record, drug dealer Thurman "Red Dog" Burns, and who later on that same day shot her and left her body on the street.

But only comparatively free, relatively unimpeded in both cases: in all kinds of ways and at every other moment, the centrifugal energies of the full *socius* exert their pressure on our hero's movements and actions. In *Slow Tomatoes*, to choose just one example, Balzic also has to pay the price at home for drinking too much wine and falling asleep in his chair with the TV on, in the coin of his Italian mother's not-so-gentle hectoring, and the renewed twitching of conscience over his neglect of his wife and family. Likewise at the opening of *Always a Body*, in exchange for keeping his officer Rugsy Carlucci running down information on the burglaries, abduction, and murder that have just taken place, he reluctantly agrees to make a call to Carlucci's mother to say her son is too busy to come by. Moreover, throughout the latter book, Balzic is burdened by the un-welcome attentions of Rocksburg's new, obtusely idealistic mayor, Kenny Strohn, who assaults him with a barrage of stupid recommendations (for example, instituting a mandatory program of physical training for his officers) and obstructs his attempts to leverage the shady edges of the legal system as he improvises his way to solving the crime. Finally, too, we must take note of all those often prolonged and perfectly typical stretches in both books in which our hero just runs out of leads or steam. Here, for example, is Mario in a Rocksburg drug store, running out of both:

> He went to a clerk who was chewing bubble gum and buffing her fingernails, and asked her for change for a dollar bill. She acted as though she could tolerate his imposition, but only barely. She placed the change on the counter without a word, and went back to her nails.
>
> Balzic was tempted to respond to her rudeness, but thought better of it. He scooped up his change on the counter without so much as a glance in the clerk's direction.
>
> He checked his address and phone book for the number of the Bureau of Drug Enforcement, dialed it, asked for Agent Russell, and was told that Russell was out of the office and wasn't expected back until five or so. The speaker asked if there was a message.
>
> Balzic said there was not, and hung up. He rubbed his chin and then his lips and then his forehead. He could have rubbed his entire body, for all it mattered; he didn't have the faintest idea what to do next. And when he didn't know what to do, he headed for the place where not knowing what to do was best done, and that was Muscotti's Bar and Grille. (*Always a Body to Trade* [1983], pp. 74–75)

So for the next six pages or so we'll get the scene at Muscotti's, where Vinnie the bartender is bitching about the building's other tenants' bitching to him because the heating system has gone on the blink, and Iron City Steve is going on about the nature and existence of God while Mario is trying to enjoy his wine, until somebody calls from the station to job him grudgingly back to work again.

Certainly none of our other authors – indeed, no other author that I know of in contemporary detective fiction – stoops to such a level of pointedly quotidian, even banal registration; nor does any other affect and deploy such a flatly declarative, "zero-degree" style. Such foregrounded verbal performances as there are in Constantine's works belong to his characters and are to be found, as we have already seen, in their speech, to which his narrations and descriptions simply function as informative integumenta, the anonymous writer (K.C. Constantine is the pseudonym, we are told at the back of these books, of a man who "lives in Pennsylvania and belongs to the world Mario Balzic lives in") simply doing his workaday job. In this sense, albeit perversely, Constantine himself is like our other authors, whose poses on their various book jackets – James Lee Burke and Robert Parker, tall strapping guys with their big arms akimbo, sloe-eyed Jonathan Kellerman with his soft, sensitive hair – invite us to conflate them with their main characters. Only here the transparency of his prose and the anonymity of his authorship insist on the democratic equivalence of author and hero as guys too ordinary to require description: both are the kind of guy who sometimes gets snubbed by drug-store clerks when he tries to get change and rubs his face when he doesn't particularly know what to do next.

Such a white straight guy is, I need hardly add, scarcely an avatar of proper male consciousness; or if he is, it is only by dint of Mario's always improvised, flawed attempts in his personal and work life alike, to do the often disappointing best he can. In his personal life, as we have seen, he constantly juggles the demands of his public responsibilities and bread-winner obligations against the needs of his family, amid the recriminations of his live-in mother and, especially after the mother's death, his increasingly – and, we are clearly invited to think, justifiably – disgruntled wife Ruth. And a similar sense of rather desperate moment-by-moment bricolage characterizes Mario's attempts to do his job. We have already noted how often he has to switch from one case or crisis to another, bandaging or postponing one situation to run off to something else, or rubbing his face and sliding off to Muscotti's. But even his detective work on the central case and its results often enough leaves something to be desired. In *The Man Who Liked Slow Tomatoes*, for example, Balzic's efforts to investigate the missing Jimmy Romanelli's connections with a state-wide drug-dealing operation turn out to be both misguided and damaging – far more so, we might add, than those of the other detectives in any of the other books we have discussed. When, following the confidential lead he has wormed out of his contact at the state Bureau of Drug Enforcement, Mario pays a visit to the old roadhouse where these new low-lifes hang out, he blows the cover on the state's investigation, sours his BDE connection, and brings the contact's blustering new boss down screaming on his butt. Moreover, when at the end of this visit, he indulges in a rare fit of violence by rolling up his car window on the young gunsel who has been threatening and ridiculing him, Balzic is quick to recognize his action as "one of the stupider things he had ever done," something that "only satisfied him emotionally" (p. 104). Constantine implicitly both lets that verdict stand and lets his hero off the hook by dropping the matter there, without any of the further repercussions or consequences Mario quite justly worries he might have to deal with from now on.

The contrast of such behavior and its effects with that of our other detective-heroes old and new is so stark that it scarcely requires any further elaboration: while the latter's violence is always significantly consequential, even when (in Burke's work) it is coded as mistake, here and throughout Constantine's writings the hero's violence is viewed as reprehensible, stupid, and with luck, irrelevant to the matter at hand; while their investigations are smoothly linked and invariably productive, his sporadic, faltering efforts often enough only lead to dead ends. Moreover, when Balzic does finally discover or improvise a solution to the main mystery that concerns him, it frequently either fails to prevent further damage or wrongdoing, or to answer all the questions raised. In *Slow Tomatoes*, the tip-off he finally gets from Mike Fiori's senile neighbor that leads Mario to find Jimmy Romanelli's body planted in the old man's garden solves the mystery of Jimmy's disappearance; but this solution only brings about the beleaguered Frances's suicide followed by the old man's death. Likewise, in *Always a Body to Trade*, though Balzic is finally able to bring the men behind the break-ins, the abduction, and the murder of the anonymous woman to justice, he is never able to find out who she was. Moreover, he only learns what he does and resolves what he can through various morally and even legally suspect efforts – for example, booking and jailing suspects on charges that will not stand up in court, then taunting and threatening them until one cracks, and, together with a colleague from the feds, hammering out a sleazy deal with a couple of very bad guys who stop by to trade some information for a clean sheet – and with the aid of one Rev. Rufee Feeler, community leader and criminal chieftain from the Black side of town.

In fact, the final revelation of this latter novel is that of the degree to which the corrupt Reverend has been playing Mario himself all along. So just as Mario has had to explain to his naive mayor the variously speckled means by which deals are really struck and convictable evidence obtained, Mario himself must receive instruction from Rufee as to how and why he was fed a bogus story about the corrupt white Drug Enforcement boys he has brought to justice with Rufee's help. The story concerned how the head of the Drug Enforcement team not only had been ripping off local drug dealers and making them pay protection fees, but had actually raped and tortured two Black girls just for kicks. Here is Rufee, chuckling over Balzic's shock and anger and the mayor's consternation at finding out the rape and torture part was a pure-D lie:

> "And there you stand, Balzic, lookin' like a motherfuckin' jive honky, trying to get yourself in order. Balzic, how was I goin' do it without chu? I went your way, mon. I went the way of law and motherfucking order. I just came in the back-door, that's all. Shee-it. Us niggers been usin' that door a long time. Now why you lookin' at the floor? Balzic, the good guys won! All you got to do is 'splain to Mr. Mayor here, that's all. Mr. Mayor need to know how this shit works."
> (*Always a Body to Trade*, p. 237)

The point is that for all his exasperated sermons throughout the book to his new mayor, Balzic himself has not known enough about "how this shit works" to claim full control or knowledge of the investigation he has just successfully completed. Behind his back and to his face alike, Feeler has been working the levers and pulling the strings the whole time. Clearly enough, the Reverend Feeler's exultant baiting at the close of *Always a Body to Trade* emphasizes and invites us to enjoy with him the kind of limited, incomplete, and sometimes downright inadequate mastery that characterizes Balzic's distinctively drab heroism throughout the series, and that stands in such a striking contrast to the completely achieved mastery of our other detectives over both their plots and their *récits* (in which respect, moreover, the Balzic series is the only one of those we have examined written in third-person).

But just as clearly it invites us to consider the equally imperfect state of Balzic's own racial attitudes towards African-Americans as well. In *Always a Body to Trade*, and in several other books as well, these attitudes are depicted and examined with some precision. On the one hand, Balzic is clearly shown to be less racist than many if not most of the other white townspeople with whom he has to work and deal. As early as *The Man Who Liked to Look at Himself* (1973), he confronts one of his young white officers with his suspicions that the officer is racist, and orders him to report to a Black psychologist to work on the problem. In *Upon Some Midnights Clear* (1985), the diatribes of Reaganite racism that pour out of the mouths of the town's fire chief and the white working-class woman whose bogus cause the chief has taken up inspire in Balzic only a weary disgust. But weary disgust, it turns out, is not enough; nor is it enough for Balzic to stop the woman's racist allegations against "the nigger" that supposedly mugged her. For by the time he does so, they have already been circulated widely enough to prompt a few of his local bad-boy whites to jump a young Black bad boy named Billie Lum, beat him up and partially castrate him. Likewise in *Always a Body to Trade*, where, as throughout the series, Balzic's comparatively enlightened racial attitudes do not prevent him from using words like "nigger" and "spook," until he talks on the phone to a Black prison guard who soberly informs him twice that "'I do not like that word'" (p. 227); and even then, the correction does not dissuade Mario from playing on a white suspect's racist fears of what the big Black men will do to him in jail to get the suspect to crack and finger his buddies in order to plea-bargain his way out of a stretch.

Nor, for that matter, and as we already know from his dereliction of his domestic responsibilities and emotional neglect of his wife and mother, is Balzic offered to us as anything like a perfect version of the pro-feminist man. The best that can be said of his gender politics is about the same as can be said of his racial attitudes: that he is better than many of the other male characters we meet, and that he is still in process and open to change. *The Man Who Liked Slow Tomatoes* amply demonstrates both Mario's relative superiority and his limitations with regard to gender. On the one hand, as we have seen, he listens sympathetically to Frances Romanelli's eloquent complaints against her father and her husband. On the other hand, though, he is markedly reluctant to give full credit to the portrait she paints of her father Mike Fiori as a harsh, unloving man. Mario remembers, and is clearly invested in remembering, Fiori as the staunch union stalwart who liked to sit drinking wine and talking union politics with his own father, before he died when Mario was still a child. But before the book is done, Mario will have to confront the fact that even this rose-colored memory is wrong, and Frances is right. Convinced of his own self-righteousness, this utterly impenitent patriarch has taken it upon himself to kill Frances's husband for beating his wife. When Mario confronts him with his crime, he responds by jeering at both the father he remembers as a weak-willed softie, and "'the mess you father makea'" of Mario himself:

"Every-a-time makea see this, see that, see top, see bottom, see backa side, fronta side, no mess, huh? You life's alla confuse."

Balzic blew out a long, heavy sigh. "Only when I run into people like you, Mr. Fiori. But I'll work it out. I don't know how just yet, and it may take me a long time, but I'll work it out. Either by myself or with somebody's help." (*The Man Who Liked Slow Tomatoes*, p. 166)

Insofar as our markedly imperfect protagonist can be considered a political hero-ideal or exemplary man at all, it is in just this sense and to this extent: insofar as he is trying, by himself and with the help of those around him, to work it out day by day as best as he can.

Before we leave *Slow Tomatoes*, there is one more aspect of its workings and thematics we should mark as exemplary of the series as a whole — and, again, as quite distinct from the workings of the other new detective fiction we have read here. For in this book, as in the whole series, an altogether different set of relations obtains between the psychological and the social, the inner life of the mind and the inner world of the family, and the other world of the socioeconomic structure and public life, than that we have seen modeled and staged in the works of Kellerman, Parker, and Burke. To characterize that relationship with a few phrases and a single example is, in fact, a challenging task, given the complexity and quietly understated surefootedness of Constantine's depictions, all the more so because the only word I can think of that catches the weave of their interaction is apt to be dismissed out of hand these days as the outmoded jargon of yesterday's obscurantist Marxist hacks. I refer, of course, to the word *dialectical*, here in the sense of a movement and relationship between two planes or entities that are simultaneously co-constitutive and interpenetrating, yet autonomously determined and separately developed and developing as well.

Bear with me, then, while I try to show how *Slow Tomatoes* models such a relationship between the psychic-familial and the socioeconomic. I hope I have already demonstrated the extent to which the former is registered in the text: in the anguish and despair that will ultimately drive Frances to end her doubly oppressed life; in the rigid patriarchal superego of her cruel father; and even, for that matter, in the wild acting-out of the husband whom we never see. Likewise, I hope it is clear enough by now that the primary vehicle in these texts for the expression of these feelings and the revelation of their inner dynamics is the vibrantly particularized speech of the characters themselves. If so, what then remains to be noted and characterized is the way that vibrancy and all its psycho-emotional resonances play off against Constantine's doggedly flat and faceless rendering of what Sartre called the "practico-inert": that whole obdurate complex of all that has already been built and is already given, from the streets and buildings that must be lived in, to the jobs that once were there and now are gone, and all the history-that-hurts which goes with them.

> He [Balzic] looked at the small clapboard houses on both sides of the street.
>
> They were one of the hundreds of coal patches in Conemaugh County, all built in the late nineteenth and early twentieth centuries when deep mining for bituminous coal was second only to farming as an industry. This patch, Kennedy Township, was incorporated as a township rather than a village only because some earlier inhabitant had gotten political ambitions, more likely for himself than for his village, and had persuaded enough of his neighbors to agree with him that their patch ought to be called a township instead of a village. He probably was among the first elected supervisors.
>
> Whatever the coal patches were called now – company towns, villages, townships, patches – there were two major differences from what they had been. Now, the houses were privately owned because, now, there was no more coal coming out of the ground. It was easy enough to recognize those two facts. What was not easy to recognize was the change of attitude over the generations about who owned the property and how it was to be cared for, both financially and physically.
>
> Balzic glanced around in the rapidly failing light of dusk. Across the street was a house with three cars parked on the grass, two on one side and one on the other – all the cars six to eight years old, all with their rear ends higher than their fronts, with dual exhaust pipes and wide tires with white lettering on the sidewalls, and with body colors that ranged from the seemingly careless gray of primer paint to the outrageous sheen of metalflake orange or yellow. Balzic could not be sure of the colors. One thing he was sure of: the house sandwiched between the cars seemed on the verge of collapse. (*The Man Who Liked Slow Tomatoes*, pp. 25–6)

My quotation, long as it is, represents less than half of the entire passage, which goes on for more than another page before the action resumes; but you can trust me that what follows is more of the same. And I trust, in turn, that I have quoted enough here to convey such writing's qualities: its drab impersonality and doggedly exact recounting of history and retailing of salient features. I have already spoken of the way the emphatic anonymity of such a narrative style generally contributes to our sense of Balzic and Constantine alike as common workaday men. But there is something more to say now about the function and effects of such writing as it is congealed into concrete slabs of socioeconomic description we must traverse more or less literally on our way into the next house, and the psychologically revealing, verbally energetic speech-performance of whoever lives there. In this case, we are on our way to hear Frances herself, whose manic speech we quoted some pages earlier; and the point I want to make here is simply that, having read the long, drab typological description of the coal patch she lives in, we cannot but understand her speech within the historical, economic and cultural context that description provided; yet the energy, vitality and rich particularity of that speech prevent us from conflating it or the anguish it expresses with that context in any crudely naturalistic way. Frances's problems are emblematic, perhaps even paradigmatic, of the problems of working-class white women in such a context; but the antipodal relationship of the dead, factual prose of the practico-inert to the desperate liveliness of her unforgettably individualized speech keeps reminding us that her problems are, as lived, as psychological as they are social, and as vividly and inescapably personal as they are drearily, ineluctably collective.

In just this manner throughout the Balzic series, Constantine stages the interaction of the psychological-individual and the socio-historical, the private and the public, with a characteristically quiet and self-effacing brilliance as the ongoing and untotalizable dialectic between two "torn halves" of a social universe "to which however they do not add up."[42] And it is this staging above all that makes these books such exemplary progressive political fictions for us today, in the dotted lines they draw between a vivid parade of familial dysfunctions that demand therapeutic insight and intervention, and the grim forced march of historical, political, and economic forces that can only be halted and changed by a new mobilized collective will and grievously hard and protracted political work. I hasten to add that, except in the case of Constantine's newest (and, it must be said, least successful) book, *Bottom-Liner Blues* (1993), no explicitly political notes are struck in his work; readers of his books hear no calls to arms, nor are they harangued with any strident critiques. But just as Mario Balzic himself models only an unfinished, unmastered and unmastering masculinity-in-process, rather than the neo-masterful masculinity-in-relation whose aggregate portrait we have derived from the works of Kellerman, Parker, and Burke, so too his books' modelings of the *socius* we live in doggedly resist the subsumption of the social into the therapeutic, while granting the latter its own sectoral legitimacy and truth, and implicitly leave the political question of what can and will happen radically open and up to us.

Will the model of masculinity-in-process offered by Constantine's Balzic as he flails around improvising his way, getting it wrong sometimes but at other times getting better by degrees, be one with which other straight white men will want to identify, to claim and use to help them describe themselves? For that matter, will it be one, is it one, that white feminist and post-feminist women and non-white people care to recognize and at least partially endorse? And how about the model of the *socius* that goes with it, the one his fiction offers us all as a way of thinking the familial and the social, the sex/gender system and the socioeconomic, psychological dysfunction and social "restructuring" against and together with each other? On the one hand, it hardly seems likely, with Alex Delaware, Dave Robicheaux and Parker around – not to mention their actually existing would-be counterparts out here in the ever more therapized and de-politicized world beyond the text. On the other hand, though, there the Balzic series rests alongside those others, at my local Barnes & Noble Superstore, and across the way at the new and even bigger Borders (great art, said Whitman, requires great audiences...). There are even, or so I like to think, some other unmasterful white straight men here and there outside those books, and at least the tattered remnants or glowing embers of a more politicized *socius* here and there as well. It all comes down, I suppose, to the question of what we decide we want to believe in and work for, into what models and sources we choose to dive for our assumptions and pleasures, and which of these we eschew and which we push further. Right now, when it comes to white straight men, it seems to me that these are – for each and all of us, both individually and in our various classed, raced, gendered, and sexualized tribes – still entirely open questions at best.

NOTES

1. Ann Snitow, "Mass Market Romance: Pornography for Women Is Different," in Ann Snitow, Christine Stansell, and Sharon Thompson, eds., *Powers of Desire: The Politics of Sexuality* (New York: Monthly Review Press, 1983), pp. 245–63; Tania Modleski, *Loving with a Vengeance: Mass-produced Fantasies for Women* (New York and London: Methuen, 1982), pp. 35–84; and Janice Radway, *Reading the Romance: Women, Patriarchy, and Popular Literature* (Chapel Hill: University of North Carolina Press, 1984).

2. McKenzie Wark, "From Fordism to Sonyism: Perverse Readings of the New World Order," *New Formations* 15 (Winter 1991), p. 44.

3. "The Simple Art of Murder," from *The Simple Art of Murder* (New York: Vintage, 1978), p. 18.

4. Quoted in William F. Nolan, *Dashiell Hammett: A Casebook* (Santa Barbara: McNally and Loftin, 1969), p. ix.

5. John G. Cawelti, *Adventure, Mystery, and Romance: Formula Stories as Art and Popular Culture* (Chicago: University of Chicago Press, 1976), pp. 139–161. All those who know Cawelti's groundbreaking survey of the field will recognize my debts to this work throughout the section that follows.

6. Dashiell Hammett, *Red Harvest* (New York: Vintage/Black Lizard, 1992), p. 85.

7. David Geherin, *The American Private Eye: The Image in Fiction* (New York: Frederick Ungar Publishing, 1985), p. 22.

8. Frank Krutnik, *In a Lonely Street: Film Noir, Genre, Masculinity* (New York and London: Routledge, 1991), p. 43.

9. *Red Harvest*, p. 3.

10. Raymond Chandler, *The Big Sleep* (New York: Vintage Books, 1988), p. 3.

11. For this point, I am indebted to David Reid and Jayne L. Walker, "Strange Pursuit: Cornell Woolrich and the Abandoned City of the Forties," in Joan Copjec, ed., *Shades of Noir* (London and New York: Verso, 1993), pp. 66–69.

12. For the historic contestation between the vision of the "middle-class Republic" and the "producers," see Michael Denning, *Mechanic Accents* (London and New York: Verso, 1987), pp. 45–6; and for a glimpse of the former vision as promulgated in mainstream literary culture in the 1920s and '30s, see my "Montage Dynasty," in *Another Tale to Tell* (London and New York: Verso, 1990), particularly pp. 151–61. Finally, see Mike Davis's insightful comments on middle-class *ressentiment* in Los Angeles and its literary expression in the hard-boiled fiction of Chandler and others, in the first chapter of his *City of Quartz* (London and New York: Verso, 1990), pp. 17–54.

13. Marc Vernet, "*Film Noir* on the Edge of Doom," in Copjec, ed., p. 29 n. 38.

14. Dean MacCannell, "Democracy's Turn: On Homeless *Noir*," in Copjec, p. 287.

15. For a lucid summary of feminist critiques of the Hegelian Subject and his relations to the world, and of feminist alternatives to them, see Kathy E. Ferguson, *The Man Question: Visions of Subjectivity in Feminist Theory* (Berkeley, CA: University of California Press, 1993), pp. 36–68 and passim.

16. Krutnik, *In a Lonely Street*, p. 128. Krutnik's analysis of hard-boiled fiction as "an emphatic process of masculinization" (p. 42) has been an inspiration throughout the following pages of this section.

17. Ibid., p. 43.

18. In, for example, "The Simple Art of Murder"; see pp. 14–17.

19. Cawelti, p. 176.

20. Raymond Chandler, *Farewell, My Lovely* (New York: Vintage Books, 1988), p. 43.

21. *Red Harvest*, p. 164.

22. Fredric Jameson, "The Synoptic Chandler," in Copjec, ed., p. 37.

23. As, for example, in the following passage from *Farewell, My Lovely*, which contains more than its share:

I felt for the white stool and sat down and put my head down on the white table beside the milky globe which was now shining again softly. I stared at it side-

ways, my face on the table. The light fascinated me. Nice light, soft light.
Behind me and around me there was nothing but silence.

I think I went to sleep, just like that, with a bloody face on the table, and
a thin beautiful devil with my gun in his hand watching me and smiling. (pp.
94–5)

24. Klaus Theweleit, *Male Fantasies: Women, Floods, Bodies, History*, vol. I, trans. Stephen
Conway et al. (Minneapolis: University of Minnesota Press, 1987), pp. 3–228.

25. *The Big Sleep*, p. 133.

26. Andreas Huyssen, "Mass Culture: Modernism's Other," in Tania Modleski, ed.,
Studies in Entertainment: Critical Approaches to Mass Culture (Bloomington: Indiana University
Press, 1986), p. 196.

27. Dashiell Hammett, *The Maltese Falcon* (New York: Vintage Books, 1972), p. 226.

28. Dashiell Hammett, *The Dain Curse* (New York: Vintage Books, 1962), p. 61.

29. My terminology and my general understanding of Fordism are derived from
Michel Aglietta, *A Theory of Capitalist Regulation: The US Experience*, trans. David Fernbach
(London: New Left Books, 1979).

30. The terms "deterritorialization" and "reterritorialization" come to me from the
work of Deleuze and Guattari, especially *A Thousand Plateaus: Capitalism and Schizophre-
nia*, trans. Brian Massumi (Minneapolis: University of Minnesota Press, 1987). But my
use of them here owes more to the essays by Fredric Jameson and Jean Franco in
Marshall Blonsky, ed., *On Signs* (Oxford: Basil Blackwell, 1985): respectively, "The Realist
Floor-Plan," pp. 373–83, and "Killing Priests, Nuns, Women, and Children," pp. 414–20.

31. This last phrase is a quotation from Frederick Wiseman's unforgettable documentary *High School* (1968), uttered proudly by a high-school teacher reading a letter
home from a graduate of Northeast High School now on active duty in the Vietnam
War.

32. In her *Brave New Families: Stories of Domestic Upheaval in Late Twentieth Century
America* (New York: Basic Books, 1990), Stacey defines "post-feminism" as those ideologies which have been influenced by feminism even as they insist on their difference,
and distance, from it – as in "the gender consciousness and strategies of vast numbers
of contemporary women and men [who are] subscribers to the doctrine, 'I'm not a
women's libber, but...'" (p. 19).

33. The following is a list of the books I read by each author, in chronological order
by date of first publication. Where relevant, I have listed the original date of publication
in brackets when citing the publication information for the later edition I read. Hence-
forward, references to individual works by these authors will be given in the text, with
page numbers corresponding to the editions listed here.

Works by Robert B. Parker: *The Godwulf Manuscript* (New York: Dell Publishing, 1987
[1973]); *God Save the Child* (New York: Dell Publishing, 1987 [1974]); *Mortal Stakes* (Bos-
ton: Houghton Mifflin, 1975); *The Judas Goat* (New York: Dell Publishing, 1987 [1978]);
Looking for Rachel Wallace (New York: Dell Publishing, 1987 [1980]); *Early Autumn* (New
York: Dell Publishing, 1987 [1981]; *Ceremony* (New York: Dell Publishing, 1987 [1982]);
The Widening Gyre (New York: Delacorte Press, 1983); *Valediction* (New York: Delacorte
Press, 1984); *A Catskill Eagle* (New York: Delacorte Press, 1985); *Pale Kings and Princes*
(New York: Dell Publishing, 1988 [1987]); *Stardust* (New York: G.P. Putnam's Sons,

1990); *Pasttime* (New York: G.P. Putnam's Sons, 1991); *Double Deuce* (New York: G.P. Putnam's Sons, 1992).

Works by K.C. Constantine: *The Rocksburg Railroad Murders* and *The Blank Page* (Boston: David R. Godine, 1982 [1972 and 1974, respectively]); *The Man Who Liked to Look at Himself* (New York: Garland, 1983 [1973]); *The Man Who Liked Slow Tomatoes* (Boston: David R. Godine, 1993 [1982]); *Always a Body to Trade* (Boston: David R. Godine, 1993 [1983]); *Upon Some Midnights Clear* (Boston: David R. Godine, 1985); *Joey's Case* (New York: Mysterious Press, 1988); *Sunshine Enemies* (New York: Mysterious Press, 1991 [1990]); *Bottom-Liner Blues* (New York: Mysterious Press, 1994 [1993]).

Works by Jonathan Kellerman: *When the Bough Breaks* (New York: Signet Books, 1986 [1985]); *Blood Test* (New York: Atheneum, 1986); *Over the Edge* (New York: Signet Books, 1988 [1987]); *Silent Partner* (New York: Bantam Books, 1989); *Time Bomb* (New York: Bantam Books, 1991 [1990]); *Private Eyes* (New York: Bantam Books, 1992).

Works by James Lee Burke: *The Neon Rain* (New York: Pocket Books, 1988 [1987]); *Heaven's Prisoners* (New York: Pocket Books, 1989 [1988]); *Black Cherry Blues* (New York: Avon Books, 1990 [1989]); *A Morning for Flamingos* (New York: Avon Books, 1991 [1990]); *A Stained White Radiance* (New York: Hyperion, 1992); *In the Electric Mist with Confederate Dead* (New York: Avon Books, 1994 [1993]).

34. Two sample instances, plucked randomly from Parker's and Burke's work respectively, will make my point, especially in the admixture of the other narcissistic pleasures of the text I have just described.

It is hilly country around Wheaton. No mountains but a steady up and downness to the terrain that makes a five-mile run in the morning a significant workout. Susan had given me one of those satiny-looking warm-up outfits for Christmas and I was wearing it, with a .32 S&W zipped up in the right-hand jacket pocket...

My new jogging suit was a shiny black with red trim. I felt like Little Lord Fauntleroy chugging along. I had on brand-new Avia running shoes, oyster white with a touch of charcoal that understated the black jogging suit. I didn't have crimson leg warmers. Maybe for my birthday.

Back at the motel, loose, warm, full of oxygen, I did some push-ups and sit-ups in my room and took a shower. At quarter of ten I was in my car heading into downtown Wheaton. I had my Colt Python in a shoulder holster under my leather jacket. Since I'm a size 48 and so is the Python, I'd had to shop extensively to find a leather jacket that fit over both of us. (*Pale Kings and Princes* [1987], pp. 41–2)

I put on my gym trunks and running shoes and pumped iron in the backyard. I did dead lifts, curls, and military presses with a ninety-pound bar in sets of ten and repeated the sets six times. Then I ran four miles along the dirt road by the bayou, the sunlight spinning like smoke through the canopy of oak and cypress trees overhead. Bream were still feeding on insects among the cattails and lily pads, and sometimes in a shady cut between two cypress trees I would see the back of a large-mouth bass roll just under the surface. (*Black Cherry Blues* [1989], pp. 10–11)

35. Barbara Ehrenreich, *The Hearts of Men: American Dreams and the Flight from Commitment* (New York: Doubleday, 1983), p. 143.

36. Kathleen Gerson, *No Man's Land: Men's Changing Commitments to Family and Work* (New York: Basic Books, 1993), pp. 141–81 and passim, where Gerson views this orientation alongside the persistence of the breadwinner-provider ethic on the one hand, and new models of interdependence and equal partnership on the other.

37. At the climax of *A Catskill Eagle* (1985) – surely the most spectacularly unsublimated of Parker's novels in the violence it stages and the transcontinentally gothic landscape of corrupt power it constructs – Spenser finds his way to the lair of the evil Costigan family via a secret tunnel that leads him under and through a mountain, and issues out into the terrible wife/mother's closet, from which he sees her "face ... squinched up like a withered apple, a trace of saliva ... at one corner of her mouth, and her posture ... bunched up like a fist" (p. 243).

38. Byzantine, that is, insofar as it turns out that Nona is not mad Garland Swope's daughter, as he thinks, but the child of a brief affair between his wife Ellen and the local Sheriff, Raymond Houten – who himself, in turn, has sex with the compulsively nymphomaniacal girl without knowing that he is committing incest, causing further complications in the novel's typically convoluted and distended plot.

39. Theweleit, *Male Fantasies*; and Peter Stallybrass and Allon White, *The Politics and Poetics of Transgression* (Ithaca, New York: Cornell University Press, 1986).

40. The racist paternalism of this portraiture of so many gentle and/or primitive Black people serving, by the way, throughout Burke's work, to balance the occasional appearance of more viciously racist images: for example, Robicheaux's nightmare conjuration of "an enormous black man in a child's T-shirt, in lavender slacks at least three sizes too small for him, so that his scrotum was outlined like a bag of metal washers, squatted down with a .410 pistol resting on his thigh ... toothless, his lips purple with snuff, his eyes red-rimmed, his breath rank with funk" (*A Morning for Flamingos*, p. 21).

41. For a rare critique from within the profession of the complicity of contemporary psychotherapy with other forces and processes generated by "Sonyist" capitalism in the production and maintenance of depoliticized "life-styled" selves, see Philip Cushman, "Why the Self Is Empty: Toward a Historically Situated Psychology," *American Psychologist* 45, 5 (May 1990), pp. 599–611.

42. I borrow the phrase in quotation marks from Adorno's tonic warnings to Benjamin against the conflation of the psychic materials of the artistic imagination with the material realities of the outer world, in the correspondence quoted in Ernst Bloch et al., *Aesthetics and Politics* (London and New York: Verso, 1977), p. 123.

CHAPTER FIVE

GUERRILLAS IN THE
MIST: WILD GUYS AND
NEW AGE TRIBES

Those readers who have made it this far will not have failed to notice the comparatively detached tone of the preceding chapters, whose analyses have tended to roll out as though I were safely set apart from and above whatever texts I happened to be reading. Such an appearance is partly enabled by the degree to which I have been able to treat the objects of study in those chapters *as* objects, or at least as relatively delimited fields defined and structured by specifiable meaning-effects. But the men's movement of the late 1980s and early 1990s in the USA, however many commodities and column inches it may have spun off, does not really offer itself up for inspection in this way; to take it as a single object, even a contradictory and disunified one, would be a mistake. Rather, the men's movement is better defined as an inherently unstable and variegated set of vertiginously alternative discourses and practices arising out of a structure of feeling located on a particular patch of sociopolitical ground in the contemporary United States. Such a phenomenon calls less for analysis and description of an operative system of interactive thematic positions than the area-mapping and archaeology of a particular *domain* – a work more familiar to sociology and anthropology than to the kind of text-based cultural criticism that has been practiced through this book thus far.

Yet this change in the nature of the subject, and therefore of the mode of its analysis, is not all that makes this chapter different from the rest of the book; there is the matter of my own complicity as well – *complicity*, from the Latin *complexus*, past participle of *complecti*, to encircle or embrace – with the practices I describe, my own location on the terrain I survey.

However much I may wish to disclaim membership in this men's move-ment, I cannot deny having been not only a spy but a "native witness" of it, and close kin to its core constituency. The structure of feeling that fuels the men's movement is one I have experienced as well as observed; its social and cultural domain is, in many respects, the country I come from as well. It seems only right, then, to steer this book towards its end by charting my way around, within, and through a place where many of the themes and contradictions explored in the preceding pages have shown up and imposed themselves on their author as personal perplexities and up-close discomforts, where the chickens have – and do – come home to roost.

1. WISDOMS OF THE TEXTS

To commence this more open-ended project, I propose a brief tour of a few of the most influential texts produced, as it were, under the sign of the men's movement: not to "read off" the movement from the pages of these texts, as though the relation between the two were that of theory on the one hand, application in practice on the other, but to use them as a relatively fixed and firm staging area where we may equip ourselves to enter that more diffuse and fluid space in which the movement acts itself out.

This is not to suggest, however, that this literature is itself of one mind. Reading in and across it has more than once given me a taste of the same headachey blur that assails any eyewitness trying to track all the ideological organelles swimming in the soup of the movement's meetings, conferences, and retreats. But for now, let us hold the blur at bay, and risk being overly schematic. In the four texts I will be discussing here, and in practically every piece of movement literature I have looked at over the past few years, it is possible to detect three types of source material or discourse, blended together in not always compatible ways: the anthropo-logical and/or historical; the mythopoetic or Jungian-archetypal; and the psychotherapeutic. More specifically (and reductively) still, we might even assign to each flavor of discourse the name of the authority most often invoked as its sage: anthropologist David Gilmore, author of *Mankind in the Making*, a cross-cultural study of masculinity purporting to reveal certain "ubiquitous" but not "universal" patterns and emphases around manhood; Joseph Campbell, popularizer of Jung's psycho-mystical theories of universal myths and archetypes, himself popularized by the PBS-television series produced by Bill Moyers and first aired back in 1988; and John Bradshaw, psychotherapist and defender of the so-called "inner child" whom we all supposedly carry within ourselves and to whose needs and sensitivities we are all prompted by his writings to attend.[1] And finally, I should add, each of these texts carries its own particular political tinge as well – though this may appear less a fully articulated discourse in itself than an implication of each book's way of arguing for the redemptive progressivity of the masculinity it prescribes, a subtext whose very liminality, combined with its insistence, suggests a defensiveness we will get a closer look at later on.

Various linkages between these three kinds of sources are then forged by the texts, with differing degrees of emphasis and coherence. On one end of the spectrum, the mythic-archetypal element predominates in Robert Moore and Douglas Gillette's *King, Warrior, Magician, Lover*; on the other, in Sam Keen's *Fire in the Belly*, Gilmore's generalizations are supplemented and problematized by a distinctive attention to the specificities of twentieth-century Western culture and recent American history, and to the changes in the sex-gender system running through both. Yet for all their variations in foregrounding and emphasis, these books enjoy a similar advantage in combining their source materials, and face a similar problem. The advantage lies in the ease with which a Jungian metadiscourse on signs, symbols and sundry archetypes may be combined with *either* the "inner-child" therapy talk *or* the anthropological long view; the problem to be finessed or faced up to is the difficulty of squaring Bradshaw's emphasis on the "inner child" to be honored in men as well as women with Gilmore's implicit (re)valorization of the apparently imperious and invulnerable "Warrior" constructed and reinforced within many diverse cultures, via various hardening and mutilating techniques and rituals, out of biological men.

Our works thus roughly sort themselves out according to how and how much they frame and/or fudge the question of whether men now should shed and disavow the conventional qualities of what Gilmore calls "the pressured type of manhood" – such attributes as "self-direction and discipline," "toughness and autonomy" – to gain or recover "soft" behavioral traits such as emotional sensitivity and vulnerability traditionally ascribed to women (and children) and proscribed for men.[2] Fudgers will, neither surprisingly nor accidentally, be those who cling most tenaciously to the dispensations of the Jungian mythopoetic cosmos, and most aggressively assert the transhistorical, cross-cultural truth of a masculinity both empathic and empowered. Framers will have to go in for a bit of manifest reconstruction and, accordingly, be that much more apt to concede some elements of those feminist critiques that view normative masculinity as a constitutive element of the inequity, violence, and degradation that characterizes white Western late-capitalist culture. But neither position as embodied in these texts absolutely excludes the other; none of them – if taken at face value, anyhow – is wholeheartedly devoted *either* to trashing feminism, *or* to critiquing masculin(ist) myth. Accordingly, to represent these texts in spatial relation to each other, and to their source materials, we come up with something like the following:

historical					mythopoetic
←	Keen	Kipnis	Bly	Moore/Gillette	→
pro-feminist					anti-feminist

where the texts are arranged along a spectrum whose endpoints represent the extremes of tendencies that nonetheless continue to include some degree of their attenuated opposites, and where the whole spectrum, for all its differences, is marbled through with the terms and assumptions of the psychotherapeutic self-help and recovery "movements."

To see how all this sampling and mixing works, we might as well begin with the movement's biggest bestseller, poet and movement avatar Robert Bly's *Iron John: A Book About Men*, which opens with the following audience-defining statement:

> it is clear to men that the images of adult manhood given by the popular culture are worn out; a man can no longer depend on them. By the time a man is thirty-five he knows that the images of the right man, the tough man, the true man which he received in high school do not work in life. Such a man is open to new versions of what a man is or could be.[3]

But Bly will go on to insist that the version he is offering is quite the opposite of new: it is the old truth that the new has supplanted, eroded, covered over and destroyed. Likewise, the preface goes on to insist that "this book does not seek to turn men against women, nor to return men to the domineering mode that has led to repression of women and their values for centuries"; nor does it "constitute a challenge to the women's movement" (x). Yet the first claim in the text that follows is that feminism, working hand-in-glove with the emasculating tendencies of what Bly calls "the mode of industrial domination" (98), has produced a feminized "naive" masculinity that is entirely too weak, too listlessly soft and peace-loving – that is, no real masculinity at all.

One way to sidestep this contradiction is, of course, to define the river of feminism only by the most essentialist currents running within it, especially those that ascribe to women such qualities as interconnectedness with others and with nature, love of peace, the capacity for nurturance, and so on, as natural attributes denied to men. Thus, for Bly and others like him, the way lies open for a similarly essentialist counterdefinition of men's natural qualities and tendencies – that natural wisdom of "patriarchy" which, along with that of "matriarchy," has been denigrated, deformed and effaced by the relentlessly leveling and desacralizing processes of modern industrial culture. This form of life, it seems, just came along at some point – was it around 1000 AD, when Western culture according to Bly lost the ability to think mythologically (107), or in the eighteenth century when the factories first came in (19)? – and took over. Readers are not encouraged to speculate about how this happened, who did it, or why. To do so might lead to historical, or even, Lord help us, political thinking, rather than to the revelation of spiritual and poetical Truth; and Bly is having none of that.

Rather, what Bly is after is an ahistorical, transcultural, and openly mythological definition of full-fledged masculinity, the deep and holy truths of the masculine psyche – that, and a set of instructions for how we his readers can get access to it too. *Iron John* purports to give us both definition and instruction in the stored-wisdom form of the heretofore rather obscure Grimm's fairy tale for which the book is named. In fact, the book basically consists of Bly's slow exegesis of this tale; those who grew up poststructuralist in the academy might think of it as a kind of *S/Z* designed for Jungian self-help freaks, with even more and loopier digressions, riffs and undefended pronouncements than in Barthes. The stages of initiation Bly extracts from his fairy tale go something like this: separate from mother, let yourself be mentored by a wise father figure, accept your woundedness and go into your sadness, honor the father energy, find your playfulness and creativity, take on your warrior energy, get another wound, perhaps or probably from the fathers, then hook up with your princess and become yourself Wild Man, King, and Lord. And in that order, too; skip steps and you'll just have to go back.

If, stripped of Bly's fustian, these instructions look as silly as the psychospiritual box-mix recipe they are, we should still not rush too dismissively past the insistent motifs underlying them. Perhaps most notoriously, there is the emphasis on wildness, here conceived in classic antinomian terms as that manly individualist spirit which resists both the suffocating blandishments of womanly domestication and the homogenizing, rationalizing tendencies of industrial society. "During the last thirty years," Bly intones,

> men have been asked to learn how to go with the flow, how to follow rather than lead, how to live in a nonhierarchical way, how to be vulnerable, how to adopt consensus decision-making. Some women want a passive man if they want a man at all; the church wants a tamed man ... the university wants a domesticated man ... the corporation wants a team-worker, and so on. (61)

The complicity of women with industrial society as taming agents is as clear and traditionally American as the more novel alliance between wildness and restored hierarchical authority, the Law of the Father rediscovered and submitted to out in the woods in the person of Wild Man Iron John or such real-life surrogates as Bly himself.[4] When the male initiate separates from the mother and goes into the wilderness, as well as later on when he leaves it, there must be "older men" to "welcome the younger man into the ancient, mythologized, instinctive male world" (15).

But this conjunction of antinomian rebellion and patriarchal authority constitutes both an ideological masterstroke and a bit of a problem, for historical reasons that lie at the heart of the movement's appeal for the men it attracts. As Bly readily concedes, within white American culture today this is precisely a "Time with No Father" when the "Hunger for a King" goes unfed, a time when the corruption and violence of our political leaders from Johnson through Reagan at the top has been complemented by the absence and emotional distance of fathers without wisdom at home. Indeed, in the 1960s, the two fed into one another in a most alarming and debilitating way, according to Bly's perverse reading of the origins of the counterculture and the white New Left:

> The students' fear that their own fathers were evil was transferred to all male figures in authority.... The unconscious intuitions come in, not because the father is wicked, but because the father is remote. (22)

The fact that many of these "male figures in authority" turned out to be complicit in a racist, genocidal, imperialist war is here tossed aside as no more than an unfortunate coincidence. The real problem was, and is, the failure to make "a good connection with adult male energy, especially the energy of an adult man in a position of authority or leadership." (22)

How then, where then, are men to make this connection if it is not available within the culture? *Iron John* gives two answers to this question: outside the culture, in the wilderness; and inside the psyche, through one's "wound." In the course of the book the wilderness becomes a space quite near if not equivalent to that of preindustrial European and non-Western culture alike, the two taken in classic racist fashion as co-equal and conjoined in the same invariant and wise tradition stretching from African tribal custom to Greek mythology and Old Norse myth. Within this wilderness, moreover – or, more accurately, perhaps, within these cultures recoded as wilderness – we may take as our Iron John guides and mentors either those remembered and recuperated elders of non-Western or pre-industrial culture who knew and revered the old ways and wisdoms, or their contemporary representatives, that is, such authorized patriarchal non-fathers as Bly himself. On the other hand, though – or is the right logical connector here "moreover"? – we are also encouraged to come into our true masculinity via the wound, that grief variously described as the tragic sense of life that our "Disneyland culture" denies, in this "world of shopping malls and entertainment complexes in which we are made to believe that there is no death, disfigurement, illness, insanity, poverty, lethargy, or misery" (81), and a sorrow specifically visited on the male initiate by "the King's men": the wound of the father's rejection and/or damage, in effect. Here at any rate, as with wildness and wilderness, the forces to resist include both overly nurturant women who might shield us from our necessary wounds, and those features of industrial modernity that repress life's tragic dimension. Thus Bly manages to acknowledge the damaging effects of that emotional distance and numbness which pervades so many white men's lives and has so often been remarked and analyzed by feminism, while not only refusing any common cause with women but at least partially extolling that damage as part of the process of making real men.

The project of *Iron John* is, then, to honor the wisdom of preindustrial patriarchy and restore the rule of the male elders, without whose wise understanding no regulated wildness can exist, no meaningful pain can be inflicted and worked through. Yet the very redundancies of the template Bly constructs from the Iron John story hint at the vagueness of the anti-modern solution he proposes, and the reactionary anti-capitalism to which he holds. Why is it one has to keep on going back to the father figure, first to be mentored, then to honor his "energy"; why the trip to the wilderness near the beginning of the story, the plunge into warrior energy later on; why the dive into grief at the beginning, the wound from "the King's men" toward the end? What *Iron John* proposes as teleological narrative looks on closer inspection more like an invitation to take up a masculinity defined by its perpetual oedipal oscillations between rebellion, submission, and emotional pain – albeit to take it up as an aggressively defended counterpoint to those matriarchal truths and strengths only women can know.

At first glance, it might not seem fair to place Moore and Gillette's *King, Warrior, Magician, Lover* to the right of Robert Bly's book, since for them "patriarchy" is a dirty word, with a surprisingly accurate historical definition:

> the social and cultural organization that has ruled our Western world, and much of the rest of the globe, from at least the second millennium B.C.E. to the present [in which] male dominance ... has been oppressive and abusive of the feminine – of both the so-called feminine characteristics and virtues and actual women themselves.[5]

Correlatively, the authors concede that the "mature masculine" they are attempting to define and recommend might never have existed, that theirs might be a progressive construction to be implemented rather than a displaced God to be restored. Yet this same candor elsewhere manifests itself less as rectification than as a kind of coarsened clarification – an "outing," in effect – of the regressive ideology of *Iron John*.

In *King, Warrior, Magician, Lover* Moore and Gillette propose not a narrative, but the straightforward set of archetypes their book's title lists. The task is not to move through, but around and within them in the prescribed ways. More specifically, we men are advised to access "the powerful resources of the four masculine archetypes within every man" (144), and to learn to discriminate between their positive, "mature" forms and their disabling and excessive, "immature" shadow versions, each of which is profiled through various cross-cultural and historical references, including ones drawn from contemporary politics, popular culture, and daily life. Positive, enabling "King energy," for example, "seeks peace and stability, orderly growth and nurturing ... not only for all people, but for the environment, the natural world," while the "Shadow King" oscillates between the "Tyrant and the Weakling" (62–63). Yul Brenner in *The Magnificent Seven* displays good "Warrior energy," while "the sadistic Warrior" is exemplified by carnage-loving George C. Scott in *Patton* (83, 90). The overriding message is that you can have it all – power and technique, fierceness and sensitivity – so long as you take the good, healthy parts of each archetype and leave the rest alone.

In addition to drawing on the good energy and eschewing the bad, we have to learn to "admix" these positive archetypal energies via a complex inner carburation into the perfectly balanced, high-octane "mature masculine" fuel. Yet Moore and Gillette are better at describing what we are to do than telling us how to do it. The techniques they sketchily describe towards the close of their book – "active imagination dialogue," "invocation," "admiring men," and "acting 'as if'" – are pretty obviously pulled straight off the shelf of contemporary psychotherapy, particularly its West Coast versions, much taken these days with technologies of imaging, emulation, and "subpersonality" or "voice dialogue"; here they have simply been infused with the equivalent of what the advertisers of Irish Spring soap used to call a "manly odor" before being peddled as stock. Altogether more telling and substantial are the anecdotal pointers Moore and Gillette scatter through their text on the enabling effects of "mature" energies properly accessed, and the disabling effects of the "immature" Shadows, as in the two excerpts below:

> Another man found himself needled and attacked by several female co-workers for his self-confident, manly ways. He found strength in a crystal pyramid that he kept on his desk. (The pyramid form, as we have seen, is a symbol for the masculine Self.) Whenever he felt overwhelmed, he would take a sixty-second breather. He would turn to his pyramid and imagine it inside himself, in his chest. The waves of the emotional attacks on his manhood crashed against its sides, trying to fragment it. But the waves always fell back, eventually spending their fury. His work situation didn't improve, but he was able to keep his balance, his calmness, and his centeredness most of the time, while he sought a better work environment. (153)

> Many people in corporate America today are not at all interested in the companies they work for. Many are just "treading water," looking for a way out and up. Here we find the executives who are more interested in furthering their own careers than in being good stewards of the "realms" placed under their authority.... This is the CEO who negotiates, for his own financial benefit, to sell his company, to see it dismembered and rendered impotent, who is willing to see his friends and loyal employees fired as excess baggage in the now popular "leveraged buy-out." (67)

Here, as in Bly, the moment of gender politics and/or political economy is transmuted and resolved under the sign of archetypal energies and mythic struggle. The first man defends himself from what we may assume is probably some "shadow" energy from the feminine side of things by taking shelter in his archetypal space; the second does his dirty deeds not because of the vicious logic set loose by the deregulation of American business during the Reagan 1980s, but because his "shadow King" is running him. These two male protagonists, moreover, pretty much define the socioeconomic spectrum from which most of Moore and Gillette's examples will be drawn, from mid-level professional–managerial (he does have his own office, after all, beleaguered though he may be) to guy at the top.

This unselfconscious bias towards the upper end of the class scale suggests that Moore and Gillette are clearly most comfortable there – or, perhaps more charitably, that up there is where they expect to find most of their readership, anyhow. Certainly their work, for all its occasional gestures against militarism, violence against women, and environmental degradation, is unconcerned with any external or institutional power inequities between men and women, or for that matter between men and men. Instead of such changes, *King, Warrior, Magician, Lover* recommends the construction of a mode of masculinity whose powers are made more, not less comprehensive, an ability to rule, war, play, *and* love (the order of the archetypes in the title and the book's exposition is instructive in itself): a "kinder, gentler" kind of dominance, a patriarchy redeemed and fulfilled. So Moore and Gillette's book ends much as it began, by acknowledging that "It may be that there never has been a time when the archetypes of the mature masculine … were dominant in human life." But the authors are now quick to add that "at least there used to be structures and systems – rituals – for evoking a greater level of masculine maturity than seems to be the rule in our antisystem, antiritual, antisymbol world today" (143). We are back in the land of anti-modernism – by now without Bly's bluster to obfuscate the schizophrenic ambivalence of our authors' back-to-the-future logic: "If contemporary men can take the task of their own initiation from Boyhood to Manhood as seriously as did their tribal forebears, then we may witness the *end* of the *beginning* of our species, instead of the *beginning* of the *end*" (156).

Finally, just *because* they are avowedly anti-patriarchal, Moore and Gillette don't want to be confused with the pro-feminist softies Bly calls "naive" men. The mixed signal in their call to go beyond patriarchy by returning to the ways of the "tribal forebears" is accompanied by a proclamation that explicitly pushes back against *les femmes*. "[I]t is clear," they remind us,

> that the world is overpopulated with not only immature men but also tyrannical and abusive little girls pretending to be women. It is time for men – particularly the men of Western [that is, white] civilization – to stop accepting the blame for everything that is wrong with the world. There has been a veritable blitzkrieg on the male gender, what amounts to an outright demonization of men and a slander against masculinity. But women are no more inherently responsible or mature than men are.... Men should never feel apologetic about their gender, as gender. They should be concerned with the maturation and the stewardship *of* that gender and of the larger world. (155–6)

A similar note of beset belligerence is struck more than once in Aaron Kipnis's *Knights Without Armor*, whose title succinctly expresses one of the principal goals of so much movement literature: to get that warrior energy back but still stay sensitive, to take one's place proudly in the long and honorable tradition of Gilmore's "protector-providers" yet still stay in touch with one's own tender "inner child." If anything, Kipnis is more insistent than Moore and Gillette on the abuses and inequities that contemporary "Western" men must endure: their bodies repressed, their emotions numbed and silenced, their rights and even lives seen as secondary and expendable compared with those of women and children, their self-image shamed by feminist mockery and rage. Yet at the same time this book, whose first page proudly acknowledges its origins in "the equal rights, recovery, and mythopoetic wings of the men's movement," comes the closest yet to calling for an autocritique and overhaul of the regulative masculinity that at other moments it insists we must honor and preserve.[6] All this, plus Kipnis's comparative willingness to come down off the mythopoetic throne and talk straightforwardly about his own experience and history, both sharpens the contradictions of *Knights Without Armor* and lends them a distinctly different pitch.

Kipnis is the first of our authors to declare openly the need to construct "*new* [my emphasis] templates" for masculinity that will be more "in balance" not only "with nature" but "with the political, economic, and social needs of women than the older dominating ... ideals for men" (6); the first to charge the fathers of his baby-boom generation with responsibility for the "Vietnam war, the squandering of natural and economic resources, global pollution, and many other ills," with having "hoarded wealth and held tightly to the levers of power" (204); the first to suggest explicitly and in detail that the "alienation, loneliness, isolation, shame, substance abuse, distrust of women and emotional numbness associated with the heroic model of masculinity may be both symptom and cause of the breakdown in the social fabric" (34). Yet even as Kipnis approvingly rehearses the linkages that feminist mytho-histories have constructed between monotheism, phallocracy, and the emergence of hierarchically structured urban civilization,[7] he insists on the power and virtue of the "earth-based masculinity" (114) which must be found to accompany if not precede any pre-phallocratic, matriarchal principle or Gaia myth. Likewise, of the "Twelve Tasks of Men" around whose exposition and rationales the book is structured, in what is surely a deliberate rhyme with other psycho-social "twelve-step" programs in recovery, for every task that calls on men to "Improve Relationships Between the Sexes," or even to "Admit That We Have Been Wounded" by the duties and deformations of the old heroic protector-provider model, there is at least one other that calls on us to "Reclaim the Ancient, Sacred Images of Masculinity," "Rebuild Self-Esteem on Deep Masculine Foundations," "Rediscover Male Initiation and Reunite Fathers and Sons."

If, despite their sharper edges, such contradictions seem all too familiar, at least Kipnis embeds his aporias in an immediate sociopolitical context that our other writers keep practically out of sight. Amidst the usual welter of references to such figures as Hades and Kali, Chinese "Earth Father" Pan-Ku, and ancient Egyptian "sky goddess" Nut, for example, he tells some helpful stories about himself and the other men in his own men's group. Perhaps the most striking of these tales is one intended to illustrate how hard it is for "many of us [men] to find a place of solidarity with them [here, feminist women] that does not hold our own self-abasement as a prerequisite" (59). Kipnis describes a late-night pre-demo ritual preceding an anti-nuclear protest at the Lawrence Livermore Labs, at a time in his life when he still "felt that women were going to save the world with the help of a few of us *enlightened* men." Despite this avowedly pro-feminist outlook, he found himself increasingly uncomfortable as the speeches, songs, and incantations of the women conducting the event shifted their target from the military-industrial complex to "the evils committed by men against women and the earth" and thence to patriarchy itself, as the statue of a man made of branches with a "large stick representing the man's penis" was put to the torch, to the Goddess-worshipping cry of "'Blessed be She! Blessed be She!'" (63). At this point, Kipnis says,

I realized that when these women said they hated men, they were essentially talking about me as well. Somehow along the way, I had disidentified myself as a man. I wasn't like *those* men who were wrecking the world with their chain saws, bulldozers, and war machines. The reality, however, was that ... my body and orientation toward life were and are very male. (64)

"It was no better to burn wicker men than to burn witches," Kipnis declares in what we might adjudge a somewhat hysterical equation of referent and representation: "The Goddess showed a dark face that night, which felt just as dangerous as the so-called patriarchy" (64) – a patriarchy with which Kipnis now admits he is deeply identified, especially in the no-man's-land of these fire-lit woods.

Through stories like these, objectionable and risible as they may be, Kipnis begins to give us some sense of the charged social field on which men's-movement advocates like himself call out for a version of gender as part of a "polytheistic, culturally plural, partnership society" in which "both men and women ... are firmly established in their own gender identity" and so "can cooperate without dominating one another" (246). Which formulation, by the way, also suggests Kipnis's comparatively advanced sensitivity to another hot potato, that conjured up and handled in the progressive-liberal discourse of "multiculturalism" and "diversity." Interestingly enough, Kipnis's only mild criticism of the men's movement concerns how "odd" it is "to witness hundreds of white, middle-class American men ... performing African, Caribbean, or American Indian music as their primary ritual forms" and taking up "the teachings of other cultures in search of meaningful reconnection with spirit, earth, and soul." Warning against the "tendency to romanticize cultural traditions far removed from our own," he insists that "[o]ur [white, Euro-American] personal and ancestral histories are also rich cultural resources" and that "our own individually unique movement and poetics ... shouldn't be underrated or seen as inferior to any other culture's exotic tradition" (243). And conversely: just as we Euro-Am whites can compose one rich, diverse nation of tribes vis-à-vis non-white or non-Western cultures, we men can make a strong nation full of "masculine soul" to counter as well as cooperate with that of women, following a foreign policy of Peace Through Strength.

Such a tendency towards defensive reaction is, it seems, a constitutive characteristic of the men's-movement books. It is even peripherally there in the most feminist-friendly of them, Sam Keen's *Fire in the Belly*, on the nether side of an expressed agreement with broad feminist perspectives that is, especially by comparison, impressively large:

> Western culture has been dominated by patriarchy – rule by the men, of the men, and for the men.
> Patriarchy is rooted in hierarchy, obsession with power, control, and government by violence.
> Warfare, rape, and ecological destruction of "Mother" nature are rooted in patriarchal habits of thought and modes of social organization.
> Misogyny and gynophobia – a devaluation of all things considered 'feminine' – form the subtext of Western "history."
> A feminist vision demands sexual, artistic, economic, and political equality.... It further demands that men assume an equal share in the private sphere – the creation of hearth and the rearing of children.[8]

Keen explicitly links these defining features of patriarchal history to the social reproduction of what he calls "the warrior psyche" in men and the "economic-warfare system" in Western society, and emphatically refuses any interest in recuperating Gilmore's "protector-provider" mode of masculinity (37). The opening chapters of *Fire in the Belly* even offer its presumably non-academic and largely male readership what might well be its first exposure to something like the feminist-materialist psychoanalytic arguments posed by Dorothy Dinnerstein and later elaborated by Nancy Chodorow and Jessica Benjamin, on how this "warrior psyche" – that is, the aggressively defended autonomy seen as normative male subjectivity – is constructed through an individuation process whose general outcomes are determined by this sex/gender system's economic, ideological, and affective insistence on keeping women in their place as the first Mother/Other on whom all nurturance depends.[9] Moreover, Keen's next section, "The Rites of Manhood," follows up this introduction with a telling catalogue of the "secondary" ideologies and institutions that compound and extend the hardened outcomes of the male subject-formation process, from the lessons of school sports in violence and competition to the instrumentalist anti-ethics of careerist professional work. Along the way, Keen even manages to critique those Bly-like perspectives that posit a conspiratorial linkage between the eviscerating effects of capitalist rationalization and the putatively emasculating effects of smothering, belittling women. "[I]f men lack the lusty pride of self-affirmation," he says in a clever twist of the Wild Man's tail, "if we are burned out without having ever been on fire, it is most likely because we have allowed ourselves to be engulfed by a metabody, a masculine womb – The Corporation" (62).

Finally, Keen's is the only one of these books sufficiently conversant with feminism to draw any distinctions *within* it. In effect, he sees the difference between what Kathy Ferguson calls "praxis" and "cosmic" feminisms – that is, between those that hold genders to be socially constructed, historically and culturally mutable categories and those essentialist versions that assume that ascribed gender characteristics are to a significant degree biologically and/or spiritually hardwired and invariant – and criticizes the second from the vantage point of the first. He warns against any mythology of Fall and Return, including and especially the matriarchal version so prominent in New Age feminist circles, with the tonic admonition that "It is always a good idea to be suspicious of nostalgic histories that look back to golden ages, because they hide an inquisitorial program for the future.... There is no reason to suspect that reversing the gender and worshiping the goddess will produce anything except another program for genderal supremacy" (200). Likewise, he insists that the result of "the simplistic effort to assign responsibility for violence to men and peace to women is to confirm the very stereotypes of women that feminists have otherwise been fighting against" (203). And he refuses attempts undertaken in the name of feminism to depict women in terms of race or class: "The notion that women are a class or a repressed minority like migrant workers, blacks, Indians in America, or Jews in Germany, trivializes the pain involved in class structure and the systematic abuse suffered by ethnic minorities" (204).

In placing the primary blame for white men's contemporary discomforts on a "corporate-industrial-warfare system" (204) that produces, regulates, and disciplines both masculine and feminine subjectivities, by describing this system in broadly structural and historical terms, and by refusing to celebrate the masculine "warrior psyche," *Fire in the Belly* might seem to lift off the terrain of men's movement literature altogether, and to be more properly categorized as a feminist book on men to be placed alongside such works as Lynne Segal's *Slow Motion* and Barbara Ehrenreich's *The Hearts of Men*. Yet in other respects it earns the prominent place it has achieved on the men's-movement shelf. For starters, like Kipnis and such godfathers to the movement as Herb Goldberg, Keen is more concerned than Segal and Ehrenreich with the mutilations inflicted on men who "are systematically conditioned to endure pain, to kill and die in the service of the tribe, nation, or state" (37), and more explicitly sympathetic to the suffering of the men who must undergo it.[10] And he is also far more passionate than either Ehrenreich or Segal in his insistence that feminism is "disastrously wrong in excusing women from responsibility and culpability for the destructive aspects of a cultural system that can only be created and perpetuated by a consensual interaction of men and women" (204). This system will not change, Keen argues, until feminist women agree to mourn the cost of its damage to men as well as women, and cop to women's complicity in its co-construction: "Until women are willing to weep for and accept equal responsibility for the systematic violence done to the male body and spirit by the war system, it is not likely that men will lose enough of their guilt and regain enough of their sensitivity to weep and accept responsibility for women who are raped and made to suffer the indignity of economic inequality" (48).

Equal reponsibility? That measurement is debatable, to say the least. Yet the general direction of Keen's argument converges with that of praxis feminism in its claims that the "artificial separation of masculine and feminine qualities" is "an act of intellectual and psychological fascism" (208), and that the "difficult task" before us now must be "dismantling the social system that has made men the way they are and women the way they are" (207) and constructing a new one in which women have full "sexual, artistic, economic, and political equality" (196) with men. All the more surprising, disappointing and symptomatic, then, are the book's final two chapters. "Becoming Together" and "Travel Tips for Pilgrims" are meant to bring us back into the present moment of tension and malaise within the sex–gender system for white middle-class and professional men and women, after the broad survey and analysis we have been through, and to offer us – Keen's male readers, especially – practical advice and instructions for what to do. And Keen begins the former task promisingly enough, by linking the eighties re-emphasis on gendered division in PMC circles – Jean Bolen's *Goddesses in Everywoman* as well as Bly's *Iron John* – to a recoil from the gender-blind, asexual competitiveness of the new professional's careerist world. But then something strange happens: while deriding this phenomenon, Keen himself falls prey to it; he begins to insist there is some important truth *beneath* all this fol-de-rol about "masculine" and "feminine" – "the real mystery of man and woman," as it turns out (214). "Peel away the layers of the social conditioning," Keen now tells us, "and there remains the prime fact of the duality of men and women" (218). This "preconscious, presocial duality of the sexes" cannot be explained or even analyzed, but it must not be ignored. For it is, in turn, the basis of heterosexual marriage, that sacred institution which, together with the family, "may provide the best hospital for our ancient wounds" (221). In a few more pages, Keen is even speculating that "the lack of substantial manliness one finds in some gay communities is a result not of a homoerotic expression of sexuality, but of the lack of a relationship of nurturance to the young" (227). Such an "enlightened" variation on homophobia is, in effect, a spin-off of the hetero familialism that erupts in these closing pages to insist on the redemptive linkage connecting the words "Heart," "Hearth," and "Earth."

What accounts for this reactionary recoil back to the Yeatsian mysteries of hetero binarism? The answer is to be found in the hostile anxiety Keen expresses here and there throughout his book towards the leveling and eviscerating effects of advanced consumer society, in its tendency to produce a depthless, decentered, nihilistic "postmodern man" unconcerned with "the age-old quest for consistency, for forging a single identity, for a unifying vision" (111). Keen's "postmodernity" – its terms borrowed from Todd Gitlin's popularized pastiche of Fredric Jameson's essay[11] – is, in effect, the cognate term for the consumption side of that same capitalist modernity which most of our other movement texts have lumped together with modern feminism, and against which they have reacted with their own turns back to the old "truths" of le différence. Yet this same strain of romantic anti-capitalism in Keen's book feels more perverse in the degree to which it undermines what had been a far more progressive gender politics, and overdetermines the devolution of the book's final chapter into yet another therapeutic list of individual and group exercises and "tips": advice, for example, on "Cultivating Solitude," or constructing "Rituals, Ceremonies, and Symbolic Events," or undertaking "Spirited and Virile Action," most of which could be neatly shuffled with the bag of self-help goodies we got at the end of Moore and Gillette's tour of the archetypes.

To the extent that it just barely succeeds at being a men's movement book, Keen's *Fire in the Belly* helps us see more clearly what bases must be hit, what motifs deployed, to count as one. From the preceding summaries, we can extract at least five such themes and motifs, for all the differences in and between the four books surveyed. First, and most obviously, Dysfunctionality: contemporary white middle- and/or professional-class American masculinity is said to be somehow not working. It is without sufficient substance, integrity, and/or honor; it is without emotional sensitivity, openness, or depth. Correlatively, neither within contemporary white American culture as a whole, nor from the present generation of male elders, have the present generation of white American men been able to receive any instruction or initiation into a mode of masculine being and behavior whose blend of strength and depth would render it (once again? for the first time?) truly respectable.

Second, there is the ubiquitous motif of Wildness/Fierceness, which must be kindled, or rekindled, within men. Even Keen, for all his refusal to buy into protector-provider modes of masculinity, runs with the pack in his assertion that "So long as the world is less than perfect the warrior can never wholly retire. It still takes gentleness and fierceness to make a whole man" (48). And then there is his book's title itself, despite its odd and no doubt unintended suggestion of a bad case of heartburn. At any rate, what we have seen about this – what, figuration? somewhere, anyhow on the bounce between modality and metaphor – is that it can be tipped in at least two directions, or towards two enemies sometimes seen virtually as one. Wildness, that is, may be most strenuously invoked as the counter to the eviscerations of instrumental rationality and capitalist technocracy at their soulless work; or to the emasculating tendencies of women, including and perhaps especially feminist women, whose impulses to vilify, shame, and cow all those with penises aligns them, in some works, as hand-in-glove allies with "industrial society." The anti-capitalist note is never wholly absent, and indeed sometimes predominates; but the same is true of the anti-feminist note as well.

Both these themes converge and contribute to a third, yet more complexly ambiguous and multivalent one, that of Going Back. Each text, even *Fire in the Belly* when faced with the hideous specter of postmodernity, calls for some sort of return: the question is, return to what? We are back, in other words, to the problem of how to square a putatively traditional and honorable protector-provider model of masculinity with the emotionally labile "inner child" whose sensitivities must, it would seem, be repressed for the protector-provider to armor up: how to work a *historical* regression to preindustrial gender roles together with a *psychological* regression to that tender openness to the world and all experience we presumably enjoyed before we were scarred. (One thinks again of the figure of the "wound" so frequently invoked by Bly and his Jungian cohorts: of how, in his male melodrama, it is always to be both mournfully tended and valorized.) Not only do our various texts attempt to blend the two regressions in different proportions; they also, each and all, run through a sometimes bewildering range of contradictory attitudes towards each one, critiquing and denying what they simultaneously admit.

Fourth, out of all this mélange and ambiguity, there nonetheless emerges a relatively consistent preference for the construction – or reconstruction, as most of this literature most of the time would have it – of a Separate but Equal relationship between the two sexes. The meaning of this slogan, especially in terms of the actual power relations it advocates, is characteristically both slippery and variable, not only between but within our four texts. But just as obviously, there are real if implicit differences between those that place more emphasis on "Separate" – by my reading, Bly and Moore/Gillette, not by accident those with the greatest appetite for "mythic" thought and argument – and those like Kipnis and Keen, that pay more attention to what "Equal" might mean.

Finally, though, what must also be marked as a constitutive feature of these writings is precisely their subordination of the political to some combination of the Archetypal and the Therapeutic. The former is taken to be above and beyond the level of political action and event, which it is nonetheless assumed to subtend; the latter is beneath it, on the level of internal/emotional individual and group action and practical technique. What more or less explicitly connnects these two realms is the category of the *ritual*, by which most of these books most of the time appear to mean any practice that works to make you feel better individually through the invocation of some larger and more collective meaning – for example, Moore and Gillette's threatened man placing the pyramid within himself. Here again, the proportions vary, from Bly's meagre and vaguely disdainful attention to the Therapeutic, to Keen's implicit distrust of Archetypes.

2. CALLS OF THE WILD

We will have more to say later on about the social history and location of all these themes and motifs. But first we need to examine how they show up and are dealt with in the various spaces in which the movement acts itself out. In what follows, I will be drawing mainly on my own witness and experience of several different forums, attended during the years 1990–92, mainly in the greater Seattle–Tacoma area of the Pacific Northwest, a hotbed of men's-movement activity. As participant-observer, I took part in monthly meetings of the Men's Wisdom Council, a city-wide half-day gathering of 200–300 men held in the parish hall of a downtown non-denominational church; attended a "Day for Men" retreat conducted by Robert Bly and his storytelling colleague Michael Meade for an audience of several hundred men; dipped into a few men's groups meeting on a neighborhood-by-neighborhood basis, and informally interviewed a small number of men in other groups meeting here and there in other towns and localities across the Pacific Northwest. To supplement and bolster my direct observations, I will also make some use of material from a documentary film called *Wild Men* (1992),[12] whose subject is a weekend-long retreat for men, conducted by Marvin Allen of the Austin Men's Center, in the Hill Country outside Austin, Texas.

But before diving in I should confess to both my squeamishness and my lack of expertise. The latter first: I am not a trained ethnographer; and I made no effort to insure that either the groups I entered, the people I talked with, or the activities I witnessed and participated in were representative of the men's movement as a whole. Frankly, I do not know enough about such work even to know how such an effort would be undertaken with a phenomenon like the men's movement, so much of which is, virtually by definition, intensely localized in its self-organization yet so centrifugal and diffuse in its energy. Moreover – and here is where the squeamishness begins to creep in – I was often reluctant to push too hard or too openly for background histories and sociological detail in spaces declared to be both ritualized and intimate, at once too private and too sacred to abide people walking around asking about age, income level and occupation. When names are given out or traded within a movement space or forum, they are almost always first names only; the standing rule governing most if not all communication situations is for you to take whatever information about the other person as comes your way in the course of his conversation or truthtelling as sufficient. In this context, a guy asking too many questions and/or writing down notes is apt to be seen as a hostile alien intruder in a movement "community" whose defensiveness towards snide mainstream media and sneering feminist critics alike is high and widespread.

One example of such defensive distrust may be in order: one Saturday morning following the opening ritual, the monthly assembly of the Men's Wisdom Council had an issue to discuss. The Council's unpaid volunteer coordinators wanted us to make a collective decision whether to allow a reporter from *The Seattle Times* to "shoot" the opening drumming ritual and run a photo of it in the paper. Reaction to this proposal came from all around the circle of perhaps 250 men, and was largely negative. Most who spoke expressed the view that the majority of media coverage of the men's movement, both nationally and locally, had misrepresented, caricatured, and ridiculed the movement; accordingly, these speakers assumed that, regardless of the photographer's best intentions, a photo of their drumming would be used to similar effect, especially in the absence of any safeguards or guarantees concerning whatever text would be used to frame it. At the very least, it was argued, such a photograph must necessarily fail to "catch the energy" of the ritual and the "community" it brought into being – not, I gathered, just because of its being a merely visual representation of a primarily auditory phenomenon, but because no vestige or sample of that sacred and communal energy could possibly survive in the outside world.

My own attitude towards this discussion and decision was, and is, both simple and complex in a way that I hope both "outs" and clarifies the deeper sources of my squeamishness. I was, and am, skeptical of movement claims for the mystical significance of drumming, especially when that significance is reserved for drumming by and with men. Drumming as a communally binding or constructing practice is hardly reserved for or unique to men, white (Lord knows) or otherwise; if I ever had any doubts on that score, they were cleared up the day in February 1991 when I went straight from the closing beats of the Men's Wisdom Council to the rhythms being put out by a multiracial women's group helping to inspirit a very mixed crowd showing up in Seattle's Central District to protest the Gulf War. On the other hand, that same experience among others has also shown me how effectively polyrhythmic drumming can help to create a kind of kinesthetic group feeling among and within any assembled group, by virtue of the strong and common temporalities it so physically insists. Drumming thus provides men gathered within the "space" of the men's movement a common experience whose literal, physical depth is easily linked, via a readily accessible repertoire of quasi-racist pop-anthropology images of non-white and/or non-Western "tribal custom," to a sense of ahistorical archetypal significance. Such a linkage is at best hilariously deluded, at worst patently offensive. Yet men's-movement drumming should not be judged entirely apart from what I am tempted to claim is the main effect it is meant to achieve: the partly physical, partly ideological construction of a separate yet still public space in which it is safe for these men to say what they feel.

In fact, for all my criticisms and reservations concerning this movement's tendencies and practices, I must still cop to my own partial agreement with the premiss that such safe space is lacking for most men – and that the desire to find or make such a space and collectively inhabit it is a legitimate one. This premiss for me contains most of whatever Gramscian "good sense" the men's movement possesses: the sense that I would wish this essay to help rescue from both the movement's detractors and adherents, and make available for a more radical elaboration. But this is to anticipate; the real point at issue concerns the degree to which my sense of the legitimacy of these white men's desire for such space has translated into a personal reluctance to blight or diminish its secure openness for the participants I have met.

Still, from what I was able to pick up from a combination of direct questioning, overhearing and inference, a general profile of Northwest men's-movement participants emerged: one, moreover, that was reassuringly congruent with the profiles drawn up by other commentators or participants from other regions of the country. From all these accounts and observations, it would seem that the member-constituents of what is known as the men's movement are overwhelmingly white, as were more than 97 per cent of the men I saw taking part in movement events; that the great majority of them are between their mid-thirties and mid-fifties; and that in their occupations, careers, and incomes, they tend to range from small-time and, in many cases, alternative or New Age small businessmen, artisans and entrepreneurs across and up through the ranks of professionals, managers, and technicians of all stripes, including a few at senior professional or even executive levels of rank, status and income, with very few from working-class backgrounds or traditionally blue-collar trades.[13] Notably, though, younger men involved in movement-based groups and activities – that is, those in their twenties and early thirties – exhibit a markedly less affluent character, and not just quantitatively; rather than occupying the lower rungs of the career ladders up which their older "brothers" have climbed, in many cases such men are eking out a living from low-paying service-sector jobs like restaurant work and store clerking with scant job security and little or no possibility for advancement. Such reduced livelihoods and prospects, of course, speak eloquently of reduced employment and income possibilities across the board in a "deindustrialized" and downsizing economy, particularly for those "Generation X" kids who came of age in Reagan time and in the wake of the post-World War II baby boom.

But now let us turn from the group's profile to its activities within the various movement forums. As the example of the Wisdom Council drumming suggests, such forums are almost invariably structured around a sequence of ritual–interaction–ritual. Within local and/or neighborhood meetings, sometimes the opening is a silent meditation; more often, though, the meeting begins with a drumming circle that goes on for twenty minutes or half an hour. Such ritual invocations of secure and separate convocation prepare the ground for whatever type of dialogue or therapeutic interaction is to follow. The latter may – once again, on the local level – include a brief "check-in" from and with each group member, followed by a decision as to who and what subject to fix attention on that evening; or there may be a more prestructured discussion of a given reading or topic. In either case, the emphasis during this part of the meeting is on the legitimacy, the "truth," of each man's experience: a truth typically respected and affirmed by both the group's attentiveness and the prohibition against any analytical or critical reaction to whatever is said. Many groups, following long-established tenets within the recovery movement from Alcoholics Anonymous on, have explicit rules against "cross-talk." Moreover, while there is every encouragement to add one's own testimony to what has just been shared, whether as a further instance of or in contradiction to it, there is a strong and at times even explicit sanction against drawing overt conclusions or constructing generalizations. On the rare occasions when it, or the threat of it, appears, such activity is regarded not only as a violation of the sanctity of each individual's experience, but as "going to your head," a fault in itself.

One result of such an in-built predisposition towards experience over analysis, the "heart" (or "gut" or "belly") against the "head," is that group meetings customarily fail to gather towards any summation or dramatic climax. Such dramatic momentum, surges of interest, or intuitions of pattern as are temporarily established by a spate of randomly convergent individual narratives and testimonies, or at times by a single galvanizing act of witness, are typically dissipated by the centrifugal tendencies implicit in the assumption that each man's contribution is as valuable and true as any other's, and that no generalizations beyond the realm of one's own personal experience are allowed. In this important respect, the inner workings of the men's movement are a far cry from those of the consciousness-raising days of the women's liberation of the early 1970s with which, by movement men, they are so often equated. "Back then," as one local group member told me, "the women were talking to themselves; now we men are." But in virtually the same breath, he insisted, "I don't want to talk about men and women; I want to talk about you and me." He was speaking here in response to my invitation to respond to charges from some feminist circles that meetings like his, and the men's movement as a whole, were anti-feminist. But in these words of defense he was perhaps saying more, with a more precise and telling accuracy, than he knew. It is true that on the local level of the neighborhood meeting and at the monthly Wisdom Councils I heard very few explicitly anti-feminist or misogynist sentiments expressed. But then I heard relatively little conversation about women, or about relationships with women, at all – and virtually nothing about the large structural inequities that the present sex/gender system in white middle-class America continues to run on and reproduce.

Behind such a silence around both women and questions of power lies a complex mixture of lack of interest and reluctance. It is not just that these men want to talk mostly about their relationships with other men; not just that they are dupes as well as beneficiaries of the anti-intellectualism and anti-political individualism that pervades not only the recovery movement, New Age and other alternative cultural formations, but virtually all of contemporary American cultural life; not even just that they are too uncomfortable or oblivious to face up to the unjust gender relations in which they are enmeshed and by which they are privileged. Along with all these other currents, I have the sense that for many of these men feminism is – that is, has become – an untouchable subject, an unspeakable tongue. Or almost unspeakable. It appears along the edges or on the peripheries of these meetings, as a perspective they must agree with yet can never share – as, for example, in one of the small group meetings into which the monthly Wisdom Council gatherings break down, when one of the younger guys in my small group spoke of growing up the only male in an all-female, feminist-identified family. Assuring us all that he had nothing, nothing whatsoever, against feminism, he went on to say how glad he was a men's movement had come along, and how hungrily he had grabbed onto it when it arrived: "Maybe now," he said, "if we learn to know and love ourselves and each other, we'll be able to reach out to those weird bastards someday too." Or, as another informant from a local meeting told me, "Let's be men *for* something – for equality, for feelings."

For equality, for feelings: it's an interesting and symptomatic coupling, a characteristic one, over on what we might think of as the Kipnis–Keen side of the haze. The ultimate goal of this same informant, the project of his group and of the men's movement as a whole as far as he was concerned, was to come out of this drumming and sharing with nothing less than a "new vision for men"; but "to get to that, men have to learn how to talk, how to feel, and have to *not get tromped on for feeling* (my emphasis)." Here the prospective trompers clearly include not only other, straighter men out in the world, but also, and perhaps especially, the specter of those feminist women for whom men's feelings are more or less by definition irrelevant and/or pernicious. For this man, then – though he would not come out with it until I ventured the conclusion myself, at which point he vehemently agreed – hegemonic masculinity and feminism are in cahoots when it comes to denying emotional fluency and expressivity to men. Moreover, when encouraged to open up on the subject, he freely admitted to feeling some resentment towards what he perceives to be the contradictory pressures and demands placed on contemporary men by feminist women: "listen to my feelings, change the baby's diapers – *and* fix the car, bring home the paycheck, and take care of me."

If such resentments feed the stream of the men's movement – and I feel pretty sure they do – in my experience they are nonetheless rarely if ever given direct voice there, not even in the protected "sacred" space secured by the opening and closing rituals. Their open expression is blocked, not only because even here feminism must not be openly disagreed with or criticized, but probably also thanks to a related confusion among these men themselves as to just what characteristics and power their reconstructed masculinity is to include. We are back, in other words, at the contradictory crux at the heart of the movement and its texts, out of which, and in the disguise of which, so much mystified, mystifying, incoherent noise issues. Is the new (or reconstructed) man to be *both* strong *and* sensitive, self-reliantly individualized *and* interdependent with women, children, and animals in the gentle flux of nature – both warrior and nurturer, provider and playful child? What, finally, do these men – these white middle-aged professionals, technicians, and entrepreneurs – really want?

We have already seen how hard it is to get an answer to this question from the men's-movement texts; to get an answer from what men say at these forums would be harder still. The very format of what I have been calling the "interaction" time of movement meetings, with its taboos on generalization and analysis plus its undialogic one-voice-at-a-time code of speech, virtually guarantees that the question neither can nor needs to be faced. Instead, it is negotiated mainly by a kind of bland serial dispersal floating on a bed of generalized agreement: one man stands up at the center of the Wisdom Council circle with the sacred, putatively Native American "speaking stick" in hand to say he works long hours in a high-pressure job to give his family the security they need, and that is a proper, masculine thing to do. Another takes the floor just after him to say that his way of "following his bliss" (the phrase floats in, I believe, from Joseph Campbell by way of the Bill Moyers PBS series) is to be a devoted fan of the Seattle Mariners; another, primary caregiver in his household, grabs the stick to assert that nurturance is manly too. The testimony of the guy who spoke with defiant, defensive pride about working hard at his job to support his family was a rare, and perhaps even singular one; the "men's" work I heard about most concerned either relationships and emotions or domestic responsibilities (especially child care, though obviously I had no way of knowing for sure how much real time of any kind or quality anyone was spending with his kids) and came tagged with the insistence that these too are – dammit – properly masculine. Still, the main point here is that none of these acts of witness and assertion are either intended or taken as comments on one another; we endorse and seal off each one as it happens with the sacred, affirmative "Native American" grunt of "Ho," and wait expectantly, appreciatively for the next.

There is one area of discussion, though, around which the question of what men want masculinity to be comes closest to focusing: when the subject of fathers comes up. There is lots of talk, lots of witnessing, at these meetings about our baby-boom generation's fathers, almost regardless of whatever the official stated topic of the meeting might be; and almost all of it is freighted with disappointment, guilt and rage. Through all the testimonies, moreover, if only by dint of sheer frequency and elaboration, certain themes and patterns inevitably emerge. Categorically speaking, there are two types of failed-father stories (or failed fathers), though the same story, and the same father, may well combine and overlap both types. A good example of the first, concerning the relentlessly judgemental, disapproving father, may be found in the sobbed and shouted testimony of Michael Moller in the *Wild Men* documentary. Moller's father, he tells his brothers on retreat, inspected and regimented his every action, up to and including his choice of an engineer's career, but judged his son to have fallen short of full masculine achievement in every task. On the other hand, there is the testimony of the forty-something man who rose one Saturday in the Men's Wisdom Council to tell of a visit to his parents undertaken after many years away. The terms this man laid down for his visit, he told us, were that he would stay in a motel rather than with them, and would insist on spending at least half of each day with his father, just the two of them alone and away from the house. This was, he told us, because he had never had any direct relationship with his father, who was off at work most of the time and extremely distant when at home, leaving his wife to serve as mediator and facilitator of such relations as he enjoyed with his children. And, said this speaker, his plan had worked out pretty well. He and his father were stiff with one another at first, but slowly managed to warm up as they spent the week hiking and golfing together, until the morning of the son's departure, when the two of them, his father driving, pulled up at the airport's curbside. The son turned to his father and said, "I love you, Dad." "We love you," the father replied, speaking for his wife and himself. "Yeah Dad," the son said, "but how do *you* feel?" The father had been squinting straight ahead, through the windshield; now he slowly moved his gaze down to his lap. "Well," he said at last, "I don't hate you. I've never hated you..."

One set of stories, then, about fathers who were too close, omnipresent even, with their censorious judgements; another, about fathers too emotionally or literally absent to have had much of any feeling towards their sons. Both kinds of story are legion (and I might add here that, for better and for worse, in all my time wandering around this movement I have yet to hear the subject of our mothers come up directly). So a close-kin variant of the question of what kind of masculinity these men want for themselves eventually begins to hover over all their – to me at least, often quite moving – anger and grief: what kind of father do they *wish* they'd had; how to combine the stand-up with the sensitive, the father who judges and the father who cares? "Young men today," say Moore and Gillette, "are starving for blessing from older men, starving for blessing from the King energy" (61); but they too leave it open as to whether, and to what degree, that desired blessing would come in the form of empathetic sensitivity or self-authorizing power. The same ambivalence helps explain the appeal of the contradictory thematic blend of paternal incorporation and denial that Bly squeezes out of his Grimm's fairy tale, including his construction of a place for a figure like Iron John or Bly himself, a father too wildly good and wildly "out there" to be anybody's actual Dad.

All this may help us understand the peculiar effectivity of Bly's own performances as wacky oracle in his public appearances before groups of men. I am thinking here, for example, of his first remarks to the crowd, after the inevitable ritual opening of the "Day for Men" I attended in Tacoma in February 1991: "We don't know why we're here," he announced, speaking of himself and Michael Meade, the movement guru with whom he was sharing the stage, "and we don't know why you're here either ...

It's mostly bullshit anyway."[14] A few poems and rambling thoughts later, though, Bly's understanding of why we were all there seemed perfectly clear: "For twenty or thirty years there's been so much doubt of the male personality, the male being, with many women and some men saying all men are rapists et cetera, and there's a great doubt as to whose code we should live by. Is that right?" Most of the audience said Yes or Ho or simply whooped out their assent; and the event was well and truly under way.

What followed, excluding a few more rituals and a break for lunch, was some five or six hours of overwhelmingly one-way, stage-to-audience instruction in the old wisdom and the true masculine path, through poems and folk tales and rambling addresses, in which the dispensation of advice and the exhortation to action – for example, "to get into the wound and work with it," or carry the relevant folk and fairy tales into the public schools, where "young boys are swimming and drowning in female energy, way too much of it" – got mixed in with Bly's own disarmingly personal confessions about the wounds, rituals and daily routines in his own life. The main result of all this formatted drift, together with the gruff dis-avowals that introduced it, was less a set of messages or a take-home package of wisdom than a kind of "wisdom-effect" pitched somewhere in between the relative fixity of the movement's written texts and the diffusion of the local, grass-roots gathering – perhaps not all that far, come to think of it, from daytime talk-show TV, Phil Donahue or Sally Jessie Raphael. Moreover, in the construction of that wisdom-effect, Bly's (and Meade's) patriarchal yet anti-establishmentarian authority was sustained and extended precisely by dint of both their self-deprecating jibes of dis-avowal and lack of fixity, through the very formlessness of the day's eccentric drift through the wilderness mist. There had been some laughs, some tears; some stories told, some ancient wisdom shared. Only now, at the end of the day as we trudged back out of the auditorium and back towards the outside world of women and children, relationships and jobs, it seemed hard to recall just what heavy stuff we had learned or been reminded of. That was, I think, a good part of the reason why so many men queued up so eagerly in the lobby of the auditorium they'd just exited to buy their audiotapes of the very event they had just heard and witnessed, for thirty bucks a pop on top of the seventy-five they had already paid: because already they could not quite seem to remember what important stuff had gone on.

It may well be that the largest and most important function of all the murk we have been examining over the past few pages, is to allow for an acknowledgement that there is *something* wrong with normative white heterosexual masculinity that nonetheless remains uncoupled from any clear statement or diagnosis of what that something is. We have seen how schizzy all our movement texts are on the subject of what's wrong with contemporary masculinity, how even the most progressive of them wants to keep a place for the warrior, and how even the most reactionary at least occasionally takes up an anti-patriarchal stand. Yet compared with the unassimilable diffuseness we have found built into the movement's enactments of itself, such contradictions and ambivalences seem models of monological clarity. In practice, the men's movement relates to that theme of Dysfunction we found in its literature through a set of behaviors reminiscent of the approach–avoid syndrome of the garden-variety neurotic towards a traumatic event that can neither be worked through nor left alone; it keeps on signaling towards an issue it is hellbent on covering over, defending itself against a set of charges that are almost never directly addressed.

Likewise with the trope of wildness and its near neighbor, the theme of Going Back; in movement gatherings, their meanings are both fleshed out and diffused far beyond those we found in the books we surveyed. For example, in the "Day for Men" hosted by Bly and Meade, we participants were introduced to the nondescript college auditorium in which the day's events would take place by being urged down through a friendly gauntlet of other men grunting, chanting, cheering, and dancing to the rhythm of the drumming up on the stage, all of which we were to join, until nearly one and all (not me) were swaying by our seats chanting "Go *back, back* / Go *back, back* / Go *back, back* / Go-o-o-o-o / *Go back!*" like a chthonic football shout. This ritually licensed display of unfettered masculine exuberance was not without its plaintively ironic aspects, given that we were about to sit meekly down in our padded seats and attend for several hours to what the two star attractions had to say.

But that very irony may serve as the clue to how the relationship between ritual, wildness, and regression works, and what it works to do. Following the Foucauldian tip, we might say that the point is not to take either wildness or regression at face value, but instead to look for the actual behaviors and discourses for which they serve as alibis. In the case of the "Wild Man Weekend" documented in the 1992 film, for instance, what all the hybrid accoutrements of wildness appear both to sanction and disguise is primarily the expression of otherwise potentially unmanly sentiments: inevitably, of course, disappointment with cruel or absent fathers, but other forms and modalities of vulnerability, grief, and physical closeness and affection as well. For these men, weekend tent-camping, maintaining a campfire and campsite, sleeping out in the cold and hunching together in a sweat-lodge all serve – along with the drumming, of course – to guarantee their wildness, a compound of masculine strength and closeness to nature that in turns serves as a cover for getting weak and going soft. Hence the lame jokes and nervous laughter over "wildness" – "Hey man, you feelin' like a wild man this morning? You ready for your wild man breakfast?" – that, passing from participant to participant, echo regularly through the film.

And roughly the same was true in the monthly Seattle Wisdom Council gatherings: the yelps, whoops, growls and howls that always accompany the opening drumming reassured us that our strong wild blood was up, so that we could proceed – or is it return? – to the business of exploring how we play, what we feel, what touches and moves us, and what we are worried and uncertain about. The difference between historical and psychological regression that appeared in movement texts as a contradiction to be faced or fudged reappears here in movement activities as a way of licensing the second by ritually invoking the image of the first. Having passed into and through the stimulating, sacred, sanctioning arches of rituals designed to conjure up simultaneously both authority and transgression, tradition and the wild, we invigorated white guys can throw off our protector-provider armor, get tearful and play, in the sure and certain knowledge that our lachrymose and/or ludic outpourings are safely sealed off from the rest of the world. As a member of one of the small groups I briefly entered put it one night, in the group hug that closed off the interaction part of the meeting and led back to the closing drumming: "For a bunch of hairy-chested nutscratchers, we sure are sentimental shits, aren't we?" But this was secret knowledge, not to be let out.

If time spent inside the movement thus gives new meanings and inflections to the foregoing themes and tropes, we have seen that on the subject of the differential relations or definitions of the sexes that movement mainly keeps up a complex silence. The most pronounced exception in my experience to this rule was, unsurprisingly, Bly himself during the "Day for Men," with an occasional assist from Meade. I have already had occasion to quote Bly's remark, replete with unabashedly pre-oedipal imagery, on the dangers to young boys of being taught by women in elementary school. It came not long after an extended ramble over the supposed differences between stages in life's journey for women and men, expressed in *Iron John* and up on the stage as an unbelievably simple-minded difference between two sets of colors (men need to go from red to white to black, women from white to red to black, as I recall), and not long before a spirited defense of the "Warrior's" capacity to hold the boundaries: "You gotta have your Warrior really up if you're gonna deal with marriage!" our wise and wild elder fairly crowed. And employ some stealth and guile as well, it would seem. Though one of the day's several closing gestures involved giving "honor" to "our wives and lovers, women or men," we were also warned by Bly not to tell them too much about what we had heard, felt, and learned that day, and were advised to "Buy a little gift for your wife or lover, so that when she asks what you got out of this day, just give it to her." Throughout the day, in effect, whenever the subject of male–female relationships came up, Bly's remarks and responses were congruent with his early assertion that "Men and women feel and talk differently – they're different tribes." Different and, apparently, innately inimical as well; so that if you're a guy you'd better keep your guard up when members of that other tribe are around.

In Bly's live rendition of the Separate-But-Equal theme, then, there's a lot more emphasis on Cold War and a strong defense than negotiation and détente. And I did hear of – though without actually witnessing first-hand – various events supported by or at least publicized through move-ment channels in which such paranoid views held sway (for example, a weekend retreat for men and women on an island in Puget Sound, in which the two sexes first gathered, consolidated, and affirmed their tribal natures in separate locations, then, quite slowly, with some dramatic out-bursts of screaming and shouting and considerable mutual distrust, began to meet and talk, one tribe to another, by the end of the final day). Mainly, though, the view from within the movement of men's relations with women (and, implicitly, towards feminism) seems, in the very charged silence in which it is typically let hang, both less aggressive than Bly's and less well worked out. Obviously, the movement as a whole is premissed on the assumption of *some* difference or differences between men and women; equally obviously, it runs off a widespread sense on the part of its adherents that men like themselves, if not men as a whole, are all too likely to be misunderstood in the outside world, by either "straight" mainstream society, or women, or both. But for the most part the "tribal" assertions ventured by movement participants do not lash out at female "others"; men in local groups and monthly Wisdom Councils seem more concerned with finding and holding onto what is supposedly theirs as men, what is worthwhile or even honorable about what they feel to be masculinity, and on "doing the inner looking ... that women have done," as one informant put it, than on drawing sabres in defense of their turf. What Separate-But-Equal is mainly about for them is simply how not to feel ashamed.

But perhaps this is the place to begin to speak at greater length of the flip side of Othering in the men's movement, that is, of its appropriations of objects and practices from other non-white and non-Western cultures, presumably under the guise of their putative status as elements of Men's culture, that great empowering cross-cultural tradition with which we white middle-aged baby-boomers and our fathers have somehow lost touch. For example, during the introductory remarks that come between the opening drumming ritual and the speaking/sharing part of the Wisdom Council's monthly program, we are solemnly informed by one of the Council's volunteer conveners that the speaking stick we are to hold while standing in the center of the gathered circle to share our truths was made by "Native American men" and "has been held" since then "over two thousand times by men." This "tradition" of the speaking stick is thus affiliated and aligned on a continuum with other so-called "traditions" – the word is quite frequently employed, the concept readily invoked – such as the "tradition" that, in the words of the same convener, "we recently began" of "honoring men who have for the first time made their way to the Council." In other words, the activity we are looking at here involves not just the appropriation but the slapdash *construction* of tradition, and the feverish conjunction of the two. What we must eventually consider, then, is not just the political and ethical implications of the appropriations themselves, but where this ravening hunger for tradition comes from and what it is about.

First, though, I should note that not everyone who employs or cites "rituals" and "traditions" taken from non-white cultures as a part of his practice in the men's movement is oblivious to the moral and political implications of his actions. One local group leader, granting that his group used "lots of Native American stuff" as part of its practice, was quick to add in his and his group's defense, first, that "we all have our own wisdom" and "wouldn't want to be laying any stuff on anyone else," and, second, that he uses the objects and procedures he has found in Native American culture – the drums and sweats and mythological/cosmological wisdom – only insofar as he "found something that spoke to me." "I am who I am," this man said, "and I'm taking what I can, with great honor." The logic here, so far as I can make out, would seem to defend against an identitarian ethic of cultural authenticity (as the t-shirts say, "It's a Black thing – you wouldn't understand") by invoking a kind of extreme Protestant-individualist notion of *sincerity*: no one has a right to lay down the law about what can or can't be appropriated from another culture's repertoire. But neither does anyone have a right to draw items from that stock, unless they resonate deeply with one's own inner spirit – and even then they must be taken with proper humility and respect.

Moreover, it seems important to point out the obvious about all these appropriations, beneath and beyond all the rationalizations: that their frequency and urgency is inversely related to the wisdom, resonance and value these men find in the white straight middle-class culture to which most of them, however antagonistic their own consciousness and however alternative their own practices, must nonetheless live in near relation. As Michael Meade, Bly's cohort, said in the "Day for Men," "Modern means no ritual"; and no ritual for these men means no meaning and no depth, merely the yawning vacuity Weber described seventy-odd years ago as the terminus of bureaucratically administered capitalism and instrumental rationality.[15] On the other hand, what is equally clear from the comparatively self-conscious self-defense of the movement guy quoted above is its righteous assumption of the consumerist freedom to pick and choose among the goods of assorted cultural traditions, albeit according to the dictates of the "true self." Such license, as we have seen, is then extended as well by sprinkling virtually any set of habits or customs within the movement, no matter how recently formed, with the pixie dust of "ritual" or "tradition." In short, we are back in the neighborhood of that symptomatic circuitry that connects up the Archetypal and the Therapeutic in the literature; only here, on the grounds of conventional speech and practice by non-gurus within the movement, the invocation of the magic "r" and "t" words stands in for and does the work of the former concept. If you hang around inside the corners of this movement I've visited, you are likely to hear the occasional expression of gratitude to "Robert," and, now and again, a fleeting reference to "doing my ashes work" or "dealing with my wound" as introduction to or wind-up of one's rap; but allusions to "King energy" and the like are altogether far less common. (Because they might sound too much like ideas, or because some concepts simply sound too silly out loud?) Instead, it is the more or less arbitrarily ritualized meeting format itself that connects one's own experience, situation, and the therapeutic techniques with which one deals with it to some larger whole: to the "tradition" of "deep masculinity," if it happens you need all that much.

In any case, whatever else such an elevation and separation from the mundane may accomplish – and we have seen that it is capable of working in a wide variety of ways to achieve a diversity of effects – it also works the way Archetypes do in our texts to establish and maintain a connection with the social while continuing to avoid any brush with questions of politics, viz. of the socially structured distribution of power. In this sense, of course, the so-called men's movement scarcely deserves to be called one, not even in the blandly general terms my old Webster's Collegiate hands out ("a series of organized activities by people working concertedly toward some goal"). Working concertedly? Some goal? This movement's blend of anti-intellectual expressivism, radical (and consumerist) individualism, contained as they are inside tall *bricolaged* hedges of tradition and myth would seem to militate against the possibility of collective will and social project alike. Yet many feminists, especially those who simply equate the movement with *Iron John* and Bly, have been quick to charge that the movement does have a political agenda, or at least exhibits a distinct and singular tendency: to wit, patriarchal reaction. Likewise, as we've seen, some movement "theorists" and participants, like Kipnis or Keen or the man who spoke to me about eventually, collectively emerging from the movement as "men *for* something – for equality, for feelings" – seem to suggest that the movement as presently constituted is but a necessary inward-looking prologue to a rejuvenated radical politics to come. This politics is sketched mainly in terms of a redefined commitment to gender justice within a redefined but not deconstructed conception of the two genders, the "masculine" and "feminine" in resonantly co-constituting equipoise. This latter vision is, moreover, typically affiliated with other putatively progressive stances, including and especially a Green-style commitment to global interdependence without domination, responsible stewardship of the earth, denuclearization, and world peace, that is, with those forms of 1980s radicalism least disturbing and therefore most congenially practicable to white Americans with middling incomes and up.

Despite such narcissistically self-enclosed limitations, however, this vision of where the movement is heading is obviously different from, and far more sanguine than, the estimations offered by most of the movement's feminist critics. Which is right, then? If I have done my work well enough to this point, if my description of the movement's literature and, *a fortiori*, its practice, has been anywhere near "thick" enough, you will anticipate and join me in answering "Neither" and "Both." Better, in my view – more illuminating, and finally more politically useful, too – to turn the question of men's movement's politics towards an exploration of the social history of its adherents' formative relationships to politics, especially but not exclusively to the various feminist perspectives they encounter in the particular, peculiar, alternative cultures and lifeworlds in which many movement adherents spend at least part of their time.

3. OF ENCLAVES AND TRIBES

As an introduction to this topic, I want to recount a few stories about some interactions between various individuals and (minimally defined) groups within the Seattle men's movement on the one hand, and, on the other, the broad coalition that was thrown up in Seattle first to mobilize against and then to protest the 1991 Gulf War. I do not pretend to know the whole story of those interactions, or to offer a "master narrative" of them here. However, as a particular conjuncture of research interests, academic leave-time, and moral and political commitments would have it, I was on sabbatical in Seattle in the winter of 1990–91, dividing much of my time between working for the anti-war coalition, and dipping around in various movement forums and events. So, as my earlier anecdote about the similar effects of two very different sets of drummers suggests, I was well situated to get some sense of whatever contacts between these two "movements" might occur.

On that day in early February 1991 I was, as I have said, coming from the monthly gathering of the Wisdom Council to a coalition-organized protest rally and march against the war the Bush administration had started a few weeks before. Much of the talk in the circle that morning concerned the war, and all of it was in opposition to it. There was, predictably, little analysis beyond a few scattered references to "oil" and to Bush and Hussein acting like "big babies"; mainly, even on this subject, the point was the truth of your own individual feelings. But the feelings expressed were those of anger, fear, and disgust; one man, hazarding a rare generalization, spoke of us all having a "fever of a certain kind – a low-grade infection that spikes." Some men invoked their past experiences as Vietnam vets or anti-war student protestors and, either way, said that it was "happening again." Several said they'd come to the Council directly from the anti-war encampment that still surrounded the Seattle Federal Building at the time; others vowed to do "whatever it takes to stop this thing – and I hope some of you guys'll be there with me." "*Ho!*" said the crowd to that, including me. But oddly enough, no speaker so much as mentioned the widely publicized rally and march that was about to begin just as this Council would be drumming itself back out to the world.

Nor, for that matter, did I spot anyone else from the Council gathering just past in the crowd at the Central District, the African-American neighborhood where the coalition's rally would be held, and from which our march would step off (though of course that is no proof that no one else from the gathering was there). But downwind of stage left, standing off to the side of the Queer Nation info and t-shirt-sales table, was a white guy in his mid-thirties with thinning brownish hair, handing out as many fliers as he could (business was not brisk for him) stating Seattle M.E.N.'s position on the Gulf War. Under a rebus-like insignia that went ♂ 4 ⊕ it read, in part, as follows (grammar and punctuation as in the original):

> Seattle M.E.N. an organization dedicated to supporting men, and raising public consciousness about men's issues is absolutely opposed to and abhors any form of violence in the Middle East and Worldwide. Our mission state-ment reflects nonviolent conflict resolution. We are distressed and angry that our culture socializes from birth our men to be warriors, expects them to sacrifice their lives for unjust causes, and are forced to register for the draft and face possible combat.
>
> We urge our members and the general public to call their elected political representatives and demand a peaceful resolution of the Middle East Situa-tion. We encourage our members and the general public to contact their representatives in support of peace and become actively involved through participation in and financial contributions to peace organizations. For more information about Seattle M.E.N. call 285–4356.
>
> Men are NOT disposable!

The M.E.N. here stands for Men's Evolvement Network, a coordinating body composed almost entirely of volunteers that puts out a small monthly newsletter (of which more later), maintains an information-referral phone, and helps to organize and publicize events such as the meetings of local neighborhood circles, the monthly Wisdom Council, such special events as the one-day Bly–Meade event I attended, and other goods and services targeted for movement-identified men. Somewhere around this same time, M.E.N. itself had been admitted into the anti-war coalition as one of the latter's forty-odd member organizations, ranging from the Palestine Solidarity Committee to Queer Nation, through the whole alphabet soup of the local and national anti-racist, feminist, anti-imperialist, non-sectarian Left – though only after extensive and at times somewhat heated discussion between M.E.N. representatives and delegates from other already admitted organizations on the coalition's steering committee as to whether M.E.N.'s commitment to drawing the links between the war abroad and, especially, sexist oppression at home was sufficiently strong and genuine. The men from M.E.N. kept insisting it was; and eventually, with varying degrees of goodwill, their word was at least momentarily taken. Already though, as our newest anti-war rally slowly came into focus on that drizzly afternoon in early February, the crowd's general lack of interest in M.E.N.'s point of view, and occasional revulsion from its presence – "Oh *ugh*!" I heard one woman say to her companion as she realized what she had just unknowingly taken, dropping the sheet she'd just been handed as though it were a poisonous snake – seemed to indicate that in the minds of the constituency our coalition was drawing on, the alliance was neither a secure nor obvious one, to say the least.

On another Saturday afternoon just two weeks later, I was sitting in the auditorium at my "Day for Men," listening to the supposedly open-ended discussion of the war for which Bly and Meade had announced at the beginning of the day they would set aside some time: an open-ended discussion that both of them, and Bly in particular, were in fact fairly carefully stage-managing. First of all, though I don't doubt that most of the 600–odd men who had arrived at this event were opposed to the war, Bly and Meade had, in effect, encouraged their audience to take such a stand with the very words they used to announce the forthcoming discussion (for example, Meade: "To me, it's a woeful time..."). Then, when the time for that discussion arrived, Bly made clear that he wanted to hear only "statements from the heart – statements from the soul," as opposed, of course, to any ideas of what the war was about. He made no bones about not only cutting short anyone who tried to offer the latter – "What's your *feeling*?" he and the crowd snarled back at the one poor sap who attempted to trot out a political analysis – and snapped back even at those whose particular flavor of emotional reaction seemed off to him: to a man who had stood up to say he felt guilty "doing this yuppie thing while people are dying," he snuffed back, "You're not in a feeling there; guilt is the opposite of feeling." ("Beautiful statement," he told the next speaker, who recounted an appropriately inchoate dream.) Bly himself, though, was hardly short of ideas when, after some of us had spoken, it came his time to offer "a few comments from the years of working with men that seemed to apply to this war." And you can probably guess by now what kind of ideas they were. "Underneath the male psyche," we were told (again), "lie a number of very powerful and ancient beings – among them the King, the Warrior, the Lover ... the Magician." But in this particular case, with the onset of this War, it was the "shallow, aggressive Warrior" that was "being activated" (as opposed, you see, to the good, deep, peace-loving one). George Bush was "caught inside of a myth," stuck in the "white" of his own incorruptible rightness: a "*defective* myth," it was important to add, since in some sense being stuck in myths is, of course, not only a good but an inevitable state of affairs. In this case, however, what he was now doing was akin (or was it identical?) to Agamemnon's sacrifice of his daughter Iphigenia for the sake of his success in the Trojan Wars. "I just want to say that mythologically, that's what it looks like. It doesn't look like a good prospect."

The preceding pages will, I hope, have made it clear that Robert Bly and *Iron John* in themselves hardly represent the full range of tendencies, energies, and possibilities tied up in the men's movement. But there is still something symptomatic in this treatment of both the audience and the War. In the first place, the audience is, in terms of the traditional binarism of our white Western gender categories, both invited to occupy the terrain of expressive and irrational emotion conventionally denied to men and assigned to women (and children, non-white Others, and so on), while only our resident elder, Bly, is allowed anything like the conventionally male-identified power to invoke rationality, to compose and put forward arguments and analyses. Such a division of labor is arguably a fixed feature of wide stretches of the movement as a whole, in its willingness to let others – those "elders" who as therapists, institute directors, and authors conduct the retreats, supervise the larger gatherings, and write the books – do its thinking for it, so long as the emotion-ridden confessions and effulgences of all non-elders in the group are both literally and ritually contained, and (therefore?) condoned there as *also* Male. Secondly, though, what is most noticeable about Bly's mythological analysis of the origins and nature of the Gulf War, aside from the now familiar way it renders politics into myth and so relieves us of the need to do anything political at all, is the degree to which it is so patently *non-falsifiable*. When the times are good, the leaders benevolent and wise, it is because the good sides of the archetypes are being accessed and held in equipoise, the best and healthiest of myths are being used. When they are bad, it is because the negative side of the archetype has surfaced, the balance is off, a "defective myth" has gotten hold of things. It is a game, really, anyone can play; one, moreover, with the pleasant or maddening feature, depending on your point of view, that whoever plays it can by definition never lose or be wrong; nor, for that matter, need the game ever come to an end.

We will return to fix this relationship between contingent social event and overarching archetype in its own cultural-historical environment in a minute. First, though, I want to get to what I know of the end of this fragmentary drama of the movement and the War, if only because like all good last acts, it brings the principals together for a final face-off. It begins with one of Bly and Meade's closing announcements near the end of that same "Day for Men": to wit, that on the Friday of the following weekend, starting from a large old church in downtown Seattle, there would be a "Poetry Reading and Grief Walk" in response to the Gulf War, one attended and conducted by (I am trying not to say "starring") the late Northwest poet William Stafford along with Bly and Meade. What I didn't witness first-hand, though, but heard about later, was the steering committee meeting of the coalition at which the delegate from M.E.N. asked for coalition endorsement for the event – an imprimatur of more than symbolic value, given the publicity the coalition could still generate for the actions it organized and/or sponsored – and was turned down. From what I got from friends in and around the steering committee, it sounded as though people made their decision on various grounds, some of them convergent with my evaluations here – as, for example, the suspicion that the event would be too emotionally focused, so concerned with the ritual enactment and exorcism of "grief" as to have no political content at all. But everyone with whom I spoke about this decision allowed that their judgements were influenced as well by their general suspicion of any activities organized by group(s) whose main focus and constituency were white men, and their disinclination to have their coalition too publicly identified with such groups.

In any case, the effective result of the steering committee's decision was to end whatever working relationship had existed between the various forces behind the anti-war coalition and those of M.E.N. This breakdown coincided neatly enough with the success of our government/media's campaign to whip up support for the US adventure in the Gulf that it would be impossible to tell how much it had to do with the nearly complete silence on the War that fell over the men's groups I looked in on through the rest of that winter and spring. But I do think that the breakdown, and perhaps other incidents like it, involving M.E.N.'s relationship to the relatively large progressive community in Seattle, probably had something to do with discernible shifts in self-definition and focus in the organization's monthly newsletter, *Seattle M.E.N.* Between December 1990 and March 1991, for example, M.E.N.'s "Statement of Goals," reprinted in each newsletter, somehow mutated into a "Mission Statement" with a significantly different spin to it.

Statement of Goals (12/90)

The goal of Seattle M.E.N. is to assist men, women and families struggling to adapt to and recover from the sweeping changes affecting them and the planet. Seattle M.E.N. provides networking, referrals and workshops related to those concerns and changes. We support and reflect the values of equality, non-violence, health, spiritual connectedness and ecological soundness. We share our joy, love, respect and care for each other and the planet with our community.

Mission Statement (3/91)

The Mission of Seattle M.E.N. is to assist men in their evolvement, to raise public consciousness about issues affecting men and to support the values of equality, non-violence, health, spiritual-connectedness and ecological soundness.

Within another year, moreover, this mission statement was to gather itself in yet further; by the following spring, it read simply, "The mission of Seattle M.E.N. is to provide support, information, and advocacy for men."[16]

Let me be clear here about what I do not mean. I am not claiming, and could in any case not persuasively argue, that the suspicion with which Seattle M.E.N.'s overtures were met in the anti-war coalition, and the eventual rebuff it received from that group, were solely, or even primarily, responsible for the narrowing of its institutional self-definition. Nor do I mean to plant the false suggestion that the change in definition was accompanied by any corresponding reduction of the often dizzyingly contradictory play of voices and perspectives within the newsletter to a grunting chauvinist monotone. In fact, though the organization's center of gravity clearly lies somewhere within the mythopoetic men's movement we have been discussing, its newsletter continues to announce the national conference of NOMAS, the explicitly pro-feminist National Organization of Men Against Sexism, right alongside notice of the annual meeting of some Men's Rights group; to run side-by-side contributions from local writers on the barbarous violence of male circumcision, and on the wisdom and necessity of reviving male rites of initiation into the deep masculine qualities of stoical, self-disciplined courage, autonomy and strength; and, on virtually a monthly basis, to publish pieces by local men active in the movement that exfoliate the murky contradictions we have found in its texts and practices again and again, as in this succulent extract from a piece with the provocative title "Staking Myself Down":

> The most courageous thing many men can do today is to cry in front of men. In today's battlefield of the heart, to cry as a man is to stake oneself down.... In many ways, crying in front of a group of men is akin to the training of boys who learned stealth and to listen to their hearts and the Spirit. Yet it is only training for the greater battles to come.[17]

On the other hand, though, I do mean to suggest that the troubled patterns of interaction and reaction between and within M.E.N. and the anti-war coalition exemplify various overlapping and often hostile interrelationships between and among alternative culture, radical politics, and the men's movement in contemporary white America, relationships that we may now begin to spin out of those examples. Let me begin by pointing out the broad continuity in the reactions to the war between the parts of the Seattle-area men's movement I was involved with, and those of other "neighboring" constituencies. It was not Seattle M.E.N. alone whose anti-war rhetoric revolved around the specter of American bodies coming back from the Middle East. To our local coalition's detriment, such an emphasis – expedient in the immediate run-up to the outbreak of hostilities, but both politically disastrous and morally monstrous in the long run, given the fish-in-a-bucket slaughter that followed – was pretty near the center of our own strategy for mobilization as well. Nor was Bly's mythologizing rap the only anti-war discourse around that foreclosed on the political; around the coffee houses and left-feminist bookstores of the area, and in the pages of local underground papers and handouts, the air was thick with therapy-talk of Bush's need to prove his masculinity, and the state as a "dysfunctional family." Likewise, the Poetry and Grief Walk for which coalition endorsement was denied was hardly the only public event devoted to the expression of grief and lamentation; I myself attended one of these, a candlelit ceremony of song, meditation and prayer sponsored by an interdenominational group of local churches with the blessing of – you guessed it – the Seattle Coalition against War in the Persian Gulf.

In the context of these other similar if not identical forms of rhetoric and action – all of them left uncriticized if not actively endorsed by those most active in mobilizing anti-war response – it becomes clear that what could not be approved about Seattle M.E.N.'s anti-war perspective was its concentration on men. In every other respect, its ways of handling the issue of the war were akin if not identical to those of large sectors of Seattle's progressive/alternative community. And to a great extent the same is true, I want to argue, of the overall relationship between that community and the men's movement which, after all, grows in and out of it. Fleshing out that claim, and speculating on its political implications, for feminism and progressive politics in general, will be the burden of the rest of this chapter.

It is, for starters, no accident that the epicenters of men's movement activity lie within those nouveau-urban regions ranging from the Twin Cities of Minneapolis and the area around Austin, Texas, out through Santa Fe, Albuquerque, and the Denver–Boulder hub to the Bay Area and the cities of the Pacific Northwest, where enclaves of the white counter-culture of the 1960s and 1970s have managed to survive the economic and ideological assaults of the Reagan–Bush eighties. What such areas have in common – aside, that is, from the aesthetic appeal of most of their easily accessed surroundings – is an economic base centered largely around "clean" industries, from tourism and financial services to aerospace and microelectronics, and dependent on a large and relatively skilled white-collar workforce. Where alternative or countercultural white communities have had no such economic base to piggyback, no such workforce to connect with as clients and consumers for countercultural artisans and entrepreneurs, or as fellow employees, they have tended to be economically and/or culturally squeezed out.

How, then, to characterize the way the post-sixties middle-aged baby-boomers who largely compose these alternative white enclaves relate to the "straight" world to which, economically anyhow, they necessarily remain connected? Here is one useful formulation: denizens of these enclaves

> took to heart the sixties languages of personal and everyday life transformation, grafting them on to the grammar of self-determination that eschewed the materialism of acquisitive self-interest espoused by the New Right, while offering a weak vocabulary of social responsibility somewhat removed from the politics of class, race, gender, and sexual preference waged by the post-sixties left.[18]

Somewhat, as we shall see, and somewhat not; and sometimes more than others. But this is Andrew Ross, clapping with one hand for the political culture of those placed under the rubric of New Age culture.

The appropriately broad terms of such a political-discursive definition work well to define the characteristic ways in which most white Americans living today within alternative cultural communities construct, encode and justify their social behavior, whether they or we want to call them "New Agers" or not. Indeed, in its most inclusive definitions, New Age is neither more nor less than the *lingua franca* of whatever alternative political culture is left in white America out beyond the groves of academe; so we are probably doomed to have something of the same kind of argument over its possibilities and limitations as a resource for radical politics as that conducted a generation ago on the effects of Methodism among the subaltern classes of early-nineteenth-century England. Indeed, at the conclusion of his own long exploratory essay on New Age culture, Ross rehearses some of the most likely positions to be taken up in just such a debate. The one in opposition to which he develops his own point of view is that New Age cultures represent the "maturing of a generation, who have inevitably made their peace with capitalism." But this version is capable of further elaboration in various quite different directions: from a cynical or right-wing perspective, as the triumph of the market's engulfing capacity over all would-be challengers; from one close to some sectors within New Age communities, as the victorious recognition of the primacy of consciousness and individual responsibility over social structure and politics as usual; or from what Ross describes as a "patrician" left, as a "narrative of decline" into commodified self-indulgence whose deleterious effects can only be countered by a "call for self-restraint, deference to public interest, and heroic affirmation of traditional reason."[19] Against all these variants, however, Ross argues that New Age culture is not simply a containment and commodification of the New Left's radical sixties energies, but also works as a preservation and continuation of what was best and most distinctive about that radical will: its attempt to come up with an "alternative (left) politics of social individualism," one that could "account for the importance of 'private' or personal acts in people's everyday lives."[20]

It is far from my intention here to settle these arguments. The problem is rather to figure out how far each truth stretches, where they cut across each other and where they overlap, and how certain forms of progressive political action on this cultural terrain are *both* enabled and distorted by the results. As my first move in this direction, I offer a friendly amendment to Ross's description of the political inflections of New Age culture, placing a question mark alongside the distinction its concluding phrase posits between New Age culture and left politics. For my own experience of doing progressive politics through the 1980s – chiefly but not exclusively anti-interventionist work around the conflicts in Central America, mainly but not exclusively in the Pacific Northwest – has seemed to suggest that once you get beyond the academic left and academic feminism within white America, much if not most of the "politics" that still gets "waged by the post-sixties left" happens out of the countercultural enclaves I've described, and is thus in crucial ways indissolubly commingled with New Age inflections, assumptions, and key terms.

To give this claim the supporting evidence it deserves would obviously require another essay as groaningly long as this one. In lieu of such argument, then, let me try to evoke some sense of the political culture I have been in with a few more observations and anecdotes, starting with the extent to which political identities are conceived within this culture first and foremost as *cultural* identities, that is, as memberships in this or that particular tribe. For example, among the parts of the Central America solidarity movement I was in and around in the Northwest USA, the predominant characterization of the Guatemalan or Salvadoran people, and even of Sandinista Nicaragua, was not unlike that of the rainforest Indians of the Amazon region: each (and, to some extent, all together) were assumed to be enfolded in a single preindustrial culture, a wise and coherent way of being and living, now under assault from an equally single-minded anti-tribe of predatory modernized elites in thrall to instrumental rationality, imperial domination, and the good life in Miami. Likewise, inside this same political imaginary, with regard to the struggles of African-American or Native American people to preserve their constantly preyed upon yet still intact wisdoms and truths from something often simply called "white America." And, coming closer to home, ditto for women, whose wise and natural, interdependent and compassionate ways of knowing and behaving have been demeaned and brutalized for untold centuries (just how many is a matter of amiable dispute in the literature), along with the wise and true culture they have somehow kept alive in the teeth of the unrelenting, top-down oppression of men.

In my experience, it is only within gay male culture, grounded as it has been in urbanity and abused as it has been by sexual ideologies of "the natural," that such naturalized tribal self-descriptions have been eschewed as the basis of political claims. Otherwise, the list is quite readily, even mechanically expandable, from ecology, particularly in its "ecofeminist" or "deep ecology" variants, to (especially, but far from exclusively non-academic) currents in lesbian communities with whom I've had some contact and done some coalition work. The hydraulic logic of their common social algebra is easily summed up. Each of these tribes has its own nature, a culture that *is* nature; that is, if you will, *its* Archetype, or its own collection of several, a kind of ever-resurgent geyser of truth and wisdom that is simply held down, without any other effect or alteration, by the Powers That Be. Among and between these tribes there is, in the strong sense of the term, a natural affinity, one based not only on their common oppressor but equally on that shared relationship to natural truth that the oppressor lacks. What that oppressor possesses and inflicts is instead, by definition, neither a culture nor a nature in the oppressed's common understanding of those virtually identical terms, but a pathology: the need to dominate, the inability to perceive self or world in interdependent and nurturant terms, the compulsion to objectify, calculate, ratiocinate, and "go to one's head" instead of to the body and/or heart where the real wisdom resides. The oppressors are thus responsible for bringing us the wretched psychic and physical squalor of "straight" culture, "mainstream" values, indeed modernity itself; these sickies are the anti-tribal secularizing group whose lack of wisdom, devotion to domination, and ruthlessly imposed anti-culture have brought all the other tribes to the state of common victimage they all now occupy; and these sickies are – I have withheld their name but you will have guessed it – straight white men.

Such a culturalist vision of the political landscape offers manifest psycho-political rewards to those who hold it, by conferring upon them a strong sense of their own purity, and permitting them to presume their solidarity in a natural confederation of tribes that appears in the mind as a kind of planetary Rainbow Coalition – albeit one from which considerations of social class have usually been discreetly withdrawn. One small problem, though, is precisely the extent to which that Coalition must remain confined to the mind, especially for countercultural white New Age progressives for whom the sight of such "contradictions among the people" as those between, say, the Miskito Indians and the Sandinista government in the early 1980s, the Salvadoran FDR and FMLN in the later years of the same decade, or, for that matter, between professional, working-class, and poor Blacks inevitably come as a well-nigh unassimilable shock, and in any case with whom many an actually existing member of these other putative tribes may signally fail to recognize their organic affinity. However, it is perfectly possible to avoid such snubs and disappointments by the simple expedient of never subjecting the assumption of natural equivalences and alliances to the test of actual contact with members of very many other tribes: except, that is, through the mediating channels created and confirmed via intuitive recognition and selective appropriation of those other tribes' cultural practices and objects, from the sweat-lodge to the natural-dyed, hand-woven Guatemalan skirt, items to be shuffled into an ensemble that, given the logic we have described, may well include the purchase, employment and display of a lunar calendar based on that devised by the Goddess-worshipping Druids of what is now Great Britain, more than twelve centuries ago.

Such acts of appropriation and consumption-in-solidarity may then come to constitute a large and even predominant dimension of a left-countercultural politics (or political culture) that duly registers "the importance of 'private' or personal acts in people's everyday lives." Indeed, it may be clear already how effectively the Archetypes of tribalized truth underwrite and warrant a countercultural common sense that equates journeys of "self-discovery" towards "personal fulfillment" and "deep emotional growth" with radical politics, especially if not exclusively for all those whose true and tribal selves – as women (or "womyn"), Native Americans, lesbians, and so on – are one and the same. To find one's self beneath the damage, to discover one's tribal affinities: these are, according to this reading of that originary slogan of late-sixties feminism "The personal is political," inherently subversive actions beyond which it is by no means clear what more or else is to be done.

This blur between self-discovery and politics, this mix-and-match jumble of New Age myths and therapies with conceptions of political oppression and empowerment, is perhaps most marked in the case of non-academic feminism, as even a casual perusal of the shelves and stacks of Red and Black Books, Seattle's most successful left-feminist bookstore, makes plain. Worker-members of the co-op that owns and runs the store freely admit the extent to which steadily increasing sales of books on dysfunctional families and co-dependent relationships issuing out of the recovery movement, together with other New Age titles on witchcraft and Goddess worship, channeling and crystals, are making the difference for them between red ink and black. Such titles, moreover, sit easily alongside other, more explicitly political works devoted to feminist therapy (to feminism *as* therapy?), such as Marion Woodman's *Leaving My Father's House: A Journey to Conscious Femininity*: "The renowned analyst and author here provides deep insight into the process required to bring feminine wisdom to consciousness in a patriarchal culture – a struggle in which many women are more fully engaged today than ever before," the back-cover copy reads.[21] Or we might move to the front door of a typical Seattle-area coffeehouse (the epicenter of the counterculture's public sphere in the Northwest) to read off the flier announcing a "Women's Empowerment Group now forming," whose means and modalities will include "Meditation," "Journaling," "Drumming," and "Spiritual Growth." "Each week," the flier declares, "we will meditate, journey and drum. Brooke Medicine Eagle's new book *Buffalo Woman Comes Singing* will be used extensively."[22]

Further examples could be heaped up virtually without end, since such uncontainably syncretic and eclectic forms of what Alice Echols calls "cultural," and others "difference feminism," percolate and permute along and through the length and breadth of the white countercultural land-scape, from the narrow defiles of local political activism to the mountain peaks of pure consciousness and the "flight into light."[23] But what most needs emphasizing about that feminism here is the extent to which its mobility and viral appropriative powers depend on the assumed equivalence and fixity of the categories "straight" (as in "mainstream," "hegemonic," society) and "(white) male." Within this culture, that is, the pervasive assumption is that all white men by birth and definition conform to Kathy Ferguson's concisely summarized view of Hegelian man as constituted and constrained by his

> desire for the consumption and control of nature; desire for recognition via domination; desire for the other's desire. The kind of person who could have these desires turns out to be characteristically modern, western, and male: an intersubjectively impoverished individual locked into a variety of combative stances, seeking dominance in relationships, mastery over nature, and absorption of differences.[24]

Only if this twisted individual exists among white men alone, and is hard-wired in all of them, are women of even the most privileged races, dominant classes and mainstream walks of life licensed to bond, in-discriminately and, as it were, in-differently, with each other and with all non-white, non-male, non-Western, and/or pre-modern groups, in fact and, *a fortiori*, in fantasy.

Numerous feminist and pro-feminist critics have called attention to the political liabilities and blind spots written into this version of feminism;[25] and Andrew Ross has brought us still closer to home by focusing on the reactive relationship between various holistic, New Age and ecofeminist versions of women's culture, identity and history articulated in and across a variety of influential countercultural and political texts, and the appearance and success of Bly and Keen.[26] The problem with such critiques, indispensable as they are, is that they still fail to get out past the texts to that country of unpaid everyday intellectuals where many self-described feminist women have not yet heard of Carol Gilligan, but will readily agree that "women's ways of knowing" and of making moral judgements are inherently different from, and superior to, men's.[27] Here is where Kathryn Robinson, writing for Seattle's main (meaning, among other things, mainly white) alternative newspaper, took an informal survey of her boomer friends, male and female, aged from late twenties to mid forties. She found that when asked what "they believed to be the inherent positive qualities of each gender" both men and women could readily recite the standard feminine virtues, "using words such as empathy, nurturing, creativity, gentleness, and sensitivity." But with few exceptions – and none of them male – no one could make, or even imagine, a connection between a meritorious quality of any kind and masculinity. Even the few exceptions – those women who cited being a "good protector" or being good at "taking action" as positive male traits – did so only "sheepishly, looking down at their feet."[28] Here is where, sitting on a bus-stop bench reading the newest installment of a five-part series in one of the city's "straight" dailies on the rising tide of domestic violence, I looked up to find a middle-aged white woman staring down over my shoulder at the same horrific article. Our eyelines tangled and I shook my head. "Terrible stuff," I said. But the implacable hostility in her gaze never wavered. "Are *you* in a group?" she asked. From instinct bred of long experience, I knew instantly what she meant: was I in a recovery group for batterers, was I working on my own program? I threw my desperate hands as open as my eyes were hysterically wide. "Hey!" I said, "I don't hit women! I don't hit women!" By this time, though, the bus was pulling up, and she was ahead of me in line; but the face that turned one last time to mine was the same. "Yeah," she said, "sure," and got on. Here is where a radical lesbian-feminist I have known for years gleefully laughed off my assurances that in this book I would "try to get it right" (as she will, no doubt, laugh off this chapter if she hears of it): "You *can't* get it right," she said, with a certainty so perfect as to verge on goodwill. Here is where one of the more popular graffiti, especially suitable for coffeehouse wall or john, is "DEAD MEN DON'T RAPE."

And here, finally, is where my partner and I had dinner one night out on one of those islands in Puget Sound where even the local class structure – basically, split between scrabbling downscale hippies and high-end alternative yuppies – is incorporated in the counterculture and inflected by its terms. We were visiting a family on the upscale side that night, one of my partner's fellow grad students in an alternative Master's program in psychology and social work. The husband and father – George, I'll call him – clearly made a good living practicing law in the city across the Sound; the wife and mother – Ellen, let's say – had her RN and had worked years ago as a nurse, but for several years stayed home to take care of their two kids, now a senior-high girl and a junior-high boy. Clearly, both parents put considerable effort into spending time with the kids, taking weekends and extended summer vacations with them, and, in general, co-parenting as much as the division of domestic and salaried labor they had chosen permitted. Just as clearly (and, arguably, homologously) they had continued to identify with and at least financially support various progressive causes, especially those concerned with environmental, peace, and human-rights issues, as much as the same cultural, economic, and familial choices allowed. They lived in a nice old farmhouse whose integrity they'd taken care to maintain even as they opened it up to more light and air on the inside, and added a deck and sauna without; they had opposed, and continued to condemn, the now formally concluded Gulf War. Already, before we sat down to eat, I had noticed among the books on their shelves a slew of titles on female spirituality and empowering archetypes; and, peeking in at a sideroom, I had spotted copies of Bly and Keen piled up on what looked like George's home desk. So, somewhere in between our tasteful dinner and the tasty dessert, I mentioned that I had been poking around the men's movement, intending eventually to write something about it, and had seen George's books. Did he consider himself in the movement? Was he a member of a local men's group?

As I recall, at this point George had already been gently chided at least once, this over his failure to walk away from the sensitive case he had been arguing in order to get home and take charge of the household during the freak icestorm and blizzard that had hit the December before last. And along with the opprobrium attached to this specific instance of the provider failing to protect, there was an undertone that explicitly surfaced now and then in the talk of both Ellen and the kids concerning the quite real moral–political compromises and complicities built into the practice George was in. Now, though, at the mention of the men's movement George's complexion took on a still deeper shade of red as the kids' faces, and Ellen's, were transfigured by the same spiteful joy. "Oh," said the grinning senior-high girl in a voice soaked to reeking with ironic portentousness, "you mean Daddy's male-bonding rituals..." And from the ensuing silence – on George's part mortified, on the rest of his family's, hugely entertained – we passed on to some other topic.

This microdrama of gender and familial relations needs to be placed, of course, somewhere near that nether edge where New Age counterculture shades into the "straight" world and its white upper-middle-class norms. But its very location there arguably only throws the issues I am trying to raise into sharper relief. Even though as of 1980, two-thirds of all boomer-generation women worked outside of the home for pay, George and Ellen have together exercised their option for a division of labor now in decline even as an ideology, thanks to the combination of feminist upsurge and economic collapse over the past twenty years: he has a career, she has children and a home. But if our dinner conversation that night was any indication, it would seem that as far as Ellen and the kids are concerned, George alone is guilty of those compromises with the immoral straight world through which the farmhouse and its grounds are sustained, the tuition bills for the kids' groovy alternative schooling are paid, and so on. And however sympathetic he may be to the environment or the cause of peace, he can never know the deep, intuitive connection to either – or for that matter, to feeling itself – that women know (not to mention what he can't know or join with as a white). And he was wrong for not leaving his job and coming home to protect his family during the storm. And his interest in the men's movement and its literature is maybe the stupidest thing of all.

And finally, I'll bet – partly from George's silence, and softness, and clear caring for his family, all of which I would have several occasions to witness again, and partly, frankly, from my own projection – that a good part of George himself believes a good part of all this. So, to some degree, do most of the white men in this counterculture, once again virtually by definition, and regardless of the directness or distance between their livelihoods and straight or mainstream business culture and its in-strumentalist, profit-maximizing ideologies. Some of the men I came across who were involved in the men's movement in the Northwest were house-husbands; several worked in alternative businesses, like co-op grocery stores or hot-tub manufacturing and sales, or various forms of alternative "body-work"; some worked in small- and medium-scale computer firms, and several had various comparatively low-level engineering jobs at Boeing. But from the house-husbands to George, I would submit that each of these men turned to the men's movement to some degree to seek its help in resolving the ongoing external and internal crisis flowing from their inevitable complicity with the evil of white masculinity, their membership in a bad tribe.

This crisis is, moreover, at least partially created, or at any rate exacerbated for them, by the degree to which our current theories of oppression, especially those circulating inside the counterculture we have been exploring, typically assume that the relationship between an individual subject – here, any straight white man – and what Peter Middleton calls a "collective singular subject" – white straight men as a group – is one of simple and direct instantiation on the one hand, coextension on the other. "One man," that is, "represents and is represented by all men." Of the utility and longevity of this assumption in relation to arguments within feminism in particular, Middleton writes as follows:

> In the past ten years the women's movement has been faced by a parallel dilemma to that of politically conscious men who wish to support feminism ... Black women have confronted white feminists with their complicity in racism.... The theory of multiple oppressions explains such conflicts by concluding that an individual can be oppressed in a cumulative way. Someone with several oppressions could claim a kind of political priority and existential authority over someone with only one oppression. The tendency to do this, and also to assume the right to speak for an oppressed group purely on the basis of one's identity as a member of this oppressed group (and not one's activities, allegiances or conscious principles) has been criticized by some feminists, but its influence in political debate remains strong. To claim oppression gives one an identity and an understanding of one's history.[29]

As long, that is, as one remains a member of at least one oppressed group: so that the "parallel" dilemma is, in effect, resolved along only one side of the tracks.

On such a politico-cultural terrain, it should come as no surprise when white men who do not wish to conform to the terms set out in Ferguson's description of the masculinist "Hegelian subject" – and whose lives and perspectives in many cases do evidence some real (if highly variable) degree of disengagement from and/or refusal of that model for themselves –

should come to announce and negotiate that disengagement in the same terms of tribalistic assertion and via the same techniques of crosscultural and transhistorical *bricolage* that have characterized other alternative groupings on the same ground. The arcs traced and retraced in the movement between individual and archetype, emotion and ritual, true feeling and true myth, for that matter even the invocation of wildness: for all their particular inflections and functions within the men's movement, these too are no more than defensive replications of, especially, that New Age "cosmic" cultural feminism against and with which the men's movement must – and does – both react *and* interact. So it only makes sense that the Wisdom Councils I attended in Seattle were first initiated four years earlier in a form and under a title (Divine Masculine Men's Gatherings) derived – with, we may now assume, all symptomatically defensive, due respect – from the Divine Feminine Women's Gatherings that blazed the cosmic-tribal trail for New Age men in the very actions and forms by which they sought to deny men's access to it. So, too, beneath the flier for the Woman's Empowerment Group on the coffeehouse door was posted another, inviting local men to help "start a men's support group to enable us to grow closer in understanding ourselves and our problems," one that, according to the same announcement, plans to "begin discussion with *Iron John.*" And so we may find, in our quarterly directory of alternative/New Age goods and services, such parallel and complementary notices as the following:

Wy'East Healing Center Presents

WOMAN • Wisdom • Strength	MAN • Power • Action
• Woman's Relationship with Mother Earth & Grandmother Moon	MAN – the Warrior and Protector
• Power through union with Great Spirit	• Sweat lodge ceremony
• Ritual and Ceremony	• Safety, support, trust
• Balance of male/female energies	• Power and union with Great Spirit
• Shields	• Relationships and intimacy
• Relationships and intimacy	• HAVE FUN!!!
• HAVE FUN!!!	TUITION: $295.00[30]
TUITION: $245.00	

where the terms set for men and women seem, if anything, more reactionary than anything we found in the darkest corners of the most retrograde movement text.

Or, you can get up close to the celebrity summit of alternative culture by purchasing a tape or reading in *New Age* magazine an edited transcript of the entirely amicable encounter (and why not?) between Iron-Bly himself and Deborah Tannen, author of *You Just Don't Understand*, a putatively feminist bestseller you can get in paper at Red and Black, on the differences between women's ways of talking and listening and men's.[31] Or, for that matter, if you've got more cash and want to go hard-core mythopoetic, you can snarfle up the entire series of six hours worth of videotaped "storytelling, dialogue and encounter" with Robert Bly *and* Marion Woodman on "Men and Women" for $149.75 (thereby receiving one "Episode" free).[32]

Yet I would not want to leave the impression that most feminists, even and perhaps especially those possessed by a strong cosmic streak, find the men's movement or its avatars welcome allies and close kin. Quite the contrary: practically every feminist-identified woman I know who learned that I was planning to write on the men's movement responded with a hoot of derision and expressed her grim hope that I would give them — those wild men, those drummers, those Bly Iron-John guys — the drubbing they deserve. In this and other respects, their univocally hostile reactions to the movement rhyme with most of those assembled in Kay Leigh Hagan's self-described "feminist collection," *Women Respond to the Men's Movement*, whose overwhelming majority opinion is put most succinctly by contributor Margo Adair: "This 'men's movement' is not about social change. It is a backlash — men clamoring to reestablish the moral authority of the patriarchs."[33] All the more ironic, then, is the extent to which the terms and tones of their condemnations reveal the very ground — in a double sense here, as homeland of its presuppositions and as a permanently hostile terrain — on which the movement circles its wagons and constructs itself.

Here, for example, is where Seattleite feminist therapist Laura Brown's voice kicks in, once she realizes that her confusion in the face of the topic can only be a function of patriarchy at work:

> how do I feel about the mythopoetic men's movement? I feel frightened, and angry, and critical, and amused. I think that anything which is so terrifically attractive to white, middle-class, heterosexual men (for who else is buying *Iron John* in hardback, who else able in these recession times to fork out the dollars for a "men's wisdom retreat") is probably very dangerous to women.[34]

If They're going for It, in other words – "They" being straight white guys, among whom no further distinctions are required or possible – It must by definition be pretty bad. And the closer you get to feminist mytho-poetics, by and large, the more strident grow the denunciations – as this one, from "feminist shaman healer" Vicki Noble, whose contribution begins:

> At my speaking engagements, men (or sometimes women) ask me, "What about men? What can we do? How can we be a part of what women are experiencing? Can men be close to the Goddess?" Some men have talked about a "new model of masculinity" that deliberately diverges from the patriarchal, mechanistic one in which they were raised.
>
> But then I started to get worried. What has emerged from the new media and the plethora of recent books written by Robert Bly, Sam Keen, and their younger protégés, is a clearly stated antifeminist backlash ... a "movement" of white men that reaffirms and reestablishes the traditional male-dominant values of Western patriarchal culture.[35]

Or from Zsuzsanna Emese Budapest, whose contributor's note describes her as the "first genetic witch in the USA, who put together feminism with witchcraft and sparked/created the Women's Spirituality Movement, otherwise known as the Goddess Movement":

> it will take more than fairy tales, therapy and abstinence from eating yogurt to turn a Shadow Male-dominated society into a secure mature masculinity. Goddess help you![36]

Or my favorite, by co-authors Jane Caputi and Gordene MacKenzie:

> During the past two decades, the contemporary women's movement has questioned and rejected rigid sex and gender stereotypes, creating new myths and definitions of female power, and naming ourselves to be "Wild," that is, undomesticated and outside of the bounds of patriarchy.... The feminist movement also challenged men to invent new definitions of "masculinity" and to make a qualitative break from a world ordered by a "masculinity" understood to be aggressive, violent, and unemotional. At first some women might be hopeful that the men's movement would concern itself with these sorts of radical changes, but despite some double-talk to the contrary, the song these wild men are singing is "Return to Gender" (that is, rigid bipolar gender roles).[37]

At the risk of belaboring the obvious, let us pause to note the symptomatic assumptions and contradictions at work in this latter passage. Only women, clearly, can be "Wild"; and can do so, moreover, simply by "naming" themselves to be so. This triumphant act of relabeling is, moreover, in no way to be understood as a continuation of "rigid sex and gender stereotypes," despite its effective relegation of women to wild nature and men to dull rational (and/or evil patriarchal) culture. In fact, men are specifically challenged to break from binarism – though it is unclear, to say the least, where they could go or how they could do so, once the terms are set up in this way. At any rate, "despite some double-talk" they have failed to do so (perhaps because they "can't get it right"?); and accordingly, in the next sentence, Caputi and MacKenzie, having triumphantly issued the condemnation that was waiting from the get-go, breeze on to equate the emergence of the movement to the appearance on the national political scene of white supremacist and former Klansman David Duke.

There are some more scrupulous and discriminating responses in Hagan's volume, but they are few and far between. More commonly, the movement is reduced not only to its literary avatars, but specifically to Bly, with Keen mentioned here and there as, almost always, simply a second instance of the same. Then, with a few side-sneers for the drums or the expression and sharing of feelings (the latter tried and condemned for failing to take into account the violence men mete out to women and the power they have over them), the overall politics of the movement are simply read straight off Bly's own most reactionary pronouncements – of which, as we have seen, there is no lack. Thus the movement is adjudged no more than another patriarchal ruse, unworthy of any more prolonged consideration or more nuanced delineation, and certainly unrelated to any of the practices or tenets of actually existing feminism, whose claims to truth and purity thereby remain inviolate.

With enemies like these around it in the white alternative culture in which it has grown up and taken root, the men's movement arguably needs few friends. And a good thing too, since in the major media (with the unintended exception of *Dances with Wolves*, starring Kevin Costner as wild – that is, Native American; that is, less civilized and closer to the earth – yet sensitive, apostate white guy), in *Esquire* articles and *Newsweek* cover stories, TV sitcoms and *Primetime* clips of "wild man retreats," the movement has at best been treated with faint praise admixed with a good deal of amused contempt.[38] Such treatment at the hands of the gate-keepers of mainstream popular culture might indeed itself be taken as a clue that something more, or at least other, is going on in the movement

221

than a simple reinvestment strategy in hegemonic masculinity. In closing off this broad but all too patchy survey, I would maintain that for all of us within or even near this alternative politico-cultural ground, a good deal more *is* at stake than that; for the men's movement raises some questions about the state and direction of left-feminist political culture to which even those of us who don't give a rap about the movement itself either way might want to attend.

4 . INCONCLUSION

Let me wrap up, then, by making the best case I can, given the facts I know and the experiences I have had, for the men's movement as it presently exists. Such a case would focus on a claim I hope most readers of this piece will by now find indisputable, however often it has been ruled out by most feminist observers: that the movement has grown out of an opposition to hegemonic white masculinity as usual, and is genuinely, if inchoately, about formulating and promoting alternatives to it.

That this intent is not more frequently discerned and acknowledged in feminism has something to do, among other things, with the failure of many versions of feminist theory, and perhaps most of feminism's walking-around common sense, to allow for the possibility of any more or other than a single, unitary mode of masculinity in a given society at any given time (or, in some of the more extreme variants, anywhere on the planet, anytime). If patriarchy is, even just in the white Western world, the name of a relation between the sexes that is in most or all respects historically and positionally invariant, and characterized everywhere by the same simple, top-down oppression, it makes no sense to attend to the difference that R.W. Connell, among others, notes between "tradition-centered patriarchy" and the other "masculinities organized much more around technical rationality and calculation" that superseded and marginalized it in the course of and as part of the long transition to capitalist modernity in the West. Yet the relevance of just such historical distinctions is eloquently marked in Connell's further elaboration of this one: specifically, in the uncanny yet perfectly appropriate reappearance of a movement keyword on whose multiple meanings we have spent no small amount of time here. As he puts it, the advent and accession to hegemony of this new, detached and inexpressive mode of capitalist masculinity "created conditions for new versions of masculinity that rested on impulses or practices excluded from the increasingly rationalized and integrated world of business and bureaucracy ... *'wild'* masculinities."[39]

The men's movement plainly fits into this broad typological narrative, and rests on just such "impulses" and "practices." What makes it cohere, despite its manifest contradictions and multiple tendencies, is hardly anti-feminism or misogyny, which are neither endemic to the movement's leaders nor typical of its adherents, but rather first and foremost its antagonism to Connell's rational-calculative masculinity and/or Ferguson's Hegelian man. The forms those refusals take, the directions in which the disclaimers lead, are indeed "wildly" variable, as we have seen. Within some groups, in some men's minds, in the oracles of some movement gurus like Bly, the new alternative masculinity may revolve around the dream of a restored, pre-industrial patriarchy of wise but distanced elders thoughtfully scarring and instructing young men willing to be hurt by them to gain the power they have. In other locations and writings and minds, though, including many of those at work under the cover story of either "wildness," "tradition/ritual" or some combination of the two, it is more concerned to register, affirm, and extend the changes many men in the movement have actually made, most often in the direction of shedding the body-armor that Keen and others (and before them, of course, Wilhelm Reich) understand men to be bullied and cajoled into putting on in order to take up their assigned places and functions in the "economic-warfare system"; of counting the costs, to themselves and their fathers in particular, of taking up those places and celebrating the joys of refusing or detaching oneself – internally or externally, as the admittedly privileged choices present themselves – from them; likewise, of developing an open, articulate, and expressive emotional life of a type denied to and prohibited by Hegelian man; and, finally, exploring issues related to their engagement in the "attempt to create egalitarian households and non-sexist environments for children to grow up in." This latter Connell quite rightly names as "the only form of progressive sexual politics in which significant numbers of heterosexual men have been involved in a continuing and active way."[40]

At still other times and places, around other subjects, the men's movement exists as a place where these putatively alternative men may roll around in the ambivalences in which they are enmeshed. I am thinking here, for example, of the extent to which men too might share in (or, if you like, have their own version of) that nostalgia for gender in which Keen is surely right to locate one component of the attraction many a mid-level professional-managerial feminist feels these days from her position deep inside the layers of a thoroughly instrumentalized and rationalized, secular work-world for a "natural" spirituality centered on the "Goddess" – and to which, as we have seen, even he himself is susceptible. Within such dreams of a restored or reconstituted gender binarism as the basis of a "true identity" that fronts for one's real complicity with a world many boomers and post-boomers cannot quite afford to spurn – and in at least some cases in response to cosmic feminists from the same alternative neighborhood who, as Kipnis has it, "hold our own self-abasement as a prerequisite" for "solidarity with them" (59) – the vision of an egalitarian "partnership society" might well get mixed up with fantasies of lost authority restored in the social imaginary of many a movement man. Something of this same oscillation between benign redefinition and baleful restoration is manifest in the case of the movement's fitfully aggressive defenses of both the figure of the "warrior" and the "protector-provider role": in one breath reclaimed as functions of that fighting spirit peculiar to men in their unique ability to dole out and receive violence for what they cherish, and in the next redefined as aspects of a loving nurturance, sense of interconnectedness, and quickness of emotion that is of course claimed as masculine too. Such fluctuations testify obviously enough to the ambivalence of the men in the movement towards their own economic location – that is, to the fact that most of them remain tied fairly directly to the mainstream economy, regardless of how "wildly" they drum on the weekend, and the probability that many if not most still function as the main source of the family income. But as Kathryn Robinson's *Seattle Weekly* article suggests – not to mention the example of George and Ellen – that ambivalence towards defining men as defenders and protectors may not be men's alone.[41]

The upshot of all this, at any rate, is a roiling lump of breakthrough, reaction and equivocation wrapped in the Indian blanket of anti-modernism, from which the back-to-the-future sign language for "wildness" and "tradition" may serve as trigger for a fantasized return to preindustrial patriarchy, warrant for physical and emotional liberation from the repressive regulations of capitalist masculinity, legitimation for a more attentive and nurturant co-parenting, or, indeed, flight from the contradictions of all of these. In all these ways, moreover, with responses that vary from reactive to reactionary, the men's movement simultaneously matches, mimes and opposes its counterpart and predecessor, that New Age feminism so near to the movement and so influential in the non-working lives of many of the movement's adherents that even its gestures of disavowal and condemnation have their co-constitutive effects. Small wonder, then, the proud confusion of that befuddled warrior quoted in the Bay Area movement mag *Quest*, summing up the result of his most recent weekend workshop for men devoted to "binding the primal energy of the mythopoetic experience with the latest information from the recovery movement":

> I was very confused before I came to this conference. I hoped to clear up this confusion by being here. Now, as we finish, I realize I'm as confused as ever. But, I know now that I am confused about higher issues and more important things than I ever imagined.[42]

Likewise, within the tidepools of alternative culture we have been studying here, both the men's movement and the versions of feminism it attempts to appease and resist share the same anti-modernist assumptions about personal and social amelioration and the connections between the two. Both share, that is, the tendency to leap over history for myth, the polity for the tribe; and both tend to conflate political and personal change, finding in ritually blessed therapeutic journeys towards individual authenticity, affirmation and fulfillment the fundamental basis for larger social change. As T.J. Jackson Lears observes about the anti-modernism pervading the emerging layers of the professional-managerial class in the USA a century ago,[43] and as the growing market for all manner of New Age-feminist and men's-movement mystic goods and therapeutic services demonstrates today, such a combination of a regressive nostalgia and idealist subjectivism is easily coopted and degraded into little more than a new market niche. But while noting this point, I would rather concentrate on another problem raised by virtually all the movements – anti-nuclear, peace, anti-interventionist and environmentalist, that is, as well as men's movement and cosmic feminist – that grow up in this way and on this terrain: their failure, indeed their virtual inability, to understand social relations and social change in terms of historically and structurally constituted relations of power.

As Lynne Segal says, "Dismantling gender hierarchies necessitates the pursuit of changes in the economy, the labour market, social policy and the state, as well as the organization of domestic life, the nature of sexual encounters, and the rhetorics of sexual difference."[44] Yet I think it is fair to say that among what is left – and Left and/or Feminist – of white alternative culture today, our focus and energies have been very much more on and with the latter than the former. Likewise, even in the peace and environmentalist movements, the predominant emphasis has for some time now seemed to rest on making peace a central dimension of one's personal life and immediate community, living a green life of voluntary simplicity, taking individual responsibility for one's own relationship to the earth, and so on. To some extent, this tendency towards personalism may be indigenous to a culture as individualist and market-driven as this one, in which case Louis Hartz's 35–year-old term "Americanism," here summarized and usefully extended by Herbert Kitchelt in a powerful critique of New Age environmentalism, is an apt concept for today's alternative cultural politics across the board.

> In its libertarian vein, it recognizes individuals as free agents in the marketplace, discounts the collective and institutional bases of social life, and considers large organizations as antagonistic to individual liberty. From this vantage point, social innovation occurs as a process of spontaneous change in markets or as a result of individual self-reform; social innovation is not viewed as a collectivized process, mediated by large social organizations. In its communitarian vein, it recognizes all people as equals. Dissolving the tension between individuals and equality calls forth a repressive conformity. The formal freedom of markets is renounced for the material unfreedom of a repressive "consensus" about social norms. The frequent occurrence of moral crusades in American politics is rooted in this conception of society. Beyond Hartz, one may observe that the contradiction between freedom and equality has been practically resolved through ethnic and cultural segmentation in the United States. Society fragments, smaller social reference groups form islands of mutual support and control within the larger framework of a competitive market order.[45]

Moreover, as even some sharp critics of "difference" feminism and other forms of mythopoetic-personalist politics concede, the impulses toward such a restrictive, circular, and accommodationist politics within white alternative culture in our own recent past have received added impetus from the enormous political success of Reaganism, with its intransigently – indeed monolithically – reactionary opposition to any and all imaginable types or modalities of progressive social change, throughout and beyond the decade just past. Faced with that opposition, infiltrated by despair, and no doubt at least in part infected ourselves by the new mood of sanctioned selfishness, many of us retreated to the task of shoring up our own immediately surrounding support systems, both in our heads and within our clans and tribes.

The men's movement glaringly exemplifies the limits and shortcomings of such a politics – so much that it may be misleading to say it has a politics at all. Certainly its critics are right to say it omits or even actively evades acknowledgement of what Connell calls "the *global* or macro-relationship of power, in which women are subordinated to men in the society as a whole," in favor of a diffuse, psychologized and mythically mystified focus on the "*local* or micro-situation in particular households, particular workplaces, particular settings."[46] Its tribalistic self-assertions are indeed pathetic, hilarious, and offensive, sometimes all at once; and the fantasies it encourages and ritually, compulsively, re-enacts of wild flights and clear breaks from instrumental rationality and the "economic-warfare system" are, in many if not most cases, scandalously ideological, in the old bad sense of the word. Yet in recasting themselves as yet another minoritized, marginalized and oppressed tribe, the white men in the movement have not only been expressing a real if partial truth about their place on the cusp between straight and alternative culture, but claiming their "difference" in the same terms and on the same ground rules by which other groups within left-feminist alternative culture have constituted and "empowered" themselves.

One of this chapter's major points has thus been to suggest that feminists and others within this alternative culture should own up to their responsibility for this bastard child, acknowledging the genuine likenesses of its bleary, misbegotten, and despised visage, posture and movement to their own. But the very last thing I want to say is that my recognition of that likeness draws me finally towards a problematic yet (I hope) productive seam out beyond that chartable by any simple plus-and-minus balance sheet of the assets and debits of New Age identity politics. To show you that place, to go there with you, let me quote two responses to the men's movement from the Hagan book that, though practically antithetical to one another, nonetheless both make sense to me. The first is from Elizabeth Dodson Gray, "feminist theologian, environmentalist, and futurist":

> when men gather in a circle not to talk of football or how many notches they have on their shooters but talk instead of their own interior life so long concealed and coerced by a John Wayne model of manhood, then I think I must also honor as sacred these spaces being created by men.... It is true that only men are going to be able to redefine masculinity, and shape it into new personal and cultural formulations that are not woman-hating. Robert Bly does not do it. Sam Keen begins it. And as men do it, it is sacred work.[47]

The second, from another feminist theologian, Rosemary Radford Ruether:

men must begin by acknowledging their public reality as males in patriarchal society, and not retreat to a privatized self that avoids accountability for that public world. They must see that the private self is not an autonomous entity but a dependent appendage of these social power relations.[48]

My problem – and *our* problem too, I think, along whatever remains of alternative culture and progressive cultural politics out beyond the academy – is that I agree with both these positions, but cannot yet imagine or discern the lines along which their mutually opposed logics and strengths might be combined. The first suggests that redefining masculinity *is* men's work; insists that the recovery and expansion of interiority and emotional expressivity is an essential aspect of that work; and acknowledges and applauds the fact that in at least some parts of the movement and some places in its literature, a new masculinity based on compassion, empathy, shared responsibility in and for the home and children, and interdependence with others and with nature, is indeed being articulated, encouraged, and affirmed. The second flatly insists that we men "must begin" from a diametrically opposed position and perspective, objectively and unflinchingly viewing even our private selves and most intimate feelings as mere reflexes of the objective power relations by which they are determined. The first allows and encourages men to break with the attitudes and behavior of Ferguson's "Hegelian man" in immediate and palpable ways, but also lets them retain "masculinity" as the sign of not only a significant but an honorific difference, and confine their changes only to their immediate subjective and interpersonal lives. The second insists that their subjectivities are indelibly tainted by the patriarchal structures under whose laws they were constructed; and that there is thus no independent men's work to do, no break with Hegelian men to be effected on a local or individual level, no better "masculinity" to be rediscovered or constructed. Rather, men's responsibility, once they have come to an objective understanding of their complicity, is, first, to disavow any and all available concepts of "masculinity" along with it; then, either to join feminists (albeit, of course, as untrustworthy troops by definition) in the struggle to dismantle those large objective structures in the state, the economy, and in ideology, that compose and reproduce patriarchy – or, in some streetside versions, to accept their guilt, shut up and stay out of the way.

Should the arguably progressive aspects of the men's movement be encouraged; or should the movement as a whole be condemned and deplored? Should men be let off the hook, and allowed to change without "refusing to be a man" as radical feminist fellow-traveler John Stoltenberg would have it? Would a so-called "deep masculinity that does not oppress women, children or other men" (in the words of an ad for a "Pacific Northwest Wildman Gathering") be good enough? Or should men remain wriggling on their own historic guilt, and defer to the leadership and wisdom of the women they as a group have oppressed? The same questions, it practically goes without saying, might be asked instead or as well in terms of whites vis-à-vis "blacks" and other minorities, and/or of "straights" vis-à-vis lesbians and gays. These questions seem – to me, anyhow – both badly put and unavoidable, unanswerable yet painfully insistent. "Dismantling gender hierarchies" – or racial or sexual ones – "necessitates the pursuit of changes in the economy, the labour market, social policy and the state, *as well as* the organization of domestic [and psycho-emotional] life, the nature of sexual [and other interpersonal] encounters and the rhetorics of sexual [and other sorts of] difference." Quite right: but where is the analysis that can mediate (to use the old *argot*) or articulate (to use the new) the complex and variable relations between the personal and the public, the local and the structural, the second set of tasks and the first, without reducing one to the other? By what social agency, through what conjunction of vision and social organization, can the "languages of personal and everyday life transformation" that Ross rightly sees as the enduring heritage of the New Left in New Age alternative culture be brought into effective coalition with the equally necessary terms and strategies of a more public and collective politics? How, finally, to keep a progressive politics moving to reconstruct and deconstruct the terms of difference from miring itself down – wherever it is, in the men's movement, in New Age feminism or elsewhere – in a post-political lifestyle of complacent self-affirmation, bolstered by discreet cross-cultural appropriation from some other tribes, and invigorated by regular jolts of blame for the Enemy, whoever They are, and however variously and differently They behave? Though the men's movement is by now no longer a hot subject for a *Newsweek* cover story, TV sitcom, or even, probably, a radical critique, and though I too have found much of it inadequate, alarming, or just plain silly, I must still be grateful to it for putting these questions before me in its own ridiculous, perverse, yet at times, startlingly moving way.

NOTES

1. David D. Gilmore, *Mankind in the Making: Cultural Concepts of Masculinity* (New Haven, CT: Yale University Press, 1990); Joseph Campbell and Bill Moyers, *The Power of Myth* (New York: Doubleday, 1988); and John Bradshaw, *Homecoming: Reclaiming and Championing Your Inner Child* (New York: Bantam Books, 1990).

2. Gilmore, p. 220.

3. Robert Bly, *Iron John: A Book About Men* (Reading, MA: Addison-Wesley, 1990), p. ix. Page numbers of subsequent quotations from this book are cited in the text.

4. Ann Douglas traces the emergence of these dialectically related cultural forces in *The Femininization of American Culture* (New York: Avon Books, 1977); and Tania Modleski supplies an important critique of Douglas's masculinist and anti-modern sympathies, without disputing her basic account, in *Feminism Without Women: Culture and Criticism in a "Postfeminist" Age* (New York and London: Routledge, 1991), pp. 24–6.

5. Robert Moore and Douglas Gillette, *King, Warrior, Magician, Lover: Rediscovering the Archetypes of the Mature Masculine* (New York: HarperCollins, 1990) p. xvii. Page numbers of subsequent quotations from this book are cited in the text.

6. Aaron R. Kipnis, *Knights Without Armor: A Practical Guide for Men in Quest of Masculine Soul* (Los Angeles: Jeremy P. Tarcher, 1991), p. 1. Page numbers of subsequent quotations from this book are cited in the text.

7. Riane Eisler, *The Chalice and the Blade: Our History, Our Future* (New York: Harper and Row, 1987); Merlin Stone, *When God Was a Woman* (New York: Harcourt Brace Jovanovich, 1970).

8. Sam Keen, *Fire in the Belly: On Being a Man* (New York: Bantam Books, 1991), p. 196. Page numbers of subsequent quotations from this book are cited in the text.

9. Dorothy Dinnerstein, *The Mermaid and the Minotaur: Sexual Arrangements and the Human Malaise* (New York: Harper & Row, 1976); Nancy Chodorow, *The Reproduction of Mothering: Psychoanalysis and the Sociology of Gender* (Berkeley: University of California Press, 1978); Jessica Benjamin, *The Bonds of Love: Psychoanalysis, Feminism, and the Problem of Domination* (New York: Pantheon Books, 1988).

10. Lynne Segal, *Slow Motion: Changing Masculinities, Changing Men* (New Brunswick, NJ: Rutgers University Press, 1990); Barbara Ehrenreich, *The Hearts of Men: American Dreams and the Flight from Commitment* (New York: Doubleday, 1983); Herb Goldberg, *The Hazards of Being Male* (New York: Nash Publications, 1976).

11. Todd Gitlin, "Postmodernism Defined, At Last!", *Utne Reader* (July/August 1989), pp. 52–61 – excerpted from Gitlin's piece in the Winter 1989 issue of *Dissent*.

12. *Wild Men* was made for, and first broadcast by, the BBC; it was shown in the USA on Connecticut Public Television in July 1993. I regret that I have been unable to discover any further information about this documentary film.

13. For another demographic assessment that matches mine here, see Don Shewey, "Town Meeting in the Hearts of Men," in *The Village Voice* (11 February 1992), pp. 36–46.

14. This and all subsequent direct quotations are taken from the audiocassette recording of *A Day for Men* (Vashon, WA: Limbus, 1991).

15. Most famously, in the closing sentences of *The Protestant Ethic and the Spirit of Capitalism* (New York: HarperSanFrancisco, 1985 [originally published in 1920]).

16. *Seattle M.E.N.* (March 1992).

17. Jeff Albin, "Staking Myself Down," in *Seattle M.E.N.* (March 1992).

18. Andrew Ross, *Strange Weather: Culture, Science and Technology in the Age of Limits* (London and New York: Verso, 1991), p. 68.

19. Ibid., p. 67.

20. Ibid., p. 68.

21. Marion Woodman, *Leaving My Father's House: A Journey to Conscious Femininity* (Boston, MA: Shambhala, 1992).

22. Here, too, I am compelled to mention the phenomenal success of Clarissa P. Estés's book, *Women Who Run with the Wolves: Myths and Stories of the Wild Woman Archetype* (New York: Ballantine Books, 1992). Since the publication of this runaway bestseller, Estés has been interviewed by a warmly approving editor of *Seattle M.E.N.*; the result, "Wild Man, Wild Woman," may be found in the November 1992 issue.

23. See the closing chapter of Alice Echols, *Daring to Be Bad: Radical Feminism in America 1967–75* (Minneapolis: University of Minnesota Press, 1989); and Katha Pollitt, "Are Women Morally Superior to Men?", *The Nation* (28 December 1992), pp. 799–807.

24. Kathy E. Ferguson, *The Man Question: Visions of Subjectivity in Feminist Theory* (Berkeley: University of California Press, 1993), p. 153.

25. In addition to the works by Ferguson, Pollitt, Echols and Segal cited above, see Donna Haraway, "A Manifesto for Cyborgs: Science, Technology and Socialist Feminism in the 1980s," in *Socialist Review* 15 (March–April 1985), pp. 65–107; and Biddy Martin, "Lesbian Identity and Autobiographical Difference," in Henry Abelove et al., *The Lesbian and Gay Studies Reader* (New York and London: Routledge, 1993), pp. 274–93.

26. Andrew Ross, "Wet, Dark and Low, Eco-Man Evolves from Eco-Woman," in *Boundary 2* 19, 2 (1992), pp. 205–33.

27. The texts I refer to here are, of course, Carol Gilligan, *In a Different Voice: Psychological Theory and Women's Development* (Cambridge, MA: Harvard University Press, 1982); and Mary Field Belenky et al., *Women's Ways of Knowing: The Development of Self, Voice, and Mind* (New York: Basic Books, 1986).

28. Kathryn Robinson, "Are Men the New Victims? In Search of the Positive Attributers of Masculinity," reprinted from *Seattle Weekly* (13 April 1991) in *Seattle M.E.N.* (May 1991).

29. Peter Middleton, *The Inward Gaze: Masculinity and Subjectivity in Modern Culture* (New York and London: Routledge, 1992), p. 149.

30. Taken from the advertisements on pp. 34–35 of the Spring 1992 issue of *Reflections: Quarterly Resource Directory*, a publication devoted to the promotion of New Age goods and services in the Portland, Oregon area. I am indebted to Mary Nolan-Smith for drawing my attention to this exemplary ad, and for many fruitful discussions on the politics of New Age tribalism in the spring of 1992.

31. "Where Are Women and Men Today? Robert Bly and Deborah Tannen in Conversation," in *New Age* (January/February 1992), pp. 28 ff.

32. I have found advertisements for this product scattered through various movement publications. Here I am quoting from one published in the April 1993 issue of *Seattle M.E.N.*

33. "Will the Real Men's Movement Please Stand Up?", in Kay Leigh Hagan, ed.,

Women Respond to the Men's Movement (New York: HarperSanFrancisco, 1992), p. 55.

34. "Essential Lies: A Dystopian Vision of the Mythopoetic Men's Movement," in ibid., p. 94.

35. "A Helping Hand from the Guys," in ibid., p. 101.

36. "In Search of the Lunar Male," in ibid., pp. 91, 83.

37. "Pumping Iron John," in ibid., p. 71.

38. See, for example, Doug Stanton, "Inward Ho!", *Esquire* 116, 4 (October 1991), pp. 112 ff.; and Jerry Adler et al., "Drums, Sweat and Tears," *Newsweek* (24 June 1991), pp. 46–53.

39. R.W. Connell, *Gender and Power: Society, the Person and Sexual Politics* (Stanford, CA: Stanford University Press, 1987), p. 131.

40. Ibid., p. 283.

41. See note 28, above; and see also the Conclusion of this book, in which I sketch out the economic context that helps determine the complex ambivalence even avowedly feminist white middle-class women are apt to feel towards the protector-provider definition of masculinity.

42. *Quest Men's Resource Newsletter* (1991; no volume or issue number), p. 12.

43. T.J. Jackson Lears, *No Place of Grace: Antimodernism and the Transformation of American Culture 1880–1920* (New York: Pantheon Books, 1981), pp. 300–312.

44. Segal, p. 294.

45. Herbert P. Kitschelt, review of F. Capra and C. Spretnak, *The Global Promise of Green Politics*, in *Theory and Society* 14, 4 (1985), p. 528. Kitschelt is paraphrasing Louis Hartz, *The Liberal Tradition in America* (New York: Harcourt Brace, 1955).

46. Connell, p. 111.

47. "Beauty and the Beast: A Parable for Our Time," in Hagan, ed., p. 162.

48. "Patriarchy and the Men's Movement: Part of the Problem or Part of the Solution?", in Hagan, ed., p. 17.

CONCLUSION

CHIPS OFF THE OLD BLOCK

As I near the end of this book, I am well aware of the extent to which the blurry snapshot its pages have provided of the contortions of white straight masculinity in the popular culture of the late 1980s and early 1990s is already artifactual, a period piece of the moment just past. Yet by gesturing towards a few subsequent developments, elaborations, and re-directions of the configurations I have sought to analyze, I hope to demonstrate that the constitutive tensions and ambivalences that gave rise to them are still very much with us today.

Here, then, are a few symptomatic straws in the wind. In the Pacific Northwest, we have it on the good authority of canny Kathryn Robinson that the men's movement, which just a few years ago swept like wildfire through the region, is now banked down to glowing embers. The monthly Wisdom Councils still take place, though their numbers are diminished; and Seattle M.E.N. still puts out its newsletter. But its head James Smethurst now says that movement events are increasingly devoted to "gender reconciliation: mythopoetic grief workshops where women and men cooperate in working out their gender problems." Given the tribal and archetypal assumptions behind both movement discourse and the New Age feminism to which, I have argued, the movement largely con-stituted itself in reaction, one can hardly feel much optimism about how these days and weekends turn out. And we may greet with similar doubts and reservations movement avatar Michael Meade's new insistence that his workshops be "multicultural" and focus "on the need for men to do the necessary work to combat violence in our society."[1] Nonetheless, the fact that any dialogue is taking place across the lines of race and gender under the aegis of a movement so exclusively devoted just yesterday to affirming what was good and right about being both "white" and "man" must be taken as something of a heartening sign.

Before offering one or two cautious cheers, though, for what has become of the movement, I have another more ominous bit of news to toss into the mix. This one, from my home-town paper, ran recently under the headline "600 gather for all-male message: Real men love God." The piece beneath the headline concerned a newly formed group of self-proclaimed "Godly men" who hope eventually to be accepted into "Promise Keepers," a national "interdenominational network" of evangelical guys, but who in the interim are calling themselves "Connecticut Men of Integrity." The guest speaker at their convocation that Saturday morning a few weeks back was "Rev. Jack Haford, a California pastor and prolific author who is a celebrity ... in the growing movement of male spirituality, which parallels" – as you might have guessed – "the spread of Christian feminism." In his address to the large and enthusiastic crowd, the good Reverend exhorted them, ambiguously at best, not to think of "feminists and homo-sexuals" as their antagonists, but rather, as Christian "men of valor," to set their warrior energies to work against "a national spirit [that has been] castrating the society for quite a long time." To fortify and sustain them in their struggle against this obscure emasculating force, he encouraged them to lend emotional support to one another; after all, "guys tend to be loners ... We are terrible at admitting our needs."[2]

Meanwhile, even as the simultaneously therapized and militantly re-invigorated figure of mythopoetic white man has been spinning itself off and being reappropriated towards such hopeful and/or alarming uses, the synthesis of emotionally vulnerable wild man and intransigent protector–provider that once generated those mega-hits *Lethal Weapon*, *Die Hard* and their sequels seems to have devolved into something of a red nova, still throwing off a certain amount of heat and light, as well as a few new spectacular events, even as it dissipates and collapses into itself. *Hudson Hawk* (1991) was such a silly, self-preening monument to Bruce Willis's ego that it promptly fizzled at the box office and scarcely deserves mention here. But the two subsequent Silver productions, *The Last Boy Scout* (1991) and *Lethal Weapon 3* (1992), both made big money (*Lethal 3*, in fact, took in the third highest domestic grosses in 1992) while working some salient variations on the Silver formula, souping up the surface intensity while slacking off on the old thematic tensions. Most obviously, the actions and characterization in these newer films are simultaneously more brutal, more spectacularized, and more self-mocking than their predecessors, up to and, if possible, beyond the point of self-parody. In terms of brutality, *Boy Scout* holds a slight edge over *Lethal 3*: at the end of the former, for example, we are to understand that our hero, Joe Hollenbeck (Bruce Willis) is getting back with his wife by the wry tonality he employs as he tells her "Fuck you." But what Mel Gibson's Riggs in *Lethal 3* lacks in nastiness, he makes up for with sheer nutsy appeal: for example, in that wacky scene early on when he completely freaks out a nerdy white guy by acting crazy enough to shoot him for jaywalking in downtown LA – pretty funny stuff, huh?

Beyond and beneath these blandishments, however, and the ever more spectacular explosions – for example, *Boy Scout*'s climactic scene in the football stadium with its literally exploding scoreboard, in which the organized mayhem of the NFL game gives way to a yet more gleefully vicious chaos – that punctuate what little story line remains, there is not that much juice left in the underlying circuits I analyzed in Chapter 1. Danny Glover's Murtaugh in *Lethal 3* and Damon Wayans's Jimmy Dicks in *Boy Scout* are mainly just a couple of Black guys along for the ride; likewise, the tensions of hetero romance have either congealed into something close to permanent hostility (in *Boy Scout*) or found their happy resolution in a coequal partnership of shitkickers (Rene Russo with our Mel in *Lethal 3*). The question that such sour or spectacular dissipations and slaphappy resolutions of our conventional rampage story press upon us concerns what has happened to the social tensions and ambivalences that once gave the subgenre its internal vitality. Has the conflict within this 1980s figuration of white straight masculinity between fluidly related wet and wild on the one hand, and stand-up tall and official on the other, somehow gotten itself resolved? Or has the contradiction moved on to elaborate itself somewhat differently elsewhere?

Obviously, I think the latter; but before I go on to indicate where it's gone and sketch out what it's doing there, it may be useful to review some features of the socioeconomic context that keeps this and related contradictions we have examined both in motion and in place. Let me begin by reeling off a few statistics whose implications must by now be vaguely familiar to us all. First, since 1973, when the average wages of American workers reached an all-time postwar high, real earnings, adjusted for the rate of inflation, have been generally going down. However, within the overall picture of economic decline, there is a startling discrepancy between men's wages, which since the early 1970s have moved more or less steadily downward, especially for those in the middle-income bracket, while women's wages have moved more slowly yet still gradually upward for women – again, especially for those in the middle. "In 1979," Doug Henwood tells us, "women's hourly pay was 64% of men's (for full-time workers); in 1993, it was 80%." Moreover, in each of the past five business downturns since 1970, women have lost fewer jobs than men, and gained more on the subsequent upswing. Coming out of the recession we are supposedly now past, for example, "[m]en did not recover all the jobs lost ... until March of this year [1994]," while the numbers for "women's employment" are "up over 2.6 million since mid-1990, over six times as much as men's."[3]

Needless to say, such figures do not spell out the unheralded end of gender discrimination in either compensation or patterns of employment. Moreover, when they are sorted out along racial lines, it becomes clear that most non-white people of both sexes remain caught in a vicious and seemingly endless downward spiral of declining wages and lost jobs. What interests me most here, however, is the action in the predominantly white middle-income bracket, where in the years 1979–92 "the share of men earning middle-level wages ... fell from 53% to 45%, while the share of women ... rose from 27% to 38%." Even for men with "college or more, polarization was the rule" – that is, wages went up for some, down for most – while the share of college-educated women earning middle-level incomes ($24,000–47,999 in 1992 dollars) rose from 38 per cent to 53 per cent.[4] As Stephanie Coontz has observed, though women's incomes have increased relative to men's to the tune of 70 cents to men's every dollar – up from 60 cents in 1979 – "[a]lmost half of women's improvement relative to men ... has been due to falling real wages for men";[5] and the same general trend is especially marked for those in the middle.

One obvious result of this trend is, of course, a decline in men's ability to fill the role of breadwinner for their families and homes. Coontz's figures eloquently convey the enormity of the shift. "Between 1949 and 1973," through the long postwar boom, she writes,

> the average man passing from age twenty-five to thirty-five saw his real wages rise by about 110 percent. Job pressures and rewards slowed down after age forty, but men could still expect to see their earnings rise by 30 percent between the ages of forty and fifty, while the homes that a majority of such men had bought in their early years of marriage continued to rise in value.[6]

This, in effect, is the deal that subtended the definition of the white straight middle-class man as protector–provider, and that, together with intense discrimination against women in both employment and income opportunities, guaranteed their subordination as mothers and wives; and this deal is now decisively and perversely off. For if, in 1963, "60 percent of men aged twenty to twenty-four earned enough to keep a family of three out of poverty," whereas "by 1984, only 42 percent could do so," it is now requiring more money and more work for two-income families with children to maintain any semblance of a middle-class lifestyle, with a single-family home, one car per wage earner, and the costs of college education shooting up. In this reconfigured middle-class home, it is increasingly likely that the husband and father puts in more work around the home. Henwood points out that in two-income homes, they are good for "about 10–12 hours of unpaid work around the house every week"; the problem is that the woman in the couple puts in no fewer than 30–35, three times more and nearly the equivalent of another full-time job.[7] Needless to say, moreover, aside from a weak-kneed and miserly Family Leave Act, even in the age of Clinton there is no help forthcoming in the form, for example, of publicly subsidized child-care programs, comparable worth legislation, or for that matter a rise in the minimum wage, forthcoming from the state.

Coontz tersely draws the lesson from these developments. "The male breadwinner no longer provides the central experience for the vast majority of children," she writes – and, we might add, for most of the rest of us as well – "but it has not been replaced by any new modal category."[8] Quoting Gramsci, we might well add that during such interregna, a variety of morbid symptoms appear, particularly when and insofar as the incomplete redistribution and equalization of economic power between men and women is further pressurized and distorted by the downscaling and out-sourcing propensities of a domestic economy straining to retain and augment its position in an increasingly internationalized and competitive world capitalist system. Reduced to its crudest terms, we could put it this way: in a situation in which middle-class men make less than they used to, and middle-class women make more than they used to but still not enough, the material conditions that once enabled men to construct and valorize a normative protector–provider masculinity for themselves, with all the rites and rituals of male supremacy that wash up in its wake, are no longer in place; but neither are the conditions under which the gender coding of the protector–provider role would be either undone or reversed. At the same time, while under the pressure of long-term national economic decline, increasing numbers of Americans, male and female alike, cling to "trappings of the postwar *economic* dream by sacrificing ... aspects of the postwar *family* dream," the anxieties and resentments they incur by doing so are ever more apt to take on the anti-social tribal form exhibited by so many other overlapping groups, from white middle- and upper-class neighborhood organizations with their "'armed response' security systems" to the Black and Latino gangs fighting over their turf in the projects. In the men's movement and in the tribalized versions of feminism to which it reacts, we can discern the presence of that same "seeming inability to recognize the humanity of those who don't belong to their own 'gang' or 'lifestyle enclave'" that Coontz rightly perceives to be one of the most alarming signs of our times.[9] And until the glacial drift of this deadlock within and around the normative terms of gender is altered by a collective political will that, as of this moment, does not seem to exist here, there is no reason to think we will find anywhere in the popular culture that gets made for and peddled to us any answers to the question of what's left of white straight masculinity after and aside from the protector–provider role that are any better than so many more morbid symptoms in their turn.

Let us return, then, to our look at a few more recent morbid symptoms; and to do so, let's go to the movies for one final triple-bill. Our first feature will be, predictably, *Falling Down*, Hollywood's most explicit attempt in recent years to cash in on the crisis of white straight masculinity, by appealing to our ambivalence towards to what it should be or become. Its portrait of the anonymous man known until the last stretch of film only by his customized license plate D-FENS, as he treks his way across the multiracial urban jungle of LA in a havoc-wreaking final day, is intended to "out" and exacerbate our mixed feelings towards this failed and flailing protector–provider gone wild. In the first scene in which he runs amok, trashing a Korean mom-and-pop store because its owner has been rude to him, for example, my partner Ann nudged me and whispered, "Are we supposed to like this guy?" Clearly enough, the film ultimately invites us to answer this question in the negative – he has caused too much mayhem, he is too much of a rigid, judgemental control freak, and he was probably out to kill the wife and child a restraining order has forbidden him to see, then shoot himself. But the politics of the pleasures it offers along the way are harder to assess. For the most part, we are invited to feel that his responses to the abuse he receives from those below and above him in our current hierarchies of race and class – for example, rudeness from the Korean store owner, a scary shakedown from a couple of ganged-up Latinos, crummy food and smugly impersonal, smiley-faced service at a fast-food joint, and the peremptory demand from a self-righteous rich white golfer that D-FENS get off the fairway of his private club – are all excessive in varying degrees. But at the same time, as with the similar exploits of our rampaging heroes Riggs and McClane, we are also invited not only to sympathize to some extent with the aggrieved, but also, even as we disavow it, to enjoy the excess of the response.

On the other hand, though, in certain respects it would not be far afield to describe *Falling Down* as a rampage film that comes wrapped in its own critique. Not only has our hero been demystified and diminished into the figure of the 1950s middle-class man virtually no one wants to be – Michael Douglas at his most carp-mouthed, in high-water pants and a short-sleeved white shirt with pens clipped to its pocket, a brush-cut leveling his head and a cheap briefcase hanging off the end of his arm – but the visual strategies used by more conventional Hollywood films to keep the hero wholly and centrally positioned in relation to the film's action and our sympathies have been knocked askew as well. You might recall, for example, the film's bravura opening shot, which begins with an extreme close-up of D-FENS's mouth and sweating upper lip, then swivels to the side as it draws back to pan the other cars and people around him in the frozen tumult of the traffic jam in which he is stuck – followed, as the film's diegetic sound bleeds in and mounts to a chaotic uproar, by a metric montage alternating between his face still in claustrophobically tight close-up and the things outside him, until its tension breaks with his frenzied pursuit of the buzzing fly stuck in the closed-up car with him. Or perhaps you may have noticed how often, when the film returns to him in a fresh scene, the establishing shot begins as an extra-long shot, one that has to pan across and/or tilt down until it discovers him as more or less merely another figure in the midst of whatever crowd we are in now. After such humbling shots, we may find our eyes moving through the scene in a more typical fashion, tracking a protagonist who is basically positioned in or near the middle of the frame, and given to us in *plan américain*, middle shot, and/or mid close-up. But often enough, before the scene is done, such shots give way in turn, at or near its climax, to more extreme close-ups: for example, when D-FENS is at the phone booth calling his wife while the gang members he has dissed are cruising the neighborhood for him, and the shots intercut with the car give us, first, Douglas in mid-shot from behind; then a tight close-up of his face on the phone; then an even tighter, more uncomfortably close shot of that face from below.

As *Falling Down* shrinks the narrative pretexts for this rampager's mayhem from the type of transnational conspiracy that legitimated it in *Lethal*

Weapon or *Die Hard* to a pathetically, egregiously prosaic and mundane size, the expanded extremes of its visual style stretch our formerly reliable sense of the hero's literal and psychological relation to us to its breaking point, pushing him in our face one minute, dissolving him in the Brownian movement of the street in the next. The result of this dual maneuver of style and plot is less to deny us the familiar pleasure of the rampage film's play between protector–provider and wild rampaging guy than to ensure that our indulgence in it will perforce be off-kilter and queasy all the while. Meanwhile, the film more or less explicitly offers us two contradictory if not outright opposed ways of reading the valence and significance of D-FENS's character in the two sets of affiliations it proposes for him. Along one line or spectrum, he is situated in between two other men in white short-sleeve shirts: between the Black man he sees being arrested and hauled away for demonstrating outside a branch bank office where he has been ruled "not economically viable" (that is, turned down for a loan), a man who looks out of the squad car, locks eyes with our hero, and says "Remember me" just before the car drives off; and, on the other end, Prendergast (Robert Duvall), the domestically henpecked cop who picks up the scent of D-FENS's trail from the desk job where he's supposed to be logging in his last day, and ultimately tracks him down. But the film also suggests another quite different convergence or identification: that of D-FENS with Nick, the racist-fascist-homophobic neo-Nazi our protagonist kills in the back room of the Army–Navy surplus store Nick runs.

Fired from his job and in trouble with his family, D-FENS is metonymically linked by resemblance to Prendergast and the protesting Black man, like them but different. But the film's rendering of D-FENS's encounter and relationship with Nick as its dramatic climax and most intense scene plainly flirts with more than similitude – and "flirts with" is surely the right phrase to use. The scene between D-FENS and Nick in the back room plays out as a virtual incarnation and re-enactment of the homophobic/homoerotic impulses Klaus Theweleit has helped us see as a core component of proto-fascist masculinity.[10] When D-FENS denies Nick's assertion that "We're the same, you and me," Nick's admiration turns to the fury of a lover scorned. When at gunpoint he forces D-FENS to turn around and spread his legs, Nick closes in behind and virtually atop him, ecstatically simulating the prison-rape he hissingly prophesies D-FENS will suffer from the "big buck nigger" he will meet in jail. His punitive erotic delirium increases as he forces D-FENS to the floor, where the intercut shots that follow build towards the climax more or less in every sense of the word, by ever more rapid cutting between D-FENS's face and extra-close-ups of a panting white mouth that now belongs to Nick, whispering "Give it to me now, give it to me" – until, in effect, D-FENS does grant him something like the consummation he has been asking for, by stabbing him with the gravity knife he previously obtained from the Latino gang members he chased away. Finally, the scene ends as D-FENS says, "Feels good to exercise your rights, doesn't it?," while dispatching Nick with a final gunshot. Except that just as the earlier stabbing played as both consummation and escape, this murder is depicted as a rejection that is simultaneously an act of merger: D-FENS's face now rises over that of the fallen Nick, the two of them caught in reflection so that as the image of Nick's face rises in the murky glass toward that of D-FENS, the shot that kills him breaks the glass at the spot where the faces coincide.

If the metonymic affiliations suggested between our protagonist and his short-sleeved, white-shirted Others thus invite a reading of this white man and those like him as decent, responsible citizens and husbands unfairly deprived of their rights, the metaphorical identification with Nick enacted in this climactic scene, even as it is denied, invites a view of white straight men as pathogenic fascist monsters whose sense of rights is based on their entitlement to exploit and conquer others even unto death. The peculiar distinction of this film lies in the degree to which it offers us both readings side by side, as it were, rather than admixing or commingling them in a mystified, speciously reconciled totality or wholeness. Yet there remain at least two respects in which *Falling Down* fudges the issues and muddies the alternatives it otherwise so admirably lays out. One has to do with the depiction of D-FENS – or, more specifically, with the excess of motivations the film proposes for his character and behavior. On the one hand, and for the most part, his anonymity through most of the film, together with the iconic typology of his physical appearance, offers him to us as a socially *representative*, even allegorical, figure of normative, white straight middle-class masculinity, and so invites us, in judging his action and gauging the degree of our sympathy and antipathy for him, to take that judgement as our assessment of the regulative construct he incarnates. On the other hand, however, late in the film, as we follow Prendergast and his Latina sidekick Sandy into D-FENS's mother's house and learn his name, we are suddenly given a mass of particulars that invite us at more or less the last moment to reconceive his character in psychological terms as the portrait of a particular individual: the specific product, that is, of a neurotically sterile, petty-bourgeois household under the sway of an obsessive-compulsive, hysterical mother and the ghost of an absent father killed by "the Communists" in the Korean War.

If this last-minute introduction of a psychotherapeutic explanation for our protagonist's character and behavior offers both the film and its audience a back-door out and away from the Lukácsian work of socio-political typing and assessment, in another way and on a whole other level, *Falling Down* also hedges its bets and ducks its own implications by alternating the story of its protagonist's falling-down with that of another white man whose power and legitimacy the film works to restore. I refer, of course, to Prendergast, the cop whose apprehension of D-FENS occurs as the final term in a series of small triumphs with large, even allegorical, implications. For the Prendergast we first meet is, like D-FENS, a diminished and slightly ridiculous character. Exiled from the streetwork he loves by the anxieties of the hysterical wife to whose wishes and whims the film manages to suggest he remains both touchingly devoted and excessively submissive, this good cop and loving family man has to make his way to D-FENS's case through both her neurotic phone calls and the scarcely veiled contempt of younger male officers, Latino, Asian, and white, who view him as a cowardly has-been. So, for him to be the Good White Guy who answers D-FENS's final, fateful question – "I'm the bad guy?" – in the affirmative and who, by shooting him off the pier and into the water in effect replaces him in the end, Prendergast will have to tell his beloved nutsy wife to shut up and make his dinner, hang up on her, punch out one of the contemptuous younger cops (the white one, of course), and provide for his Latina sidekick when – good cop that she is, but not *quite* up to Prendergast's level – she is wounded by D-FENS as he flees from the home of his wife and child in Venice to the pier, where the confrontation between our two white men finally takes place.

Through these operations, then, the track of the secondary plot that *Falling Down* sets in tandem with the story of our dismissed defense worker's last day invites its viewers, if they wish, to downplay and forget the very ambivalence it is the film's main project to interrogate and excite, and cling to such desires as they may still possess to believe in a protector–provider masculinity whose essential goodness warrants its ongoing right to put and keep the Others in their place. If *Falling Down* is thereby rendered a thematically incoherent text, arguing for a model of masculinity it simultaneously depicts as fallen in both moral and social terms, that incoherence eloquently attests to the mixed-up blend of anxiety, yearning, anger and *ressentiment* surrounding that model in the audience the film attempts to attract. So too, as we shall see, with the equally complex and contradictory response we are invited to make to the conventional model of white straight masculinity reconfigured in our second and far more successful feature *In the Line of Fire*, even as it carries its hero through to the end Prendergast at the last minute escapes: the retirement of the normatively male hero. But to get to that ending and to the regret and ambivalence it invites, we will first have to make our way through and across a complex field of other related thematics as well.

Let me begin with the most obvious: that is, with the degree to which the central conflict in this box-office smash of summer 1993, between Secret Service Agent Frank Harrigan (Clint Eastwood) and ex-CIA operative Mitchell Leary (John Malkovich), a brilliant sociopath out to kill the president of the United States, is staged in terms that almost overtly venture across the no-man's-land between the homosocial and explicitly homosexual. Think, for starters, of the breathy, "fem" softness that constitutes the tonal baseline of Mitch Leary's phone conversations with Harrigan; of the fact that in the first such conversation, he is depicted synecdochally in extreme close-up as a soft, wet whisker-rimmed mouth; of "wet boy," the "inside" term the CIA agents use to name Leary's former Agency function as professional rampager, back before he slipped his leash and ran amok. Think also of the way Mitch takes the barrel of Frank's gun into his mouth while dangling our helpless hero from a rooftop's edge, inviting Frank to shoot the bullet that in effect will kill them both, and of Frank's conflicted desire to do just that. Consider the metaphorical suggestiveness, for that matter, of Mitch's taunting challenge to Frank – "Do you really have the guts to take a bullet, Frank?" – and of Frank's confession of doubt on just this point and in just these terms in his most notable scene with Lily, standing hand-in-hand in the painstakingly secure presidential hotel suite.

Against and in counterpoint with such literally loaded flirtation, we are also given the above-board romance of Frank with his younger, hardnosed Secret Service comrade Lily (Rene Russo, fresh from her *ninja* stint alongside Gibson in *Lethal 3*). And it is worth noting that in this film, unlike the first two *Lethal*s or the *Die Hard* duo, the woman is not criticized, punished, or humbled for her professional ambitions. Rather, Lily's presence and aid are instrumental to Frank's victory over Mitch at the film's climax. Moreover, the film ends by inviting us to assume that Frank has now retired, at least in part so that he and Lily can pursue their relationship without her needing to trim her professional ambitions. In another sense, however, the functional definitions and uses of the heterosexual relationship in all these films are the same. Particularly in both the original *Die Hard* and *In the Line of Fire*, the attraction of the seductive villain – a man with a deep understanding of and admiration for the hetero hero that no woman can share – helps deflect our attention from the homoerotic implications of that hero's relationship to his sidekick; Frank in *Line of Fire* is always coaxing his young partner Al away from his concerns for his family and into a deeper commitment to his work, with lines like "Come on, pal – I need you – please." Likewise, in all these films, and many more besides, the hero's straightness grants wiggle room to the homoerotic currents of desire that may then almost explicitly "come out" as the actual energy source of the plot. Almost, I say, but not quite – and not only insofar as our hero's vaunted straightness is concerned. For the other side of the heterosexual alibi in these films, and in contemporary homophobic pop-cult in general, is the hysterically sado-masochistic imagery that constellates the demonized gay or proto-gay villain himself, from the "skin games" of "Buffalo Bill" in *Silence of the Lambs*, to the slit throats and bloody mouths of Mitch's victims in *Line of Fire* – including, it will be recalled, sidekick Al's, brought along by Frank only to be initiated/dispatched by Mitch in a primal-scene act of "taking the shot" to which we draw nigh but which we are not allowed to see.

Between the putatively straight, then, and the punitively homophobic – such are the banks within and between which the turbulent currents of queer energy are canalized into a safely domesticated, renewable energy resource.[11] But the more I have thought about this film's sexual politics, the more I have come to suspect that they might in fact be performing a complex double duty, by serving, in effect, not only as themselves but also as the containing narrative and binding sheath – the "cover story" once again, and this time quite literally – for a complicated, irresolute set of psychological and ideological negotiations going on underneath and within that familiar narrative: negotiations conducted on and about the ideological ground of the brave new post-industrial workplace and the brave new selves it needs. To unpack just what "ideological ground" I am referring to here, though, we will have to take a brief intermission from our film. Specifically, I beg your indulgence to stop for a quick look at a typical contemporary exploration of "the meaning of post-industrial transformation for our workroles and personal relationships," Jerald Hage and Charles H. Powers's widely hailed *Post-Industrial Lives: Roles and Relationships in the 21st Century*,[12] in which the "transformation" is only partially described, the dynamics driving it only selectively acknowledged, and the portrait of the new work-relations and selves that results paints a smiley face over even what little it is able to see.

The decisive move in this operation is a perfectly typical and symptomatic one in the contemporary sociological literature on "post-industrial society": the neglect of structural relations of power as explanatory or co-causal factors in favor of a technocratic emphasis on new knowledges and techniques, these last perceived as more-or-less wholly autonomous catalysts of change, unleashing new liberating and constraining forces all by themselves. Accordingly, Hage and Powers define the previous industrial age not as a regime of capitalist accumulation, that is, a system of power, but as an epoch dominated by knowledges and technologies devoted to the concept of rationalization. It is rationalization, not class struggle and not the drive for profit, that brought us the deskilling of the worker, the rule-bound specification and specialization of tasks, the centered, vertical hierarchy of corporate organization, and, not least, the internalized and lived concept of the centered, unitary self. "Industrial selves," we are told, "feel most comfortable where there is a sense of certainty about who the self is and where the self sits in relationship to other selves, and all the feedback one receives about the self is consistent" (79). Likewise, the post-industrial age runs on the new paradigm fuel of "complexification," thanks again to the interplay of new knowledges and new technologies:

> Routine jobs that have to be done frequently, and for which we can precisely prescribe straightforward procedures, are perfect jobs for robots and are made redundant with automation. Meanwhile, other jobs are being made more complex both by our improved ability to collect information about a plethora of variables and by our increased understanding of the ways in which those variables influence one another – knowledge that requires individualized skills rather than mass production and servicing. (54)

Robots? And here I thought, silly me, that it was Indonesian women doing piecework on my running shoes for far less than a living wage. Such misconceptions aside, though, what is called for in this brave new world is no longer the specialized self, "affective ... at home," "instrumental ... at work" (85), and despite this binarism convinced of the singularity of its identity. What we need and must become now instead are "complex selves who are comfortable maintaining multiple identities" (81). The new interactive selves in their fluid and ever-shifting work spaces and teams are able to network, team up, shift allegiances, translate and share specialized knowledges, come up with interdisciplinary solutions to complicated individual problems; they are those able to "'hear' feeling tones" (91), and to "remain conscious of all one's selves in order ... to look at perplexing problems from different points of view" (85). Centralized, vertical rigidity, fixity, and singularity are out; horizontal flexibility, flux, and diversity are in, in organizational and psychic structures alike – which sounds just great if you can handle it. But Hage and Powers understand that many of us cannot yet make the stretch: "the average person with an industrial mind-set does not have the interaction *skills* [their emphasis] necessary to accommodate constant role change and maintain coherent interpersonal relationships at a time of rapid change, which is why roles are failing and social institutions are breaking down" (119–20). At any rate, now that we know that it's that old retro mind-set that's at fault (rather than, say, the global restructuring of the capitalist world order, with attendant fresh offensives on the weak and the poor), all we have to do is get that new software booted up, and strip those old programs off those creaky old hard-disk drives.

With such arguments in mind, we can return to *In the Line of Fire*, for we are now in a position to see the extent to which it not only *accepts* but actually *responds to* and *negotiates* the very same ideologically loaded and limiting terms of description for the "post-industrial" situation we are now all supposed to be in. What kind of man, after all, is Frank Harrigan – and what kind of worker – if not one defined by a rigidly self-imposed adherence to codes and constraints, a man completely identified with his job yet clinging hard to his isolated individuality, as well as to his touchingly anachronistic belief in an outmoded depth model of subjectivity, so that he believes he can discern under the surface behaviors of others their innermost cores, and thus "know things about people"? It's hardly accidental or insignificant that virtually his first words in the film are a tight-lipped injunction to his youthful partner Al – "When you work with me, be punctual" – nor that in their ensuing confrontation with a gang of counterfeiters, Al is saved, if he and we are able to believe it, thanks to Frank's "instinct," which "usually tells me if there's something wrong."

But into the life of this "borderline burn-out with questionable social skills," as he is described by an old friend and former boss, this protagonist whose notions of work and selfhood, like those of the Fordist gumshoes of Hammett and Chandler we surveyed in Chapter 4, are as quaintly out of date as his love for the cool bop of the 1940s and early 1950s, comes a new and for the most part very contemporary challenge in the form of the almost infinitely protean Mitch Leary, a.k.a. "Booth." Frank Harrigan's antagonist is first known to the authorities as a man that no two of his neighbors can describe in anything like the same terms; and later on, even though his legal identity has been established, as a suspect whose shape-changing abilities require law-enforcement agencies to generate and sort through a gallery of computer-generated image possibilities. From the beginning, then, and throughout the film we are invited to think of Leary as a virtual figure for what Kristeva used to call the "semiotic," that realm of being in which the flux of signifiers over the bar of the signified can never be staunched or fixed: as, in other words, a "New Age Modeler," like the specialty magazine he likes to read. Accordingly, the primary pleasure of Malkovich's performance as the odious yet fascinating Mitch Leary derives from watching him put on and shuttle through the requisite multiplicity of vocal registers, mannerisms, and appearances he must assume to play his nefarious "game."

Our villain's malleability is thus set up in perfect opposition to our hero's fixity, just as Malkovich's hyperactive face forms the perfect antagonist to Eastwood's notoriously limited, hard-ass inexpressiveness. Even after Leary's assassination attempt has failed, and he is trapped, with Harrigan his hostage, in the plexiglass elevator of LA's Bonaventura Hotel, for him it has all still been merely a "game" that Frank has won and he has lost – which characterization Harrigan just as typically refuses with the response, "No game, Leary. I was doing my job." Even that moment when, as we are reminded again and again, our hero's character was formed and crystalized, the years of the Kennedy presidency, contributes to the allegory of this confrontation between "industrial" and "post-industrial mind-sets," insofar as Kennedy still stands in the popular imagination as a figure for the best and brightest hopes of the late-industrial era, at the high tide of American hegemony abroad and liberal corporatist consensus at home.[13] By contrast, Mitch's demonic character is, just as clearly, a product of post-Vietnam, post-Watergate malaise; for even though, like Frank, he too "used to think this country was a pretty wonderful place," he has by now been so cruelly used and deformed by his heartless masters at the CIA that he has come to play the game only for its own sake, and for himself.

Such symbolically resonant histories and imagery incarnate the terms of Hage and Powers' opposition, while complexly tilting their valences. Most obviously, and so just for starters, the film offers us Malkovich/

Mitch Leary's New Age Modeler performance (just think, by the way, of that ingeniously custom-designed gun!) as a pleasure, but codes it as a threat. Likewise, it is full of mixed messages for us concerning how much faith to place in Frank's old-fashioned methods and beliefs. True, Frank's hunch does seem to pay off in the opening scene with the counterfeiters; true also that following up a later hunch, and openly contradicting orders from above, he is able to learn the identity Leary has assumed to inveigle his way into the presidential fund-raiser at the Bonaventura; and true too that in the first of the film's back-to-back climaxes, he succeeds in picking Leary out of all the other donor-guests assembled in the ballroom by simply, instinctively spotting him (camera-work and editing give us this via a rapid cut from a point-look of Frank's to an eyeline-matched, extreme close-up of Leary, focusing on his eyes). Yet at other moments the film takes almost equal pains to suggest that Harrigan's company-man loner persona is not up to the tasks it has to shoulder. If the electronic sur-veillance team with which he's working comes up with the wrong address the first time they pick up one of Leary's taunting phone calls to Frank, in the course of the second call it is Frank who breaks down and bugs out, his rigid face first twitching with ticks in response to Mitch's taunts, then cracking open as he drops the phone and runs from the office at the instant his team has traced the call to a pay-phone at the Mall across the way. There, once again presumably thanks to his ability to see into people's depths, Frank is able to spot Leary through his disguise as a street hippie – but to no avail; the operation has been blown, and Leary beats feet down the street and disappears.

The twitching and cracking of Eastwood/Harrigan's otherwise immobile face in this scene thus stands in marked contrast to Malkovich/Leary's impeccably micro-managed *moues* in the sequence just previous, as Leary first sets up a bank account for him in a false name, then kills the bank worker who quite inadvertently nearly caught him in his lie, together with her roommate. So too with that intermediate stretch of the film whose main point seems to be the contrast between the ease with which Mitch moves from city to city along the trail of the presidential tour, and Frank's increasingly constricted and anxious uptightness in the entourage – an uptightness that, when Lily expresses concern for the fever he's con-tracted on the trip, prompts him to snap back "Stay alert in there, will you?," and that then itself cracks open in a burst of photo-flashes and whirling 360–pans of audience and stage, until a balloon neatly pricked by a comfortably ensconced Leary out in the audience throws him into a full-scale false alarm. All this suggests that even if Frank is our hero, his outlook and values are not quite adequate: to catch Mitch he will have to learn how to move more comfortably through all the space and time zones involved, to be more flexible and mobile, to slide around and mix it up.

Yet if Frank's "industrial mind-set" is depicted as simultaneously praise-worthy and inadequate, Mitch's New Age modeling as both fascinating and evil, what complicates and inflects the contrast between them still more are those aspects of their lives and histories that they hold in com-mon. Both have worked for the same employer for many long years; both have, in effect, been "company men" for an organization that appears to have disrespected and abused them. Frank admits to Lily that he took the rap for some of Kennedy's sexual indiscretions; and Mitch as a "wet boy" has done far worse, far more compromising things than that, out of the belief both once shared that "this country" and, by implication, their employer, the US government, was "pretty wonderful." Finally, even though one of these disillusioned company men is still with the company while the other has gone freelance, both exhibit the same void in the space where a private life might be. The untended, barren ranch house in Phoenix in which Al and Frank find the CIA instead of their quarry rhymes with the spare impersonality of Frank's own Washington apartment; neither man has a personal life, both are all work and no play.

To the extent, then, that for all their opposition Mitch and Frank turn out to be cut from the same cloth, it is time for us to rethink them in relation to Lily, company *woman* and the film's third principal. For through-out the film she is shown functioning smoothly and effectively as a team player, unlike either of our two men. Indeed, it will be by dint of her effectiveness as a good listener (able, as Hage and Powers say, to "'hear' the ... tones" in the double utterances hostage Frank is simultaneously transmitting to her and putting out to Mitch on the elevator in the second climax) as well as a model of efficient mobility, in that she will in the end be able to take charge of the SWAT team that shoots Mitch down and direct them effectively, even in the notoriously unknowable postmodern space of the Bonaventura Hotel.[14] Likewise, though unencumbered by idealistic commitment to her employer, she is nonetheless explicitly un-willing to give up her job for the sake of any private-life relationship. Yet she is also conspicuously more skilled and successful than either of our two male leads at moving around between the personal and the profes-sional, negotiating the interplay of occupation and emotion. Wisely, but to no avail, she warns Frank to attend to the fever that will help throw his reflexes off on the president's campaign tour; shrewdly yet compassionately, she assesses Frank's personal and professional reasons for wanting her to use her influence to get him back into the entourage; just as wisely, on the verge of the climactic confrontations, she will remind Frank that "It's not just you against Leary – you've got to have some faith in the rest of us." If, then, the domestic spaces company men Mitch and Frank inhabit are deserts of the heart, the space in which career-woman Lily will come to seem most at home will be the Presidential suite in which she stands hand in hand with Frank as he breaks down, confessing his guilt for not "taking the shot" in the Kennedy assassination. For Lily and Lily alone is perfectly comfortable and adept in a private space that is also a public space, both on the job and off.

In Lily, then, the film might be said to have constructed an ideal-type personality and employee, one capable of quieting and resolving the schizzy ambivalences and dizzying coincidences of the Frank/Mitch, Eastwood/ Malkovich contrast – yet this resolution seems to me not without regret, this valorization not without its qualms. Surely, after all, it is significant that the film *needs* two climaxes: one (in which Frank, working alone and playing his hunches, discovers Leary just in time to "take the shot" intended for the president) which triumphantly vindicates Frank's "company man" way of being and doing, and the other (in which Frank's life is saved and Leary's taken, thanks to Frank's double-tongued utterance "Aim high," and Lily's expert ability to interpret and act on it) a vindication of her team-playing, "career woman" skills. Likewise, if Frank might seem to have learned something from the latter rescue, to have become more malleable and mobile than he started out, surely any sense we might enjoy of his "growth" toward a new and better work-self is diminished by the fact that having learned this lesson, like Mitch he leaves the company as well. Could the cumulative effect of his retirement, together with the evil nature of Mitch's mobility, be to suggest that this new "post-industrial" flexibility and mobility called for today are not finally worthy of real men, whose best move is thus to retire from the postmodern space of the Bonaventura, leaving it to adept but comparatively lusterless Lily-livered women? And for that matter, how *are* we to feel about the very ending of the film: of the scene, that is, in which, sitting once again on the steps of the Lincoln Memorial, jobless Frank prattles on to his careerist lover about his hunch that a brown pigeon will fly off before the white one does? Sure it's a victory of sorts, sure it's a resolution: but does not this muted ending contain its note of pathos, despite the reassuring presence of the Washington monument's pure white phallus, its own invitation for us to feel at least a shade of resigned regret that our male hero's abilities have been reduced to this?

If so, on the basis of our reading of both *In the Line of Fire* and *Falling Down*, we might hazard a provisional generalization about how the inner conflicts and tensions of the white middle-class film audience over what is left of protector–provider masculinity, and what is to become of it, will be restaged in popular films as long as the deadlock I have outlined remains in effect: that the most secure resolutions of that conflict will necessarily be the most blatantly ideological ones – "ideological," that is, in the strongest sense of the term, as purely imaginary, self-deluded, and virtually without reference to the real. So we come to the final and most spectacularly successful of our three films, the runaway hit of this past summer, *Forrest Gump*. Released in July 1994, *Gump* took in $100 million in its first three weeks; as of the beginning of October, it had racked up nearly $270 million in domestic earnings, and displaced *Jaws* as the fifth-highest-grossing film of all time.[15] And this phenomenal success is, I am convinced, directly related to – indeed, it is a function of – the genius of its utterly ideological resolution of what a proper white straight masculinity should be.

Before we look at that resolution, however, and as our way into it, it is worth taking a brief side-tour to examine the flurry of appropriative and condemnatory responses the film's saga of one feeble-minded white Southern man's passage through the past three decades of American history has excited from liberals and conservatives alike. Martin Walker nicely summarizes the case for *Gump* from a liberal perspective as a film that "attacks war, racism, male sexism, the sexual abuse of children and upholds the pride and decency of single mothers." Yet the film has also been embraced by no less than that darling-doyen of the radical Right, Patrick Buchanan, as an eminently "conservative film" in which "decency, honor and fidelity triumph over the values of Hollywood" – an assessment that has been attacked in turn by fellow conservative Charles Moore, who echoes his liberal enemies in arguing that *Gump* is "typical Hollywood propaganda," a work that "reeks of political correctness" and therefore deserves to be shunned.[16]

Happily, we need not spend our time adjudicating between these claims, which I trot out here merely as so many symptomatic effects of the cynically deliberate stupidity practiced by the film itself. For at bottom

Gump's project is demonstrably not to take political sides, but to sidestep and evacuate the very concepts of history and politics alike. This operation is inscribed in director Robert Zemeckis's stated purpose in making the film: "to present [the postwar baby-boom] generation *without commenting on it*."[17] The same intention is more or less overtly thematized in the film itself, in the frequent musings of both Forrest and his eventual disciple Lieutenant Dan over whether our lives are governed by destiny or pure, random chance – alternatives whose opposed and complementary possibilities clearly enough foreclose the third possibility that the fates we partly endure and partly make are the results of human agency, individual and collective, present and past, and are just as clearly figured in the image of the drifting feather that wafts down from the heavens at the film's opening and back up into them at its close.

But it is also effected in three ways that, if pursued, will lead us straight into the magical reconstruction of masculinity that is really at the heart of the film. Let us start with those moments when Forrest most explicitly brushes up against what we have come to think of as official History – that is, the moments when he appears in the midst of a public event shown on TV. That the historical process of human self-activity and struggle has become equivalent to what gets shown on TV constitutes in and of itself a woeful reduction and alienation to be played here for smiles of bemused recognition, if not outright laughter. But the real yucks – ideally accompanied, of course, by uplifted brows of gee-whiz appreciation for the nifty computer-generated inserts into the old footage – are reserved for the basic joke written into Forrest's every appearance on the TV screen. Whether he is picking up a notebook dropped by a Black woman on her way past Governor Wallace and a crowd of jeering whites to enter her first class at the University of Alabama, asking JFK where the nearest bathroom is, showing his wounded ass to a hilariously amused LBJ, or getting some advice about where to stay in Washington from Tricky Dick, the comic point lies in the extent to which his naive responses "unintentionally" undercut and thereby triumph over the official significance of the moment portrayed. What the TV tells us is the politics and history of our time is, in effect, exposed as a sham – not, however, because the real historical events and political struggles have been edited out, but rather because politics and history themselves are no more than a mystified, second-order representation of a primal chaos whose real truth is only the untotalizable, intrinsically funny Brownian movement of so many blundering individual acts.

If in this way *Forrest Gump* cheerfully bears out Fredric Jameson's grimmest prophesies of the evacuation of history and politics inside a postmodernist cultural field whose practices seem by now to have spread, like designer-label knock-offs or smallpox-infected blankets, from the professional-managerial class in which they first found a home to the general public, across the porous frontiers separating hip from straight-out mass, along a whole other narrative seam, the film not only reinforces the same trivialization, but adds to it a sterner warning to those benighted viewers who might otherwise be tempted to hold out for any sense of social agency.[18] This other ideologeme emerges in the story of Gump's true love Jenny, which is interwoven throughout the film in a sort of secondary counterpoint with his own. The self-destructive, self-indulgent wayward-ness of Jenny's terminally confused life is, we are to understand, at least in part to be marked down to the sexual abuse visited upon her by her redneck father in her childhood – because of which, in accordance with the therapization of the social we have remarked upon before, we are to extend to her our sympathies and properly sensitive understanding. At the same time, however, we are all the more emphatically encouraged to view her involvement with the student anti-war Left, the Black Panther move-ment, and 1960s counterculture in the same light as her posing for *Playboy*, working at a grind house, and, later on, sniffing coke at discos and sleeping around with junkies who presumably (though the film is, of course, too obsessively anti-political to name it) infect her with AIDS. Anti-war, Black Panther, counterculture, cocaine, discos, heroin, AIDS – all are depicted, in effect, less as a road to hell than as various aspects of the same hell to which Jenny's rotten childhood condemns her. In this respect, among others, the film's excision of feminism from the historical pastiche it whips up for us in Jenny's story is symptomatic; if added into the mix, it might, to say the least, have proved somewhat more difficult – not to mention more objectionable to some in the audience – to efface the political open-ing it provided and the agency that feminism invited its adherents to seize and operate as their own. For that, of course, is how all the other political and cultural initiatives of the 1960s are presented to us: as so many self-deluded mystifications spun out by a demiurge of cultural decadence and breakdown in which poor souls like Jenny are perpetually exploited and abused – slapped up by her hyper-macho New Left boyfriend as the swaggering Panthers look on, used as a sex toy by one and all – even, and perhaps especially, insofar as they entertain the simultaneously pathetic and perniciously self-indulgent belief that they are making history.

Against and in tandem with the story of this fallen woman, then, we are given the uplifting story of the right-minded man whose failure to save her from her troubled self in time constitutes the only flaw in his otherwise perfect success. But here, of course, we come to the joke that constitutes both the film's basic premiss and its most serious and apparently satisfying response to the question of what a proper white straight masculinity must be: that the best man we can imagine, one whose goodness we can each and all warrant, can only be constituted by the negations he incarnates; that, put simply, to earn our mass approval, he can only be a particular kind of dope. In this sense, the sublimely stupid Forrest is the final term, at least for now, in the sensitive-guy films we have read, just as the frazzled D-FENS is the latest variation of and newest step beyond his rampaging progenitors. But unlike the Henrys, Peters, and Jacks from the Year of Living Sensitively, this hero is *born* brain-damaged, and so does not have to undergo any suffering in order to regress. Accordingly, the story he recounts to his skeptical or wonder-struck companions on the bus-stop bench comes across to us in the film's series of flashbacks as the can-you-top-this account, in effect, of all that has *failed* to happen to him. From all-star football to Vietnam, from ping-pong with the Red Chinese to spectacular business success, through all of Jenny's betrayals and mistakes in her doomed fall through the cultural and political vortex of the past three decades, the dramatic point offered up for our delectation is that Forrest remains immaculately unchanged.

"Ignorance," Oscar Wilde wrote, "is like a ripe, delicate fruit – touch it, and the bloom is gone"; and it is the genius of *Forrest Gump*'s creators to have realized its audience's desire to take his cynicism as its own sentiment, and hold his aphorism's sense to its heart as noble truth. But before any further consideration of his exemplary ignorance, we should note as well the significance of Forrest's single additional attribute – that is, of the related fact that he is so fast. Forrest's supernatural speed and stamina as a runner are clearly enough related to his physical defectiveness, in the form of the leg braces he wears through his childhood until the day he discovers his talent by running away from the redneck kids who taunt and torture him. But if that defect turns out, like his brain damage, to be an overwhelming strength, in another sense Forrest's running functions as the complementary obverse of his stupidity, as time and again he escapes from the scarring effects of personal and historical experience alike not only by remaining oblivious to their potential significance (which, as we have seen, in the case of political and historical events, the film denies as well), but also by literally outrunning them. So, just as the child Forrest outruns the bullies, the adult Forrest will outrun first the Viet Cong (whom we must never see, any more than Jenny's AIDS can be named), and, later still, the grief of Jenny's disappearance and his mother's death.

Bathed in the light of the philosophy explicitly proposed by the film, that life is composed of a blend of sheer whimsical contingency and iron-clad destiny, Forrest's running comes to express the truth of sheer frenzied flight or drift, his implacable stupidity that of immovable destiny, the two working in concert to dispose of any trace or possibility of humanly willed achievement or significance. Whatever happens to Forrest, that is, he either doesn't get it (thus his wise mantra *re* the assassination attempts whose televised replays dot the film, that this or that public figure was shot "for no particular reason at all"), or else he runs past it as fast as he can, both literally and in his spoken narrative ("And that's all I got to say about that"). If we think of Forrest's running ability as one of the two components of his ideal white straight masculinity, however, it takes on yet another significance and does some other work as well. For what are Forrest's flights from personal grief but so many updated, renovated, and revalorized enactments of the flights from pain and difficulty into sheer numb activity to which white straight men have conventionally resorted, often enough to the rage and compounded grief of the women left behind to do the emotional work?

If Forrest's running thus encourages the men and women in the film's audience to throw up their hands cheerfully at the challenge to men that some versions of feminism have also abandoned, even as the men's move-ment in its own eccentric manner took it up – that is, of learning ways to deal with and speak of their feelings – Forrest's stupidity helps supply the alibi for his emotional incapacity while simultaneously constituting in and of itself the innovative element in the film's reconstruction of white straight masculinity. We have by now probably said enough of what that stupidity in its wisdom cannot entertain or fathom: not only emotional but, all the more so, historical and/or political self-consciousness, which the film in any case depicts as silly, self-destructive delusions hardly worth having. What remains coupled with these wise abnegations, though, is what that stupidity is allowed to know and do. What, in other words, are the active forms of goodness Forrest embodies? By definition, of course, these must exist and operate only on an interpersonal level, given the film's insistent demonization and evacuation of any larger social and political concerns. Forrest's perfect submission to the brutality of military order while a soldier may draw a satirical smile from us if we like, but the film is hardly concerned to press the critique. The real point of its decidedly brief tour of Vietnam is, rather, his loyalty to the others in his platoon, and above all his steadfast friendship with the almost equally feeble-minded Bubba, whom he risks his life again and again to rescue in the fire-fight in which Bubba is killed. Likewise, he is doggedly loyal to Lieutenant Dan, his legless and embittered former superior officer, whose faith in life and humanity is eventually rekindled by Forrest's devotion; and, of course, to his sainted mother, whose banalities ("Life is like a box of chocolates; you never know what you're going to get") constitute his own guide to life.

But above all Forrest is faithful to Jenny, to whom he demonstrates over and over the real meaning of love: by slugging the college kid date-raping her in the front seat of his car and, later on, the New Left punk who slaps her around; by rescuing her from the stage of the grind house on which she performs folk songs naked; by providing her the haven of his family's old plantation house, first, when she wanders back in from the glittering decadence of the 1970s a burnt-out case, and, ultimately, when she brings herself and the child he has fathered back home so she can marry him and die. "You can't keep rescuing me all the time," she tells him; but of course that is exactly what our hero can and must do again and again, until, too late, she learns his lesson and submits. "I'm not a smart man," he tells her, "but I know what love is." Obviously enough, the meaning of love is our old friend, protector–provider masculinity – albeit one with a new twist. For Forrest is warranted to take up these traditional functions of masculinity only insofar as he remains a child in all other respects, immaculately innocent of any knowledge of or partici-pation in the larger world. In this recuperation of the protector–provider model we may discern a curiously obverse slant rhyme with late-nineteenth- and early-twentieth-century feminist arguments for women's participation in the public and political realm, especially in the struggle for suffrage. Then, a primary argument of middle-class white women was that, precisely because of their special access to and responsibility for moral virtue as mothers of children and keepers of the home, they deserved to be allowed to bring those values to bear on public life.[19] Now, in effect, in *Forrest Gump* white straight masculinity is likewise allowed to remain superior to the femininity it is charged to protect and provide for only so long as it holds sway within private life alone and leaves the public world to itself. In this respect, indeed, the scene when Forrest blunders into a giant anti-war demonstration in Washington and is plucked up to stand before the microphones on the stage, only to have the one thing he has to say about the war in Vietnam reduced to silence by a government saboteur who pulls out the wires, says it all. For the point is, of course, that Forrest cannot, must not, have anything to say about the Vietnam War: or, rather, that his real and only speech about it comes just after the sound has been restored, when seeing his true love in the massive crowd, he shouts out the single word "Jenny!"

I remember hearing, years ago, a grimly witty comment by a Black friend of mine about the crop of Black mayors then taking up what looked like power in some of our country's most troubled cities: something to the effect that you can tell whenever something in this country is broken down, because at that point whites give it to Blacks. The overwhelming success of *Forrest Gump* suggests that a similar satisfaction may now be enjoyed along the lines of gender: to wit, that since the social itself is widely perceived as a bottomless sink of chaos and corruption, it may be assigned to women, while childlike men stay virtuously home, taking care of their own. In this popular date-movie itself, of course, the potentially troubling question of how a mature adult woman could stand to live married to an emotionally and intellectually stunted, asexual idiot is nicely foreclosed by Jenny's death – a death that, linked as it is with her sexual escapades of the past, just as her one night of sex with Forrest results in conception, also carries the tonic message that women are around at best just to have babies, and that proper sex is procreational, not recreational. Yet the film's main through-line may finally be summed up as follows: men who give up their right to and responsibility for the social will be enabled thereby to fuse their "inner child" and their protector–provider "warrior" selves into a single seamless whole; and women, correspondingly, should give up on their efforts to make their way in the world and to force the men who provide for them to grow up. The poor babies, after all, can't help it; they can only do what they have to do.

Such a reconfiguration of white straight masculinity must remain for the most part a purely imaginary mythos in a society in which white men continue to dominate the commanding heights of politics and the economy, however much the economic and social status of middle- and working-class white men continues to slip. Nonetheless, we would be wrong to conclude that the dream of some redemptively Gump-like version of white straight masculinity is strictly confined to the dark, oneiric space of the local cineplex and our most idle, ineffectual fantasies. Indeed, even as I write these words, a virtual host of mindless protector–provider types – all of them white men, so far as I know – are running for office across this great land, each and all of them expounding a new Republican anti-politics whose fundamental premiss is that politics is bogus, government a corrupt and vicious joke. The notion that political solutions of any kind to structural problems may be arrived at through collective political struggle is precisely what these white men most stridently condemn and oppose. Since no such solutions should even be attempted, the only worthy task for politicians to take up is to reduce the revenues and public sway of democratic government to a minimum: that is, to its own protector–provider function of national defense via an ever more bright and bloated military and an ever more punitive criminal-justice system to fight off those enemies at home and abroad who would seek to disturb us in the pursuit of our partly destined and partly contingent but wholly private lives.

We could spend much more time studying and musing upon all the brilliant collateral moves *Forrest Gump* makes: for example, on the clever-ness with which its Old South setting is made to collude with its hero's stupidity in foreclosing the possibility and/or necessity of depicting the enormous economic shifts and displacements of the past two decades in any way; or on the genial racism it taps and promulgates by depicting Bubba, the only Black man with whom we spend any time, as nearly as much of an idiot as Gump himself. But to end this book, I would rather walk outside the cineplex and away from our happy idyll with Forrest Gump, to take a quick glance at a real-life candidate whose image and platform express nearly to perfection the film's gender-coded dreams. Michael Huffington, like Gump a multimillionaire, is, unlike Gump, a one-term Congressperson now spending his enormous personal fortune hand-over-fist in an ad-driven campaign to topple a seasoned female politician, Dianne Feinstein, out of her Senate seat.[20] But both his term in Con-gress and his political perspective are ones that any real-life Gump could only approve. In the House of Representatives, he has practically no record whatsoever, in happy accordance with the position he concisely outlined to Margaret Carlson of *Time*: "I want a government that does nothing." Likewise, if we are to believe the ads playing night and day on California's TV sets, Huffington made his fortune as Gump made his, with "hard work and luck." Yet in these ads, as finally in *Gump*, the main project is less to portray Huffington as a successful businessman (which could, after all, be resented much more than admired) than as the paradigmatic husband and father whose virtues as a family man, walking hand-in-hand with his wife and daughters across a sun-kissed California field, are in and of themselves his prime qualification for office. Indeed, it is the very insularity and detachment of such wholly private virtue from any involvement in public life that is promoted over his female opponent's lifelong career in the tawdry, corrupt political circus. According to the logic of Gump, that is, it is Feinstein's very knowledge of and involvement with issues of public and political life that make her unfit to hold public office.

To push such an argument and maintain the Huffington image of perfect private virtue and public ignorance, as you might expect, the Huffington campaign has had to resort to some relatively novel strategies: chiefly, an unprecedented reliance on its impeccably vacuous TV ads, coupled with a studied refusal to allow the candidate to conduct any public interviews through which he might be pinned down on any particular issues or positions. Aside from broad stands against crime, illegal immigration and welfare, and for the unregulated operation of the free-market economy, nothing is known of what he thinks: indeed, we are encouraged to believe if we like – and the success of *Gump* suggests that arguably many of us do – that there is nothing more to know. If Huffington wins his race – and he is now running neck-and-neck with Feinstein – I suppose we will get to see how he then manages to continue to keep himself, or at least his image, out of politics and public life even while in office. But whether his anti-political campaign succeeds or fails, I suspect he will hardly be the last to shape his image to the face of Forrest Gump, and to claim the right to rule on the basis of his perfect ignorance. Nor do I expect to find that claim lodged only in the realms of popular culture and political life. The task of finding out – that is, of making – all that white straight masculinity might be, both in itself and in its relation to the manifold Others that its dominance has traditionally both repressed and disordered, ripped off and held in place, awaits the time of a very different politics from even most of those we still think of as "progressive" today. As old-fashioned as it may be to say it, such progressive reconstruction will depend upon the hard-won articulation of all those others, and a few white straight men besides, whose present diffusion, dispersal, and mutual hostility is too often wrong-headedly celebrated as precisely a "profusion of leftward identities ... now expressed and reflected upon and disseminated in ways too complex and diverse to be enumerated," as though our micro- and, in many cases, post-political disaffiliations were the sign of our triumph and not the guarantor of our ongoing impotence.[21] To end this book, then, in which I have argued throughout that the normative definitions and regulative images of white straight masculinity have indeed been changing, and that those changes do, for all their manifold inadequacies and offenses, offer us so many clues and openings towards the tasks a reinvigorated left-feminist politics might take up, it seems only right to turn the floor over to another book that spells out the perspective from which this one has been written, and lays out more specifically and more comprehensively than I have both the work that must continue and all the other work that we in the USA have hardly yet begun.

> The conscious subversion of men's power ... is partly the work of those who travel the slow and grinding route taken by mainstream reformist political parties and organisations committed to sexual equality. It is also the work of those engaged in the more erratic, more radical, spurts and retreats along the volatile route of interpersonal sexual politics, as feminists, lesbians, gay and anti-sexist men refashion and live out their new visions of what it is to be "woman" or "man." It is finally, as feminists have always preached and often practised, also a matter of cultural subversion – the creative work of revaluing the lives and experiences of women and de-centring the androcentric positioning of men in all existing discourses. Though it may be difficult to perceive, these routes do intersect. Interpersonal struggles to change men, attempts by men themselves to refashion their conceptions of what it is to be a man, always encounter and frequently collide with other power relations. Men are changed by greater involvement in childcare and domestic work and by being required to pay attention to the demands and interests of women. But not all men could assume more domestic responsibilities, even if they wished to. And not all women have the same power to demand, or the same interest in ensuring, change in men. State policy, and expansions and contractions of welfare, as well as patterns of paid employment for men and for women, affect the possibilities for change in men. The competitive, individualistic nature of modern life in the West exacerbates the gulf between what is seen as the feminine world of love and caring and the masculine world of the market-place – wherever women and men individually find themselves. As some socialist feminists have always known, the difficulty of changing men is, in part, the difficulty of changing political and economic structures.[22]

Changing political and economic structures: not enough, to be sure, but neither will any other changes be sufficient in the absence of these, without which the "new" forms of white straight masculinity will only be such perverse chips off the old block, as it has been my gruesome pleasure to detail here – albeit in the frankly utopian hope, and against the odds, that in the future no other book with an agenda quite like this one's will ever need to be written again.

NOTES

1. Kathryn R. Robinson, "A Field Guide to Northwest Men," *Seattle Weekly* (31 August 1994), p. 29. A special thanks here to Mart Stewart for providing me with a copy of this useful article.

2. Gerald Renner, "600 Gather for All-Male Message: Real Men Love God," *The Hartford Courant* (31 October 1994), pp. B1, B2.

3. Doug Henwood, "Women Working," *Left Business Observer* 65 (31 August 1994), p. 5.

4. Ibid., p. 4.

5. Stephanie Coontz, *The Way We Never Were: American Families and the Nostalgia Trap* (New York: Basic Books, 1992), p. 260.

6. Ibid., p. 263.

7. Henwood, p. 5.

8. Coontz, p. 183.

9. Ibid., pp. 266, 271.

10. Klaus Theweleit, *Male Fantasies: Women, Floods, Bodies, History*, vol. I, trans. Stephen Conway et al. (Minneapolis: University of Minnesota Press, 1987)

11. Here, though I draw on none of his specific interpretations and arguments, I should nonetheless mark my indebtedness to Alexander Doty's *Making Things Perfectly Queer: Interpreting Mass Culture* (Minneapolis: University of Minnesota Press, 1993), which has provoked and helped me to construct formulations like the one just hazarded in the main text.

12. Newbury Park, CA: Sage Publications, 1992, p. 2. Hereafter, page numbers for all citations from this work are given in the main text.

13. For a cogent historical analysis of this consensus and its dialectical self-unraveling, see Samuel Bowles, David Gordon and Thomas Weisskopf, *Beyond the Wasteland: A Democratic Alternative to Economic Decline* (Garden City, NY: Anchor Press/Doubleday, 1983), pp. 62–94.

14. Made famous, of course, by Fredric Jameson's classic phenomenological evocation. See his *Postmodernism: or, The Cultural Logic of Late Capitalism* (Durham, NC: Duke University Press, 1991), pp. 38–45.

15. The estimate of domestic theatrical grosses through the beginning of October 1994 comes from *The Hartford Courant* (4 October 1994), p. E1. The $100 million figure for the first three weeks may be found in Martin Walker, "Making Saccharine Taste Sour," *Sight and Sound* (October 1994), p. 16, which also provides me with the data from which I have been able to extrapolate the film's besting of *Jaws*.

16. Quoted in Walker, p. 17.

17. Quoted in ibid., p. 17 (my emphasis).

18. I refer to Jameson's famous pronouncements in the title essay of his *Postmodernism*

(Durham, NC: Duke University Press, 1991), pp. 1–54. My own argument that the initial social site for the production and consumption of postmodernist texts lay within the professional-managerial class, resting on its peculiar and unprecedented cultural capital and reflecting its contradictory anxieties and hopes, may be found in "'Makin' Flippy-Floppy': Postmodernism and the Baby-Boom PMC," in *Another Tale to Tell: Politics and Narrative in Postmodern Culture* (London and New York: Verso, 1990), pp. 97–125.

19. See, *inter alia*, Aileen Kraditor, *The Ideas of the Woman Suffrage Movement, 1890–1920* (New York: Columbia University Press, 1965); and thanks to Joan Hedrick for breaking my bibliographic amnesia on this point.

20. Huffington has to date spent over $10 million on his overwhelmingly ad-driven campaign; his total spending is quite likely to run over $20 million by Election Day. This fact and all subsequent quotations and information on Huffington's candidacy is drawn from Sidney Blumenthal's chilling profile of "The Candidate," *The New Yorker* (10 October 1994), pp. 54–62.

21. Dick Flacks, "Response," *Socialist Review* 93/3 (1994), p. 123.

22. Lynne Segal, *Slow Motion: Changing Masculinities, Changing Men* (New Brunswick, NJ: Rutgers University Press, 1990), pp. 308–9.

INDEX